The
Ideological Origins
of
American Federalism

The

Ideological Origins

of

American Federalism

Alison L. LaCroix

HARVARD UNIVERSITY PRESS

Cambridge, Massachusetts, and London, England

First Harvard University Press paperback edition, 2011

Library of Congress Cataloging-in-Publication Data

LaCroix, Alison L.
The ideological origins of American federalism / Alison L. LaCroix.
p.   cm.
Includes bibliographical references and index.
ISBN 978-0-674-04886-7 (cloth:alk. paper)
ISBN 978-0-674-06203-0 (pbk.)
1. Federal government—United States—History.   2. United States—Politics
and government.   3. United States—History—Revolution, 1775–1783.
I. Title.
JK311.L33   2010
320.473'049—dc22   2009035216

To William

༄

Contents

Introduction: A Well-Constructed Union   1

1. The Federal Idea   11
2. Dividing Lawmaking Power   30
3. The Debates over Sovereignty   68
4. Forging a Federated Union   105
5. The Authority of a Central Government   132
6. Jurisdiction as the Battlefield   175

Epilogue: Federalism Demystified   214

Notes   223
Selected Bibliography   289
Acknowledgments   297
Index   301

Introduction:
A Well-Constructed Union

FEDERALISM IS EVERYWHERE AND NOWHERE in American legal and political history. On one hand, historians of the Revolution and the early Republic are quick to celebrate the achievements of the Constitutional Convention, lauding founders such as James Madison and Alexander Hamilton for their genius in establishing a new political architecture that apportioned authority between two levels of government. On the other hand, the precise circumstances of federalism's birth remain obscure. Its parentage unknown and its origins murky, federalism too often arrives in the historiography just in time to save the Republic, a deus ex machina springing fully formed from the minds of the founders to illuminate the nation's future legal and political landscape.

The Constitutional Convention of 1787 in Philadelphia looms enormous in many accounts of American constitutional history, serving as the set piece in which various and muddled worldviews, theories, interests, and allegiances jelled into a coherent science and structure of politics. The convention thus becomes time zero in the chronology of American political and constitutional development, a finite and forward-looking first moment defining, for good or ill, the terms according to which subsequent debates regarding the nature of American government would be conducted. The moment of origin, in other words, sometimes appears to lack origins of its own. Preconvention precedents provide antiquarian interest, perhaps, but are seen as offering little useful insight into the "real" legal questions concerning the post-1787 meaning and function of particular constitutional doctrines. Legal scholars sometimes trawl the convention records for footnote fodder but ignore the context surrounding the remarks they value. Some nonlawyer historians of the period, meanwhile, avoid writing about the convention altogether, regarding it as a spoiled field overtrampled by lawyers or else as a moment about which little of interest remains to be gleaned.

The strange place that the Philadelphia convention occupies in American constitutional history leads to several unfortunate consequences. Chief among them is a surprising shortage of scholarly attention to the convention as something other than an unassimilable outlier in historical time, a unique moment of genius that set the terms of debate but that resists efforts to place it in a broader temporal context extending before, as well as after, 1787. Scholars have long looked to *The Federalist* for insights into the meaning of federalism, but an exclusive focus on these admittedly important essays from 1787 and 1788 overshadows other valuable sources that helped Alexander Hamilton, James Madison, and John Jay arrive at the ideas articulated there.

Federalism, according to many accounts, emerged as a by-product of this foundational conversation among the men who sat in the Pennsylvania State House during the summer of 1787. Along with judicial review, federalism is frequently regarded as one of the signal American contributions to the science of politics. Both concepts' origins are typically traced to the drafting and ratification of the Constitution, despite the lack of any explicit reference to either concept in the document itself. On this view, a set of ideas about government that was later called "federalism" began to coalesce at the convention, conjured into action by the exigencies of a fraying confederation and the combined force of fifty-five creative minds. Federalism appears as a new-modeled creation cobbled together out of a mix of necessity (the existence of the states) and theory (the belief that a republic could not easily be maintained across a large territory). The product of these imperatives was not simply a constitutional doctrine but rather an entire philosophy of government. In addition to providing the theory of authority that undergirded the whole structure of the new republic, federalism took concrete form in the particular provisions of the document that established that republic, from the enumeration of Congress's powers in Article I, section 8, to the Supremacy Clause of Article VI.

The story I have just described is the story of a beginning, in which the convention debates serve as the first act in the unfolding drama of American constitutional history and therefore as the original moment for purposes of understanding American federalism. This is a familiar story, especially for constitutional scholars. To be sure, any study of the Constitution must devote special attention to the moment of the document's creation. But there is another account of the history of American federalism that focuses not only on the period between 1787 and 1789 but on a broader, more expansive time frame. This chronologically broader species of account typically approaches the question of federalism's origins from one of two angles: a focus on institutions or a focus on republican ideology.

The few scholars who have explicitly discussed the question of federalism's origins have pointed to the structures and institutions of the British Empire as the source of the concept of divided authority. Most prominent among these scholars is Jack Greene, who argues that life under the imperial system introduced American colonists to the notion that political authority could be apportioned between a ruling metropolitan center and a remote but expansive periphery.[1] In Greene's view, because colonists were subject to multiple ascending layers of political authority (colonial legislature, royal governor, Parliament, Privy Council), only a minor conceptual adjustment was needed following independence to establish the Constitution's two-level federal structure of state and national authority. Greene, like constitutional historian Andrew C. McLaughlin before him, views the transition from Britain's "composite empire" to the United States' federal republic as largely characterized by continuity.[2]

Greene's story is one of institutions, of the day-to-day political experience of British North Americans whose ideas about government followed from their interactions with what Greene terms the "negotiated authorities" that operated as a practical matter within the British Empire. Similarly, McLaughlin, writing in 1918, based his argument for imperial-to-federal continuity on what he described as Americans' "institutionaliz[ation] and legaliz[ation]" in the 1770s and 1780s of "the practices of the prerevolutionary imperial system of Britain."[3] Such accounts focus on the outward manifestations of authority rather than on political beliefs or theories of government. In this sense, they embrace a positivistic vision of political history, treating institutions and experience as more reliable—or, at a minimum, more significant—than arguments or ideology.[4]

More recent books by Daniel Hulsebosch and Mary Sarah Bilder have brought a similarly institutional focus to the question of the nature of the eighteenth-century Anglo-American constitution. Hulsebosch's book focuses on "the way people experienced constitutions rather than on constitutional theory," while Bilder's study of what she usefully terms "transatlantic legal culture" is "less interested in constructing a conceptual demarcation of the legal structure of the empire" than in offering "a practical analysis about how the legal empire worked and, more importantly, how litigants worked within it."[5] Like McLaughlin and Greene, Hulsebosch and Bilder for the most part minimize questions of ideology and theory, emphasizing the legal and constitutional experience of eighteenth-century British North Americans rather than the processes of argumentation and ideology formation that underpinned that experience.

In so doing, these more recent accounts of Anglo-American constitutional history diverge from the ideologically oriented accounts by Bernard Bailyn and Gordon S. Wood that have dominated the historiography of the founding period since the 1960s. Describing late-eighteenth-century America as undergoing a "transformation of thought" that culminated by 1787 in "an entirely new conception of politics" based on republican theory, Bailyn and Wood each place ideas at the center of the analysis.[6] The new institutional history of early American constitutionalism, in contrast, emphasizes the outward, observable emanation of ideas in the form of experience.

The institutional approach thus offers both a methodological and a substantive contrast to the view of many constitutional law scholars, as well as to the republican theorists. In addition to the distinction between ideological and institutional emphases, these approaches privilege different chronologies. The constitutional law story typically begins in 1787 and pays little regard to colonial precedents, while both the institutional and republican stories start more than a century and a half earlier, with the governments created by the first New World charters. The institutional and republican views thus treat the convention as an endpoint, or perhaps a midpoint, in the process of Anglo-American legal development, while the constitutional law approach venerates the convention as the crucial point of origin.

Substantively, these three approaches reach varied conclusions on the question of federalism's origins. In keeping with its emphasis on drafting and ratification as foundational moments, the constitutional law version of events holds that American federalism was novel, and that the creation of the Republic constituted a fundamental break with the past. Perhaps the best example of this perspective comes from the Supreme Court itself: "Federalism was our Nation's own discovery. The Framers split the atom of sovereignty. It was the genius of their idea that our citizens would have two political capacities, one state and one federal, each protected by incursion from the other," wrote Justice Anthony Kennedy in a 1997 concurring opinion.[7] In contrast, republican scholars have tended to focus less on federalism itself and more on broader moments of ideological transformation in late-eighteenth-century American politics.[8] The institutional view, meanwhile, implicitly downplays the significance of the convention and suggests instead that 1787 was one of many moments of negotiation and reshuffling among preexisting institutional forms.[9]

This book seeks to offer a different view of the origins of American federalism. It brings ideology back into the discussion of the meaning and significance of federalism in the founding and ratification periods and places the Philadelphia convention in the broader context of federal thought in the late eighteenth century. To be sure, institutions are an important part of the story, but the ideas surrounding those institutions—the words and concepts that contemporary actors used as they explained to themselves what the institutions meant—played a crucial role in defining the contours first of colonial and then of early national government.[10] To borrow David Armitage's phrasing, the purpose of this ideological inquiry is "not to expose beliefs . . . as either true or false," but instead "to show the ways in which the constitutive elements of various conceptions" of federal thought "arose in the competitive context of political argument."[11]

The phrase "federal idea," in this context, refers to a conception of political authority as capable of an enduring division between levels of government based on subject matter. This conception can be traced from the law-of-nations theorist Samuel von Pufendorf's political league and early-eighteenth-century theories of Anglo-Scottish union to the vertically structured system of legislative review that James Madison advocated in 1787. Rather than viewing federalism as a transcendent notion that was always available to canny nation builders, this book treats the federal idea as an artifact of intellectual endeavor at a particular historical moment. This approach requires that contemporaries' claims be viewed as claims rather than as statements of an essential or immanent reality. Consequently, this book focuses on what contemporary observers knew or believed and how they understood concepts such as federation, confederation, sovereignty, and empire; it tries to avoid grafting what we now know or believe onto what are fundamentally their ideas and contexts.

Building on this foundation, the central claim of this book is that the emergence of American federalism in the second half of the eighteenth century should be understood as primarily an ideological development— indeed, as one of the most important ideological developments of the period. The core of this new federal ideology was a belief that multiple independent levels of government could legitimately exist within a single polity, and that such an arrangement was not a defect to be lamented but a virtue to be celebrated. In this sense, the book emphasizes change rather than continuity in the transition from the British Empire to the federal republic.

Indeed, the new federal ideology rapidly became identified with the Republic itself. More than a mere doctrine or a rule, the belief in multiplicity, in overlap and concurrence, became a foundational principle of the entire American political enterprise. "Federal" and "republic" were the nation's twin attributes, terms so resonant that they were obvious choices for the names of the country's first political parties. From its origins in a disconnected set of pre-Revolutionary arguments about the relative powers of Parliament and the colonial legislatures to regulate colonial affairs, the federal conception of divided authority became necessary to the Republic. The "well constructed Union" required construction because it was a special species of union: a republic comprising several levels of government, all operating at once, but upon different objects. "The larger the society, provided it lie within a practicable sphere, the more duly capable it will be of self-government," Madison observed. "And happily for the *republican cause,* the practicable sphere may be carried to a very great extent, by a judicious modification and mixture of the *federal principle.*"[12]

In this way, an ideological interpretation of federalism complements divergent accounts of the founding era by Max Edling and David Hendrickson. Whereas Edling views federalists in the early Republic as focused entirely on "the need to build a powerful state and to explain how this state would work," Hendrickson warns against "exaggerat[ing] the significance of the national idea in the era of revolution and constitution-building" and instead emphasizes the role of the Confederation and the Constitution as "peace pacts" among "sovereign and independent communities."[13] An ideological approach offers one possible way to reconcile these seemingly conflicting accounts. If the organizing principle of federal ideology was divided authority, that principle might well have meant divided *authority* for some contemporaries (whom, following Edling, we might now identify as nationalists) and *divided* authority for others (whom, following Hendrickson, we might now call confederalists).

Certainly the specific consequences of federal thought shifted over the decades between the 1760s and 1800s. But a few key themes remained constant, connecting the Stamp Act controversy of the 1760s with the debates over federal-court jurisdiction in the 1800s. They included multi-layered authority as a conceptual matter; overlapping institutions (sometimes legislative, sometimes judicial) as a practical matter; and a belief that the division of authority among levels of government should be determined according to the subject matter at issue.

The path of American thinking about federalism in the latter half of the eighteenth century began with what many colonists initially believed was an uncontroversial notion of multilayered government based on a hierarchical arrangement of largely independent legislatures. Between 1764 and 1774, British and British North American political and legal thinkers promoted this theory, insisting that the provincial assemblies and Parliament could divide legislative power among themselves on the basis of various taxonomies of subject matter. To support these arguments, provincial commentators drew heavily on their colonies' charters, most of which dated to the seventeenth century and derived from royal, not parliamentary, authority. Some theorists, such as Richard Bland and Daniel Dulany, settled on a distinction between internal colonial and external imperial matters, arguing that Parliament could not reach the former but could regulate the latter. Other writers delineated a distinction between laws—or, more precisely, taxes—that specifically aimed at raising revenue in the colonies and those that levied duties only incidentally to a larger goal of regulating trade across the empire. The chief proponent of this view, and the author of one of the most widely read tracts of the prewar period, was John Dickinson. These alternative approaches to imperial organization ranged across a variety of forms, but the majority of them shared, first, an explicit differentiation between metropolitan and provincial legislative power, and second, a conviction that each of these types of power could be assigned a specific set of activities and entities to oversee. The debates of the 1760s thus explored the possibility of expanding imperial lawmaking authority from Parliament alone to encompass a number of different, coordinate bodies, each with a legislative brief defined by subject matter.

The early 1770s witnessed further conflict over the feasibility and legitimacy of divided authority within the British Empire. A particularly intense debate unfolded in Boston in 1773, pitting the royal governor against the colonial assembly in an extended public confrontation. At the heart of the controversy between Governor Thomas Hutchinson and the Massachusetts General Court lay the question of sovereignty. In the course of the debate, the parties grappled with what William Blackstone's *Commentaries* (first published in 1765) had termed the "supreme, irresistible, absolute, uncontrolled authority . . . in which the rights of sovereignty reside."[14] As each side of the debate articulated its vision of the scope of parliamentary power and the concomitant scope of the colonial assemblies' power, allegiances hardened, and visions of sovereignty began to diverge.

The relationship between the British Empire and American federal thought thus provides an important analytic theme of this book. American federalism began as a response to British metropolitan claims that only one supreme law-giving authority could exist within the empire (and the corollary claim that this authority resided in Parliament). Throughout the 1760s and 1770s, colonists and metropolitans wrangled over the possibility of dividing authority without running afoul of the traditional prohibition on *imperium in imperio,* or dominion within dominion. But the consequences of this imperial argument endured past the British surrender at Yorktown and the treaty negotiations at Paris into the first several decades of the United States' existence as a federal republic.

In the 1780s, the question became how the levels of authority the colonists had demanded would actually interact in the new government.[15] After 1787 and the defeat of Madison's proposal to give Congress the power to veto state laws, the institutional focus of this inquiry shifted. Divisions of power based on subject matter; distinctions based on regulation of commerce versus regulation of internal affairs; questions about institutional competencies—these vestiges of American whigs' complaints against metropolitan power became part of a sweeping new vision of multilayered government based on a reformulated conception of authority. The colonial embrace of the idea of multiplicity combined with a new focus on courts as the crucial intermediaries between levels of law, creating an ideological-institutional form of composite government called federalism.

As part of this increased interest in institutions, contemporaries began to consider different modes of power sharing among entities at a single level of government (the legislature, the judiciary, and the executive) as a means of carrying out their larger commitments to power sharing between a national center and a peripheral constellation of states. The Revolutionary commitment to vertical multiplicity translated into an early republican search for the appropriate horizontal balance of power among national institutions. In the years following the drafting and ratification of the Constitution, the focus of American federal thought therefore shifted again, from an emphasis on legislative authority to a new preoccupation with jurisdiction and a corresponding interest in courts. This shift is evident in the decades-long debate concerning the nature and scope of federal judicial power, which saw repeated efforts by jurists and statecrafters to establish the proper jurisdictional arrangement to mediate between the multiple levels of government set forth in the Constitution. The fruits of these struggles to cement the practical and ideological meanings of federalism were the judiciary acts of 1789 and 1801. The two acts have received remarkably disparate treatment from scholars, who have heralded the 1789 act as the basis of the federal judicial system and have regarded the 1801 act largely as an embarrassment notable only for its role in the partisan conflict over the election of 1800. Situating both acts in the broader context of the development of federal thought, however, offers new insight into the institutionalization of federalism in the early Republic—in particular, the issue of concurrent jurisdiction.

The story of federalism is not only about republicanism, or the rise of popular sovereignty, or the balance between states and union. It is also about the emergence of a normative vision of multilayered government. The story commences in the North American colonies in 1764, ranged along the Atlantic coast and still willingly tethered by language, trade, and the storied rights of Englishmen to "home," three thousand miles away.

CHAPTER 1

The Federal Idea

FEDERALISM WAS A CONCEPT created in time, not an eternally exist-ing model. The time of creation was between 1764 and 1802. Yet, as is nearly always the case with intellectual history, the idea had a prehistory. Federalism's core idea of divided governmental authority drew from sev-eral strands of political, legal, and constitutional thought, some of which originated in the late sixteenth and early seventeenth centuries, in con-texts that had little to do with North America. These precedents did not necessarily lead to federalism, nor was any one of them sufficient to bring about the development of federal ideas. Rather, taken together, they of-fered a conceptual framework through which observers in the latter half of the eighteenth century organized their thoughts about government, as well as a body of lived experience that shaped the vocabulary those ob-servers had at hand. They were the words and ideas available to eighteenth-century commentators, and so they became part of the dialogue through which those commentators fleshed out a new concept called federalism.

The antecedents of federal thought in the eighteenth century can be grouped under four headings, two of which pertain to theory and two to practice: seventeenth-century Anglo-American constitutional debates; continental European political philosophy; experiments with North American colonial union; and the Scottish and Irish examples.

Early Anglo-American Constitutional Debates

The lived constitutional experience of many colonists involved multiple lawmaking bodies. For many North Americans, the most significant laws touching everyday activities emanated from their towns or their colonial assemblies, not from Parliament or the Privy Council.[1] In addition, these local authorities operated within a long metropolitan shadow. Every regulation of an exchange between local farmers or adjudication of a dispute between merchants operated in a potentially imperial legal zone. The provincial hat trade might be shut down by act of Parliament on the theory that colonial hat production siphoned commerce away from the greater imperial mercantile system, as happened in 1732. A Connecticut intestacy law might be invalidated by the Privy Council on the ground that it was contrary to English law and the colonial charter, as happened in 1699. Although many colonists, beginning in the 1760s, challenged the plenary authority of Parliament by claiming that their local assemblies possessed jurisdiction over certain classes of matters (sometimes defined as "internal" affairs, sometimes as matters relating to taxation or the raising of revenue), these claims must be recognized as polemical and aspirational rather than as necessarily descriptive of the contemporary operation of imperial power.

The issue of the nature and location of sovereignty lay at the heart of much of the constitutional struggle that convulsed England and its empire from the sixteenth through the eighteenth century. Throughout this period, sovereignty was a highly contested and fraught concept both in the British Isles and throughout England's near- and far-flung territorial possessions. Early modern definitions of English sovereignty typically invoked the Act in Restraint of Appeals of 1533, which contained one of the earliest recorded references to England as an "empire," meaning, in the words of J. G. A. Pocock, a political entity "exercising a final and unappealable jurisdiction over itself in both church and state."[2] A state that possessed "sovereignty," then, was a state complete in itself, over which no other state (ecclesiastical or political) could claim authority.

Yet this early modern conception of sovereignty as a species of final dominion did not address the question of where within the structure of government that dominion ought to be lodged. Specifically, did sovereignty lie with the Crown, with Parliament, or with some other institution? Conflict over this issue underlay the English Civil War and the Glorious Revolution, two watershed constitutional moments that exerted tremendous influence on the minds of eighteenth-century Britons both at home and in the colonies. In 1642, Parliament's declaration of a theory of its own sovereignty helped to spark war while also laying a foundation for the theory of parliamentary sovereignty that would gain currency while continuing to cause strife over the subsequent decades.[3]

Also in the seventeenth century, an influential core of European thinkers promoted a vision of power as "both absolute and unitary."[4] One mission of such claims was to justify increased centralization of government authority. Preeminent among these thinkers were Jean Bodin and Thomas Hobbes. Bodin's *Six Books of the Commonwealth* (1576) provided the abiding definition of sovereignty as "the absolute and perpetual power of a commonwealth" which "is not limited either in power, or in function, or in length of time." In other words, according to Bodin, sovereignty was held exclusively by a single authority and could not be divided among other, lesser authorities. Indeed, Bodin rejected the very notion of a lesser authority, arguing that the powers of the sovereign "cannot be relinquished or alienated": "Just as God, the great sovereign, cannot make a God equal to Himself because He is infinite and by logical necessity . . . two infinites cannot exist, so we can say that the prince, whom we have taken as the image of God, cannot make a subject equal to himself without annihilation of his power."[5] Hobbes's *Leviathan,* published in 1651, adopted Bodin's approach to sovereignty and emphasized its consequences for rule. The authority of the ruler, Hobbes stated, must be "indivisible, and inseparably annexed to the sovereignty" as well as "greater than that of any or all the subjects."[6] For both Bodin and Hobbes, then, to divide authority was to destroy it. Seventeenth-century English statesmen were certainly familiar with Bodinian theory. The *Six Books* appeared in an English translation in 1606 and had previously been available in French and Latin editions.[7] By the late eighteenth century, Bodin's argument for the indivisibility of sovereignty had become a mantra among some English political thinkers.[8]

After the Glorious Revolution of 1688–1689, some commentators began to view parliamentary sovereignty as an accepted part of British constitutional theory. Citing the great seventeenth-century jurist Edward

Coke, William Blackstone observed in the 1760s, "The power and jurisdiction of parliament . . . is so transcendent and absolute, that it cannot be confined, either for causes or persons, within any bounds."[9] Blackstone's *Commentaries on the Laws of England* aimed to enshrine this unitary vision of sovereignty in late-eighteenth-century British legal thought.[10] In a chapter dealing with the medieval writ of *praemunire*, which punished an offense against the king and his government, Blackstone inveighed against what he termed the *"imperium in imperio"* that would result from a foreign power's interference with "that obedience . . . which constitutionally belonged to the king alone."[11] Although the writ in question had originally targeted attempts by the papacy to undermine the rule of the English monarchs in the fourteenth century, the principle allowed for broader application: multiple sources of authority could not share the same political space. Where multiple authorities did appear to exist, the theory ran, close inspection would reveal that one of the seeming authorities actually derived its entire power from the other and therefore was neither independent nor a genuine authority in any meaningful sense of the word.

Throughout the late eighteenth century, political theorists routinely denounced the notion of *imperium in imperio,* variously translated as "an empire within an empire" or "dominion within dominion," as a "solecism."[12] The idea that separate and equal authorities could exist within the same juridical boundaries offended contemporary understandings of the very nature of government power. The *imperium in imperio* principle—really a counterprinciple insofar as it sought to avoid the political creature for which it was named—appealed to the early modern desire for clear rules according to which governments were to be constructed. At the same time, it provided a relatively nuanced analytical framework by which to assess the success or failure of a given political arrangement. For example, although most eighteenth-century theorists viewed feudalism as a relic from an earlier, benighted era, it would not necessarily have run afoul of the *imperium in imperio* principle insofar as it created a chain of incomplete authorities, each of which ultimately owed its puissance to the enforcing power of the monarch.[13]

The focus on sovereignty in seventeenth- and eighteenth-century Anglo-American political theory accompanied the emergence of Parliament during the same period as the institutional repository of lawmaking authority. As Blackstone's stern phrases illustrate, by the latter half of the eighteenth century, some commentators viewed parliamentary sovereignty as an established part of British constitutional theory. Again citing Coke, Blackstone observed, "The power and jurisdiction of parliament . . . is so transcendent and absolute, that it cannot be confined, either for causes or persons, within any bounds. . . . It hath sovereign and uncontrolable authority in making, confirming, enlarging, restraining, abrogating, repealing, reviving, and expounding of laws, concerning matters of all possible denominations, ecclesiastical, or temporal, civil, military, maritime, or criminal. . . . It can, in short, do every thing that is not naturally impossible." Therefore, Blackstone concluded, "So long therefore as the English constitution lasts, we may venture to affirm, that the power of parliament is absolute and without control."[14]

This supposedly orthodox principle of sovereignty had only recently become established, however. It had originated as the centerpiece of anti-Stuart, Parliamentarian ideology during the Civil War of the 1640s and had cemented its place as the fundament of Whig—and therefore English—constitutionalism in the Glorious Revolution of 1688–1689.[15] By the late nineteenth century, theorists of British government viewed parliamentary sovereignty as integral to the nation's political and constitutional structure.[16] In 1773, however, unitary sovereignty was still contested as a positive conception of how the British constitution actually functioned, and it required assertion and argument by jurists such as Blackstone to establish its hegemony after the turmoil and uncertainty of the previous century and a half.

The issue of the "correctness" of particular seventeenth- and eighteenth-century theorists' views of the nature of the British imperial constitution is significant because it propelled much of the agenda of Anglo-American colonial historiography in the early twentieth century. Many scholars have read the American whigs to be making descriptive claims about the state of the British Empire in the 1760s and 1770s. These scholars have then made analytic arguments based on that supposed contemporary understanding, rather than considering that the colonists might have been speaking aspirationally or argumentatively. But this impulse to take the colonists at their word has an ironic consequence, for it often results in charges either that the colonists in some sense "got the law wrong" or that they in fact "got it right" but that colonial thought therefore contributed few new or interesting ideas to eighteenth-century Anglo-American constitutional thought.

The deep roots of this body of scholarship lie in the early-twentieth-century work of imperial historians Charles H. McIlwain and Robert Livingston Schuyler and constitutional historian Andrew McLaughlin. Later scholars such as Barbara Black, John Phillip Reid, and Jack Greene subsequently engaged with and elaborated on a similar set of questions. For all these historians, the central issue concerned what Schuyler termed the "legal right of the British Parliament to legislate on any subject for any or all parts of the British Empire."[17] As the imperial school has passed through alternating periods of vibrancy and quiescence over the past several decades, however, the emphasis of the inquiry has shifted slightly.

The earlier trio—McIlwain, Schuyler, and McLaughlin—focused their inquiries on the medieval and early modern precedents for parliamentary legislation over dominions outside the realm; in other words, on whether the American colonists' constitutional claims possessed any legitimacy whatsoever. Each reached a different conclusion. According to McIlwain, the question was "the simple issue as to whether the American or the English interpretation of the British constitution is the one more properly deducible from the precedents furnished by the development of that constitution in the whole period of its growth up to the time of the struggle." The answer, he concluded, "must on the whole be more favorable to the claims of the American colonists" than to those who spoke for the British government.[18] Schuyler, in contrast, disputed both the premise (the possibility of two valid interpretations of the British constitution) and the conclusion (that the American interpretation was correct or at least plausible) in what he presented as a devastating critique of McIlwain's Pulitzer Prize–winning book. "[T]he jurisdiction of parliament was never confined to the realm of England," Schuyler declared. "From the earliest times parliaments were imperial in the scope of their authority."[19] Taking a more conciliatory tone, McLaughlin noted in 1935 that the intense—and, by then, well-rehearsed—dispute between McIlwain and Schuyler demonstrated that the "very difference of opinion is of more significance than any definite assurance concerning the indubitable legal correctness of either position."[20]

For the most part, the later generation of historians accepted McIlwain's contention that the American colonists had articulated at least a plausible constitutional claim. In particular, Black's insights regarding the blurred borders between Crown and parliamentary authority during the main period of North American settlement suggest that Schuyler's argument that Parliament qua Parliament had legislated for the colonies since the earliest days of English colonization suffered from anachronism.[21] Having apparently laid to rest the early-twentieth-century interrogation of which side had the better argument in the 1760s and 1770s, this post–World War II group of scholars—notably, Bernard Bailyn and Gordon Wood—shifted the terms of imperial history away from transhistorical assertions about the relative power of imperial and colonial institutions and toward more contextual studies of the origins of the various strands of late-eighteenth-century Anglo-American political and legal ideology.[22] As one commentator puts it, "The question for the new breed of constitutional scholars was not therefore which side was 'correct.' Rather, the query was whether American patriots asserted sound claims as measured by the accepted constitutional principles of the day."[23]

For Black, Greene, and Reid—albeit according to different lines of analysis—"there were two versions of the British constitution: London's interpretation, in which Parliament was omnipotent; and the colonial interpretation, premised on the belief that there were limits to Parliament's authority to legislate for the colonies."[24] Reid's argument in support of the American view emphasizes the colonists' continued allegiance to a seventeenth-century version of the English constitution (which allowed at least some room for consent of the governed, customary rights, and appeals to the monarch), in contrast to the emerging post–Glorious-Revolution version that emphasized the supremacy of Parliament and that was gaining currency at home in Great Britain.[25] Greene, for his part, has emphasized the negotiations that shaped transatlantic constitutional and legal culture, positing an ongoing and continuous dialogue regarding the nature and location of authority that began with the first English colonial forays. This negotiation, Greene argues, endured into the early national period in the form of assumptions regarding the nature of divided authority that connected the imperial with the American constitution. On this view, the tension between the two versions of the British constitution mapped onto founding-era tensions concerning the proper division between the authority of the states and that of the general government.[26]

The work of Black, Greene, and Reid has important consequences for the history of federal thought. The shift away from questions of who was right and who was wrong in the colonial constitutional debates, and toward an understanding of the debate on its own terms, has produced new and nuanced readings of the eighteenth century that situate the American colonial experience within the wider framework of early modern political history.

Continental Ideas of Multiplicity

As the Anglo-American constitutional debates suggest, colonial legislation and adjudication operated in the uncertain penumbra of metropolitan authority. But there was another way of looking at sovereignty besides the unitary approach. In addition to reading Bodin and Hobbes, eighteenth-century observers also drew on a different Continental view that acknowledged certain systems of divided authority as legitimate, or at least plausible, governmental structures. Beginning with the work of Hugo Grotius in the early seventeenth century and continuing with the writing of Samuel von Pufendorf in the later seventeenth century and Emmerich de Vattel in the mid-eighteenth century, a long line of European thinkers had offered an alternative to the English (later, British) all-or-nothing, unitary vision of sovereignty and the belief that multiple sovereignties necessarily spelled solecism and disaster.

This early modern body of political philosophy was deeply influenced by the work of Roman thinkers such as Cicero and Plutarch, whose experience of the decline of the Republic led them to contrast "the growing corruption and disorder they saw about them with an imagined earlier republican world of ordered simplicity and [arcadian] virtue and sought continually to explain the transformation."[27] Using the classical concept of *foedera*—that is, treaties or positive agreements among political entities— the early modern European inheritors of these Roman theorists argued that leagues, compacts, and confederations offered viable modes of political cooperation among sovereign bodies.[28] Moreover, Grotius, who was born into a family of Dutch East India merchants, and Pufendorf, who was a keen observer of the German (formerly Holy Roman) Empire following the Peace of Westphalia, came to their studies with deep personal knowledge of the many varieties of formal and informal authority that characterized early modern imperial and colonial efforts.

Throughout both Europe and America, this Continental notion of divisible sovereignty jostled against the common-law vision of unitary sovereignty in the middle decades of the eighteenth century. Despite the insistence of Blackstone, the lexicographer Samuel Johnson, and others that a single sovereign power must be acknowledged to "pervade the whole mass of the community," and—perhaps more important— despite their contention that this was not an argumentative claim but a descriptive claim about the essence of the common law, the truth was that the nature of sovereignty was a contested, not a settled, issue in Anglo-American constitutional thought during this period.[29]

The Grotian vision of the law of nations emphasized what Edward Keene terms an "extra-European order" of colonial and imperial systems based on "the principle that sovereignty should be divided across national and territorial boundaries."[30] Pufendorf's *Law of Nature and Nations* (1672) offered a similar vision of nonunitary authority based on his study of the German Empire. By the mid-seventeenth century, that empire had been reduced essentially to an elective monarchy. Centralized sovereignty, if it had ever existed, had been replaced by satellite princes, each husbanding his own store of authority over his own territory. Notably, each of the member states possessed the power to negotiate its own foreign alliances. In the words of German historian Hagen Schulze, "[F]ragmentation was the abiding constitutional principle of the Holy Roman Empire, a structure without its own statehood, organization or power."[31]

For Pufendorf, however, German fragmentation was an invitation to revise the traditional Aristotelian categories of political bodies (monarch, aristocracy, democracy) to take into account the real, if unharmonious, structure of the empire.[32] Generalizing from the specifics of the empire and certain classical leagues of states, Pufendorf developed a new category: the "system of states" in which "several States are joined to each other, each by a perpetual League or Alliance" pursuant to which the states agree that "they shall not exercise some Part of that Sovereignty there specified, without the general Consent of each other." Sovereign powers that did not implicate the common interest, however, were left to each member state. "[T]hese Unions submit only some certain Parts of the Sovereignty to mutual Direction," Pufendorf noted, recommending that "the particular States reserve to themselves all those Branches of the supreme Authority, the Management of which can have little or no Influence (at least directly) on the Affairs of the rest."[33] In contrast to a unitary theory of sovereignty, therefore, Pufendorf's conception allowed for the possibility that political authority might cross jurisdictional boundaries and, on occasion, be shared among multiple states tied together in a single system.

Experiments with Colonial Union

Besides looking to sovereignty theory for inspiration, by the 1760s British North Americans could examine their own experiences with colonial union in the British Empire, some dating from the earliest decades of English colonization. Each of these efforts proposed an association among multiple colonies with some type of overarching authority to oversee the affairs of the association as a whole; at the same time, each colony retained control over its own internal matters. The most significant of these early precedents for colonial union were the New England Confederation of 1643 and the Albany Plan of Union of 1754. Both styled themselves as confederal forms of government—that is, loose leagues created for limited purposes among existing political entities, each of which retained its own sovereignty. The historical and theoretical roots of the confederation as a form of government stretched back to classical times, as many educated Anglo-Americans were aware. Let us examine these two specific cases of colonial confederation in the context of the models that they provided for observers of the political and legal situation of the 1770s.[34]

Formed in 1643, the New England Confederation—officially denominated the United Colonies of New England—comprised the colonies of

Massachusetts, Plymouth, Connecticut, and New
and the northern regions of Massachusetts, whicl
did not join the confederation.) Delegates from th
Boston in May 1643 to draw up articles of confedei
purposes and powers of the "firm and perpetual lea ͜ ͟ ͟ ͟ ͟ ͟ ͟ ͟͟ and
amity." The principal objective of this "Consocation amongst ourselves"
was to provide "offence and defence, mutual advice and succor upon all
just occasions both for preserving and propagating the truth and liberties of the Gospel and for their own safety and welfare." The last clause
pointed to the proximate cause of the impulse to join together: the threat
of attack by Indian, Dutch, or French forces. In addition to the emphasis
on mutual defense, the articles also granted the confederation authority
over boundary disputes, dealings with foreign powers, quotas for contributions of troops and funds to the confederation during wartime, and
delivery of escaped servants and other fugitives to their proper jurisdiction. A commission consisting of eight representatives (two from each
colony) would exercise the power of the confederation, meeting at least
once a year. The assent of six of the eight commissioners was required in
order for a particular provision to take effect, with a fallback option of
submitting the provision in question to the legislature of each colony.[35]

Strikingly, the articles of confederation did not refer to the Crown,
Parliament, or any other metropolitan authority. The recitation of authority that began the document referred only to the member colonies
and spoke in the language of Calvinist voluntarism. The New England
colonists, the first paragraph stated, "all came into these parts of America with one and the same end and aim, namely, to advance the Kingdom
of our Lord Jesus Christ and to enjoy the liberties of the Gospel in purity
with peace." The drive to enter into an association stemmed from "our
bounden duty" to aid fellow Christian pilgrims. The prospect of little
aid coming from England, which was embroiled in what the articles po-
litely termed "those sad distractions"—that is, the Civil War—convinced
the New England settlers of the necessity of banding together to resist
destruction and to preserve their mission of establishing a godly commonwealth in the New World.[36]

The New England Confederation endured for four decades, until
1684, when displeasure at colonial intransigence led the administration

.es II to strip Massachusetts of its charter and fold it into the newly
.eated Dominion of New England.[37] But the autonomy the colonies
displayed in setting up the confederation in the midst of a metropolitan
power vacuum, combined with the limited purposes of the confederation government, served as an important precedent for mid-eighteenth-
century colonists' efforts at union.[38]

An even more significant and proximate antecedent to the pre-
Revolutionary union plans involved several political figures who would
become principal players in the drama of the constitutional debates of
the 1770s. In June 1754, delegates from eleven colonies (all save Virginia)
met at Albany at the behest of their metropolitan overseers on the Board
of Trade and the governor of New York to discuss the possibility of
forming a union for defense, primarily against the French. British fears
of French territorial gains were real. The North American phase of the
Seven Years' War had begun a few months earlier with an encounter in
Pennsylvania between Colonel George Washington and French commander Joseph Coulon de Jumonville that ended in Jumonville's violent
death and French accusations that the British and their native allies had
engaged in war crimes.[39] In addition to bringing the colonies together to
form a defensive force that would beat back French imperial projects and
hold the line for the British Empire, metropolitan officials urged union
in the hope that the powerful Iroquois Confederacy—representatives of
which attended the congress—could be persuaded to join the British
fight against the French.[40]

During their nearly monthlong conference, the delegates, led by Benjamin Franklin and Thomas Hutchinson, later governor of Massachusetts, produced what became known as the Albany Plan of Union.[41]
Unlike the conference that had generated the New England Confederation, the Albany Congress had been called into existence by metropolitan authorities; unlike the New England Confederation's articles, the
Albany Plan proposed that Parliament create a "general government"
that would insert a new level of administration between the individual
colonial governments and their superiors in Britain. The Albany Plan
did, however, share the New England Confederation's emphasis on experimenting with new methods of joining the colonies in a union designed to serve particular enumerated purposes.

The general government described in the Albany Plan comprised a "grand council" of delegates selected by each colony's assembly and a "president-general" who would be appointed by the Crown and hold veto power over the grand council. The powers of the general government extended to Indian treaties and trade; land sales and grants; levying "general duties, imposts, or taxes" on the "several colonies"; the regulation of new settlements; and the funding of troops, ships, and forts for colonial defense.[42] Thus, as Edmund Morgan notes, the structure of the general government paralleled that of the colonies, with the grand council occupying the place of the colonial assembly and the president-general that of the governor—and, perhaps most important, the authority of the general government "would be limited to the external affairs of the member colonies and would not otherwise affect their existing governments."[43] The general government also reflected the colonial governments' relationship to metropolitan authority, for the Albany Plan required that laws enacted by the general government be "transmitted to the King in Council for approbation, as soon as may be after their passing; and if not disapproved within three years after presentation, to remain in force."[44] In other words, as was the case in many royal colonies, the general government possessed only incomplete legislative power; Crown review was mandatory in order for a given act to take effect.

From the impetus behind the initial meeting to the provisions of the plan, then, the Albany gathering represented the policies of parliamentarians in Westminster and administrators in Whitehall. In this case, colonial union functioned as a tool of empire. As Franklin put it, "Britain and her Colonies should be considered as one Whole, and not as different States with separate Interests."[45] That same year, Franklin published the famous "Join or Die" cartoon depicting the colonies as segments of a snake's body.

In spite of Franklin's urging, however, the Albany Plan failed to win approval from the colonial assemblies. Franklin believed that this rejection stemmed from many colonists' view that the grant of veto power to the president-general represented a threatening expansion of the royal prerogative power that already existed in the governor's veto and the Privy Council's power to disallow colonial acts.[46] Efforts by Franklin and his fellow delegates to send the proposal directly to Parliament foundered.

Moreover, the Board of Trade, the body that had originally promoted the congress, ultimately declined to approve the plan, preferring instead to promote its own more expansive scheme involving a commander in chief and colonial commissioners who would supervise colonial defense. The board's plan, in turn, was ultimately shelved in the face of resistance from members of Parliament who believed that the arrangement left the colonies too powerful.[47]

Despite the differences between the New England Confederation and the Albany Plan, the schemes shared one important characteristic: both operated within the confines of the existing imperial structure. Or, to put the point in the negative, neither sought to overturn the fundamental relationship between the colonial and metropolitan arms of the British imperial government. In 1643, during the earliest decades of the English settlement project in North America, colonies such as Massachusetts Bay and Plymouth still operated largely as corporate entities and thus enjoyed—or suffered, depending on one's point of view—a high degree of autonomy. Their efforts at union, therefore, represented little threat to the empire; on the contrary, to the extent that such organization succeeded in warding off native, French, or Dutch attackers, it comported with the interests of the still-lean mercantile empire.[48] The Albany Plan, meanwhile, contemplated a much more thoroughgoing reform of provincial government—most notably in its insertion of the general government as a new lawmaking layer between the existing levels of authority—but, as its origin in the Board of Trade demonstrated, the plan's principal aim was to draw the colonies more tightly into the imperial web. Both reforms aimed at connecting the colonies to each other in order to reap the benefits of union. The Albany Plan, however, like other eighteenth-century proposals for union, also tightened the connections between the colonies and Britain in order to reap the benefits of empire.

The Scottish and Irish Examples

The transformation between 1603 and 1707 of what David Armitage terms the "composite monarchy" of England into the "multiple kingdom" of Great Britain caused observers throughout Anglo-America to consider seriously the possibility of multilevel political and legal authorities that differed from the old feudal arrangements. Moreover, because the era of the Anglo-Scottish unions coincided with the era of English colonization in North America, political thinkers on both sides of the ocean frequently drew analogies between the status of Scotland and that of the colonies. In this way, as Armitage notes, the same ideology that accompanied the melding of the multiple kingdom at home drove the expansion of the empire overseas. Thus, "British state-building and British empire-building" were "continuous with one another in their origins as in their outcomes."[49] This conceptual connection between state- and empire-building in the British Isles deeply influenced the constitutional debates in British North America.

James VI of Scotland had added the title of James I of England on the death of Elizabeth I in 1603, when he ascended the Confessor's throne (underneath which sat the Stone of Scone, which Edward I had taken from Scotland in 1296). This "union of crowns," as it is typically termed, "united the kingdoms only to the extent that it gave them 'one Head or Sovereign'; it did not unite them in one body politic."[50] Full merger into a single body politic did not occur until 1707, when the Act of Union dissolved both the English and Scottish parliaments, creating the British Parliament and the new nation of Great Britain. For 104 years, therefore, Scotland was connected to England only by a common monarch; each nation retained its own parliament and thus its legislative sovereignty.

Anglo-Scottish legal and political arrangements between 1603 and 1707 were the subject of intense scrutiny by later-eighteenth-century political theorists in Scotland and in America. Colonial advocates such as John Adams mined Scottish precedent to bolster their claims that a union between colonies and Crown was not only feasible but grounded in solid British constitutional history.[51] Even earlier, during the debates over the Act of Union, Scottish political theorists had explored the nature of the connection between England and Scotland under the union of crowns in order to assess whether Scots ought to endorse the proposal to join parliaments as well. These studies from the years before 1707 generated theories of union that later reappeared in the American context; moreover, the analyses provided historical examples of alternative approaches to union and empire that challenged the official British account of an empire based on unitary parliamentary sovereignty.

Scottish theory and history also offered a vital vocabulary that North Americans borrowed to understand and articulate the various constitutional options before them. Most notably for purposes of this book, the pre-1707 debates over the union of parliaments explicitly invoked concepts of federalism. Specifically, as John Robertson has outlined, Scottish and English commentators who discussed the prospect of a full merger between the two nations distinguished between "federal" and "incorporating" unions.[52] The distinction between the two species of union depended on the consequences of union for the status of each component entity's sovereignty. In a federal union, each entity retained a measure of sovereignty and independence. In an incorporating union, by contrast, one or more of the component entities gave up its sovereignty to take on the political and legal identity of the larger entity.

Thus, in the words of the Scottish nationalist James Hodges, the many varieties of "amicable Conjunctions or Confederations of Kingdoms and States" could be grouped under "Two principal Heads, to wit, An Incorporating, or a Federal Union." Hodges began by describing an incorporating union:

> The Title of an Incorporating Union denotes that Kind, where by distinct and independent Kingdoms and Dominions parting with their distinction, and Independency do so unite themselves with another Kingdom, as to be embodied with it, and to become a particular Part, Province, or District of the Kingdom with which they do so unite, being subject to the Laws and Government thereof.

Hodges then defined a "confederate or federal union" as

> that, whereby Distinct, Free, and Independent Kingdoms, Dominions or States, do unite their separate Interests into one common Interest, for the mutual benefit of both, so far as relates to certain Conditions and Articles agreed upon betwixt them, retaining in the mean time their several Independencies, National Distinctions, and the different Laws, Customs, and Government of each.[53]

To illustrate the concept of incorporating union, Hodges offered the cases of Spain, France, and England, each of which had at one time consisted of multiple kingdoms or governments that subsequently joined to form a single incorporated kingdom.[54] For examples of federal union, Hodges pointed to Holland, Switzerland, the Polish-Lithuanian union, and the ancient republics of Greece. Although he admitted that the idea of a federal union was "a general Term of a very large Comprehension," Hodges generalized from a few key characteristics belonging to the Dutch confederacy. These included several "distinct Bodies of People" coming together "in a peculiar kind of general Government, for ordering all things relating to War, Taxes, Trade, &c. with mutual consent." The scope of this general government did not extend, however, to all matters, for "as to other things, each do retain their particular different Laws, Customs, and Government amongst themselves."[55] The crucial difference between the two types of union therefore centered on whether the component entities retained independent authority over any portion of their affairs—that is, whether they retained sovereignty.

Scottish commentators such as Hodges, Andrew Fletcher, and George Ridpath promoted federal union as an alternative to the incorporating union that many English observers, as well as some of their Scots contemporaries, advocated. In contrast to the connotations of conquest that the notion of incorporating union carried (the subsuming of a weak government by a more powerful one), Fletcher, in particular, envisioned a union of equals. This confederal idea, in which each member nation would retain sovereignty over all but a specific range of issues shared with the other members, resembled Pufendorf's "system of states."[56] Given the political and economic realities of the time, however, a union on a basis of full equality was unlikely, despite Fletcher's best efforts to extract more favorable terms of union by raising the specter of Scotland's selecting a different succession from England's choice of a successor to the childless Anne.[57]

Ultimately, contemporaries understood the union of 1707 as creating an incorporating union; the key fact was the dissolution of both parliaments and their reconstitution as the Parliament of Great Britain. This result was effectively a rejection of Pufendorf's confederal vision of a system of states, each of which retained its independence, sovereignty, and identity. The union of parliaments, in contrast, created a new, supreme, British body rather than simply joining preexisting bodies.[58]

In addition, despite the ostensible parity with which both parliaments dissolved and jointly reconstituted themselves as the British Parliament, the imperial possessions and status of what had been England gave the southern portion of the new union a disproportionate influence. Since its earliest articulations in the sixteenth century, the notion of incorporating union had carried overtones of empire—specifically, English empire. This connotation suggested that a kingdom that styled itself an empire, as England had since at least 1533, should stand in a superior position to its subordinate lands, and therefore that they be incorporated rather than allowed to remain in a coordinate or federal status.[59] For Scottish nationalists in the early 1700s, this incompatibility between federal and imperial systems posed an insuperable problem to achieving their desired union with England.

If the Scottish example was the happy story toward which eighteenth-century Americans aspired, there was also a cautionary tale of empire and colonization: Ireland. In contrast to the formal union that joined Scotland and England, Ireland labored under an "ambiguous status" with respect to England: "juridically a kingdom, though treated practically by the English as if it were a colony."[60] Although Ireland retained its own parliament, since 1495 Poynings' Law had mandated that all the acts of that legislature be sent to the king and the Privy Council for review.[61]

The uncertain position of Ireland within the empire meant that the Irish example was cited in support of a variety of propositions. In 1698, the Anglo-Irish political philosopher William Molyneux inquired, "Have not multitudes of Acts of Parliament both in *England* and *Ireland* declared *Ireland a Compleat Kingdom?* Is not *Ireland* stiled in them All, the *Kingdom,* or *Realm* of *Ireland?*" Molyneux then implied that Ireland therefore ought not to be considered in the same category as the American provinces: "Do these *Names* agree to a *Colony?* Have we not a Parliament, and Courts of Judicature? Do these *things* agree with a *Colony?*"[62] John Adams, in contrast, pointed to Ireland as an analogue for American arguments that the colonies were bound only to the Crown and not to Parliament: "The case of Ireland is enough to prove that the crown and realm are not the same. For Ireland is certainly annexed to the crown of England, and it certainly is not annexed to the realm."[63] References to Ireland appeared throughout the eighteenth-century Anglo-American constitutional debates, but its impact as a model for the colonists was blunted by the controversy over its position in the empire. The Irish example was thus much more troubling than the Scottish example for advocates of a formal division of authority between metropole and provinces.

Taken together, these antecedents formed the background against which American thinking about legislative power, sovereignty, authority, union, and jurisdiction fundamentally changed between the 1760s and the 1800s. They were the ideas and experiences that helped transform a vague and undefined notion of divided authority into an institutional and ideological commitment to federalism.

CHAPTER 2

Dividing Lawmaking Power

O N DECEMBER 17, 1765, a broadside appeared on the streets of New York, thrust into the hands of passersby and, at midday, posted for public consumption on the wall of at least one coffeehouse. The single sheet bore at its head an edited version of the seal of the city of New York, a heraldic device featuring two men—one European, the other Native American in appearance—arrayed on either side of a shield emblazoned with a pair of flour barrels and a brace of beavers statant. Beneath the shield, the creator of the broadside had replaced the usual motto "Sigillum Civitatis Novi Eboraci" (seal of the city of New York) with the legend "LIBERTY, PROPERTY, and no STAMPS."

The poster's text carried the heading "A serious Address to the Inhabitants of *New-York*." In just under ten column inches of close printing, the author, identified only as "Britannus Americanus," issued few prefatory niceties before launching into the meat of the appeal. The "British Constitution," the broadside warned, stood in peril of destruction. The Stamp Act, which had been passed by Parliament in March 1765, "is intended to deprive us of the most valuable Part of it, viz.—The Right of taxing ourselves, and being tried by our Equals." The "sacred and indispensable Duty of every Member of the Community," therefore, was "to support and defend" the constitution "by all just Ways and Means, against all its Enemies, whether internal or external."[1]

Just who were these enemies? They were fellow subjects—both at home and in America—who argued that Parliament possessed supreme authority over the colonies. The broadside described "our Adversaries" as "those whoever they be that aspire to a Superiority above their fellow Subjects." These foes were numerous and powerful, Britannus Americanicus gravely informed readers; therefore, New Yorkers must gird themselves for a struggle to reclaim the true meaning of their storied constitution, or system of government. Invoking the hallowed names of heroes who had distinguished themselves during the past century and a half of English and Scottish battles against arbitrary power, Britannus Americanicus implored the "native Sons of South and North Britain" to remember "those immortal Names" of seventeenth-century republican martyrs John Hampden and Algernon Sidney. For readers whose sympathies lay just to the west of England, with a different set of parties to the Civil War, the author offered similar encouragement, exhorting "you Sons of Hibernia" to "recount the Deeds of your heroic Predecessors, for the Preservation of their inestimable Rights of internal Representation." Having addressed readers on the basis of English, Scots, and Irish identity, respectively, Britannus Americanicus issued a final appeal to the "Descendants of the primitive Planters of this Colony." "[Y]ou I hope, will consider the least Infraction of your Liberties, as a Prelude to greater Incroachments."[2]

Placing resistance to the Stamp Act in the context of more than one hundred years of conflict concerning the fundamental nature of first the English and then the British constitution, this pseudonymous author urged North Americans whose roots lay in all corners of the United Kingdom to unite in the "great GENIUS of Liberty." This time, however, the opponent was neither a prerogative-wielding king nor the menace of a Catholic on the throne. Rather, the malevolent force behind what Britannus Americanicus termed "the most powerful Invasion" was the very institution whose ascendance had given the appellation "glorious" to the revolution that many contemporaries viewed as having ended the bloody political and religious struggles that had convulsed early modern England.[3] That institution was Parliament.

By 1765, many British North Americans had begun to undergo a subtle but important change in their attitudes toward Parliament. The Glorious Revolution of 1688–1689 had witnessed the triumph of the whig

philosophy that had emerged in the decades following the radical political and social upheaval of the English Civil War.[4] Central to this philosophy was the preeminence of Parliament in the constitution of England—
what Bernard Bailyn has called "the absolute supremacy of Parliament
over all other agencies of government."[5] On this view, the legislature at
Westminster—in particular, the House of Commons—stood as the great
guardian of popular rights and a counterbalance to the House of Lords
and the Crown.

Throughout the 1760s and 1770s, however, British and American ideas
of the proper scope of parliamentary power increasingly diverged. During this period, metropolitan British thinkers articulated an ever-broader
vision of the power of Parliament, or, as it was also termed, the "king-in-
Parliament"—the corporate legislative entity constituted by the combined authority of the Crown and Parliament.[6] British North Americans,
in contrast, began to challenge Parliament's supremacy—in particular, its
authority to legislate for the colonies—and to search for alternative constitutional theories, some of which attempted to cabin Parliament's authority within certain specific bounds, while others rejected altogether Parliament's power to make laws for the colonies.[7]

Britannus Americanicus's broadside was just one of many that appeared in New York and other towns in British North America between
March 1765 and March 1766. This single year constituted the entire life
cycle of the Stamp Act.[8] The act was passed by Parliament on March 22,
1765; it took effect on November 1, 1765; and it was repealed on March
18, 1766. During these twelve months, British colonists in North America launched a furious resistance marked not only by a steady barrage of
salvos from the popular press but also by boycotts of English imports,
burnings in effigy, looting, petitions to the king and Parliament, and,
most important, an intense and lively political debate that developed on
broadsides and in pamphlets, on street corners and in coffeehouses, on
Royal Navy ships and in dissenting congregations.

This debate connected several competing versions of political and legal
thought from throughout the British Isles and North America and mixed
them in a ferment of ideas about the nature of governmental authority. The
passage of the Stamp Act brought into focus the recurring and fundamental constitutional question of British North American colonization: could

provinces that increasingly regarded themselves as semiautonomous claim legitimacy within the imperial structure? To put it more pointedly, could a system of multiple layers of legislatures become formalized into what contemporaries might reasonably regard as a coherent framework of government? Or must it remain a de facto arrangement, a collection of authorities whose multiplicity might be justifiable in practice but that defied assimilation into prevailing political and legal philosophy? The issue, in short, was whether the idea of legislative multiplicity possessed normative content for eighteenth-century British North Americans, or whether a regime organized along such lines was better understood as a set of institutions requiring no particular theoretical underpinning.

Early documents of English colonization had alluded to but largely skirted this problem of multiple authorities. The Rhode Island Patent of 1643, for example, required that "the Civil Government of the said Plantations be conformable to the Laws of England so far as the Nature and Constitution of the place will admit."[9] The patent thus acknowledged both provincial and metropolitan regimes while also clearly placing those regimes in a hierarchical order (the laws of England above the civil government of the plantations). By 1765, however, such abstract statements of principle no longer satisfied metropolitan or colonial commentators. Many of these observers struggled to articulate a theoretical basis for the "imperial constitution," as Jack Greene terms it, "according to the practice of which authority was distributed in an as yet uncodified and not very clearly understood way between the center and the peripheries."[10] The Stamp Act debates demonstrated that not only had the early charters not settled the issue of multiplicity, but their broad language had created space for more than a century's worth of sometimes-conflicting precedents and institutions to develop. As Greene suggests, by the 1760s, the question whether multiple legislatures could coexist as a matter of practice within the single frame of British imperial government had been answered in the affirmative. Whatever officials in Whitehall, Westminster, Boston, or New York thought about it, the fact was that all colonists lived their lives within the regulatory ambit of both a colonial parliament and the metropolitan Parliament.[11]

Yet the controversy over the Stamp Act concerned something besides practice. The dry-sounding question behind the controversy—whether

Parliament possessed the power to lay internal taxes on the colonies—sparked a conflagration fueled by ideas about how government ought to operate, not just about how one's own government happened to operate. Certainly, the Stamp Act debates highlighted the importance of Greene's uncodified imperial constitution. But they also ushered in a new concern of contemporaries, particularly those in British North America, with codifying that contingent, perpetually renegotiated constitution into a new vision of government that was explicitly based on multilayered authority.[12] The story of federalism's origins, therefore, begins with the constitutional crisis of the 1760s, in which the background fact of multiplicity, of institutional overlap, that characterized the British Empire began to give way to a new normative vision in which multiplicity itself was a potential source of governmental authority. During the Stamp Act debates, the multilayered authority that had originated as a by-product of the imperial system became one of the key contested concepts of Anglo-American constitutional thought. With decades of experience of multilayered governmental authority behind them, the participants in the debates began to consider and discuss the idea of multiplicity as a political and legal value—not simply one characteristic of a government manqué but a central component of an emerging ideology.

The period between 1764 and 1769 thus saw repeated and regular efforts by American colonists to theorize the relationship between provinces and metropole. These theories were characterized by a growing sense that multilayered legislative authority was not only possible but perhaps even desirable. Building on this assumption, many commentators experimented with systems of allocating authority among institutions and levels of government. A common theme among these various experimental approaches was the possibility of changing the nature of the criteria by which governmental power was to be allocated. For example, instead of a territory-based view of authority, according to which British power emanated from Parliament and was coterminous with British dominions, some theorists in the 1760s offered a view based on subject matter that apportioned regulatory power according to the nature of the particular thing or activity being regulated. To be sure, throughout the history of British North American settlement, authorities at home had declined to regulate certain aspects of local, colonial life, instead leaving such regulation to local legislative bodies.[13] This metropolitan delegation of lawmaking power to the colonial periphery was, however, a far cry from the type of claim to exclusive jurisdiction over certain realms of activity that many colonists began to assert in the 1760s.

Many colonial commentators sought to bar Westminster and Whitehall from intervening in particular classes of matters, whether through legislative, regulatory, or administrative measures. Sometimes colonists referred to this protected category of things or activities as "internal"; at other times they denominated it "special," "domestic," or related to matters of revenue. Despite the variable terminology, these systems of classification demonstrated the colonists' common determination to carve out a category of lawmaking that was free from metropolitan oversight. In the imperial system as it had grown up, the central authority claimed plenary power to define the scope of its own powers, subject to no provincially imposed limits. Beginning with the Stamp Act crisis, though, some colonial observers challenged the territorial notion that imperial authority was coextensive with the map of Britain's North American holdings. They began to push toward a system that formally recognized two distinct levels of government within the empire, each with its proper sphere of legislative power. In this way, then, two central elements of American federal ideology were defined during the debates of the 1760s: first, structuring a government to include multiple levels of authority; and second, dividing that authority along subject-specific lines.

In his *Constitutional History of the American Revolution,* John Phillip Reid briefly discusses a form of federalism that he believes was assumed but not developed by some colonial observers, notably John Dickinson, John Adams, and Richard Bland. According to this "federalism of function," Parliament might constitutionally intervene in matters defined as imperial, but not in colonial matters.[14] A functional form of federalism differs in two important ways from the normative conception of divided authority that this book posits as a vital ingredient of early federal thinking. First, a functional conception of federalism implies that contemporaries were focused primarily on function itself—that is, on enabling government to achieve certain ends—and that decisions about initial allocations of power followed only secondarily from these ends. In this sense, a federalism of function is occupied with issues of institutional practice in the here and now, rather than attempting to construct an account of the nature of governmental authority itself. Certainly, practical concerns about taxation and regulation were part of the story of the 1760s debates, but contemporaries also explicitly engaged in constitutional theorizing in their attempts to set formal boundaries around the exercise of distinct metropolitan and provincial species of authority. The internal-external and, later, revenue-regulation distinctions were the products of a radical conviction that legislative power could be split into multiple heads, each associated with a set of particular substantive activities. Multiplicity, not function alone, was the touchstone that emerged from the 1760s debates.

Second, and perhaps more important, this limited notion of federalism treats it not as a bundle of ideas that contemporaries were actively developing in the mid- to late eighteenth century but rather as a free-floating model of political organization apparently independent of human creation or even influence. The idea of federalism, according to Reid, "had not yet been developed as a constitutional doctrine or, at best, was only vaguely understood in America" during the 1760s. Although Reid notes that some "concept of federalism . . . was developing as part of the pre-revolutionary controversy," he distinguishes this concept from "the federalism of concurrent jurisdiction that eventually became the hallmark of American constitutionalism."[15] Rather than depicting federal ideas as hovering above but ultimately only marginal to the 1760s debates, this chapter seeks to demonstrate that the concepts that would be denominated as "federal" after the 1780s in fact originated in the opposition constitutional theories of Reid's "American whigs."[16]

Although the single sheet penned by Britannus Americanus in December 1765 was only one of many such public declarations, the broadside is noteworthy because it encapsulates many of the themes of the transatlantic political and legal struggles of the 1760s. In addition to invoking the British constitution and harking back to the great political struggles of the seventeenth century, the "Serious Address" referred to the separate kingdoms of England and Scotland that by 1765 constituted Great Britain, as well as suggesting that the colony of New York was but one satellite in an imperial constellation that also included Ireland. The "Serious Address" thus gives us an initial mise-en-scène in which to observe how ideas of divided government developed in British North America during the Stamp Act crisis.

It must be noted that independence did not lie at the heart of the colonial resistance movement of the 1760s.[17] Although many of the provincial participants in the 1760s debates sought to redefine the relationship between metropole and colonies, they did not challenge the fact of the empire or their own condition as colonists. On the contrary, the colonial opposition for the most part embraced the colonies' position as components of the British Empire. Their objections focused on what they viewed as a novel and illegitimate power grab by one arm of the British government—Parliament—and the efforts of that body, in their view, to translate its newfound supremacy at home into a wholly unprecedented degree of authority over the entire empire.

The Stamp Act: Crisis Becomes Manifest

To understand the theories of divided authority that began to emerge during the crisis of the 1760s, we must begin with the piece of legislation that John Adams described in his diary as an "enormous Engine, fabricated by the British Parliament, for battering down all the Rights and Liberties of America."[18] The Stamp Act—the object of Britannus Americanicus's outrage—passed into law in March 1765 and took effect on November 1 of that year. The impulse behind the act, however, can be traced at least to March 9, 1764, when George Grenville, first lord of the Treasury, rose in the House of Commons to present the ministry's proposed budget for the coming year. As part of the draft budget, Grenville introduced a "resolution to raise the revenue in America for defending itself."[19] Such a measure was necessary, Grenville maintained, to restore economic balance between the colonies and the mother country in the wake of the extraordinary expense of the Seven Years' War. Moreover, the significant increase in territory that victory over France had added to the British Empire required additional troops, administration, and regulatory attention, all of which required increased spending. "We have expended much in America," Grenville told the Commons. "Let us now avail ourselves of the fruit of that expense."[20]

As early as the summer of 1763, Grenville had contemplated levying a stamp tax and had considered draft legislation to that effect. Indeed, Grenville suggested that the 1764 revenue bill contain a provision stating that Parliament might in the future "charge certain Stamp Duties in the said Colonies and Plantations."[21] To explain the lag between Grenville's original proposal and the passage of the Stamp Act, historians have pointed to some combination of a desire to stave off American opposition by inviting colonists to take part in the process, concern regarding reaction in Parliament and in Britain generally to a stamp tax, and a simple need for more time to determine how such an act would be enforced.[22] According to surviving reports of Grenville's March 9 speech, the minister stated that passage of the stamp tax would be delayed for one year in order to give the colonies an opportunity to devise their own method of taxing themselves.[23] Having raised the possibility of levying a stamp duty on the colonies, Grenville thus refrained from immediately recommending that Parliament enact such a tax policy. In the meantime, Treasury officials set about drawing up draft stamp tax legislation.[24]

Scholars have long viewed the period following the end of the Seven Years' War in 1763 as a moment of renewed imperial interest in strengthening the ties between Britain and the North American colonies. Grenville typically occupies a prominent place in this narrative of metropolitan leash tightening. After taking office in the summer of 1763, a few months after the Treaty of Paris ended the Seven Years' War, Grenville quickly demonstrated his determination to reform the mechanisms of colonial revenue collection while also increasing the system's yield. The British national debt had grown from £72,289,673 in 1755 to £122,603,336 in 1763 and £129,586,789 in 1764. Official estimates of the cost of maintaining ten thousand regular troops in North America—especially necessary in light of Pontiac's Rebellion in 1763—put the figure at a minimum of £220,000 per year.[25] Clearly, the end of the war did not mean an end to the enormous expense of protecting and maintaining the British colonies in North America.

Nor did the accounts-receivable side of the imperial ledger inspire confidence. Since the earliest days of American colonization, authorities in England had struggled to police colonial commerce through various navigation acts and other regulations emanating from London, most notably from the Board of Trade, which had been established in 1696.[26] In keeping with the mercantile aims of British colonization dating from the days of Elizabeth, such regulations had consistently sought to keep the colonies commercially tied to the home country. Thus, Parliament restricted—sometimes by taxation, sometimes by outright prohibition— colonial imports from non-British lands, required colonial produce to be transported on British ships, and mandated that the proceeds from American exports be turned over to metropolitan authorities.

This was the policy; the practice, however, was another story. According to figures at the time, the revenues netted by the royal customs collectors amounted to only £1,800 per year. Many collectors drew their salaries from afar, spending the majority of their time in England and delegating their duties to deputies who in turn were susceptible to bribery from fellow colonists. Rampant and effective smuggling by seasoned colonists further stunted imperial receipts.[27] Faced with mounting imperial expenditures and insufficient revenues, Grenville launched his campaign in 1764. As Edmund S. Morgan and Helen Morgan have suggested, Grenville's effort represented a qualitative departure from past attempts to bind the colonies more tightly into the imperial commercial orbit.[28] Not content merely to enhance the execution of the existing customs laws, Grenville sought new, wider-ranging regulations in addition to more rigorous enforcement. Previously, "customs duties had been designed to regulate the flow of trade rather than fill the Treasury."[29] In order to meet the pressing financial needs of the British Empire as a whole, however, Grenville and others argued that the colonies needed to increase their contribution to the imperial economy. Beginning with the Sugar Act in 1764, therefore, Grenville's reforms included a revitalized customs service involving more stringent inspection of ships and expanded jurisdiction for admiralty courts.[30] The final and most important piece of Grenville's program was the Stamp Act, which followed eleven months after the Sugar Act in March 1765.

Although Grenville appears to have anticipated some degree of opposition from the colonies (and perhaps from Parliament) to this exercise of metropolitan legislative power, he does not seem to have believed that the turn to a stamp tax to raise revenue was materially different from any other species of tax. Nor did he countenance the distinction between raising a revenue and regulating trade that would soon become a central issue of debate. The Sugar Act, he noted, had contained a reference to "improving the revenue of this kingdom."[31] As Edmund Morgan puts it,

Grenville's "chief concern was the money, not the method of raising it." Grenville himself later stated, "I have ever said, I wish to see a plan and a system. . . . I framed a plan. I framed a system."[32]

As the centerpiece of that system, the Stamp Act required that a wide array of printed materials and documents—from decks of cards to legal pleadings and wills—be printed on paper that bore an official British stamp.[33] Each type of document required a specific denomination of stamp, and the stamp in turn required the payment of a specific duty. Official printers in Britain produced the paper; the paper was then shipped to America and taken into the custody of stamp distributors, who were instructed to dispense it to purchasers upon payment of the appropriate duty. Unlike previous imperial taxation regimes, the Stamp Act required payment of the duty upon transfer of the item from supplier to consumer, rather than upon importation into the colonies. In contrast to the Sugar Act, for example, which set the duty on molasses imported from outside the British Empire, the Stamp Act provided for direct taxation on transactions within the colonies. Like the Sugar Act, however, the Stamp Act permitted violations to be prosecuted in either common-law or admiralty courts.

News of the act reached the colonies in early April, nearly seven months before it was to take effect. In May, the Virginia House of Burgesses challenged Parliament's authority over the colonies by issuing a set of resolutions that insisted on the right of representation in matters relating to taxation. By the end of October, before any stamps had been purchased or duties collected, all but two of the royally appointed stamp distributors in the colonies had resigned. Of the remaining two, one resigned in November; the other fled upon arriving and surveying the scene in Georgia in January.[34] Also in October, delegates from nine colonies assembled in New York in a gathering that became known as the Stamp Act Congress. They drafted a "Declaration of Rights," as well as petitions to the king and the House of Commons and a memorial to the House of Lords.[35]

By November 1, 1765, when the act was to take effect, mob violence, popular protest, and a cascade of pamphlets and broadsides, including the one by Britannus Americanus, had swelled to such a state of upheaval that enforcement of the act became virtually impossible. Unrest began in Boston and swept throughout the colonies, threatening stamp distributors' lives and property as colonists sought to prevent any enforcement of the act that would become precedent and thus arguably bind them to submit to the tax.[36] In late August, the Boston home of Lieutenant Governor Thomas Hutchinson was ransacked, vandalized, and nearly leveled by a particularly determined mob; Hutchinson himself, as well as other colonial officials, received repeated death threats and regular burnings in effigy. Furthermore, Americans had for months protested the imminent stamp duties by boycotting many British goods. These nonimportation agreements, adopted throughout the colonies, led to economic depression in Britain and, consequently, to pressure on the government from powerful merchants to heal the rift with the colonies.[37] The exit of Grenville and the arrival of Charles Watson-Wentworth, second Marquess of Rockingham, as first lord of the Treasury established the ascendance of the merchants, whose zeal for commercial normalization led them to band together in a committee to advocate repeal of the act. A significant public outcry in England also urged conciliation with the colonies for the sake of justice, as well as economic interest.[38]

On December 17, 1765, the day on which Britannus Americanicus's broadside appeared in New York, George III addressed Parliament, referring briefly to "Matters of Importance" in America but forbearing to mention the violence and upheaval that had taken hold of the colonies.[39] Momentum toward repeal neared its crest in January 1766. On January 14, William Pitt—brother-in-law of Grenville and, while prime minister, architect of the British victory in the Seven Years' War—argued in the House of Commons that although Parliament did possess supreme authority over the colonies, that authority did not extend to levying taxes. "[M]y opinion," Pitt declared, "is, that the Stamp Act be repealed absolutely, totally, and immediately. . . . At the same time, let the sovereign authority of this country over the colonies, be asserted in as strong terms as can be devised, and be made to extend to every point of legislation whatsoever." But, Pitt added, this broad assertion of metropolitan sovereignty did have some limits. Parliament might "bind their trade, confine their manufactures, and exercise every power whatsoever, except that of taking money out of their pockets without their consent."[40]

Pitt's comments included multiple sharp exchanges with Grenville, who maintained that the Stamp Act was a proper exercise of Parliament's power. In the words of one observer, "For some hours the debate lay between those two great masters, and the ministry stood by, like the rabble at a boxing match."[41] Pitt's speech sparked "offence" at home and "delirium" in America, according to Horace Walpole, who counted the remarks as "rank[ing] in celebrity with [Pitt's] most famous orations."[42] When word of the speech reached the colonies, many Americans fixed on one passage in particular: "If the gentleman does not understand the difference between external and internal taxes, I cannot help it; but there is a plain distinction between taxes levied for the purpose of raising a revenue, and duties imposed for the regulation of trade, for the accommodation of the subject; although, in the consequences, some revenue might incidentally arise from the latter."[43]

By distinguishing between internal and external taxes, Pitt was contributing to a transatlantic constitutional discourse that continued to structure political debate even after the repeal of the Stamp Act. Well after March 1766, the language of internal versus external regulation, and the related dichotomies of revenue versus trade regulation and taxation versus legislation, filled the pages of pamphlets and were echoed in discussions in salons and coffeehouses throughout America. Observers in the colonies and in Britain initially used these dichotomies to evaluate the constitutionality of the Stamp Act and subsequently applied them to broader inquiries into taxation and regulation per se. In pamphlets and debates between 1764 and 1768, these distinctions recurred frequently as commentators tested their application to current political events.

Historians disagree about the role of the internal-external distinction in colonial thought of 1760s. Some scholars view the distinction as a polemical device that the colonists deployed strategically in an effort to combat parliamentary regulation with the narrowest argument possible. Although this view might suggest that the distinction lacked meaningful content, and that it was more or less a fig leaf for an amorphous spirit of resistance to Parliament, it can also tend toward the subtler and more interesting conclusion that American assertions that the Stamp Act was an "internal" tax were carefully worded for maximum effect according to contemporary legal and political norms.[44] Reid, for example, argues that many colonial spokesmen's deep immersion in the "dynamics of constitutional advocacy" motivated their argumentative approach, which he describes as "limit[ing] the issues and claim[ing] no more than is necessary to establish your point." Thus, according to Reid, the colonists began their debate with metropolitan authorities by confining their arguments to the specific question of Parliament's power to lay internal taxes.[45] After 1765, this inquiry expanded to include the larger question of Parliament's power to tax for the purposes of revenue. Subsequently, Reid suggests, the issue took the broadest form of Parliament's power to legislate in any way for the colonies.[46] On this view, although the colonists' argumentative strategy might have changed over the course of nearly a decade of debate, their underlying opposition philosophy remained largely consistent.

Related to, but distinct from, this interpretation is the view of the internal-external distinction as a temporary and somewhat tentative stop on the way to a more full-throated denial of Parliament's authority not just to tax the colonies but to regulate them at all. According to this interpretation, colonial claims became more extreme during the period from 1764 to 1775—that is, the strategic change was the result of a change in ideas. In this vein, Randolph G. Adams set forth three stages of constitutional debate on the subject of taxation: first, colonial acceptance of Parliament's power to lay external taxes but denial of its power to lay internal taxes; second, colonial acceptance of Parliament's power to regulate trade but denial of its power to lay taxes at all; and, third, colonial acceptance of Parliament's broad power to oversee the colonies in some general sense, as part of the British dominions, but denial of its power to legislate for the colonies as long as they were not represented in Parliament. More recently, Robert Middlekauff has argued that in 1765 the colonists threw themselves into a debate they believed was limited to taxation and only later grasped the consequences of their ideas.[47]

A third interpretation of the events of 1765 holds that the colonists believed in the internal-external distinction, and that the idea had some basis in theory, but that metropolitan participants took advantage of the idea's implications when they concluded that the colonists' resistance to internal regulation meant that the colonists conceded Parliament's authority to engage in external regulation. Bernard Bailyn has offered a version of this view, as has Reid.[48] Still other scholars, most notably Edmund Morgan and Helen Morgan, deny that American whigs differentiated between internal and external regulation at all and argue that this distinction stemmed from mischaracterization (whether willful or not) by observers in Britain. Morgan and Morgan point to statements by James Otis, John Dickinson, and Thomas Hutchinson to the effect that the distinction originated in Britain rather than in America. Thus, for Morgan and Morgan, colonial thought proceeded in two stages. In the first stage, which began with the Stamp Act controversy and lasted through the 1770s, the colonists admitted the power of Parliament to regulate trade and legislate generally for the entire empire but denied its power to tax the colonies; in the second stage, beginning with the Coercive or Intolerable Acts of 1774, the colonists moved to the more extreme position of denying altogether Parliament's power to legislate for the colonies.[49]

Regardless of where the internal-external distinction first originated, the evidence clearly demonstrates that commentators in both Britain and America found it helpful as a tool to interpret the situation in which they found themselves after 1764. These binary approaches to lawmaking power came to possess their own interpretive power, providing a lens through which participants made sense of the arguments they heard and read and thus structuring the subsequent course of the debate. Indeed, both colonial and metropolitan commentators moved frequently among the various languages of internal versus external, revenue versus trade, and taxation versus legislation.[50] What matters here is not the nature of the particular fissures that appeared in the previously smooth facade of imperial constitutional theory, but the fact that those fissures appeared at all.

Expedience and Ideology: Colonial Theories of Legislative Power

Some of the earliest tracts distinguishing between internal and external regulation appeared in the 1750s, when the Seven Years' War gave special salience to the issue of the colonies' contributions to the imperial economy. Significantly, metropolitan as well as colonial spokespeople appear to have found the internal-external distinction useful in their efforts to articulate the respective duties of home and provinces.

Writing in 1755, when the North American phase of the Seven Years' War had already begun, Henry McCulloh, a metropolitan administrator sent to North Carolina during the 1740s to oversee the royal land offices, explored the distinction between internal, colonial affairs and the external affairs of the empire as a whole. McCulloh began his account, which was published in London as a pamphlet, by contrasting the British imperial system to that of France. He found the former wanting as compared with the "Liberty" and the "Improvement of their Trade, and Enlargement of their distant Colonies and Possessions" that he saw as central to French imperial policy. Clearly concerned that the chaos of war augured a breakdown in imperial order, McCulloh advocated that the political and commercial ties between Britain and North America be rationalized and fortified. "It is the Want of System in the Conduct of our Affairs, which is the Bane and Ruin of our *American* Colonies, and must in the end prove destructive to our Trade and Commerce," McCulloh lamented.[51]

Central to McCulloh's reform plan was knitting the colonies more tightly into the fabric of the empire by convincing observers on both sides of the ocean of their "mutual Relation or Dependance upon the general System." In particular, McCulloh argued for a clear distinction between the powers of government that were vested in the colonies and those that were retained by authorities at home. The colonies' legislative powers, which derived from royal charter and were subject to review by either the Crown or Parliament, extended to "Bye-Laws, for the better ordering their own Domestic Affairs"; they did not include the power to "make Laws which may have a general Effect, either in obstructing the Trade of this Kingdom, or in laying Restraints and Difficulties on the neighbouring Colonies."[52] For McCulloh, then, the goal of binding the colonies more tightly to the empire was best achieved by granting them a quantum of sovereign power over their domestic, or internal, affairs. His effort to draw a line between, on one hand, matters of general concern to multiple colonies or to the empire as a whole and, on the other hand, "domestic" affairs that concerned only the particular colony in question demonstrates that at least as early as 1755, some imperial agents were willing to consider experimenting with new jurisdictional arrangements.

McCulloh wrote as an imperial administrator intent on correcting what he regarded as a misalignment of interests between the components of the British Empire. Other commentators in the 1750s took a similar approach.

Archibald Kennedy, a Scot who held various imperial offices in New York, published several treatises that discussed the colonial situation. In *Observations on the Importance of the Northern Colonies under Proper Regulations* (1750), Kennedy argued that the colonies suffered under British trade restrictions. "A Situation melancholly enough! Vast Numbers of People, and daily increasing, uselessly employed, which is the worst Sort of Employment. In Debt we are, and in Debt we must be, for those vast Importations from Europe," he lamented, noting that the scant profits the colonies received from their exports "will hardly defray the Expence of the Apparatus of our Tea Tables." In a subsequent pamphlet, Kennedy returned to the theme of the "sorry figure" the colonies made in imperial revenue accounts. This time, however, he argued that the colonies ("little, diminutive, dependent States") had become too costly to Britain. Colonies such as New York had been "nursed up and indulged, at an infinite Expence to the Crown, and the People of *England*. . . . We are exempted from all parliamentary Aids; we have never added any Thing to the Revenue of *Great-Britain,* as some of our Neighbour Colonies have done, of immense Sums." In order to "relieve the Merchant, and encourage Trade," Kennedy advocated a "gentle Tax upon Lands here."[53]

As Ned Landsman has noted, many of these administration officials "approached imperial problems more from the perspective of the empire as a whole than from that of the metropolis, at least until the outbreak of colonial resistance."[54] As part of his reform proposal, McCulloh suggested that Parliament raise revenue in the colonies by passing an act requiring the use of stamped paper for all legal documents. In contrast to the 1765 act, however, McCulloh's plan would have directed the receipts from stamp duties not simply into the Exchequer but rather into "some new Funds" dedicated "only to the Security and Advantage of the Colonies." McCulloh subsequently opposed the Stamp Act of 1765, which did not provide for segregated accounts.[55]

By 1764, the end of the war and the first phases of the Grenville reforms had begun to reshape the contours of the transatlantic discussion. The tone shifted from a shared emphasis on tying the components of the empire more closely together to a new division between colonial and metropolitan interests. With the Sugar Act in force and a stamp duty looming, prominent public figures such as Richard Bland of Virginia, James

Otis of Massachusetts, Daniel Dulany of Maryland, and John Dickinson of Pennsylvania began to attack what they viewed as the ministry's corrupt efforts to expand taxation at the expense of the imperial constitution. In addition, groups of colonists—for example, those assembled in the Virginia House of Burgesses and in the Stamp Act Congress—issued official statements responding to the new parliamentary regulations.

Richard Bland's pamphlet *The Colonel Dismounted: or the Rector Vindicated* appeared in Williamsburg in August 1764, ahead of the news that officials in London were considering levying a stamp tax. The pamphlet put forth an early version of the distinction that his fellow colonists would increasingly articulate between internal and external government.[56] Responding to a controversy between the colonial authorities in Virginia and the Board of Trade over which institution would have final authority to set tobacco prices, Bland's tract undertook to investigate the proper division of authority between governmental actors within the empire. Bland distinguished between internal and external matters and argued that for purposes of external government, "we are and must be subject to the authority of the British Parliament." But with respect to internal government, which Bland defined as "exclud[ing] from the legislature of the colony all power derogatory to their dependence upon the mother kingdom," Bland was less complaisant: "[A]ny tax respecting our INTERNAL polity which may hereafter be imposed on us by act of Parliament is arbitrary, as depriving us of our rights, and may be opposed." Therefore, Bland opined, "the legislature of the colony have a right to enact ANY law they shall think necessary for their INTERNAL government."[57] In the pamphlet, Bland did not explicitly address the question of Parliament's authority to tax the colonies, but he did employ the rhetoric of internal and external governmental powers to erect a boundary around what he viewed as the special legislative province of the Virginia assembly.[58] Bland developed these ideas further in his *Inquiry into the Rights of the British Colonies* of 1766, which will be discussed later.

Another, more widely circulated tract published during the summer of 1764 rejected the internal-external distinction altogether. James Otis's *Rights of the British Colonies Asserted and Proved* argued for a broad interpretation of the scope of Parliament's authority: "The power of parliament is uncontroulable, but by themselves, and we must obey."[59] But this is not to say that Otis conceded Grenville's case. On the contrary, *The Rights of the British Colonies* became one of the touchstones of American whig opinion during the Stamp Act crisis. The pamphlet argued for certain limits on Parliament's power to regulate the colonies. The limiting factor for Otis, however, was not whether the matter in question pertained to the colonies' internal affairs; rather, it was whether the provinces had been adequately represented in the legislative process at Westminster. Thus Otis saw "no foundation for the distinction some make in England between an internal and an external tax on the colonies."[60] Otis's association of internal-external language with metropolitan arguments—despite the previous use of that language by Bland and other colonists—and his turn to representation as the chief restraint on Parliament suggest that at least some colonists feared that even the internal-external distinction might result in too broad a concession to Westminster.

Otis's writings demonstrate his belief that Parliament was supreme within the framework of the English constitution, but that legitimate methods nevertheless existed to restrict Parliament's authority over the colonies. Declaring as one of the "first principles" of "civil rights of the British colonies" that "all of them are subject to and dependent on Great Britain," Otis laid out the case for Parliament's broad power over the colonies: "[T]herefore as over subordinate governments the Parliament of Great Britain has an undoubted power and lawful authority to make acts for the general good that, by naming [the colonies], shall and ought to be equally binding as upon the subjects of Great Britain within the realm." A few pages after this strong endorsement of parliamentary supremacy over the subject and dependent governments of the colonies, Otis issued his opinion on taxation of the colonies. His comments here reflected his belief that the subjects' consent was crucial to the legitimacy of certain government acts. "[C]an there be any liberty where property is taken away without consent?" Otis demanded. He immediately answered in the negative. "[T]he imposition of taxes, whether on trade, or on land, or houses, or ships, on real or personal, fixed or floating property, in the colonies is absolutely irreconcilable with the rights of the colonists as British subjects and as men."[61] Otis's acknowledgment of the supremacy of Parliament in matters of taxation was thus premised on the colonists' consent to the tax.

This sweeping conception of Parliament's power therefore still insisted that external criteria existed by which parliamentary actions could be evaluated. Although Otis denied the validity of the internal-external distinction, he invoked natural-law concepts and customary English rights to justify his claim that Parliament's power, while extensive, was not entirely without limits. "The Parliament cannot make 2 and 2, 5: Omnipotency cannot do it," he insisted. "There must be in every instance, a higher authority, *viz.* GOD." In light of the lawyer-statesman's famous oratory in the writs of assistance case just three years earlier, in which Otis had argued that the English constitution placed limits on Parliament's lawmaking power, and that therefore Parliament could not grant search warrants (writs of assistance) to customs officials, this line of analysis was not surprising.[62]

Otis's wide range of sources extended beyond natural law and English custom to include English and Continental political theorists such as Hugo Grotius, Samuel von Pufendorf, John Locke, Emmerich de Vattel, Jean-Jacques Rousseau, and Charles-Louis de Secondat, baron de Montesquieu.[63] In particular, Otis focused on these authors' theories of the rights of colonies and, in a broader sense, states joined together in colonial or confederate arrangements. But his approach to these theories tended, as was often the case with Otis, toward ambiguity. For example, in *The Rights of the British Colonies,* Otis cited Grotius's *De jure belli ac pacis (The Rights of War and Peace)* (1625) for the principle that "when people by one consent go to form colonies," they create "a new and independent state." He then cited Pufendorf's *De jure naturae et gentium (The Law of Nature and Nations)* (1672) for the principle that a given colony might continue as "a part of the commonwealth it was sent out from," remain "united to it by a sort of unequal confederacy," or else become "a separate commonwealth" with "the same rights with the state it is descended from." After lengthy discussions of both these theorists of the law of nature and nations, however, Otis concluded, "[T]hese two great men only state facts and the opinions of others, without giving their own upon the subject."[64]

Alongside his apparent minimizing of Grotius and Pufendorf, Otis here implied that their views were so commonplace as hardly to deserve mention—a suggestion belied by both the oppositional status of Continental thought in the contemporary Anglo-American legal tradition and his own extensive canvassing of their theories.[65] He then approvingly referred to Locke (one of the "purer fountains . . . of our English writers"). Otis thus demonstrated his immersion in a political conversation that did not traffic in the notions of unitary sovereignty that soon thereafter reached their full articulation in the work of William Blackstone.[66] Consequently, Otis's tangled and seemingly contradictory arguments for the supremacy of Parliament stopped short of a fully positivistic vision of legislative authority. Instead, he adverted to "the law of nature and its author"—in addition to Parliament's own sense of what was "expedient" and "equitable"—as restraints on its power to make law for the colonies.[67]

Along with Otis's tracts, the writings of Daniel Dulany served as a prominent source of arguments for the American whigs. In August 1765, during the uneasy months before the Stamp Act was to take effect, an anonymous pamphlet titled *Considerations on the Propriety of Imposing Taxes in the British Colonies for the Purpose of Raising a Revenue by Act of Parliament* appeared in Annapolis. Demand quickly exhausted the first print run, and a second edition soon followed. Word of the author's identity soon made its way through Maryland and spread to the other colonies.[68] Dulany, a prominent lawyer and colonial official and the son of an Irish immigrant, presented two principal arguments against the Stamp Act: first, the colonists were not in fact and could not in theory be represented in Parliament; and second, the colonies were adequately and completely represented in their provincial assemblies, which were subordinate to the tripartite entity of the king-in-Parliament.

Dulany conceded that "the Colonies are Dependent upon *Great-Britain,* and the supreme Authority vested in the King, Lords, and Commons, may justly be exercised to secure, or preserve their Dependence, whenever necessary for that Purpose." This authority did not, however, extend to taxation, which Dulany viewed as the superior's "seiz[ing] the Property of his Inferior when he pleases." To keep these superior and inferior authorities in their proper spheres, Dulany proposed a solution that connected the internal-external distinction with the idea of dependence. "By their Constitutions of Government, the Colonies are impowered to impose internal Taxes. This Power is compatible with their Dependence. . . . May not then the Line be distinctly and justly drawn between such Acts as are necessary, or proper, for preserving or securing the

Dependence of the Colonies, and such as are not necessary or proper for that very important Purpose; and would moreover Destroy the fundamental and necessary Principle of Constitutional Liberty?"[69] In other words, in cases where the exercise of a particular power by the colonial assemblies might threaten the hierarchy of the empire, Parliament would occupy the legislative field.

Dulany thus seemed to envision a second-order legislative inquiry into not just the ostensible purpose of a piece of parliamentary legislation (e.g., a regulation on the colonial manufacture of hats) but also the overarching structural purpose of that legislation (e.g., to keep the colonies tied to metropolitan political and commercial systems). This approach left unresolved the vital question of which institution would make this second-order assessment—and, indeed, whether such an assessment would be made in Britain or in America. The colonies would retain all other lawmaking authority, especially in cases involving what he viewed as the Americans' customary English constitutional claims to consent.

Dulany's analysis thus combined Bland's focus on separating internal from external powers with Otis's emphasis on representation, producing one of the more nuanced contributions to the debate of the 1760s. But the question not just, to paraphrase one scholar, "who decides?" but "who decides who decides?" continued to dog colonial attempts to (as Dulany put it) draw the line between the supremacy of Parliament and some modicum of colonial legislative authority.[70] As the following chapters will show, this theme recurred, albeit in somewhat different variations, throughout American constitutional debates into the nineteenth century.

Reform and Reinforcement: Metropolitan Approaches to Divided Authority

Thus far this discussion has focused on the opinions of observers writing from the colonies as a matter of both geographic location and self-identification. But Otis's association of the internal-external approach with British rhetoric likely stemmed at least in part from his familiarity with tracts published by observers from across the imperial map. In response to Bland, Otis, Dulany, and many other authors who developed the colonial viewpoint during the debates of the 1760s, several representatives of the metropolitan government—creole and British, in America and in London—issued their own treatises that attempted to correct what they saw as the colonists' erroneous constitutional interpretations. In one way or another, each of these observers used the events of 1764–1766 to articulate his view of the possibilities for dividing authority between imperial center and colonial periphery. Moreover, each of these widely circulated analyses of the nature of the imperial constitution brought a version of the language of internal versus external regulation to bear on the difficult question of the extent of Parliament's power to tax the colonies.

The metropolitan view was far from uniform and may in fact have exhibited more diversity than the American whigs' side of the argument. Perhaps this breadth of opinion should not be surprising. After all, what one might reasonably denominate "the metropolitan perspective" ranged across an enormous spectrum of allegiances and experiences, including administrators in London such as William Knox, undersecretary in the Colonial or American Department; Thomas Pownall and Francis Bernard, English-born governors of colonies in North America; William Bollan, English émigré to and agent for the colonies; and creoles such as Thomas Hutchinson, scion of an established Boston merchant family and holder (in some cases simultaneously) of numerous Crown offices, including those of chief judge, lieutenant governor, and governor. A fundamental feature of life during this period for the actors discussed in this chapter was their dual identity as both agents—in the broadest sense of the term—of the British government and participants in colonial political life. They thus occupied a liminal status as sometimes middlemen, sometimes compradors, and sometimes dissidents.[71]

Despite the diverse backgrounds and positions of these imperial middlemen, however, their writings addressed a common theme: the difficulty of reconciling a constitutional theory based on unitary authority with an emerging countertheory that embraced multiple authorities located within a variety of sometimes-overlapping institutions.[72] Unlike the American whigs, whose identity the Stamp Act crisis helped crystallize, these metropolitan spokesmen already had in common their status as officials of the empire. Some, such as Hutchinson, were also longtime residents of the colonies, but for purposes of this discussion—as, indeed, for purposes of the discussion in 1764–1765—the salient quality connecting them all was their chosen role as agents of the empire.[73] Furthermore, the internal-external approach to imperial governance, as well as the revenue-trade and taxation-legislation approaches, were discussed and in some cases adopted by these commentators. This spirit of intellectual experimentation demonstrates the willingness of some metropolitan observers at least to consider translating the fact of multilayered authority into an ideology of multilayered authority.

Of the metropolitan commentators, the most interesting for this discussion are Francis Bernard and Thomas Pownall. In addition to sharing the distinction of serving as royal governor of Massachusetts, both men published lengthy treatises—each well more than one hundred pages long—on the relationship between Britain and the provinces. Both works displayed an interest in colonial reform, as well as an impulse to justify actions taken in an official capacity. Pownall served as governor from 1757 to 1760, when, relieved of his post, he returned to England. After a two-month interlude during which Lieutenant Governor Hutchinson served as acting governor, Bernard arrived and assumed the governorship, which he held until 1769, when certain letters he had written to officials in London appeared in a few Boston newspapers and led to demands for his removal.

Pownall's *Administration of the Colonies*, first published in London in 1764, was a substantial work; the second edition, published in 1765, numbered 292 pages (including a seven-page dedication to Grenville). The work attracted the attention of James Otis, who referred to it repeatedly in *The Rights of the British Colonies;* it continued to be published in updated editions until 1774.[74] *The Administration of the Colonies* presented a forceful argument for reform of the colonial administration at home, urging the government to fulfill what Pownall viewed as its duty to incorporate the colonies into a single commercial empire with Britain. Pownall's goal was, as he put it, a "grand marine dominion consisting of our possessions in the Atlantic and in America united into a one Empire, in a one center, where the seat of government is." In the aftermath of the Seven Years' War, Pownall argued, the European power that could bring the emerging commercial might of the Caribbean and mainland North American colonies under its dominion would become "the ruling commercial power of Europe." Besides offering bold statements, Pownall proposed specific reforms that he believed would "interweave the administration of the colonies into the British administration." His principal suggestion was to house the scattered duties of colonial oversight in one new department located in Whitehall with a secretary of state for the colonies at its head; this department must, Pownall urged, be "sovereign and supreme, as to every thing relating to it."[75]

As this language and the title of his work suggest, Pownall envisioned the British Empire as a vertical hierarchy of administrative authorities, with the new American Department at the top of the chain of authority. To that end, the former governor recommended keeping each colony separate from the others and connected only to the metropole. The colonies, Pownall insisted, "must be guarded against having, or forming, any principle of coherence with each other above that, whereby they cohere in this center." The great marine dominion would operate in hub-and-spoke fashion, with London as the "center of the system" with respect to every colony.[76]

But Pownall did concede a measure of authority to the colonial assemblies. He took pains to distinguish between "full, free, uncontrouled power, in the act of legislation" and "full, free, uncontrouled independent power, of carrying the results of that legislation into effect, independent either of the Governor's or the King's negative."[77] The colonists, he stated, possessed the former right but not the latter one. In other words, according to Pownall, the colonial assemblies had the authority to make laws within their sphere as subordinate legislatures, but that lawmaking authority was provisional until the laws in question received the approval of both the local representative of Crown authority (i.e., the governor) and the Crown itself (i.e., the Privy Council). In both cases, approval would be expressed indirectly, via the executive's decision not to veto the legislation in question. This acknowledgment of some degree of local legislative power, albeit contingent on the silence of another arm of government, was significant for colonists in 1765 who felt uncertain of the position their provincial assemblies occupied in the broad structure of imperial government.

But what, in Pownall's view, were the precise contours of the sphere of colonial legislative authority? On this question, the former governor had a well-developed theory. Each colony, he said, had two types of "services," or fiscal responsibilities: first, services that pertained to the support of the government of that particular colony; and second, services that supported the Crown and the larger empire. The former species he termed "special," the latter "general." In Pownall's scheme, each colony's legislature would be permitted to tax lands, tenements, and improved property "unincumbered by parliament"; monies raised would be "the special funds of those colonies." The general services, meanwhile, would be the province of Parliament, which would "with the utmost delicacy and regard to the colonies power of taxing themselves, raise those taxes which are raised for the general service of the crown." These included "revenues by imports, excise, or a stamp duty." Pownall justified this distinction thus: "[T]hese kind of taxes are (if I may be permitted the expression) coincident with those regulations which the laws of the realm prescribe to trade in general; to manufactures—and to every legal act and deed;—because they are duties which arise from the *general rights and jurisdiction of the realm,* rather than from the *particular and special concerns of any one colony.*"[78]

Moreover, Pownall noted, the colonists should expect to begin paying a stamp duty soon—an obligation that he suggested was equitable in order to prevent the colonies from benefiting from a less onerous tax regime than their cousins in Britain. "Whenever therefore this point, now in question, shall be decided," and the ministry had arrived at "the proper taxes, so as not to interfere with the special internal property and rights of the colonies," Americans would be subject to "an impost, excise, and stamp duty."[79]

Pownall's vision of marine dominion thus permitted the colonies to maintain a sphere of activity that was theirs and theirs alone to regulate— essentially, matters relating to land and other indisputably local, internal affairs. Everything else that moved or extended beyond the colony, or that related to matters beyond the colony—whether an affidavit of appeal to the Privy Council, a length of imported silk, or a dram of rum—fell within the external, imperial purview and was therefore subject to regulation and taxation by Parliament. Thus Pownall's plan in a sense represented the apotheosis of the internal-external distinction, for it identified as internal only those things such as land that were literally within a

given colony. If an ounce of tea or a common-law pleading crossed a colonial boundary, it entered the realm of the marine dominion and thus
became the proper object of imperial oversight.

Pownall's scheme did not rely on location alone as the defining factor
in assessing whether a particular activity was subject to colonial or metropolitan jurisdiction, however. Indeed, Pownall's language suggested
that it was not the boundary line itself but the essential nature of the matter or thing in question—its specialness or its generalness—that determined whether it was internally or externally regulated. Was the matter
associated with the general jurisdiction of the realm, or was it confined
only to the special concerns of its own colony? The terms suggest a deep
inquiry into the nature of the matter or thing itself rather than a simple
assessment of location alone, which, after all, could be entirely a matter
of chance.

Bernard's publication took a different form from Pownall's, for it consisted of a compilation of letters together with a treatise titled *The Principles of Law and Polity, Applied to the American Colonies.* Some of the
letters dated to 1763, and the treatise to 1764, but none had been published until the entire book appeared in 1774. Bernard had left Massachusetts in 1769, to the great delight of many residents who had opposed
his efforts to enforce the Sugar and Stamp acts and who had been out-
raged to learn of the nature of his correspondence with officials at home.
The first sixty-three pages of the book contained versions of many of the
letters in question; much of the publication bears the aura of an exculpa-
tion after the fact, or at least an effort to set the record straight.

For example, the letters from the period between 1763 and 1765 emphasized Bernard's efforts to moderate the rising tensions in Boston while
still fulfilling his duties to the administration at home. In a letter dated
October 25, 1763, and reprinted with the address "To the Earl of——,"
Bernard suggested the difficulty of his position but attempted to reassure
his noble correspondent of his own efforts to bring the irascible colony to
heel: "I do not pretend that this Province is entirely free from the breach
of [the] Laws; but only, that such breach, if discovered, is surely punished." He then went on to acknowledge "an indulgence time out of
mind" with respect to the importation of "a trifling but necessary article;
I mean, the permitting *Lisbon* Lemons, and Wine in small quantities, to

pass as ships stores." Explaining that the lemons were "in this climate . . . not only necessary to the comfort of life but to health also," Bernard appealed for lenient treatment of a favorite colonial antiscorbutic.[80]

In another letter, dated November 30, 1765, and addressed "To the Lord——," Bernard observed, "It must have been supposed, that such an innovation as a *Parliamentary taxation* would cause a great alarm, and meet with much opposition in most parts of America; it was quite new to the people, and had no visible bounds to it." Pressing the point, he asked, "Was this a time to introduce so great a novelty as a *Parliamentary* inland taxation into *America?*"[81] Although such assertions and questions might not have endeared Bernard to his official superiors, many London merchants reading his tract would undoubtedly have agreed with the sentiment, given their widespread opposition to the Stamp Act.[82]

In addition to these gentle pleadings of the colonial case to his audience in London, Bernard's writings suggest that he had hoped to launch a reform program similar to the one Pownall had previously proposed. The second half of Bernard's 1774 publication, titled *The Principles of Law and Polity, Applied to the Government of the British Colonies in America,* bore a drafting date of 1764. The essay resembled Pownall's in arguing for a closer union between Britain and the colonies—"a Connection between the Seat of Empire and its Dependencies," as well as a "regular, free, and equitable subordination." Within this imperial union, Bernard differentiated between the duties of subjects residing in "external [British] dominions" and those of subjects at home.[83] He disposed of the representation issue by stating that only subjects located within Britain had a claim to representation; Parliament therefore possessed the power to lay taxes on the external dominions.

Bernard then examined the various levels of taxing authorities and types of revenue within British North America. Unlike Pownall, whose plan appeared to proceed from a profound sense that certain matters (and therefore taxes) were specific to the colonies and certain others ought to be considered general to the empire as a whole, Bernard began by considering the pools of revenue that needed to be collected. He then set about apportioning them to the most convenient authority. Bernard's plan was therefore more a delegation of tax-collection duties to the colonies than a recognition of any special colonial jurisdiction over certain things or activities. Thus, Bernard charged the colonies with "pay[ing] the charge of the support of their own Governments" and collecting port duties ("most properly applicable to the defence of the Colonies"). The colonial legislatures would also be responsible for collecting "the necessary internal taxes"; these amounts would be determined by Parliament, because "[i]t would make it more agreeable to the people, though the sum to be raised was prescribed, to leave the method of taxation to their own Legislature."[84] The concept of internality thus referred more to the location of the tax's collection (for example, an excise tax) than to the nature of the underlying good or activity being taxed. Parliament would determine the amount of tax owed; all that would remain for the colonial assemblies was to choose the method of collection.

This analysis seems to have disturbed some of Bernard's colleagues in the Massachusetts government. In 1765, the Massachusetts House of Representatives expressed displeasure with the governor's willingness to grant plenary power over taxation to Parliament. "[W]e beg leave to observe that the charter of the province invests the General Assembly with the power of making laws for its internal government and taxation; and that this charter has never yet been forfeited," the House stated shortly after the Stamp Act riots convulsed Boston in August 1765.[85]

As this discussion demonstrates, by the autumn of 1765 the notion of dividing lawmaking authority between metropolitan and provincial spheres had become an established piece of the intellectual equipment that both colonists and imperial officials used to understand the Stamp Act crisis. This is not to say that the concept was not vague (it was), or that it was universally adopted as the most compelling rationale for opposing the act (it was not). Indeed, as we have seen, contemporaries from all sides of the Stamp Act debate employed versions of the internal-external distinction. Nevertheless, the ideas meant something to participants in the debate; they seemed to all parties to get at something significant about what the Grenville ministry was trying to achieve with its new laws. And, as the set of resolves passed by the Virginia House of Burgesses in May 1765 suggested, the resonance of the internal-external language, combined with the long history of bitter struggles over taxation in early modern England, conjured up equally deep-rooted ideas of sovereignty: *"Resolved,* That His Majesty's liege people of this his most ancient and loyal Colony have without interruption enjoyed the inestimable right of being governed by such laws, *respecting their internal polity and taxation,* as are derived from their own consent, with the approbation of their sovereign or his substitute; and that the same hath never been forfeited or yielded up, but hath been constantly recognized by the kings and people of Great Britain."[86]

In making this connection among consent, laws respecting the colony's internal polity, and the ancient right to petition the king, the burgesses placed their radical claim to a measure of lawmaking authority squarely within the context of the traditional rights of Englishmen.[87] By attaching the colony's jurisdiction specifically to laws respecting its internal polity and taxation, the Virginians moved toward a conception of government in which lawmaking authority was not only divided but was divided along lines that parceled out certain substantive, nondiscretionary heads of legislation to each level of government within the empire.

Repeal and Aftermath: Challenges to Unitary Legislative Power

The repeal of the Stamp Act and the accompanying passage of the Declaratory Act on March 18, 1766, changed but did not fundamentally alter the terms of the debate over Parliament's lawmaking authority for the colonies. The broad language of the Declaratory Act deliberately widened the scope of authority that Parliament claimed for itself; consequently, the scope of the debate in the colonies widened as well.[88] The act's assertion of the power of the king-in-Parliament to pass laws that bound the colonies "in all cases whatsoever" decisively shifted the discussion from a focus on taxation to broader theories of legislation per se.

Similarly, the passage of the Townshend Acts in 1767, which established import duties on tea, paint, glass, lead, and paper, among other goods, reopened the taxation question but witnessed the broadening of the colonists' argument from a denial of Parliament's power to levy internal taxes to a flat denial of the power to levy taxes at all, whether internal or external. The period between 1766 and 1769 thus saw a shift from the internal-external binary toward the revenue-trade and taxation-legislation dichotomies discussed in the writings of colonial and metropolitan commentators. These latter perspectives relied more heavily on a distinction between metropolitan and provincial authority than had the internal-external categorization. In short, observers on all sides of the Stamp Act debates were experimenting with subject-matter divisions as one means of rationalizing and formalizing multiplicity.

On the colonial side of the debate, among the most prominent and sophisticated commentators were Richard Bland, John Dickinson, and William Hicks. Bland, who had penned *The Colonel Dismounted* in 1764, invoked internal-external language but then pushed that language further than his predecessors to argue that the colonies and Britain were joined in a confederation or league for purposes of their common interests. After presenting a historical account of the colonies' constitutional history (with a particular focus on the early charters), Bland asserted that the internal-external lawmaking distinction could be traced back to the seventeenth century. The early colonists "were respected as a distinct State, independent, as to their *internal* Government, of the original Kingdom, but united with her, as to their *external* Polity, in the closest and most intimate LEAGUE AND AMITY, under the same Allegiance, and enjoying the Benefits of a reciprocal Intercourse." According to this "sacred Band of Union between *England* and her Colonies," the respective powers of Parliament and the colonial assemblies had been established more than a century earlier.[89] The idea of carving the overarching jurisdiction that obtained within the British Empire into provincial, imperial, and metropolitan segments therefore could hardly be called novel, in Bland's view; rather, the practice lay at the heart of the earliest English efforts to build governments in the New World.

John Dickinson, a prominent Philadelphia lawyer and colonial assemblyman, caused a sensation throughout the colonies with his series of essays titled *Letters from a Farmer in Pennsylvania*, published in 1767 and 1768. After initially appearing in the *Pennsylvania Chronicle*, the twelve pseudonymous pieces eventually ran in all but four of the nearly thirty newspapers published in America during the period.[90] Dickinson's chief contribution lay in his reorientation of the debate from the emphasis on internal versus external legislation that had dominated the discussion between 1764 and 1766 to the related but distinct dichotomy between raising a revenue and regulating trade.

Reviewing the Sugar, Stamp, and Townshend acts, Dickinson concluded that the significant fact about all three was their novel and explicit goal of taxing the colonies to raise funds for the imperial coffers rather than to regulate the flow of imports and exports between provinces and capital. "Never did the *British parliament,* till the period abovementioned, think of imposing duties in America, FOR THE PURPOSE OF RAISING A REVENUE," Dickinson insisted. "Mr. *Greenville's* [*sic*] sagacity first introduced this language, in the preamble" to the Sugar Act, which termed the raising of a revenue from the dominions in America "just and necessary."[91] The Townshend taxes might plausibly be defined as external taxes insofar as they took the form of traditional import levies, but they also aimed at raising revenue from the colonies, which Dickinson identified as a new and illegitimate objective. Invoking Pitt's speech on the repeal of the Stamp Act, Dickinson exhorted his readers to resist what he characterized as a newfangled parliamentary incursion. Even a single act of compliance with the Townshend duties would become binding precedent, in which case "the tragedy of American liberty is finished." The British government's claimed power to "levy money in general upon [its] subjects" must be denied, Dickinson argued, implying that the scope of Parliament's taxing power was not plenary but instead limited to certain specific objects.[92]

Dickinson's vision permitted regulation of trade for the benefit of the entire empire but objected to taxation that had no other objective than raising funds in the colonies to be sent back to London. Efforts to distinguish between supposed varieties of taxation were foolish and misguided, in his view. "The place of paying the duties imposed by the late act, appears to me therefore to be totally immaterial. The single question is whether the parliament can legally impose duties to be paid *by the people of these colonies only* FOR THE SOLE PURPOSE OF RAISING A REVENUE, *on commodities which she obliges us to take from her alone;* or, in other words, whether the parliament can legally take money out of our pockets without our consent."[93] In contrast to his contemporaries' focus on the distinction between highly visible levies such as the stamp tax and more hidden costs such as duties on the importation of molasses, Dickinson viewed himself as shifting the inquiry from the place where taxation took place to the legitimacy of the underlying governmental assertion of jurisdiction. This approach presumed that the empire could contain two legislative bodies, and, more important, that each of those bodies had a defined sphere of competence.[94] The definition of this sphere of competence in turn depended on the nature and purpose of the regulation rather than the type or location of activity being regulated.

Other commentators put forth similar arguments that attempted to limn the substantive boundary between metropolitan and colonial legislative authority. In a series of essays published in newspapers in Pennsylvania, Massachusetts, and South Carolina between January and April 1768, William Hicks offered an analysis that linked the internal-external distinction with the revenue-regulation inquiry. After considering Grenville's comment in the House of Commons that internal and external taxes had the same effect, Hicks concluded that "Mr. *G——lle*" (whom he described as "our greatest enemy") had been correct. Laws regulating or restricting trade had the potential to damage the colonial economy every bit as much as did taxes, Hicks argued. "It is taken for granted that the collection of a stamp duty would drain us of all the specie which we receive as a balance in our West-India trade. If an exorbitant duty upon sugar and molasses produces the same effect, in what does the difference consist? By either means the treasury of England will be enriched with the whole profit of our labour and we ourselves shall be reduced to [a] deplorable state of poverty."[95]

Thus, Hicks concluded, both the regulation-revenue distinction and the internal-external distinction were illusory. Hicks delivered ironic thanks to Grenville ("our *British Machiavel*") for having "kindly bestowed" upon the colonists "the most irrefragable proof that internal and external taxes are the same in effect; and that they may be as effectually ruined by the powers of legislation as by those of taxation." Hicks dismissed Parliament's claim of "sovereign jurisdiction" over the colonies as "a piece of Ottoman policy" aimed at "strangling us in our infancy."[96]

In contrast to Dickinson's suggestion that certain legislative purposes were within Parliament's proper province, Hicks insisted that colonial administrators had acted in bad faith, and therefore that all regulations emanating from London were suspect. Unlike Dickinson's continued faith in the possibility of delineating the various species of imperial jurisdiction, then, Hicks's analysis implied that administrators at home—

particularly Grenville and Pitt—did not share what he regarded as the colonists' naïve belief that divided authority was possible or desirable. For Hicks, the reality of power and "Ottoman" corruption had triumphed over abstract political theory.

As had been the case during the initial phases of the Stamp Act controversy, metropolitan and colonial observers brought a shared set of interpretive tools to bear on the post–Townshend Acts debates. While serving as lieutenant governor of Massachusetts in 1768, Thomas Hutchinson drafted a dialogue between two fictitious individuals, one speaking on behalf of America and the other on behalf of Great Britain. The dialogue, which may have been prompted by Hutchinson's perusal of Dickinson's *Letters from a Farmer,* was never published, but it provides intriguing insights into Hutchinson's highly developed constitutional theory at this time.[97]

In one of the most notable passages, Hutchinson's American speaker proposes "that no taxes should be laid upon us but by our own legislatures, that we should be governed . . . by laws of our making, but in matters of commerce we are willing to be restrained by acts of the British Parliament," because Britain protected America against other nations and therefore deserved the benefits of its colonies' trade. The English interlocutor responds skeptically to this proposal. "[W]hat assurance have we that you will not very soon complain of this restraint upon your trade; which deprives you of the means of increasing your property, as much as you now do of the revenue acts, which take from you a part of your property?" The Englishman concludes by saying, "As we concede, so you advance."[98]

Bernard Bailyn describes this exchange as illustrating that Hutchinson had "known from the start" what Dickinson "discovered" in his *Letters from a Farmer:* "that restraints of trade were only a special way of depriving people of property and that they would stir up agitation against commercial regulation just as they had against taxation."[99] Bailyn's characterization assumes that a "real" understanding of the relationship between metropolitan and colonial legislative authority existed in the 1760s, and that some observers were able to discover it (while, presumably, others remained confused or ignorant). This real grasp of the nature of imperial power, Bailyn suggests, relied on an essential similarity between taxation, trade regulation, and legislation generally. On this view, the sooner the colonists came to grips with this understanding and stopped quibbling about specious distinctions between internal and external taxation or revenue and regulatory laws, the sooner they would reach a Hicks-like conclusion that the real issue was naked power and that debates about the specific shape of that power were at best irrelevant and at worst obfuscatory.

This characterization, however, concedes too much to the metropolitan view of the state of the imperial constitution in the 1760s. Moreover, it overlooks the differences between the terms of the debate in the early years of the decade and those that dominated the conversation after 1766. Certainly, by 1768, the view expressed by Hutchinson's Englishman was shared by many metropolitan observers: in 1769, colonial undersecretary William Knox referred to the revenue-regulation distinction as "without a difference" and the colonists as "determined to get rid of the jurisdiction of parliament *in all cases whatsoever,* if they can."[100] In the early years of the transatlantic constitutional debates, however, commentators on all sides of the discussion clearly believed that the effort to distinguish between the authority of Parliament and that of the colonial legislatures was worthwhile. These issues were muddy and complex; after all, the internal-external distinction had described the modus vivendi of imperial power on the ground since the early days of North American settlement.[101] The novelty of the 1760s debates consisted in their efforts at formal articulation of previously ad hoc, pragmatic approaches to political and legal authority. In the course of the Stamp Act crisis, the practice of living with divided authority began to transform into an ideology of multiplicity.

Thinking Federally in the Shadow of Empire

Beginning in 1764, American whigs—and, more strikingly, numerous British officials and metropolitan middlemen—struggled to codify an informal system of multiple authorities into an explicit structural element of the imperial constitution. In so doing, they helped shape a new set of beliefs about the nature of government. This ideology emphasized the possibility of dividing lawmaking power between the existing arms of imperial legislative authority: Parliament and the colonial assemblies.

From Henry McCulloh's 1755 distinction between the general affairs of the empire and the domestic concerns of the particular colonies to Thomas Pownall's 1765 delineation of special and general services, commentators on both sides of the Atlantic appeared willing at least to contemplate apportioning legislative powers among multiple levels of governmental authority—provided, of course, that all levels remained subject to the overarching authority of the king-in-Parliament in its capacity as imperial sovereign. To be sure, they disagreed, sometimes violently, on the details and origins of this apportionment, but nevertheless they shared some important terms. By the late 1760s, however, this initial moment of openness had given way to a hardening of perspectives. The shared vocabulary of internal and external, domestic and general, remained, but the tone of the debate had altered. As Pauline Maier has argued, American whigs' "ordered resistance" to the Stamp Act had by 1767 shifted toward "a more serious threat to British authority."[102]

When Hutchinson penned his "Dialogue" in 1768, then, the language of subject-matter distinctions had become associated with colonial efforts to limit Parliament's authority rather than with all parties' efforts to achieve a compromise imperial constitution. Hutchinson's decision to make his American speaker state that Parliament ought to have authority "in matters of commerce" suggests that many of his fellow colonists had by that time arrived at a theory of imperial authority based largely on subject matter.[103] This theory followed directly from the distinctions that British North Americans had developed during the Stamp Act debates. Indeed, even the claims of Hutchinson's American straw man were granted the benefit of some internal coherence by his opponent and creator. In the wake of the Declaratory Act, meanwhile, that placeholder's real-world counterparts increasingly pushed back against metropolitan insistence on unitary legislative authority emanating from Parliament alone.

This discussion has not attempted to discern the "correctness" of the positions delineated by participants in the 1760s debates. Instead, the focus has been the meaning that emerged from the constitutional argumentation itself, in its own context.[104] The very fact that colonists engaged in such a serious and prolonged effort to make sense of their constitutional situation as provinces of the British Empire is remarkable in

that it signals a deep commitment to that empire and a desire to partici-
pate in the shaping of its most fundamental legal and political structures.[105] During the Stamp Act controversy, colonial and some metropolitan observers argued that the cracks and overlaps in the imperial
structure ought to be formalized into a system in which the colonial satellites of the empire received a portion of lawmaking power. In contrast
to parliamentary assertions of plenary authority over all matters—
whether within a given colony or without, in the imperial space beyond
that colony's borders—this nascent colonial vision insisted that each
component possessed its own sphere of legislative competence. More
fundamentally, commentators in the 1760s began to offer affirmative arguments for multiplicity as a foundation on which to build a new, complex, widely scattered Anglo-American empire. By 1773, some colonists
began to flesh out the consequences of divided authority in the face of
outright metropolitan denial that such division might be legitimate. By
1787, efforts to divide authority along lines defined by subject matter—as
in the Commerce Clause of the Constitution—formed an essential foundation of American federalism.

In 1765, however, this transition was still inchoate. Although the colonists were eager to stretch the meaning of empire as a species of political
organization, they did not seek to exit their own empire. On the contrary, the colonists' zeal during the 1760s for devising taxonomies to divide authority between provinces and metropole did not question the
fact of the greater imperial system in which such divisions would be situated. Nevertheless, the distinctions that fill the writings of the 1760s—
between internal and external taxation, between raising a revenue and
regulating trade, and between taxation and legislation—show a desire
to experiment with constitutional visions that differed from the official
account of metropolitan authority as coextensive with imperial dominions. Rather than accepting the unitary view of metropolitan power,
many colonial observers contested the nature of that power and offered
alternative (albeit sometimes inconsistent and tentative) schemes of
authority. These schemes took various forms, but the majority of them
shared two characteristics: first, an explicit distinction between metropolitan and provincial spheres; and second, a willingness to consider
attaching to each of these jurisdictions specific duties and powers of
government.

Increasingly in the 1760s, American colonists began to challenge traditional theories of governmental authority and to experiment with radical ideas of multilayered legislative power. The catalyst for these novel approaches was the practical reality of increased parliamentary regulation of the colonies after 1764, beginning with the Sugar Act and culminating in the Stamp Act and the Declaratory Act. In the subsequent decade, these concepts, born in the anguish of the early debate between provinces and metropole combined with further lived experience, historical arguments from the constitutional history of Britain itself, and a pastiche of Continental theory to become the basis of a newly defined federal ideology.

CHAPTER 3

The Debates over Sovereignty

J ANUARY 1773 found the town of Boston mired deep in political discontent. Since the passage of the Sugar and Stamp acts nearly a decade before, a cycle of metropolitan discipline, colonial challenge, and increased assertions of power from British authorities had become wearyingly familiar to observers on both sides of the ocean. The memory of the Boston Massacre of March 5, 1770, lingered in the minds of townspeople, as did the bitter recollection of the Townshend Acts of 1767, which had levied new taxes on imported goods, including paper, tea, glass, paint, and lead. The acts had been repealed in 1770, save for the duty on tea, an ominous reminder of the transoceanic scope of Parliament's power to tax. More recently, the *Gaspée* affair of June 1772, in which Rhode Islanders had lured aground a British revenue cutter sent to enforce imperial customs regulations, captured the crew, and burned the ship, remained a catchword in mounting political rhetoric thanks to British officials' announcement that the perpetrators, if found, would be tried in England.

Fueling colonists' seething indignation at what they regarded as the ever-increasing reach of the regulatory arms of Westminster and Whitehall, imperial administrators had in 1772 issued a pair of regulations that altered decades-old practices by ordering that the salaries of colonial governors, judges, and other law officials would henceforth be paid directly by the Crown rather than by the colonies.[1] Fearing that such a change in the source of colonial officials' salaries would lead to a similar shift in the direction of colonial officials' loyalties, colonists, led by their local assemblies, had begun to consider resistance.[2] In addition to preparing petitions to the king that enumerated their grievances and requested relief, Massachusetts colonial leaders in November 1772 organized a committee of correspondence to allow for communication among the colony's towns and with other colonies. A few months later, the Virginia House of Burgesses followed suit, launching an intercolonial resistance network.

Against this background of increased tension between metropole and colonies, January 1773 might strike observers, then and now, as hardly the most propitious moment for an imperial official to initiate a public debate on the constitutional basis of the British Empire. That month, however, a desire for such a debate simmered near the surface of everyday life in the Massachusetts capital. Since at least the Stamp Act crisis of 1765, the question of the extent of Parliament's power to regulate the colonies—most notably, through taxation—had formed the subtext of political discussion in British North America. To be sure, Boston's newspapers that January featured the usual advertisements for imported wares such as chocolate, "choice West India RUM," Irish linens, "new Raisins & Currants," and "Teneriffe and Madeira WINES."[3] By the end of the first week of the year, however, a new political debate had begun a slow burn in the upper chambers of the Province House. Soon reports of this great controversy began to fill newspaper columns alongside the merchants' solicitations. The debate helped end the career of Governor Thomas Hutchinson, finishing the work of destruction that the Stamp Act mobs had begun eight years earlier. Most significantly for the story of American federalism, the political conflict of early 1773 highlighted the growing divergence between the colonists' and their imperial cousins' conceptions of sovereignty.

The constitutional debate between Hutchinson and the Massachusetts General Court (the colonial assembly) unfolded between January 6 and March 6, 1773, in a series of widely publicized speeches and responses between Hutchinson and the General Court, the latter acting sometimes in its collective capacity and sometimes in its component parts of upper

(Council) and lower (House of Representatives) houses. These three months provide a glimpse into a moment of significant crisis in prewar America. That crisis was both political, inasmuch as it concerned contemporary arrangements of power and regulation, and constitutional, inasmuch as it concerned the structure of imperial governance itself.

At the heart of the controversy lay the issue of sovereignty: that is, determining the nature and location of the highest authority to which an individual owed duties and from which an individual could demand fulfillment of rights. Both Hutchinson and the General Court sought to identify the "final and absolute political authority in the political community" such that "no final and absolute authority exists elsewhere."[4] As each side of the debate articulated its vision of the scope of parliamentary power and the concomitant scope of the colonial assemblies' power, allegiances hardened, and visions of sovereignty began to diverge.[5] While Hutchinson hewed to a unitary view of sovereignty possessed exclusively by Parliament, the members of the General Court struggled to construct a plan by which sovereignty could be apportioned between Westminster and the colonies. When, by 1774, this scheme proved elusive, the colonists applied their fledgling conception of divisible sovereignty to their efforts to promote union among the colonies.

The debate between Hutchinson and the General Court brought together some of the most theoretically sophisticated minds of the day in a public dispute over the nature of government power. Ultimately, the controversy exposed a widening schism between the British imperial view of sovereignty and the colonial view. Spokesmen for the British Empire took their cues from developments in domestic political theory, which by the late eighteenth century increasingly insisted that sovereignty was both indivisible and possessed by Parliament alone. The great debate of 1773 thus illustrates an important break with the metropolitan conception of authority and an early instance in which colonists began to grope toward a conception of multilayered sovereignty in reaction to the theory of unitary sovereignty that they saw gaining ground among British officials. This multilayered sovereignty, in turn, provided a crucial theoretical underpinning for the development of American federalism.[6]

The Boston debates of 1773 should be understood as continuing this long history of confrontation while also signaling a new urgency in the tone of the debate—a shift from a state of relatively regular, if unsettling, dissent and discussion to a heightened atmosphere of strife in which first principles of government and constitution seemed to contemporaries to require redefinition and reexamination. John Phillip Reid, in an essay on the debate, refers to the addresses that each of the three sides delivered as "legal briefs" submitted on "the one occasion when the constitutional controversy was joined." For this reason, Reid notes, "these briefs may well be the most important legal documents of the prerevolutionary era."[7]

In their detail, their comprehensiveness, and—perhaps most important—their origin as speeches delivered in the heated context of an actual debate, the addresses offer valuable insight into the developing schism between imperial and colonial visions of the nature of British sovereignty. The debates served, on the one side, as a rehearsal of post–Glorious Revolution British political theory and, on the other side, as a debut for creole constitutional notions that pointed toward a new understanding of the nature of authority within a composite political entity. In this way, the standoff between governor and assembly in Massachusetts helps illuminate the path of colonial constitutional thought from the oppositional mode of the 1760s to the more daring and experimental assertions of the possibility of divided sovereignty that characterized the period between 1774 and 1787.

During the Stamp Act controversy of the 1760s, British North Americans had experimented with a variety of proposals to reorganize legislative authority within the empire, offering the internal-external distinction as one possible axis along which to distinguish the domain of Parliament from that of the colonial assemblies. Faced first with the Stamp Act's minutely detailed regulations and then with the bald statement of power contained in the Declaratory Act, commentators such as Richard Bland, Daniel Dulany, and John Dickinson searched for a system that could assimilate and formalize the multiple legitimate sources of lawmaking authority that they believed existed within the empire. Their arguments were for the most part institutional ones aimed at the question of dividing different legislative powers (e.g., internal and external, revenue and trade) between the assemblies and Parliament. The 1773 debate between Hutchinson and the General Court, by contrast, was a less concrete,

more open-ended conversation that began with the institutional question of legislative multiplicity and quickly moved to structural and theoretical questions. Even if one assumed more than one legislature within a
given polity, was the relationship among the multiple bodies a hierarchical or a parallel one? How, if at all, could existing theories of sovereignty
accommodate more than one source of governmental authority? Calling
for the explicit separation of governmental authority within the empire
along subject-matter lines had been a radical demand in 1765. By 1773,
the colonists were pushing even further, from a claim about multilayered
legislatures toward an idea of multiplicity itself as a new way to understand the relationship between sovereignty and space—the relationship
at the heart of federalism.

Controversy Builds in Boston

Having served as lieutenant governor of Massachusetts Bay Colony since
1758, Thomas Hutchinson became acting governor upon the resignation
and departure for England of Governor Francis Bernard in August 1769.
Nearly two years later, in March 1771, Hutchinson officially became governor when he took the oath of office in Boston. In keeping with the an-
tagonistic relationship that he had developed with the people of Boston
throughout his service as chief justice of the Massachusetts Superior
Court of Judicature and then as lieutenant governor, Hutchinson immediately became a lightning rod for the increasingly voluble critics of the
imperial administration. As Bernard Bailyn, Hutchinson's leading biographer, puts it, "He was embroiled in argument with the opposition
from almost the first day of his acting governorship."[8]

Even the most sympathetic observer must marvel at Hutchinson's
striking habit of choosing the wrong course of action—usually involving
some sort of public address or debate—at the wrong time. Yet these gam-
bits also seem to have been offered as earnest efforts to resolve misunder-
standings and reestablish political equilibrium. For example, in the summer of 1772, Hutchinson stoked the flames of public outrage over the
Crown's assumption of the salaries of royal officials when he engaged in a
written, public exchange with the House of Representatives in which he
sought to defend his own acceptance of the salary. Despite his professed

dislike of "argumentative speeches," Hutchinson's July 14 message to the House nevertheless delivered a lesson on English constitutional history that would provide a leitmotif for the coming debate. In a letter written a few days later, Hutchinson recapitulated his speech before the House: "It is part of the prerogative of the Crown, as well as of the power and authority of Parliament, to constitute corporations or political bodies, and to grant to such bodies a form of government, and powers of making and carrying into execution such laws, as from their local, or other circumstances, may be necessary, the Supreme Legislative authority of the British dominions always remaining entire, notwithstanding."[9]

Already in this early skirmish, Hutchinson's message was clear: he would uphold the complete supremacy of British authorities, whether the Crown or Parliament, to legislate for the colonies, come what might.

By late December 1772, confrontation between the governor and the assembly appeared imminent. When the Boston town meeting, led by Samuel Adams, formed a committee of correspondence to caucus with other towns on the issue of the Crown salaries, Hutchinson attempted to stanch radical sentiment by immediately exercising his prerogative to "prorogue," or terminate, that session of the General Court. Defending his actions in one of his periodic letters to William Legge, second Earl of Dartmouth and secretary of state for the colonies, Hutchinson sounded the first of what would become a series of claims of necessity to his metropolitan superiors: "I immediately prorogued the Court and sooner than I otherwise should have done to shew them that I would not give the least encouragement to their unwarrantable doings," he wrote, "there being no law to support Town in transacting any other business than what is *of publick concernment* to the Town."[10] Determined to check the spread of colonial challenges to Parliament's authority, Hutchinson attempted to silence the assembly as a means of restoring order and calm to Boston.

Despite the General Court's hiatus, dissent continued to brew. Hutchinson's proroguing of the colonial assembly could not silence the Boston town meeting. In November, a few weeks after referring to the Crown salaries in a widely reprinted message as a plot by imperial officials "to complete the system of their slavery," the members of the town meeting issued a pamphlet titled *The Votes and Proceedings of the Freeholders and Other Inhabitants of the Town of Boston,* which included "a particular enumeration of those grievances that have given rise to the present alarming discontents in America." The pamphlet thus sought to present a coherent case for the colonists "as Men, as Christians, and as Subjects."[11]

By late December, Hutchinson was reconsidering his policy of attempting to mute debate. Far from stifling murmurs against Parliament's authority to alter the source of payments to royal officials in the colonies, his suspension of the General Court appeared only to have emboldened the town meeting further. In a December 22 letter to Lord Dartmouth that, given the minimum two-month travel time for correspondence between Boston and London, would certainly arrive in London too late to serve as anything more than constructive notice, Hutchinson proposed a new approach. "I am sorry that I am obliged to acquaint your Lordship with the extravagant principles on Government which are still avowed not only by the Writers in News papers but by the Inhabitants of Towns who assemble together." Having in an earlier letter dismissed the town meeting's activities as "irregular," the governor now contemplated a frontal assault on what he viewed as the rabble-rousing General Court. "I am brought to a necessity of requiring the Assembly to be more explicit in declaring how far they approve or disapprove of such proceedings and what sense they have of their dependence upon the Supreme Authority of the B[ritish] isles and Dominions than they have ever yet been."[12] The explicit declarations that Hutchinson sought would require open public debate.

Two weeks later, on January 6, 1773, the General Court convened in a special emergency session called by the governor. Everyone knew that the session would focus on a single question: whether Parliament possessed exclusive legislative authority over the colonies, or whether that authority was shared by the colonial assemblies.

The Indivisibility of Sovereignty

Historians differ in their evaluations of Hutchinson's decision to take the highly irregular step of opening a substantive constitutional debate with the Massachusetts colonial assembly. Reid terms it "the most serious mistake made by any imperial official in the colonies prior to 1775."

Hutchinson's calling of the emergency session "laid down the imperial constitution and challenged the Massachusetts General Court to put some answer on the record." In Reid's view, Hutchinson forced the controversial question of the scope of parliamentary authority into the full glare of public attention, driving the colonial legislators to adopt a more extreme position than they might otherwise have done.[13] K. G. Davies concurs, charging Hutchinson with "forc[ing] a showdown by compelling the Council and House of Representatives to say where they stood on the matter."[14] Writing in the early twentieth century, the constitutional historian Andrew C. McLaughlin pronounced Hutchinson's decision to "measure swords" with Samuel Adams and the other leaders of the General Court "a perilous undertaking" and observed that "vigorous, talented, and determined" though Hutchinson might have been, "we still wonder at his folly."[15]

Other scholars are more sympathetic, noting the intractable difficulty of Hutchinson's position. Bailyn regards Hutchinson as a kind of tragic hero, trapped between his staunch commitment to the British Empire, based on what he viewed as the fundamental fact of American dependence, and the increasingly radical ideology of his fellow colonists. Hutchinson's fatal flaw, according to Bailyn, was his faith in his own ability to reason his interlocutors into accepting his view of the proper constitution of the empire. Describing Hutchinson's belief "on the one hand, that the authority of Parliament must reach into a given segment of the British polity or it would have no authority there at all, but on the other hand that Parliament should never use that authority to tax the colonies, which were not, and could not be, represented in it," Bailyn presents a complex figure whose belief in both the exclusive and the discretionary nature of parliamentary power could not withstand the opposition's increasingly clear denial of that power.[16] In a similar vein, an earlier commentator, Randolph G. Adams, lamented in 1922 that Hutchinson, like many others, foundered "on the rocks of sovereignty" in his efforts to explain to the General Court (as well as his wider audience) that attempts to limit parliamentary authority were fundamentally incompatible with the legal and constitutional structures of the empire.[17]

Seen in light of the development of federalism's vision of divided sovereignty, Hutchinson is both an indispensable catalyst for and an intransigent foe of alternative distributions of power between center and periphery. Hutchinson watchers from both scholarly camps make important points. From the standpoint of his and his superiors' desire to maintain the British Empire as it was, Hutchinson's decision to press for a public debate was a mistake. From the standpoint of American constitutional development, however, the controversy of 1773 served as a crucial moment of productive conflict between the British vision of indivisible governmental authority and the emerging American vision of authority apportioned among different levels of government according to specific, substantively defined principles.

In the speech that opened the 1773 debate, Hutchinson presented a forceful case for the supremacy of metropolitan rule. Adhering to post–Glorious Revolution whig orthodoxy, he took as his premise the notion that the paramount authority of the British government was vested in Parliament, by which he meant the unified political entity of king, Lords, and Commons—a political version of the Holy Trinity in which three seemingly distinct entities operated as one.[18]

Pressed, he felt, to provide a primer on the status of the colonial assemblies in the overall imperial hierarchy, Hutchinson argued for unlimited parliamentary authority to legislate for the colonies. He based this argument on a twofold vision of the empire that saw the colonies as British satellites and Parliament as the center of British imperial power—much like his predecessor Thomas Pownall's hub-and-spoke conception. Dismissing claims that the colonial assemblies possessed any powers apart from those granted to them by Parliament, Hutchinson embraced the view that at that time was becoming orthodoxy among many British political theorists: sovereignty must be undivided and indivisible within any given state.[19] Power could be delegated from the central government to agents such as royal governors, but such delegations were only temporary; power could not truly be shared. "In sovereignty there are no gradations," Samuel Johnson would write in 1775, echoing Blackstone's *Commentaries,* published a decade earlier. Instead, Johnson insisted that every society must contain "some power or other, from which there is no appeal, which admits no restrictions, which pervades the whole mass of the community."[20] Hutchinson's January 6 speech to both houses of the General Court expressed the same conviction that civil society required a single, supreme, unlimited, rule-making and -enforcing power.

In the Council Chamber that Wednesday, before both houses of the General Court, the governor wasted no time in reaching the gravamen of the matter. "That the Government is at present in a disturbed and disordered State is a Truth too evident to be denied," he announced. "I have pleased myself, for several Years past, with Hopes that the Cause would cease of itself and the Effect with it, but I am disappointed, and I may not any longer, consistent with my Duty to the King and my Regard to the Interest of the Province, delay communicating my Sentiments to you upon a Matter of so great Importance." Promising candor and entreating his listeners to the same, Hutchinson then commenced an excursus on the political history of Massachusetts Bay Colony.[21]

He began with a provocative claim: "When our Predecessors first took Possession of this Plantation or Colony, under a Grant and Charter from the Crown of England, it was their Sense, and it was the Sense of the Kingdom, that they were to remain subject to the supreme Authority of Parliament." According to the customary law of nations, Hutchinson argued, the earliest Massachusetts colonists had continued to live under the same governmental power under which they lived at home. Moreover, by settling the colony in the name of the mother country, these early residents had brought Massachusetts into the dominion of what was at that time England.[22] Colonists in Massachusetts Bay, therefore, had always been and continued to be subject to the "supreme Authority of Parliament."

Despite his lack of formal legal training, Hutchinson then engaged in a narrow reading of the provision of the colonial charter that had established a provincial legislature.[23] "The General Court has, by Charter, *full* Power to make such Laws as are not repugnant to the Laws of England," Hutchinson stated. Finding no specific statement in the charter denominating the colonial legislature the "*sole* Power" governing the province, he argued that the General Court's lawmaking power was supplemental to, not exclusive of, the legislative authority of Parliament. "Surely then this is by Charter a Reserve of Power and Authority to Parliament . . . and, consequently, is a Limitation of the Power given to the General Court," he concluded.[24]

This line of argument illustrates the zero-sum nature of the debate for Hutchinson. He appears to have believed that in order to make his case for the complete supremacy of Parliament, he had to prove the total subordination of the General Court. Any limit on the power of the colonial assembly—especially if that limit stemmed from the province's founding charter—would, he hoped, dispose of all challenges to the broad sweep of metropolitan power. Absent an express grant of sole power, or sovereignty, to the colonial assembly, Hutchinson argued that any claim of independent legislative power by colonial legislators must fail.

At this point, the accounts of the January 6 session convey the sense that Hutchinson had reached the climax of his polemic. The colonial assemblies existed at the pleasure of metropolitan authorities, he argued. Imperial officials, Hutchinson among them, had never envisioned the colonial governments as anything more than "subordinate Powers," corporations "formed within the Kingdom" with the limited brief of "mak[ing] and execut[ing] such Bylaws as are for their immediate Use and Benefit." Hutchinson then summed up his vision of sovereignty in a statement that would ring in his own ears and the ears of his fellow colonists for years to come: "I know of no Line that can be drawn between the supreme Authority of Parliament and the total Independence of the Colonies. It is impossible there should be two independent Legislatures in one and the same State, for although there may be but one Head, the King, yet the two Legislative Bodies will make two Governments as distinct as the Kingdoms of England and Scotland before the Union."[25]

The governor thus made his case clear: despite their recent pretensions to power, the colonial assemblies were nothing more than the creatures of the supreme assembly housed along the Thames. Hutchinson, like Dr. Johnson, viewed sovereignty as containing no gradations; the power pervading the whole mass of the British Atlantic community emanated from the center and tolerated no provincial competition. No line could be drawn between imperial and colonial power because, simply put, colonial power had no independent existence. No line could be drawn because, according to eighteenth-century British political theory, parliamentary power had to be absolute and plenary in order to fulfill its ancient constitutional mandate.[26] No line could be drawn because to divide sovereignty was to deny sovereignty.

Theories of Sovereignty

When Hutchinson invited the General Court to parley, some colonists in Massachusetts and beyond had at hand a broad set of interpretive tools with which to assess Hutchinson's arguments for unlimited parliamentary authority. Familiarity with alternative, Continental theories of government helped some colonial commentators respond to the Blackstonian view of sovereignty as contained entirely within a single domestic institution. Emmerich de Vattel's *Droit des gens (Law of Nations)* of 1758, for example, had been translated and published in an English edition in 1759. This version was followed in 1775 by an edition that was published in Amsterdam and distributed by Benjamin Franklin to the Library Company of Philadelphia, Harvard College, and the Library of Congress.[27] Richard Bland, writing in 1766, included a citation of Vattel in his *Inquiry into the Rights of the British Colonies,* and George Washington's library contained a copy of Hugo Grotius's *Rights of War and Peace* in its English translation of 1738.[28] As Peter Onuf and Nicholas Onuf have demonstrated, Vattel's notion of a Europe-wide system of republics inspired some British North Americans to strive toward a colonial union capable of participating in a more rational and progressive "Vattelian world" based on "a developing regime of law among nations." Vattel's theories provided a normative vision of multiplicity, positing that "a republic of republics" could be capable of operating as a "sovereign among sovereigns."[29]

Similarly, Samuel von Pufendorf's idea of a "system of states" offered a vision of multilayered political authority for those seeking an alternative to Blackstone's unitary theory.[30] Indeed, the House of Representatives cited both Grotius and Pufendorf during the debate with Hutchinson, deploying both theorists against the governor's assertion that the colonies constituted part of the realm. "We beg Leave, upon what your Excellency has observed of the Colony becoming Part of the State, to subjoin the Opinions of several learned Civilians," the House stated. "Colonies, says Puffendorf [*sic*], are settled in different Methods. For either the Colony *continues a Part* of the Common Wealth it was [sent] out from; or else is obliged to pay a dutiful Regard to the Mother Common Wealth, and so to be in Readiness to defend and vindicate its Honor, and so is *united by a Sort of unequal Confederacy;* or lastly *is erected into a separate Common Wealth* and *assumes the same Rights,* with the State it descended from." Immediately following this passage (which it was noted came from "a very able Lawyer in this Country"), the House cited Grotius for a similar proposition: "King Tullius, as quoted by the same learned Author from Grotius, says, 'We look upon it to be neither Truth nor Justice that Mother Cities ought of Necessity and *by the Law of Nature* to *rule over the Colonies.*' "[31] Hutchinson parried the reference with his own interpretation. "Your Attempt to shew that new discovered Countries do not become Part of the State, from the Authority of Puffendorff &c., will fail," he replied. "[T]he Instance given by him of a Colony erected into a separate Common Wealth plainly appears by the Context to be by the Leave or Consent of the Parent State."[32] As this exchange demonstrates, European theory formed part of the conceptual background to the Boston debates.[33] True, the Continental theorists offered little specific advice for constructing a system of states.[34] But the availability of this alternative body of political philosophy helped shape the colonists' intellectual framework, providing an important counterweight to the Hutchinsonian and Blackstonian vision of the empire as an extension of Parliament's regulatory sphere.

A faithful servant of the unitary empire, Hutchinson appears to have believed that the problem of divided authority was best answered by invoking a maximalist interpretation of metropolitan power.[35] The arguments of the Continental theorists did not sway the governor. Following Blackstonian precedent, he denied utterly the proposition that the colonial assemblies might share some portion of British sovereignty—or, indeed, that sovereignty might ever be shared. The tripartite entity of king, Lords, and Commons functioned together, a unitary sovereign from which all political power on both sides of the ocean emanated. The colonial assemblies might occasionally borrow specific legislative powers, but only in certain limited circumstances, and only as deemed appropriate by metropolitan officials. No constitutional line could be drawn between the full authority of Parliament and the full independence of the colonies, just as no political line could be drawn between the territory of Britain and the territory of the colonies. Legal and political boundaries were one and the same, and the space they encompassed was the British Empire, governed by the Parliament at Westminster.

Drawing the Lines of Sovereignty

We must now return to the Council Chamber in the Boston Province House on January 6, 1773. With his speech, especially the pronouncement concerning the line between Parliament's authority and the independence of the colonies, Hutchinson fixed the terms of debate for the next three months—and, in some ways, for the next sixteen years. The specter of *imperium in imperio* would haunt colonial, and later national, political debate at least until 1789, cropping up throughout the debates over the Articles of Confederation and the Constitution and providing seemingly limitless fodder for accusations between large-state and small-state delegates, Federalists and Anti-Federalists, and Federalists and Republicans.

In the days immediately after its delivery, Hutchinson's speech fanned controversy among Bostonians as they awaited the responses of the Council and the House of Representatives. The town's newspapers were quicker to address the debate. Most newspapers printed lengthy extracts of Hutchinson's speech, as well as letters and other commentary that folded the speech into the ongoing print discussion concerning the scope of parliamentary authority. For example, in addition to carrying the latest installment of John Adams's essays on the question of royal officials' discretion to remove colonial judges, the *Boston-Gazette and Country Journal* of Monday, January 11, 1773, printed a letter in which "An Elector" responded to the governor's speech. After quoting Hutchinson's statement that he knew of no line that could be drawn between the supreme authority of Parliament and the total independence of the colonies, An Elector requested clarification: "And, pray! what then? Which is the Conclusion,—*therefore* the Parliament have not the intended Authority? or, *therefore* the Colonies are independent of that Parliament?"[36]

An Elector went on to distinguish between British protection and British legislation, arguing that the mere fact of the colonies' membership in the empire did not necessarily compel them to submit to every law that emanated from the imperial capital. "Portugal is perhaps more dependent upon the Protection of Great Britain than these Colonies are, but does [Britain] claim the Right of Legislating for Portugal?" the writer demanded. Rather than trumpeting metropolitan power to coerce colonial obedience, imperial officials ought to recognize that a *"Principle of Gratitude,"* not constitutional obligation, had motivated whatever deference colonial assemblies had heretofore paid to parliamentary authority. Hutchinson's speech, An Elector charged, had shifted the terms of the debate—not to mention the terms of the relationship between Britain and the colonies—by suddenly speaking of obedience to supreme authority rather than of what the writer called "the binding Power of Interest." Because Hutchinson's position lacked a due appreciation of the degree to which the colonial assemblies had acquiesced in, rather than been bound by, parliamentary legislation, the writer argued, it would reduce the colonies to servitude. "NO *Line can be drawn between the usurped Power of Parliament, and a State of Slavery in the Colonies,"* An Elector's letter concluded.[37]

For this commentator, then, the issue of sovereignty was susceptible to a more subtle reading than it had received from Hutchinson. Malleable concepts such as "interest" and "gratitude" might buffer or mediate raw metropolitan power. If imperial officials persisted, however, in viewing the colonial assemblies' past adoptions of parliamentary acts as working a kind of estoppel on the colonists' power to challenge subsequent acts, then talk of lines with absolute endpoints would be warranted. The dramatist and historian Mercy Otis Warren provided her own gloss on the debates, publishing a satire titled *The Adulateur: A Tragedy,* in which a thinly veiled Hutchinson appeared as "Rapatio," the brutal, Caesar-like tyrant who oppressed "Brutus" and other citizens of "Servia."[38]

While commentators throughout the colonies debated the consequences of Hutchinson's remarks, the members of the Council and House of Representatives considered their responses. Each house designated a committee to craft written replies to be delivered to Hutchinson. Slightly more than two weeks after Hutchinson's address to the General Court, the two houses delivered their answers, the Council on January 25 and the House on January 26. Each answer had received unanimous approval in its respective house, as the *Boston-Gazette* gleefully noted.[39] Both responses took up the governor's rhetoric of supremacy and sovereignty; both responses proceeded from the premise, widely held among colonists and shared with British officials, that the colonies were indeed part of the empire, and that consequently they were subject to some amount of imperial authority. In contrast to the public statements of Hutchinson and other members of the administration, however, the responses of the General Court suggested that a line could—and, indeed, must—be drawn between complete subordination and complete independence.

Picking up Hutchinson's theme of lawmaking supremacy, the Council's answer nevertheless resisted the governor's conclusion by invoking traditional imperatives of limited governmental authority. Citing Magna Carta, the Council argued that Hutchinson's phrase "supreme authority" actually translated into "unlimited authority" and then charged that this was an untenable proposition according to the ancient, fundamental law of England, which held that no authority could legitimately claim to be unlimited. "[I]f Supreme Authority includes unlimited Authority, the Subjects of it are emphatically Slaves," the Council argued. Moreover, the Council objected to Hutchinson's use of the term "supremacy," contending that the word was a term of art with a specific, nonterrestrial meaning. "Supreme or unlimited Authority can with Fitness belong only to the Sovereign of the Universe. . . . But with Truth this can be said of no other Authority whatever."[40] After thus chiding Hutchinson for confusing mere political power with divine dominion, the Council moved on to consider the limits that must necessarily attach to the former species of authority.

As these claims suggest, Anglo-Americans in the 1770s did not consider the terms "supremacy" and "sovereignty" to be necessarily synonymous. In general, the idea of sovereignty in this period can be seen as an ill-defined concept relating to the legitimate source of "right," as opposed to mere "power," within a given polity. "Supremacy," in contrast, was a more relative term that dealt with the question whether a particular lawmaking body was the final authority within its particular jurisdiction.[41]

Whatever difference existed between sovereignty and supremacy did not matter greatly, however, as long as the British nation and the British Empire were viewed as coterminous. And this was precisely the view of British officials. From the standpoint of imperial administrators, because Parliament was domestically sovereign, it was imperially supreme.[42] Sovereignty and supremacy therefore were synonymous for imperial spokesmen, which allowed them to make the type of sweeping claims that Hutchinson's speech asserted. The colonial opposition, however, sought to break this equivalence between rule over nation and rule over empire, especially in the wake of the Stamp Act crisis of 1765. Still regarding themselves as British in the larger sense, they accepted Parliament's authority over them, but only to the extent that that authority did not encroach on that of their local assemblies.[43]

Furthermore, the American whigs differentiated between the sphere of law and that of politics. John Adams's *Novanglus* letters of 1774 emphasized this distinction: "[T]he terms 'British Empire' are not the language of the common law, but the language of newspapers and political pamphlets." He continued: "I would ask, by what law the parliament has authority over America? . . . [B]y the common law of England, it has none, for the common law, and the authority of parliament founded on it, never extended beyond the four seas; by statute law it has none, for no statute was made before the settlement of the colonies for this purpose; and the declaratory act, made in 1766, was made without our consent, by a parliament which had no authority beyond the four seas."[44]

Adapting "the old English constitutional doctrine of resistance to arbitrary power" to the new circumstances of the empire, Adams built his argument against parliamentary supremacy on the premise that sovereign power at home did not necessarily translate into sovereign power in the colonies.[45] Parliament might be sovereign in Britain, according to the common law of England. But Adams resisted what he viewed as an extension of this power beyond its legal boundaries. He therefore did not accept Hutchinson's claims of parliamentary supremacy, arguing that the word "supremacy" implied a lack of limitation. Rather, Adams believed that Parliament's authority over the colonies was limited both by English common-law principles and—more significantly for this study—by other, parallel assemblies that occupied specific portions of the legislative field.

The willingness of American theorists to contemplate a system in which colonists lived under two layers of legislative authority suggests that they had begun to abandon existing understandings of supremacy as requiring a single dominant power. They were also beginning to reject the Blackstonian concept of indivisible sovereignty. Instead, they acknowledged a limited authority in Parliament to regulate trade and reserved the other legislative powers for the colonial assemblies. Although the members of the colonial opposition might have agreed with Hutchinson that the colonies were part of Britain (whether empire, realm, or dominion was a separate issue), they disagreed with the governor's assertion that no line could be drawn between submission and independence. Parliament's authority over England, Scotland, and Wales could and must, they argued, be distinguished from its authority over America.

The House's answer to Hutchinson displayed this more aggressive tone. The answer, which filled twenty-six pages when it was published in pamphlet form, met Hutchinson's brief for parliamentary authority with a point-by-point rebuttal of his theory of empire. Its critique used several lines of argument, but its two most significant targets were Hutchinson's interpretation of the original Massachusetts charter and his larger theory of sovereignty.

The House began its investigation into the colony's early history by disputing one of Hutchinson's key premises: his claim that because the charter had not contained an express grant of "sole power" to the colonial assembly, it had therefore reserved the bulk of the legislative power to Parliament, which in turn obligated the colonial assembly to pass only such acts as were not repugnant to the laws of England. In Hutchinson's view, therefore, the colonial assembly was entirely the creature of Parliament. House members challenged this hierarchy by offering their own construction of the charter, based on seventeenth-century political understandings. At the time of the English arrival in America, the House reply contended, the prevailing theory held that the new colonial lands belonged to the king's dominions, not to the kingdom. They therefore possessed a special legal status that placed them under Crown authority alone. "[T]he Right of disposing of the Lands was in the Opinion of those Times vested solely in the Crown."[46]

The chain of argument proceeded thus: if the colonies were under the exclusive control of the Crown at the time of the charter, then they were at that time not part of the realm; if they were not part of the realm then, they could not now be part of the kingdom of Great Britain; if they were not now part of the kingdom of Great Britain, they were not now under the control of Parliament. "If then the Colonies were not annexed to the Realm, at the Time when their Charters were granted, they never could be afterwards, without their own special Consent, which has never since been had, or even asked," the House stated. "If they are not now annexed to the Realm, they are not a Part of the Kingdom, and consequently not subject to the Legislative Authority of the Kingdom."[47] House members thus insisted instead that the constitution of 1629 and the constitution of 1773 were one and the same.

This argument made historical sense: the Massachusetts Bay Company had obtained its charter from Charles I in 1629, sixty years before the Glorious Revolution supplanted royal prerogative with parliamentary sovereignty as the basis of English government. At the time of the charter's drafting, therefore, English constitutional theory placed the king at the top of the ladder of sovereignty. Hutchinson's argument, in contrast, read the parliamentary sovereignty of his own, post-1688 period backward on the assumption that the revolution settlement had applied retroactively and for all time.[48] Hutchinson's approach might have been good whig orthodoxy, but the House's answer charged that it was not good history.

By challenging Hutchinson's interpretation of the charter, the House attacked imperial officials' assumption of equivalence between parliamentary sovereignty at home and supremacy over the colonial assemblies. Just as the Council had invoked Magna Carta as a talisman of the ancient constitution against overweening parliamentary power, the House sought refuge in the traditional, pre-1688 vision of Crown prerogative. The Massachusetts colonial legislature therefore invoked what John Phillip Reid terms the "authority of custom" to challenge openly Parliament's authority both at home and in the far reaches of the empire.[49]

Was the colonists' argument in favor of Crown rule purely instrumental? Perhaps; after all, England had fought a savage civil war over the issue of Crown prerogative versus parliamentary sovereignty. But members of the colonial opposition routinely pledged loyalty to the king during this debate, adhering to what scholars have variously termed the theory of dominion status or the "doctrine of allegiance," which emphasized membership in a loosely defined association with the monarch alone rather than membership in the British nation.[50] As the eminent Scots-American jurist James Wilson put it in 1774, "[A]ll the different members of the British empire are distinct states, independent of each other, but connected together under the same sovereign in right of the same crown."[51] Adams made a similar distinction between the kingdom of Britain and the dominion of the king: "We are within the dominion, rule, or government of the King of Great Britain," he acknowledged; however, he added, "[W]e are not . . . a part of the British kingdom, realm, or state."[52] Although they chose different terms, Wilson and Adams endorsed what Randolph Adams terms the "commonwealth of nations" view of empire, which held that the colonies were independent states, "that their sole connection with Great Britain lay in the crown; that the parliament at Westminster was but one of many co-equal legislatures, analogous, for example, to the General Court of Massachusetts Bay." Rather than a choice for the Crown, such arguments should be seen as a choice against Parliament: the colonists sought to place their own legislatures directly under royal authority by cutting Parliament out of the hierarchy altogether.[53]

The central role played by James Wilson, who emigrated from Scotland to America in 1765 at the age of twenty-three, in developing the doctrine of allegiance was not a coincidence. For Wilson and other colonists who argued that the colonists owed loyalty to the king alone, the example of Scotland provided a rich trove of legal arguments. The union of crowns of 1603, in which James VI of Scotland also became James I of England, "united the kingdoms only to the extent that it gave them 'one Head or Sovereign'; it did not unite them in one body politic."[54] By 1707, when the Act of Union formally dissolved both the English and the Scottish parliaments and brought England and Scotland into a new entity called the British Parliament, English subjects—and, after 1607, American colonists—had lived through more than a century of debates about the practical meaning of sovereignty and the many varieties of Pufendorfian "systems of states" that could join two polities.[55] (Recall Hutchinson's January 6, 1773, statement that he "knew of no line" that could be drawn between parliamentary supremacy and colonial independence that would not create "two Governments as distinct as the Kingdoms of England and Scotland before the Union.")

Although Adams lacked Wilson's firsthand knowledge of Scottish politics and law, he, too, looked to the case of Scotland to bolster his arguments against parliamentary authority.[56] In particular, Adams focused on the period after the union of crowns but before the Act of Union, which he believed provided useful precedents for the situation of the colonies in the 1760s and early 1770s. Just as Scotland had shared a king but not a legislature with England between 1603 and 1707, Adams contended, the American colonies should be seen as owing allegiance to George III but not to Parliament. Just as Scotland had maintained its sovereignty until it formally merged with England in 1707, the colonies remained sovereign in 1774. In each case, one state had contracted its own arrangement with a sovereign who just happened to be the sovereign of another state—a fact that did not affect the relationship between the sovereign and the first state, which existed independent of the sovereign's relationship with any other state. "Distinct states may be united under one king. . . . Massachusetts is a realm, New York is a realm, Pennsylvania another realm, to all intents and purposes, as much as Ireland is, or England or Scotland ever were," Adams wrote in his *Novanglus* letters. "The King of Great Britain is the sovereign of all these realms." Should Britain and the colonies mutually determine that a complete union was desirable, the full formalities of annexation—notably, consent, in the form of legislative acts on each side—would be required.[57]

Another key element of the House's response was its depiction of Hutchinson's argument as relying on outmoded theories of authority.[58] In his January 6 address, Hutchinson had offered a twofold argument: first, the colonists were British subjects for purposes of their obligations to Parliament, but not British subjects for purposes of the rights that they might demand from Parliament; second, the colonists were not physically situated within the realm for purposes of rights, but they were physically within the realm for purposes of obligations. The governor had asserted that by "their voluntary Removal," the colonists had "relinquished for a Time at least, one of the Rights of an English Subject" (i.e., they had fewer rights because they had left the kingdom). But despite the nonportability of English rights, Hutchinson argued, it did not follow "that the Government, by their Removal from one Part of the Dominions to another, loses it's [*sic*] Authority over that Part to which they remove" (i.e., they had the same obligations despite their having left the kingdom).[59] Thus, while English rights might not weather the transatlantic voyage, English authority could be salted away and then produced on colonial shores. The early colonists had left behind their homeland and some quantum of the rights granted to them by their government, but this relocation had not removed them beyond the reach of the long arm of English authority. In terms of jurisdictional theory, Hutchinson's argument mixed elements of Roman law's emphasis on personality with medieval law's emphasis on territoriality.[60] According to Hutchinson's reasoning, then, neither principles of personality nor principles of territoriality could aid the colonists in their attempt to escape parliamentary authority.

The House challenged both the premise and the conclusion of Hutchinson's jurisdictional interpretation. Rejecting the governor's mixed approach to determining which law governed the colonies, the House's answer reiterated one of its fundamental arguments: the colonies had never been part of the realm; therefore, Parliament never had—and, absent colonial consent, never would have—plenary authority over the colonies. Placing great weight on the claim that the colonies had never been within the realm, the House argument thus relied on the territorial principle of law. By crossing the ocean and establishing colonies in America— colonies formed pursuant to royal authority alone—the earliest settlers had removed themselves from the realm and, therefore, removed themselves from the ambit of parliamentary power. Parliament's authority was "constitutionally confined within the Limits of the Realm and the Nation collectively, of which alone it is the Representing and Legislative Assembly," the House reasoned. "[I]f that Part of the King's Dominions to which they removed was not then a Part of the Realm, and was never annexed to it, the Parliament lost no Authority over it, having never had such Authority; and the Emigrants were consequently freed from the Subjection they were under before their Removal."[61] In short, the House argued, domicile mattered more than nationality for purposes of authority.

For purposes of rights, the House offered a winding and delicate argument that skated quite close to Hutchinson's reasoning but reached the opposite outcome. Although the burdens of English nationality had not accompanied the early colonists on their voyage to the New World, some of their English rights had made the trip, pursuant to a grant from the king. The most significant of these rights was the right of representation in Parliament. "They never did relinquish the Right to be governed by Laws made by Persons in whose Election they had a Voice," the House stated. "The King stipulated with them . . . that they should be as free as those who were to abide within the Realm." According to the House, then, the territorial principle controlled in determining that the colonies were not included in the realm, but a special, affirmative stipulation by the king—under whose exclusive authority the colonies continued— allowed the colonists to claim English rights. In this way, the House argued, its vision of colonial duties and rights was, both logically and practically, more coherent than Hutchinson's vision. "We cannot help observing, that your Excellency's Manner of Reasoning on this Point, seems to us to render the most valuable Clauses in our Charter unintelligible," the response noted. "As if Persons going from the Realm of England to inhabit in America, should hold and exercise there a certain Right of English Subjects; but in Order to exercise it in such Manner as to be of any Benefit to them, they must *not inhabit* there, but return to the Place where alone it can be exercised."[62]

With this argument, the House called into question Hutchinson's assertion that no line could be drawn between total parliamentary authority and total colonial independence. Obviously struck by Hutchinson's metaphor, the House draftsmen went on to offer their own version, confirming its role as a leitmotif of the debate. "[I]ndeed it is difficult, if possible, to draw a Line of Distinction between the universal Authority of Parliament over the Colonies, and no Authority at all," the House's response observed.[63]

The blandness of this statement concealed a radical divergence from imperial orthodoxy. Drawing lines remained difficult, but suddenly the House insisted that it was possible. Rather than following Hutchinson's lead and treating the outlines of British constitutional law as congruent with the geopolitical boundaries of Great Britain, the colonial opposition attempted to separate political lines from constitutional ones. Adams, Wilson, and many of their fellow American whigs agreed that the colonies were part of the British nation, but they did not view this political authority as necessarily determinative of final, legal authority. Instead of accepting Hutchinson's all-or-nothing, totalizing vision of imperial structure, the colonists sought to adapt what had originally been an ad hoc structure of royal charter and local assembly into a newly conceived vision of divisible legislative sovereignty.

The 1773 debates are significant because they marked the beginning of a transition, not because they witnessed the completion of that transition. Despite the slowly shifting meaning of the term "sovereignty," the members of the House feared—or at least pretended to fear—the unnatural creature of the *imperium in imperio* sufficiently to deploy it against Hutchinson in their reply of January 26. To bolster their claim that the original charters had placed the colonies under the exclusive control of the king, the members of the House committee reinterpreted the *imperium in imperio* principle as precluding Parliament from exerting its power over the colonies. "[T]o suppose a Parliamentary Authority over the Colonies under such Charters, would necessarily induce that Solecism in Politics, *Imperium in Imperio*," the House's answer contended. Premising their argument on the existence and authority of the assemblies from the earliest moments of colonial settlement, the House members demurred to Hutchinson's claims, using his own argument to conclude "that the Colonies were by their Charters made distinct States from the Mother Country."[64]

Throughout the debate, then, both sides employed the *imperium in imperio* argument. Hutchinson relied on it to underpin his claim that the colonial assemblies did not possess legislative sovereignty; the members of the General Court relied on it to support their challenge to parliamentary authority. Both sides espoused the underlying principle that multiple sovereigns could not exist within the same political entity. But while Hutchinson took this principle to mean that the sovereignty of Parliament at home must translate into its supremacy abroad, the members of the General Court used it to build a novel argument for the sovereignty of the colonial assemblies on the basis of a reconfiguration of the lines of authority between Britain and America. And, the House added, if such line drawing proved beyond the capacities of the royal governor, Massachusetts—in concert with the other colonies—was prepared to essay it: "If your Excellency expects to have the Line of Distinction between the Supreme Authority of Parliament, and the total Independence of the Colonies drawn by us, we would say it would be an arduous Undertaking; and of very great Importance to all the other Colonies: And therefore, could we conceive of such a Line, we should be unwilling to propose it, without their Consent in Congress."[65] More than a year and a half before the Continental Congress convened in Philadelphia, the members of the General Court were contemplating not just their own redefinition of sovereignty but a continent-wide redrawing of the lines of authority.

The Boston newspapers, hawkishly monitoring the debate, waded into the midst of the controversy. In addition to printing excerpts from each side's statements, the newspapers began publishing anonymous commentaries, as well as unsigned statements that presumably articulated the editors' views. Much of the commentary focused on whether Hutchinson had had the blessing of his metropolitan superiors when he initiated the debate, and on the related issue of whether the administration intended conciliation. Admittedly, Hutchinson was caught in a difficult position, as "A True Friend" allowed in the *Boston Evening-Post:* "Thomas is the servant of George, who has a right to command him in all things—but Thomas is also the servant of the people, and so is George his master; government being appointed by Him who is higher than all, for the service and benefit of all."[66]

In an open letter to the governor signed "A Friend to the Community" and published in the *Boston-Gazette,* another commentator who described himself as "an Englishman" and "a sincere lover of the best constitution that ever had an existence" nevertheless criticized Hutchinson for appointing himself "the grand *arbiter* between Great Britain and her colonies." By forcing the issue of parliamentary authority, A Friend argued, Hutchinson had either assumed that his arguments would easily carry the day or else had hoped to draw the General Court "to give such an answer as should lay the parliament of Great-Britain under the necessity of either totally relinquishing all right of jurisdiction over us; or force us by coercive measures to submit to whatever terms they may impose upon us." Throughout the recent years' controversies, the writer noted, he had held out hope for an end to "the unnatural dispute between the *parent state and her colonies*"; now, however, Hutchinson's pronouncements had "blasted all those hopes, and set me afloat in an abyss of gloomy reflections."[67] Meanwhile, the newspapers noted, the judges of the superior court had not yet received their Crown salaries; this news seemed to vindicate fears that administrators at home were withholding payment in order to ensure the judges' obedience.[68]

Despite colonists' speculations about Hutchinson's support from colonial administrators, correspondence between the governor and Lord Dartmouth demonstrates that Hutchinson had at least initiated the debate with his superiors' blessing. Shortly after receiving Hutchinson's letters of December 30 and January 7, Dartmouth wrote a reply, dated March 3, in which he temporized somewhat but ultimately agreed with Hutchinson's plan to broach the subject of parliamentary authority. Unrest among the towns of Massachusetts had "made it necessary that you should call upon the Council and House of Representatives to be explicit with regard to their sentiments of those proceedings and of the doctrines they adopt." Dartmouth added that reports of open opposition to metropolitan control "made it incumbent upon you to speak out upon the occasion." After a carefully phrased caveat ("But how far it was or was not expedient to enter so fully in your speech into an exposition of your own opinion in respect to the principles of the constitution of the colony I am not able to judge"), Dartmouth ended his letter with a measured endorsement of Hutchinson's plan: "[W]hatever the effect of that speech may be, it was certainly justified in the intention and I hope it will have the consequence to remove those prejudices which the artificers of faction" had attempted to foist upon the minds of the colonial opposition.[69]

Hutchinson, meanwhile, was planning his rejoinder to the two houses' answers to his initial speech. After each party had aired its position, the subsequent round of statements predictably became more vitriolic and demonstrated not movement toward concord but rather growing entrenchment. "I shall at the close of the Session give both the Council & House a full reply & shew them from undeniable Authority what was their Constitution at the beginning and what it still continues to be and what must be the fatal consequences of departing from it," Hutchinson wrote to Dartmouth on February 1.[70] The determination of the House and, to a lesser extent, the Council to challenge imperial orthodoxy by asserting that the lines of sovereignty could be redrawn had raised the stakes of the debate for all parties.

Hutchinson addressed the General Court twice more before proroguing the legislative session on March 6; between his two speeches, each house issued a response. The issue of sovereignty dominated the remainder of the discussion. In a speech of February 16, Hutchinson first addressed the Council before directing the bulk of his comments to the House. As his comments to the Council suggest, his "drawing a line" phrasing had again returned to haunt him. The Council's "Attempts to draw a Line as the Limits of the Supreme Authority in Government, by distinguishing some natural Rights as more peculiarly exempt from such Authority than the rest, rather tend to evince the Impracticability of drawing such a Line," Hutchinson stated. The governor thus stuck to his original observation that the sovereignty of Parliament was complete and indivisible. Addressing the House, Hutchinson noted that Massachusetts Bay Colony had formerly been "holden as feudatory of the Imperial Crown of England." The colony was therefore "subject to one supreme legislative power"—Parliament—and was part of the dominion of the British Empire.[71]

Just over a week after Hutchinson's second speech, the Council issued what would be its final salvo; the House followed with its answer five days later. Previously, the House had produced the fierier response. Here, however, the Council struck directly at the heart of the issue: whether two coordinate authorities, in this case Parliament and the colonial assemblies, could ever exist within the same polity. The Council based its argument on Hutchinson's previous statement, uttered as part of his initial address on January 6, that "although from the Nature of Government there must be one Supreme Authority over the whole, yet this Constitution will admit of Subordinate Powers with Legislative and Executive Authority, greater or less, according to Local and other Circumstances." The Council heartily endorsed Hutchinson's assertion. "This is very true," the Council noted, adding that allowing for the existence of subordinate as well as supreme powers implied that "the Supreme Power has no rightful Authority to take away or diminish" the authority of the subordinate power. The supreme power lacked such authority to police the subordinate power because, the Council argued, the subordinate power was constituted independently of the supreme power. If the subordinate power were not independently constituted, then it would not need to be denominated a subordinate power; instead, it would be a subset of the supreme power. But this was not the case. Each power had its own grant of authority and its own zone of responsibility. Therefore, the Council observed, "[T]he two Powers are not incompatible, and do subsist together, each restraining its Acts to their Constitutional Objects." The constitutional objects of each power were distinct, and they were defined by their subject matter.[72]

In other words, the colonists might consider consenting to Parliament's supremacy if that supremacy was accompanied by an independent acknowledgment of the colonial assemblies' subordinate authority. Such an arrangement would keep the two levels of legislative authority separate by assigning to each a specific array of responsibilities: Parliament would supervise, regulate, and legislate for the entire British Empire, including America; the colonial legislatures, meanwhile, would oversee all matters that did not relate to the empire as a whole.

This arrangement tracked the distinction between internal and external affairs that observers such as Richard Bland, Daniel Dulany, and Thomas Pownall had articulated when the Stamp Act debates had raised the issue of the scope of Parliament's authority over the colonies.[73] In the context of the 1773 debates, however, the Council's delineation between superior and subordinate powers moved beyond the specific issue of taxation and toward the theoretical problem of *imperium in imperio,* as well as the practical difficulty of having two legislatures operating over the same territory. Without necessarily intending it, the members of the Council had taken a crucial step toward articulating a new vision of sovereignty. This reconception permitted sovereignty to be divided—not simply along the territorial lines that some early modern thinkers had posited, but along substantive lines defined by subject matter. Parliament would regulate matters relating to the empire as a whole, while the colonial assemblies would have authority over all other matters. The Council's proposal, then, attempted to rebut Hutchinson's claim that one could not draw a line between complete parliamentary sovereignty and complete colonial independence by arranging Parliament and the General Court along parallel rather than overlapping planes.

In a broader sense, the proposal laid the foundation for American federalism's parallel arrangement of national and state legislatures. Hutchinson's equivalence between political and legal boundaries based on territory would begin to give way to legal boundaries based on subject matter: in 1773, imperial versus colonial matters; sixteen years later, national versus state matters. Such an arrangement would satisfy Blackstone's maxim that "there is and must be in all [governments] a supreme, irresistible, absolute, uncontrolled authority, in which the *jura summi imperii*, or the rights of sovereignty, reside" through the granting of the aforementioned supreme authority to a specific arm of government depending on the particular substantive issues at stake.[74] No *imperium in imperio* would result, and there would be no need for recourse to the type of unitary, monolithic sovereign enshrined in the British constitution.

Several scholars have pointed to the theory of popular sovereignty as the key that allowed the colonists to circumvent the problem of *imperium in imperio*. Most notably, Edmund Morgan has described popular sovereignty as an agreed-upon "fiction" that first emerged in England in the mid-seventeenth century as an antidote to the Stuart theory of the divine right of kings. During the ratification period, Morgan argues, James Madison and other advocates of the Constitution used popular sovereignty to justify the creation of a national rather than a confederational government.[75] Placing the rise of popular sovereignty somewhat earlier, Bernard Bailyn argues that by the 1770s, Americans' questioning of the idea of unitary, indivisible sovereignty had been followed by a new belief "that the ultimate sovereignty . . . rested with the people."[76] On a related note, Larry Kramer has emphasized colonists' growing belief throughout the 1760s and 1770s that popular sovereignty was "the central principle of American constitutionalism."[77]

As these debates demonstrate, however, a transformation in the understanding of sovereignty preceded—or, at least, accompanied— American discussions of a revesting of sovereignty in the people. The essence of the General Court's break with imperial constitutional theory was its members' insistence that the ultimate source of political authority could be divided, rather than that it could be shifted wholesale to reside, still unitary, in a different location within the political community.

Downfall of a Governor

To his credit as a servant of the empire, Hutchinson resisted to the end the Council's reformulation of the concept of sovereignty. On March 6, he delivered the final installment in the exchange with the General Court. The Council's distinction between supreme and subordinate powers was specious, he insisted, citing the "Inconsistency" of "supposing a *subordinate* Power without a Power *superior* to it." Adhering to the Blackstonian idea of sovereignty, the governor refused even to consider the possibility that authority could be divided along subject-matter, as opposed to territorial, lines. "[I]f you are still of Opinion that two Jurisdictions, each of them having a Share in the Supreme Power, are compatible in the same State, it can be to no Purpose to Reason or Argue upon the other Parts of your Message," Hutchinson asserted. "It is essential to the Being of Government that a Power should always exist which no other Power within such Government can have Right to withstand or controul." And, as had been the case since 1688, when the English nation "*returned* to a just Sense of the Supremacy of Parliament," that uncontrollable, supreme power resided at Westminster.[78] Having made his last stand, the governor, in the words of one pamphlet, "was pleas'd to put an End to the Session."[79]

By the spring of 1773, Hutchinson seems to have realized that the debate with the General Court had strayed far beyond the bounds of whatever initial approval his plan had received from imperial administrators. In a letter to General Thomas Gage, the commander of British military forces in North America, Hutchinson set down his version of events as if in anticipation of litigation. Noting that reports of the Massachusetts controversy had appeared in newspapers throughout the colonies and in Britain, Hutchinson defended his decision to bring the question of parliamentary authority into open debate. The circular letter drafted by the Boston town meeting in response to the news of the Crown salaries had contained "Sedition & mutiny" insofar as its radical views "expressly den[ied] Parliamentary Authority." Hutchinson's concern that allowing such agitation to spread "would be deemed a great neglect of my duty to the king" had motivated him to take steps that, he acknowledged, some observers might have considered drastic. True, he could have issued a written statement or asked the General Court to suppress the circular letter. "I saw the impropriety of such argumentative speeches or messages to an assembly," Hutchinson admitted. But he felt that he had chosen the best approach, given that "the people are more attentive to any matters which come from the Governor in this way than to any other Publication." The governor thus insisted that he had been "compelled . . . to shew the unwarrantableness of the Proceedings by laying before them the true Principles of the Constitution in as simple & concise a manner as I could."[80]

Moreover, Hutchinson's correspondence with Lord Dartmouth became increasingly strained in the spring of 1773. Dartmouth, who had taken office as secretary of state for the colonies in 1772 (and who was the stepbrother of Lord North), had followed a policy of conciliation in his dealings with the colonies.[81] Faced with a royal governor whose zealous advocacy of the official government position had clearly ignited the simmering colonial opposition, Dartmouth appears to have reconsidered the limited approval of Hutchinson's plan that his March 3 letter had conveyed. News of Whitehall's increasing disapproval, as well as the firestorm of public commentary that the debate had sparked, seems to have begun to affect Hutchinson around the time of his March 6 speech to the General Court. A marked decline in the quality of his handwriting, in addition to his self-exculpatory letters to correspondents such as Gage, suggests the governor's anxiety, but he continued to alternate between ringing affirmations and defensive self-justifications. On March 10, he wrote to an unknown correspondent that the "contagion" that had begun in the town meeting "seems to have been stopped by my speech to the Assembly and the consequent Proceedings there." By April 25, however, a letter to Dartmouth contained the following apologia: "If I could, consistent with my duty to the King, have avoided any controversy with the Assembly upon Constitutional Points, it would have been most agreable to me. . . . It affords me relief that the propriety of the measure appears to His Majesty and that he is pleased to approve of it."[82]

Hutchinson's fears were well founded. By June 1773, his imperial superiors had moved to sacrifice him in the hope of stanching the flow of unrest in Massachusetts. Following reports from Benjamin Franklin, London agent for Massachusetts, confirming that the debate had thrown the colony into an uproar, Dartmouth, the colonial secretary, took the extraordinary step of drafting a "private and confidential" letter to Thomas Cushing, speaker of the House of Representatives. In this letter, Dartmouth took pains to note that he was writing as a private individual rather than in his official capacity; he then opined that although Parliament's power to tax the colonies could not be disputed, the power ought to be used sparingly in order to avoid just these sorts of disputes with the colonies. Dartmouth then invited the General Court to reconsider the extreme declarations that it had made during the course of the debate with Hutchinson and suggested that a retraction might persuade Parliament to "overlook the mistakes of a well-intentioned, though perhaps not well-informed, part of His Majesty's subjects."[83] Despite these entreaties, however, the House refused to recant its statements. Cushing informed Dartmouth that although Hutchinson had foisted the debate upon an unwilling General Court, the House regretted nothing in what Cushing argued were measured and carefully considered answers. The responses, Cushing noted, had judiciously refused to "draw a line of distinction between the supreme authority of Parliament and the total independency of the colonies."[84] Cushing's response thus strongly implied that the General Court had behaved as prudently as possible, given the predicament into which the governor's reckless challenge had forced them.

The exchange between Dartmouth and Cushing damned Hutchinson. Sometime in June, he began receiving letters from Dartmouth of an altogether different tone from the secretary's earlier correspondence. Dartmouth rebuked Hutchinson in no uncertain terms for provoking the General Court to articulate positions "of the most dangerous nature . . . subversive of every principle of the constitutional dependence of the colonies upon this kingdom."[85] In letters dated April 10 and June 2, Dartmouth essentially ordered Hutchinson to halt the debate before he caused more damage to the delicate imperial arrangement. Before the first of these letters arrived in Boston, Hutchinson had already drafted an apologia to Dartmouth in which he again explained his reasons for initiating the debate and attempted to portray a stoic resignation in the face of both the constitutional debacle and the blame that had already begun to attach to him. Hutchinson reiterated his conviction of the supremacy of Parliament: "My Sentiments of the Relation between the Kingdom & its Colonies have been the same ever since I have been capable of conceptions of the nature of Government. From the remote situation of the Colonies I always supposed a different and more extensive Legislative Power to be necessary for a Colony than for a Corporation in England, a Supreme controuling Power nevertheless remaining in the

Legislative Authority of the whole Dominion." He reminded Dartmouth that he himself had opposed the Stamp Act and had instead argued for parliamentary "forbearance" from exercising its power. He then offered what was essentially his resignation, citing the need for a governor "of greater abilities" to stand against the "Principles of Independency" that were on the march in Massachusetts.[86]

Around the time of the arrival of Dartmouth's April 10 letter, Hutchinson appears to have changed his mind. He scrapped his tormented apologia and instead sent a crisply worded response to his superior. "It gives me pain that any step which I have taken, with the most sincere intention to promote His Majesty's Service, should be judged to have a contrary effect. . . . [A]s far as I shall know His Majestys pleasure upon any point whatsoever I will, as I have hitherto done[,] endeavour strictly to conform to it." He did not mention resignation to Dartmouth until June 26, when he asked permission to visit England in order to seek an alternative post.[87]

In the intervening weeks, another catastrophe had befallen Hutchinson: the release and subsequent publication of thirteen letters that Hutchinson, his relatives, and his friends had written to Thomas Whately, the former British undersecretary of the Treasury (and, not incidentally, author of an early draft of the Stamp Act) in the late 1760s. The letters, in which Hutchinson argued—as he had elsewhere—that preserving the empire would require tightening metropolitan control over the colonies, "set in motion an almost unstoppable landslide of public opinion."[88] Nearly a year later, on June 1, 1774, Hutchinson departed for England, leaving Massachusetts to the military governorship of General Gage. That day, Hutchinson's son-in-law Peter Oliver, Jr., who remained in Boston, noted in his diary, "Nothing but mobs and riots all this summer."[89]

Redrawing the Lines of Sovereignty

On the same day on which Hutchinson departed for England, where he would spend the rest of his life, the first of five parliamentary acts that boldly asserted Parliament's authority to legislate for the colonies took effect. Derided by colonists as the Intolerable Acts, these laws (also known as the Coercive Acts) comprised the Boston Port Bill, which shut down the transport of goods through the city's harbor; the Massachusetts Government Act, which replaced the colony's charter government with a military regime under Gage; the Administration of Justice Act, which permitted British officials charged with capital offenses to be tried in England or another colony; a new version of the 1765 Quartering Act, which ordered the colonies to house British troops in occupied American houses and taverns; and the Quebec Act, which granted the land between the Ohio and Mississippi rivers to Quebec rather than the colonies.[90] As John Phillip Reid puts it, the Coercive Acts represented the first time that Americans "were confronted by the ultimate constitutional issue of executed parliamentary sovereignty."[91]

To be sure, the passage of the Declaratory Act in 1766 had asserted Parliament's "full power and authority to make laws and statutes of sufficient force and validity to bind the colonies and people of America . . . in all cases whatsoever," but Parliament's subsequent exercises of authority over the colonies had been confined to taxation (e.g., the Townshend Acts and the Tea Acts).[92] The passage of the Coercive Acts signaled that Parliament intended to enforce the full sweep of its lawmaking authority over the colonies. Despite Hutchinson's sad downfall and retreat, imperial policy remained as the governor had described it: Parliament's sovereignty in the colonies was just as complete and indivisible as its sovereignty at home.

The competing theories articulated by Hutchinson and the General Court demonstrate the collision between the Blackstonian vision of sovereignty as indivisible and unitary and the colonists' increasingly federal vision in which divided authority was neither a solecism nor an ad hoc practice, but a foundational principle.[93] This story has been told in the context of the drafting and ratification of the Constitution, but as the Massachusetts debates of 1773 demonstrate, the emergence of an American conception of legislative multiplicity predated the Philadelphia convention by more than a decade. The confrontation between Hutchinson and the General Court is therefore important to the history of American federalism because it illustrates the way in which theories of multilayered authority emerged in the 1770s to complement the institutional arguments that had characterized the debates of the 1760s.

By the mid-1770s, the idea of drawing lines between levels of legislative power—and thereby acknowledging that multiple lawmaking sources could legitimately exist within a single polity—became a frequent theme in American whigs' writings. In 1774, John Dickinson adopted the metaphor of line drawing that Hutchinson had first employed and that both houses of the General Court had then adapted for their own use. "The authority of parliament has within these few years been a question much agitated, and great difficulty, we understand, has occurred in tracing the line between the rights of the mother country and those of the colonies. . . . Whatever difficulty may occur in tracing the line, yet we contend that by the laws of God and by the laws of the constitution a line there must be beyond which her authority cannot extend. . . . We assert, a line there must be, and shall now proceed, with great deference to the judgment of others, to trace that line."[94] As in his widely circulated *Letters from a Farmer in Pennsylvania* of 1768, Dickinson then proceeded to draw a line between regulating trade and legislating for the colonies' internal affairs. The former, he contended, was permissible; the latter was not. Dickinson thus emphasized a subject-matter distinction separating the areas that a legislature might permissibly oversee and those that it might not.

Also in 1774, James Iredell invoked a similar substantive vision of the scope of lawmaking authority when he argued that the *imperium in imperio* principle was "not at all applicable to our case, though it has been so vainly and confidently relied on," because the emerging system of federalism relied on "several *distinct and independent legislatures,* each engaged within a *separate* scale, and employed about *different* objects."[95] For both Dickinson and Iredell, then, the objects of the law determined which authority could legitimately pursue it.

Hutchinson had refused to grant such a distinction, arguing that Parliament's sovereignty at home translated into full authority over the colonies because the colonies, like the British Isles, were part of the realm. In other words, Hutchinson understood legislative authority as coterminous with territorial boundaries, while Dickinson, Wilson, and the members of the General Court permitted legislative authority to be segmented according to the boundaries of subject matter.[96] Hutchinson might have scored a temporary victory for the empire in 1773 (albeit at the immense personal cost of his own career), but the substantive inquiry proposed by the General Court and embraced by Dickinson lived to fight—and win—another day. In 1787, Alexander Hamilton would describe the powers of the proposed federal government as similarly bounded by subject matter, not by political space: "[T]he laws of the confederacy, as to the *enumerated* and *legitimate* objects of its jurisdiction, will become the SUPREME LAW of the land."[97] The enumerated, legitimate objects of an authority's jurisdiction, not the reach of its might over a given piece of territory, would determine whether its laws or those of a concurrent authority would apply.

Rather than tying sovereignty to territory, the members of the General Court and their successors connected sovereignty with its particular substantive objects; rather than insisting on sovereignty as monolithic and unitary, the colonial opposition viewed it as divisible into parallel and nonoverlapping repositories. From the earliest disputes of the 1760s concerning the scope of Parliament's authority, colonists and some imperial officials had attempted to draw lines limiting that authority; every time, imperial administrators had refused to consider that lines could be drawn, let alone the specific lines that the colonists proposed.

The debates of early 1773 signified an important transition in Anglo-Americans' thinking about sovereignty, a moment of divergence between imperial and colonial theory, and an illustration of a key conceptual breakthrough that helped bring about the development of federalism. Whether the General Court or Hutchinson—or neither—had the better constitutional arguments at the time is less relevant for the story of the intellectual history of federalism than the following two facts: first, each side was deeply committed to its particular constitutional vision; and second, one can clearly see here elements of the political-theoretical moves that would enable the General Court and its successors to develop a domestic version of Pufendorf's system of states.

Eighteenth-century American federal thought was defined by a belief not only that lines could be drawn between sources of authority, but also that such line drawing was desirable as a normative matter. In 1773, imperial officials, citing the increasingly powerful theory of parliamentary supremacy, argued that such delineations were impossible. The General Court suggested, however, not only that could lines be drawn around sovereign authorities, but also that they could be drawn according to novel, subject-matter-specific principles. Despite their tendentious origins, arguments such as these ultimately provided the foundation for the American federal experiment. The Constitutional Convention delegates' enumeration of the powers of the national government, and their accompanying reservation of powers to the states, expanded on the Massachusetts General Court members' assertion, fourteen years earlier, that sovereignty could be apportioned among authorities—and preserved against competing claims—according to the substantive ends toward which that sovereignty was directed.

CHAPTER 4

Forging a Federated Union

D ESPITE THE CHOLER and controversy that accompanied the debates between Governor Thomas Hutchinson and the Massachusetts General Court in the early months of 1773, the confrontation in some sense ended in a draw. True, opposition to his policies and outrage following the publication of his correspondence with metropolitan officials forced Hutchinson to quit Boston for an uncertain future in England, an ignominious exit that many of his fellow colonists regarded as a victory.[1] But the coincidence of Hutchinson's departure on June 1, 1774, with the arrival of the new regime of the Coercive Acts dampened the sense of relief that Bostonians felt upon the sailing of their governor. Just as repeal of the Stamp Act was accompanied by passage of the Declaratory Act (a sober reminder that Parliament's legislation bound the colonies "in all cases whatsoever"), the combination of Hutchinson's exit with the advent of what Bostonians termed the "Intolerable Acts" made clear that the American whigs' victory was only partial and temporary.

In the summer of 1774, the nuances of internal versus external taxation and the intricacies of construing charters began to give way to broad metropolitan assertions of power, on one hand, and sharpening colonial demands for political and economic accommodation, on the other. Arguments that colonial leaders had used for more than a decade against parliamentary supremacy and in favor of provincial legislative power developed into more abstract and ambitious proposals to reshape imperial governance entirely. During the 1760s, political observers had articulated a distinction between legislative powers that were specific to the colonies and those that were general to the empire as a whole. This distinction shaped the arguments of writers on both sides of the Atlantic, such as former Massachusetts governor Thomas Pownall and Pennsylvania legislator and pamphleteer John Dickinson. By the early 1770s, however, controversies such as the debate between Hutchinson and the General Court signaled the end of the previous decade's spirit of experimentation with divisions between metropolitan and provincial lawmaking authority.

The years between 1774 and 1777 witnessed profound developments in American constitutional thought. Political and legal thinkers responded to what they regarded as a newly acute set of exigencies by offering creative theories of governmental organization that carried dramatic consequences for the development of American federal ideas. In 1774, prominent commentators on both sides of the Atlantic, such as Thomas Jefferson, John Cartwright, and Joseph Galloway, proposed various plans for formal union between Britain and the colonies. Their efforts to revise the map of imperial authority drew on three strands of thought: first, the experience of British North Americans' handful of earlier efforts at confederation; second, the history of England's union with Scotland, a process that had unfolded over the course of a century; and, third, several early modern political thinkers' studies of the law of nations and the messy reality of political authority in Europe. By 1777, the colonies—now in the form of a political entity called "the United States in Congress assembled"—were attempting to institutionalize these nascent ideas of confederation in order to transform themselves from a collection of imperial satellites into a perpetual union.

Throughout this period, the theories of divided authority that had been implicit and inchoate during the 1760s and early 1770s became increasingly explicit.[2] A few common threads had run through the crisis over imperial taxation and regulation that had accompanied the Sugar and Stamp acts, as well as the dispute over the relationship among Crown, Parliament, and colonies that had dominated the debate between Hutchinson and the General Court. These shared themes included repeated inquiry into the nature of sovereignty (was it indivisible, as William Blackstone's *Commentaries* of 1765–1769 argued, or could it be partitioned?); the rights of British subjects who inhabited lands beyond the realm pursuant to agreements contracted with a monarch in what was essentially a different constitutional era; and, most important, the possibility of harmonizing the values of empire with notions of shared authority that appeared to some observers to reflect the reality of imperial political organization.

After nearly a decade of transatlantic conversation, by 1774 these issues became concrete in the form of several proposals to reorganize first the empire and then the colonies alone. This increased explicitness makes the period between 1774 and 1777 a crucial moment in which students of the history of American federalism do not have to search to find the terms "federal," "confederation," and other cognates of the classical *foedus* concept.[3] Ten years' struggle with various scenarios of divided authority made the proposals of this period both more sweeping and more fully theorized than any that had come before.

At least initially, these comprehensive reform plans issued from desks in London, as well as in the colonial hotbeds of Massachusetts and Virginia. As in the previous decades, observers in both Britain and America challenged Parliament's assertions of plenary legislative power by proposing alternative arrangements that apportioned lawmaking authority among multiple governmental institutions. In 1774 and early 1775, this was still possible within the confines of the British Empire as contemporaries knew it. By 1776, however, the outbreak of sustained combat in North America had irrevocably altered the tenor of the debate. Actual military conflict among armies with equal claims to British identity necessarily shifted the controversy from a reexamination and refinement of the constitutional issues that had emerged out of the Glorious Revolution of 1688–1689 to a mortal struggle over what ownership of and membership in an empire meant.

The commentators of the 1760s and early 1770s had built their claims on the premise that the theory of empire could be retooled to incorporate what they viewed as the reality of empire: namely, a system in which legislative authority was attached to specific things or matters of governance, as opposed to territorial boundaries. The failure of the plans proposed by Jefferson, Galloway, Cartwright, and others to win accommodation for the colonial view, however, demonstrated a profound incompatibility between the increasingly unitary constitution of the British Empire and the provincial drive to divide lawmaking authority among multiple jurisdictions. By 1777, American observers had moved beyond remarking on the mismatch between the practice of multiplicity and the ideology of unitary power within the empire. Instead of attempting to rebut the claims of metropolitan spokesmen such as Hutchinson or to fit their counterideology within the contours of official imperial theory, the colonist-revolutionaries shifted their focus to constructing what Murray Forsyth terms "a federal union of states."[4]

The major proposals for union that appeared in 1774 and 1775 aimed at restructuring the broader political and legal structure of the British Empire, starting with a renegotiation of the place of the colonies within the imperial constitution. The locus of this negotiation differed among the various proposals. For John Cartwright, the solution required metropolitan officials to realize that Britain would benefit more from a consensual league with independent American states than it would by continuing in a coercive imperial relationship. For Thomas Jefferson, the key was to tie the colonies directly to the Crown without the intervention of Parliament. For Joseph Galloway, the answer lay in formalizing the important legislative role that the colonial assemblies played and raising them to the level of Parliament, at least for some purposes. All three plans emphasized the idea of confederation as a tool to maintain the substance of the British Empire, albeit in a slightly changed form. Following a brief discussion of each of these theorists' work on the subject of imperial restructuring, this chapter will take up the question of what influences—besides those of the earlier colonial constitutions already mentioned—informed their writing and guided their thinking about the manner in which political authority could be organized within an empire.

Cartwright's Plan: Fealty to the Crown Alone

In 1774, John Cartwright, a Royal Navy officer who had served in the Seven Years' War and upon retirement took up the post of major in the Nottinghamshire militia, produced a radical plan to reform the empire into a league of independent states joined only by treaty. After this initial foray into public debate, Cartwright became a vocal and prominent advocate of parliamentary reform. His 1774 contribution took the form of a pamphlet; the title, lengthy even by eighteenth-century standards, began, *American Independence the Interest and Glory of Great Britain.* The seventy-two-page pamphlet consisted of a series of letters addressed to "the legislature" (Parliament) that examined the state of Parliament's sovereignty over the North American colonies, specifically the question whether Parliament possessed the power to tax the colonies.[5] Cartwright answered in the negative. "To every man of candour, I apprehend it must be evident, that Parliament hath not the rights of sovereignty over his Majesty's American subjects," Cartwright insisted. "The respective governments in America, are no longer dependent colonies; they are independent nations." For Cartwright, the impossibility of Americans' consenting to parliamentary legislation meant that they could not be bound by that legislation, for this result would violate their "inherent right to liberty."[6]

Cartwright thus rejected Parliament's claims to represent the colonies either by innate authority or by virtual representation. But he did not view the Crown as similarly lacking in authority over the colonies. "That the King should have the sovereignty of the colonies is but reasonable, is consistent with the spirit of the English laws." Cartwright based this assertion on the original royal grant of permission to settle on lands in the New World. The early colonists had thus bound themselves to the monarch as subjects, similar to the subject status they had possessed in England. But this did not bind them to Parliament as well, for the result would be to make them "subjects of subjects," which Cartwright denounced as a "despicable" situation.[7] The North American colonies' relationship to Britain thus hinged only on their tie to the Crown, not to any broader membership in the realm that would give rise to the general jurisdiction of Parliament.

In its emphasis on the early settlers' connection to the Crown alone, Cartwright's proposal resembled the arguments of the Massachusetts General Court and others in the early 1770s who insisted that the colonies, properly understood, were subject to the authority of the king alone and not to Parliament. But Cartwright pushed even further than those earlier commentators. The members of the General Court had by and large accepted their status as subjects of the empire; they had disputed the nature of that imperial connection and the ultimate authority at the top of the imperial hierarchy, but they had not challenged the political category of "empire." Cartwright, in contrast, flatly denied that the colonies belonged in any sense to the British Empire. "It is a mistaken notion, that planting of colonies, and extending of empire, are necessarily one and the same thing," Cartwright contended. "As to the imagination of Great Britain and America being *one empire,* these are only words that serve to blind, to amuse, and to confound inconsiderate reasoners." The British Empire, he maintained, was "confined to the British Isles, and to the various *settlements and factories of our trade* in the different parts of the world, including *the government of Newfoundland;* together with the garrisons of *Gibraltar* and *Minorca.*"[8]

Cartwright argued that even his bête noire Josiah Tucker—dean of Gloucester Cathedral and himself a prolific pamphleteer—had conceded that the colonies were not part of the empire, insofar as Tucker had proposed granting the colonies representation in Parliament "in order to incorporate America and Great Britain into one common empire."[9] Cartwright's reform plan thus began from the premise that the North American provinces were not incorporated into the British Empire, and, therefore, that they could rightfully claim to possess independent legislative authority.

Without a binding imperial connection, Cartwright argued, Parliament ought to acknowledge the colonies' independence. When this ratification had been dealt with, the path would be clear for the former colonies voluntarily to form a "league" or a "general treaty between Great Britain and the states of America."[10] This league, Cartwright observed, would benefit Britain, as well as the colonies, for it would replace the existing state of conflict between metropolis and provinces with a new and amicable bond that would in turn allow transatlantic commerce to thrive. Indeed, a declaration of the colonies' independence would tie the colonies even more tightly to Britain by ensuring their willing reliance on the mother country's trade and protection. As the "common umpire," Britain would "become in effect the general sovereign, so long as she interposes her good offices for maintaining the common independence"—

and so long as Britain comported itself as "*not a conquering*, but a commercial state."[11]

True, in this scenario Parliament would lose its claims to jurisdiction over the colonies, but the benefits of the league would redound to the glory of the king. "[H]is Majesty will be a gainer, inasmuch as he will thereby receive fifteen independent kingdoms in exchange for as many dependent, and *hardly dependent* provinces, and become the father of three millions of free and happy subjects, instead of reigning joint tyrant over so many discontented slaves." Cartwright's plan for a "firm, brotherly, and perpetual league" between Britain and the erstwhile colonies thus sought to move beyond the existing imperial framework to a new form of organization limited to a discretionary league with Britain. In other words, Cartwright envisioned a structure that accepted elements of union but lacked the full apparatus of empire.[12]

Galloway's Plan: Union within Empire

Other commentators writing in 1774 and 1775 offered proposals to reshape the colonial-metropolitan relationship that were less radical and, in some cases, more nuanced than Cartwright's scheme. Thomas Jefferson's *Summary View of the Rights of British America* (1774) fit both these descriptions; Joseph Galloway's "Plan of a Proposed Union between Great Britain and the Colonies" (1774) fit the former, if not the latter. In contrast to Cartwright's plan, which assumed an imminent split between the colonies and Britain, Galloway's proposal explicitly aimed to bring the colonies back into the metropolitan fold. If Cartwright's objective was union without empire, Galloway's was a firmer union within a firmer empire.

A Quaker and a longtime member of the Pennsylvania colonial assembly, Galloway took a conservative stance during the Stamp Act crisis that led some observers to accuse him of supporting parliamentary taxation.[13] Nevertheless, Galloway won election to the speakership of the assembly in 1766 and again in 1771; moreover, in 1774, he represented Pennsylvania in the Continental Congress. In Congress, Galloway presented his plan of union, which undertook to bring the colonies and Britain into a closer and more formal relationship. Despite some early support for the plan, after Galloway's initial presentation it never reached

the floor again. Eventually, the delegates rejected the plan, and references to it were excised from the minutes.[14] In 1775, Galloway published
the plan, with commentary, in a pamphlet titled *A Candid Examination
of the Mutual Claims of Great-Britain and the Colonies.* The plan drew
fierce attacks in public debates and in pamphlets, to which Galloway
responded in kind. By 1775, Galloway was the target of repeated threats
of violence; by 1776, he had decamped for New Jersey to seek safety behind British lines.

The first line of the "Plan of a Proposed Union" announced Galloway's objective of knitting the colonies more closely into the empire.
The plan envisioned a "British and American legislature, for regulating
the administration of the general affairs of America," which would consist of a president-general appointed by the king and a grand council
elected triennially by the colonial assemblies. The president-general and
the grand council would together constitute "an inferior and distinct
branch of the British legislature, united and incorporated with it," with
authority over matters relating to general colonial affairs. Under the
plan, legislation might issue either from Parliament or from the grand
council; the acts then required approval by the other body in order to
become effective. Finally, the plan concluded with a resolution pursuant
to which Congress would assure the king that "the Colonists hold in
abhorrence the idea of being considered independent communities on
the British government, and most ardently desire the establishment of a
Political Union, not only among themselves, but with the Mother State"
in the form of "the foregoing plan, under which the strength of the whole
Empire may be drawn together on any emergency."[15]

Both the debate on and the responses to Galloway's plan emphasized
certain characteristics that it shared with the Albany Plan of 1754. To
begin with, both plans had been authored by Pennsylvanians; indeed,
Franklin and Galloway corresponded regarding the 1774 plan. "[W]hen I
consider the extream Corruption prevalent among all Orders of Men in
this old rotten State, and the glorious publick Virtue so predominant in
our rising Country, I cannot but apprehend more Mischief than Benefit
from a closer Union," Franklin wrote to Galloway from London. "To
unite us intimately, will only be to corrupt and poison us also." Even
Franklin, who in 1774 still held out hope that the British Empire in North

America could be salvaged, regarded Galloway's plan as too focused on tying the colonies to Parliament.[16] Despite Franklin's disapproval of Galloway's plan, some observers attempted to tie the new plan to the rejected Albany Plan; other commentators, meanwhile, compared the two plans' provisions to assess what each might have meant for the colonies.[17]

In contrast to Cartwright's proposal, which had proceeded from a presumption that Parliament lacked authority over the colonies and that the colonies had never been incorporated into the empire, Galloway's plan required action by the king-in-Parliament for its enactment ("the Colonies . . . will humbly propose to his Majesty and his two Houses of Parliament, the foregoing plan") and explicitly aimed to draw the provinces more tightly into the structures of the empire ("the foregoing plan, under which the strength of the whole Empire may be drawn together on any emergency"). Galloway's plan centered on the new "British and American legislature," which would be "united and incorporated" with Parliament to create a unified legislative body with jurisdiction as broad as the empire itself.[18] This integration and incorporation stood in stark contrast to Cartwright's rejection of metropolitan oversight, his embrace of colonial legislative independence, and his desire to build a league based on mutual benefit.

Jefferson's Plan: Union on Colonial Terms

Cartwright's plan took as its premise the radical position that the colonies did not belong to the British Empire and thus were free to enter as equals into a league with Britain. Galloway's proposal embraced empire and worked toward closer union in the service of that empire. In contrast to both Cartwright's and Galloway's plans, Thomas Jefferson's *Summary View of the Rights of British America* focused on shifting the relationship between metropolis and provinces from one of empire to one of union. Jefferson thus attempted to work within the structures of the empire to extract greater legislative autonomy for the colonies. In so doing, he directly challenged Parliament's claims of both metropolitan and imperial sovereignty.

According to Jefferson, his *Summary View of the Rights of British America* began life as a set of remarks to be delivered to a select group of fellow Virginians but quickly reached an eager public when it was published as a pamphlet in the summer of 1774. Jefferson had originally drafted the essay in anticipation of presenting it at a gathering in Williamsburg held in advance of the initial meeting of the Continental Congress, which was set to convene in Philadelphia on September 1, 1774. According to Jefferson's 1821 autobiography, however, a case of dysentery contracted en route prevented him from attending the meeting; instead, Jefferson sent on two copies of the essay—one to Peyton Randolph and one to Patrick Henry—and requested that they make it known to the other delegates to the Virginia convention. "It was read generally by the members, approved by many, but thought too bold for the present state of things," Jefferson noted, "but they printed it in pamphlet form under the title of 'A Summary view of the rights of British America.'"[19] Subsequently, the pamphlet "found its way to England, was taken up by the opposition, interpolated a little by Mr. Burke so as to make it answer opposition purposes, and in that form ran rapidly thro' several editions." The pamphlet had also earned Jefferson inclusion on a list of individuals to be subject to bills of attainder by Parliament, or so Jefferson claimed Randolph had informed him.[20]

Just what was so sensational about a pamphlet penned by a thirty-one-year-old planter and member of the Virginia House of Burgesses? The answer lay in the measures that the pamphlet proposed in order to reform the empire and the premises that underlay that proposal. By presenting an explicit argument for union, Jefferson showed that he did not believe that a union currently existed between Britain and the colonies. Indeed, he exhorted his metropolitan audience to "be ready to establish union on a generous plan."[21] Provinces and center might be joined in an empire, but they lacked a formal, regular, consensual relationship. Metropolitan officials might have agreed with Jefferson this far; after all, the British Empire had not been aimed at establishing a coordinate nation with which to unify. But the further significance of Jefferson's statement lay in its assumption that the colonies could legitimately propose a union with the mother country—that they were not barred by some fundamentally peripheral status from entering into a consensual relationship with Britain.

The bare fact of the proposal for union was likely striking enough to warrant an attaint. But the *Summary View* went much further. The essay built on earlier arguments focusing on the particular British institution to

which the colonists owed allegiance and extended those arguments to offer a systematic account of precisely how the provinces would agree to be
bound to the home country. In keeping with, for example, the refusal of
the members of the Massachusetts General Court to accept Parliament as
the supreme imperial authority, Jefferson phrased his comments as a series of petitions to George III. This posture invoked the ancient right of
Englishmen to request relief from the king, as well as sounding in the
more recent tradition of colonial resistance to the post–Glorious Revolution ascendancy of Parliament. Jefferson thus followed the General
Court's strategy of appealing to the Crown against Parliament (although
he did not scruple to mention a few instances of what he viewed as the
king's overreaching his constitutional power). But he went further than
the Massachusetts legislators when he offered this rearrangement as more
or less the price of keeping the colonies in the empire. Jefferson therefore
sought in the *Summary View* to bring concepts of confederation to bear
on the problem of sovereignty within the British Empire.

As previous chapters have demonstrated, colonial commentators
since at least the early 1770s had argued that they owed allegiance and
subordination only to the Crown, not to Parliament (nor even to the
mystical tripartite legislative entity of the king-in-Parliament).[22] This assertion gained new salience when theorists such as Jefferson employed it
as the basis for asserting a measure of colonial power to bargain over the
terms of the empire. For Jefferson, the history of English settlement in
North America provided dispositive evidence for a direct link between
colonies and Crown without Parliament. "America was conquered, and
her settlements made and firmly established, at the expence of individuals, and not of the British public," Jefferson observed. Commercial interest had drawn Parliament into the business of colonial oversight, beginning with aid to the colonies against France in the Seven Years' War. But
this submission to Parliament had been mere expedience; the colonies
had not thereby acceded to the jurisdiction of Parliament, Jefferson contended: "[T]hese states never supposed that, by calling in her aid, they
thereby submitted themselves to her sovereignty."[23]

According to Jefferson, therefore, the otherwise-autonomous colonies
had freely joined with the home country by adopting English common
law and, more important, by accepting Crown jurisdiction. The colonies' act of "submitting themselves to the same common sovereign" as

that governing subjects in England made the Crown "the central link connecting the several parts of the empire thus newly multiplied." Thus, on Jefferson's view, the colonies had chosen "to continue their union" with Britain on their own terms.[24] Those terms included the retention of a measure of sovereignty by the colonial legislatures such that the North American provinces would function parallel, not subordinate, to Parliament.

Having thus painted an edenic picture of the early decades of the American colonies' existence, Jefferson moved to the inevitable narrative of decline. Despite what Jefferson viewed as its certain lack of authority over the colonies, Parliament had passed a series of regulations that explicitly claimed jurisdiction in that regard. The Post Office Act of 1710; the Hat Act of 1732; the Iron Act of 1750; the Sugar Act; the Stamp Act; the Declaratory Act; the Townshend Acts—all were mentioned, and all added weight to Jefferson's litany of the "connected chain of parliamentary usurpation."[25] Jefferson saved the full force of his attack for the Coercive Acts, by which Parliament undertook to punish Bostonians' dumping of tea and general intransigence with the closure of the port and several other punitive measures. He then launched his institutional critique of the failure of the Crown and Parliament—in different ways—to accord due respect to the colonies' place in the imperial constitution.

Enumerating what he regarded as the specific legislative enormities worked by the acts already described, Jefferson used the by-then-familiar distinction between internal and external colonial lawmaking to charge Parliament with "intermeddl[ing] with the regulation of the internal affairs of the colonies." He thus rejected the notion that Parliament possessed plenary legislative authority over all colonial matters. Jefferson's challenge to the Crown, however, presented a more profound accusation: that the executive's failure to police the institutional boundaries between Crown and Parliament had permitted Parliament to grasp at powers that were beyond its proper jurisdiction—in particular, "a new executive power, unheard of till then, that of a British parliament."[26] Jefferson thus criticized Parliament for exceeding its authority but blamed the Crown for allowing this breach of the imperial constitution.

The *Summary View*—which, it must be remembered, was phrased as a petition to George III—presented a series of four related complaints against the Crown, all of which stemmed from what Jefferson viewed as a lack of puissance in keeping Parliament in its place. Jefferson thus charged the king with neglect of the Crown's constitutional role in the legislative body of the king-in-Parliament. The first of these "deviations from the line of duty," according to Jefferson, was the king's failure to exercise the royal veto against parliamentary acts that oppressed the colonies. Although, as Jefferson noted, the monarchy had for several decades "modestly declined the exercise of this power," he argued that the time had come for the Crown to shake off modesty and regain some of its constitutionally prescribed vigor. Jefferson entreated George III to "resume the exercise of his negative power" to "prevent the passage of laws by any one legislature of the empire which might bear injuriously on the rights and interests of another." Choosing to deemphasize the fears about royal prerogative and overweening monarchical power that had formed the core of British—and therefore American—whig thought since the early eighteenth century, Jefferson suggested that the colonies' special relationship to the Crown required the king to monitor the boundaries between regulating and taking advantage of the colonies.[27]

Jefferson's second critique stemmed from the converse problem: namely, the frequency with which the Crown—in the form of the Privy Council's Board of Trade—disallowed colonial statutes upon review of the acts of the provincial assemblies. "For the most trifling of reasons, and sometimes for no conceivable reason at all, his majesty has rejected laws of the most salutary tendency." Jefferson cited colonial attempts to curtail the slave trade as the most prominent example of what he termed "the wanton exercise of this power."[28] Thus while urging the king to exercise his power to veto acts of Parliament more frequently, Jefferson contended that the Crown and its representatives were overzealous in their disallowance of colonial acts.

The third complaint charged the Crown with dilatoriness in reviewing acts of the colonial legislatures. Whether the act in question was ultimately approved or disallowed, Jefferson argued, metropolitan administrators' delay in deciding threw the colonies into uncertainty. This problem was acute regardless of whether a colonial legislature operated subject to a suspending clause, which made all acts provisional pending action by the Board of Trade. "[S]uch of them as have no suspending clauses we hold on the most precarious of all tenures, his majesty's will, and such of them as suspend themselves till his majesty's assent be obtained, we have feared, might be called into existence at some future and distant period, when time and change of circumstances shall have rendered them destructive to his people here." Furthermore, delay often vitiated whatever purpose the act in question was designed to serve, because in some cases the law could not be enforced "till it has twice crossed the Atlantic, by which time the evil may have spent it's [*sic*] whole force."[29] Whether or not metropolitan administrators were justified in striking down any given colonial law, Jefferson argued that North Americans were entitled to certainty about the status of those laws.

Finally, Jefferson objected to what he viewed as the Crown's eagerness to dissolve colonial legislatures. Since the Glorious Revolution, he argued, the Crown had not possessed the power to dissolve Parliament; why, then, did it have this power over the provincial assemblies? Moreover, if the stated reason for dissolving certain colonial assemblies included the fact that they had "lost the confidence of their constituents" and "assumed to themselves powers which the people never put into their hands," Jefferson queried whether it would not "appear strange to an unbiassed observer that that of Great Britain was not dissolved, while those of the colonies have repeatedly incurred that sentence."[30] Jefferson thus questioned the metropolitan assumption that despite the legal and practical inability of the monarch to dissolve Parliament, the analogous power of the Crown (and its representatives, the royal governors) over the colonial assemblies remained intact.

Summing up these structural arguments concerning what he viewed as an imbalance of power between Crown and Parliament, Jefferson insisted that the king's duty to his subjects compelled him to protect the lawmaking domain of the colonial legislatures. "From the nature of things, every society must at all times possess within itself the sovereign powers of legislation." At least with respect to matters such as taxation and the billeting of troops in America, Jefferson articulated a vision of primary legislative authority lying with the colonial assemblies; this legislative power would be complemented by Crown executive power. The Crown possessed "the executive power of the laws in every state; but they are the laws of the particular state which he is to administer within that state, and not those of any one within the limits of another."[31]

The union established on a "generous plan" for which the *Summary View* argued, then, was a limited union between only the colonies and the Crown. Jefferson's plea to the king to intervene on behalf of the colonies was significant because it demonstrated his Crown-centric vision, in 1774, of the ideal imperial structure. Despite Jefferson's radical critique of what he saw as the Crown's neglect of its own duties to the North American settlements, the *Summary View* posited a reform plan in which the colonies remained tied to metropolitan authorities.[32] The difference for Jefferson lay in the nature of the authority to which the colonies would be bound.

Jefferson's vision of the British Empire consisted of an overarching Crown authority connected to each of the colonial legislatures. Parliament would be kept outside this imperial structure—restricted, presumably, to regulating domestic British affairs. The *Summary View* thus sought to create what scholars have variously termed a "commonwealth of nations" or a "theory of imperial federalism."[33] Central to both these conceptions of the empire were the views that each component of the British Empire ought to be governed by its own local legislature; that each local legislature stood in parallel to, rather than in a hierarchical relationship with, the others; and, most important, that the several component polities were connected only through the Crown. As Jefferson's repeated use of the modifier "British" to describe the Parliament at Westminster suggests, he regarded the empire as consisting of multiple parliaments, each of which could legitimately claim lawmaking authority with respect to a given portion of imperial space.[34]

In this regard, Jefferson's *Summary View* echoed James Wilson's "dominion status" theory, according to which the members of the British Empire were "independent of each other, but connected together under the same sovereign in right of the same crown."[35] Writing, like Wilson, in 1774, John Dickinson made a similar point: "The colonies have no other head than the king of England. The person who, by the laws of that realm, is king of that realm, is our king." But, Dickinson hastened to add, this relationship did not entail subjection to the realm of England itself. "To be subordinately connected with England, the colonies have contracted. To be subject to the general legislative authority of that kingdom, they never contracted."[36]

James Iredell of North Carolina, also writing in 1774, endorsed a related vision of the empire as comprising multiple legislatures joined by shared allegiance to the Crown. Addressing the *imperium in imperio* dilemma, Iredell inquired, "[W]hat application does this make to the case of several *distinct and independent legislatures,* each engaged within a *separate* scale, and employed about *different* objects. The *imperium in imperio* argument is, therefore, not at all applicable to our case, though it has been so vainly and confidently relied on." In distinguishing between the specific purposes and objects of each legislature, the future United States Supreme Court justice adopted the subject-matter-focused approach to jurisdiction that had emerged out of the Stamp Act crisis of the 1760s.[37]

Thus, just as the members of the Massachusetts General Court had distinguished between the colonists' obligations to the Crown and those they owed to Parliament, commentators in the period between 1774 and 1777 attempted to identify alternative forms of union that would permit some provincial autonomy while also keeping the colonies within a version of the existing empire.

Scottish Precedents for Union

Where did this rehabilitated idea of empire come from? By Jefferson's own account, it followed from the example of Scotland. In his autobiography of 1821, Jefferson described his underlying theory that "the relation between Gr. Br. and these colonies was exactly the same as that of England & Scotland after the accession of James & until the Union, and the same as her present relations with Hanover, having the same Executive chief but no other necessary political connection."[38] For American whigs in the 1770s considering the Scottish case, the precedent to be cited was clearly the period between 1603 and 1707—the halcyon century that, viewed from the distance of nearly seventy-five years, appeared to offer the ideal example of coordinate states joined only at the level of the monarch, each with an independent legislature. But this vision required a theory of union, a fact that troubled American commentators in the 1770s, as it had their Scottish predecessors in the 1700s.

Although Jefferson's *Summary View* stopped short of advocating independence, the Scottish distinction between a federal and an incorporating union continued to inform American debates even after armed conflict had begun and a break with Britain appeared imminent. In the summer of 1776, members of the Continental Congress engaged in a comprehensive debate regarding the Scottish precedent and its significance for the project of independence. The Congress's discussion on June 7, according to Jefferson's notes, focused on the constitutional status of the colonies. Jefferson noted that John Adams, George Wythe, and others had identified the relevant question as "not whether, by a declaration of independance [*sic*], we should make ourselves what we are not; but whether we should declare a fact which already exists." Central to answering this question was understanding the precise nature of the colonies' connection to the various arms of the British government. Even at this stage in the long-running dispute with Britain, some colonists insisted that they had owed different duties to Parliament from those owed to the king. Jefferson's notes reported that Adams, Wythe, and others argued "that as to the people or parliament of England, we had alwais been independant of them, their restraints on our trade deriving efficacy from our acquiescence only & not from any rights they possessed of imposing them, & that so far *our connection had been federal only,* & was now dissolved by the commencement of hostilities."[39]

With respect to Parliament, then, the delegates argued that the colonies stood in a relationship more or less of equals, in which the provincial assemblies legislated for the colonies in parallel to Parliament's domestic power of legislation. The colonies' connection to the Crown, however, was different, they insisted: not parallel but subordinate, albeit voluntary. The following sentence of Jefferson's notes recounts his colleagues' contention "that as to the king, we had been bound to him by allegiance, but that this bond was now dissolved by his assent to the late act of parliament, by which he declares us out of his protection, and by his levying war on us, a fact which had long ago proved us out of his protection."[40]

In this exchange, the delegates used the language of federal union as it had come to them from the Scottish union debates of more than seventy years earlier. The colonies' connection to the people of Britain through Parliament was "federal only"—that is, to paraphrase James Hodges, the colonies and Britain had been distinct, free, and independent kingdoms, dominions, or states, united only for certain agreed conditions, and each retaining its own independence, laws, customs, and government.[41] True, the colonies offered allegiance to the king, but only on a discretionary basis. According to this formulation, the substance of lawmaking authority and therefore sovereignty remained with the colonies themselves. The arguments of Scottish nationalists such as Hodges therefore provided a vocabulary through which American colonists could assert their continued claims to legislative—and, increasingly, national—independence.

More than language connected the American debates of the 1770s with the negotiations leading up to the union of the Scottish and English parliaments. As Ned Landsman has demonstrated, throughout the eighteenth century a corps of Scots and Scots-Irish officials had been involved in imperial administration, both at home in Great Britain and in North America. These greater British agents of the empire included figures who have already appeared in these pages, such as Henry Mc-Culloh, Archibald Kennedy, and William Knox; the motivation for their service, Landsman argues, was less empire than a vision of "an expansive commercial union" that stemmed from Scottish political ideas and a distinctively provincial outlook shared by many North Americans.[42] This class of imperial middlemen brought with them a special appreciation for the many varieties of union, as well as a confederal vocabulary that was crucial for American federal thought.[43]

Another broad category of Scots émigrés included ministers and educators who traveled to North America to spread the Presbyterian faith and the particularly Scottish brand of moral philosophy.[44] Most notable among these churchmen was John Witherspoon, who emigrated from Paisley in 1768 to become president of the College of New Jersey, where he supervised the education of James Madison, among others. A vocal and thoughtful contributor to the American political debates of the later 1760s and 1770s, Witherspoon served as a delegate to the Continental Congress. There he brought both personal and theoretical knowledge of the forms of union to bear on the debates, in particular with respect to the type of association, if any, that should bind the colonies after independence.

Many of Witherspoon's comments on the floor of the Congress invoked the history of unions and confederations. As the delegates debated the proposed articles of confederation, Witherspoon argued for a permanent rather than a temporary association among the states. "Shall we establish nothing good, because we know it cannot be eternal? Shall we live without government, because every constitution has its old age, and its period?" he demanded. "A confederation of itself keeps war at a distance from the bodies of which it is composed." Citing the Dutch and Swiss examples, Witherspoon noted that the confederate form had allowed both those unions to stave off internal conflict despite their respective economic and religious heterogeneity. "[E]very argument from honour, interest, safety and necessity, conspire [*sic*] in pressing us to a confederacy," Witherspoon concluded.[45]

On August 1, 1776, Witherspoon made the connection to Scotland explicit during a discussion of the manner in which each state would be represented in the confederation. Would it be equal or proportional, and if it was proportional, would it be based on population or some other metric? According to Jefferson's and Adams's notes, Franklin and others likened the situation before them to the debates on the union of parliaments. Adams noted that Franklin observed, "[T]o sett out with an unequal Representation is unreasonable. It is said the great Colonies will swallow up the less. Scotland said the same Thing at the Union." In reply—and, apparently, clarification—Witherspoon "[r]ises to explain a few Circumstances relating to Scotland. That was an incorporating Union, not a federal. The Nobility and Gentry resort to England."[46] Jefferson's notes give a similar report: in response to Franklin, Witherspoon "distinguished between an incorporating & a federal union." According to Jefferson, Witherspoon explained, "The union of England was an incorporating union; yet Scotland had suffered by that union, for that it's [*sic*] inhabitants were drawn from it by the hopes of places & employments."[47]

In both Adams's and Jefferson's reports, Witherspoon appears to have been keen to distinguish between the incorporating British union (which he indicated had led to suffering on the part of Scotland) and, implicitly, the planned federal union of the American states (which, he hoped, would bring about "a lasting confederacy, if it was founded on fair principles").[48] On Witherspoon's view, the incorporating British union—and Scotland's consequent loss of its parliament to Westminster—had drawn the Scottish elite to the metropolis in the hope of gaining preferment and political power, a scenario that he appeared loath to repeat in America.

Witherspoon's focus on the distribution of political power led him to the conviction that the states ought to be represented equally in the new confederation. The broader import of Witherspoon's comments, moreover, was that the Scottish precedent was important both for its theoretical distinction between federal and incorporating unions and for its practical illustration of the potential dangers of a union that was too much a unitary empire and not enough a confederation.[49] Witherspoon's and his colleagues' comments demonstrate that "federal"—like "incorporating"—was understood in the 1770s as a term of art with specific reference to scenarios in which one nation either joined in league with or engrossed another nation. The former was called a federal union; the latter was called an incorporating union. If the lesson of 1707 demonstrated anything to participants in the American debates of the 1770s, it was that a state with imperial aspirations would not easily consent to a truly federal association with another, less powerful state. Thus, although a federated union might be possible, a federated empire was unlikely to thrive. For the fledgling association of the former American colonies, then, the difference between empire and union was profound.

The Influence of Continental Political Theory

The Scottish example thus provided a key source for the retooled theories of empire that emerged in 1774 and 1775—in particular, the theory elaborated in Jefferson's *Summary View*. Embedded within the Scottish precedent, as the foregoing discussion has suggested, was another important source of influence on Jefferson and other commentators who wrote in 1774 and 1775. That source was Continental political philosophy—the writings of early modern theorists of the law of nature and nations, such as Hugo Grotius and Samuel von Pufendorf, as well as more recent authors, such as Emmerich de Vattel and Montesquieu. This Continental strand was prevalent in Scottish Enlightenment thought and, through that and other channels, was funneled into the North American debates of the 1770s.[50]

As discussed earlier, Continental political theory—particularly that of Grotius and Pufendorf—exerted a notable influence in the debates of the 1760s and 1770s. These writers on the law of nations provided observers (especially the colonists) with a vocabulary of authority, empire, and confederation that offered an alternative to the increasingly dominant, Blackstonian view of sovereignty as indivisible within a given political entity. The American whigs appear to have found Continental ideas increasingly relevant in the 1770s, for the connections between law-of-nations theory and the colonial commentaries of 1774 and 1775 can be traced even more directly than the lines of influence of a decade earlier.

The lines are perhaps clearest in this period in the case of Jefferson. One scholar has noted that beginning in 1769, Jefferson had plunged into a study of political theory, reading John Locke, as well as Jean Jacques Burlamaqui, Montesquieu, Henry Home Kames, Algernon Sidney, and Pufendorf.[51] Indeed, as his commonplace book demonstrates, Jefferson devoted substantial effort to research into confederal systems of government, reading both historical and philosophical works in an effort to find what he called "articles worthy of attention in constituting an American Congress." To this end, he noted some details regarding the constitution of the Swiss confederation. Jefferson's studies also led him to investigate the Union of Utrecht, Denmark, Sweden, and Poland. Other citations included Grotius on the rights of neutrals according to the laws of war and Pufendorf on the natural law of rule by majority.[52]

The commonplace book also records Jefferson's notes on the *république fédérative* Montesquieu outlined in his *L'esprit des lois,* as well as Jefferson's rebuttals to Blackstone's assertion that every state must contain a single "supreme, irresistible, absolute, uncontrouled authority in which . . . the rights of sovereignty reside."[53] At the end of his comments on Blackstone, Jefferson included a reference to James Wilson's *Considerations on the Nature and Extent of the Legislative Authority of the British Parliament.* In that work, Wilson challenged Blackstone's unitary view of sovereignty and argued instead that "all the different members of the British empire are distinct states, independent of each other, but connected together under the same sovereign in right of the same crown."[54] As this entry in the commonplace book suggests, Jefferson's reading in history, philosophy, and law followed his needs and interests as he and his contemporaries tested the boundaries of parliamentary sovereignty.

Other colonial commentators in this period chose a less subtle path than Jefferson's and displayed the fruits of their research not only in private notes but also in public writings. Most notable in this regard is Alexander Hamilton, whose *Farmer Refuted* of February 1775 granted no quarter to his opponent, "The Farmer" (Samuel Seabury). Attacking Seabury's assertion of Parliament's authority to legislate for the colonies, Hamilton, who was no more than twenty years old at the time, wrote, "I shall, henceforth, begin to make some allowance for that enmity you have discovered to the *natural rights* of mankind." He continued: "If you will follow my advice, there still may be hopes of your reformation. Apply yourself, without delay, to the study of the law of nature. I would recommend to your perusal, Grotius, Puffendorf [*sic*], Locke, Montesquieu, and Burlemaqui."[55]

Jefferson's notes and Hamilton's gibes might appear to have little in common, but the great reliance each placed on study of political theory—in particular, Continental political theory—is striking. As the political and constitutional crises of the past decade began to spill over into warfare, the need for interpretive avenues to work through issues of union and confederation became ever more urgent. Previous colonial experiments with confederations—the New England Confederation of 1643 and the Albany Plan of 1754—provided Americans in the 1770s with practical examples of how a commitment to confederalism might be institutionalized. These attempts at joining together the colonies remained outliers, however: undertheorized attempts to accommodate the fact of provincial multiplicity within the confines of a metropolitan commitment to unitary authority. The true innovations in federal thought took place not in these formal attempts at constructing colonial unions, but in the back-and-forth of imperial constitutional debates such as the Stamp Act crisis, the controversy between Hutchinson and the General Court, and the polemics of Cartwright and Jefferson.

The First American Union

By the time the Continental Congress began discussing a colonial confederation in the early summer of 1776, several North American observers had produced important works that examined the interrelated problems of union, confederation, and empire. Many precedents informed these and subsequent discussions of whether and how the colonies—

states, now—ought to be joined together in some form of league. Indeed, three distinct strands of precedent for thinking about union were represented in individuals who were present in the Congress. An observer in the chamber in 1776 might glimpse Benjamin Franklin, author of the Albany Plan, participating in the discussions of the form that the new colonial union would take. Also in attendance might be John Witherspoon, spokesman for the Scottish influence and that nation's long history of negotiation and ultimate unification with England. Nearby might be Thomas Jefferson, author of the *Summary View* and student of Continental theory. All these lines of precedent, history, and theory converged in Philadelphia. They contributed learning and experience, as well as a sense of possibility, to the process of debate and drafting that led to the ratification of the Articles of Confederation in March 1781.

The Articles of Confederation were born and grew up largely in parallel with the Revolution, beginning with early drafts by Benjamin Franklin and Silas Deane in 1775 and culminating in a final version written by John Dickinson and approved by Congress in 1776–1777 before being ratified in 1781. In their final form, the Articles established a framework for the general government of the United States, bringing the thirteen states together in a "firm league of friendship . . . for their common defense, the security of their liberties, and their mutual and general welfare."[56] From an institutional standpoint, the powers of the general government were lodged entirely in "the United States in Congress assembled," an occasional gathering rather than a freestanding branch of government. The Articles gave Congress authority over specific substantive areas of government, notably foreign affairs, postage, and currency, but reserved to the states "every power, jurisdiction, and right, which is not by this Confederation expressly delegated to the United States in Congress assembled."[57] Indeed, the general government and Congress were essentially one and the same, for the Articles made no provision for an executive or a judiciary, instead allocating some of those functions to Congress. The Articles thus established the leanest possible union—"simply a delegation of specific powers," as Murray Forsyth puts it—and left the vast majority of governance to the states.[58]

As several scholars have noted, the drafters of the Articles appear to have spent little time debating or even articulating the theory of confederation underlying the text. "At the outset of the Revolution, the problem of confederation received little sustained attention," Jack Rakove observes. "When it was first considered in 1774 and 1775, the task of dividing the powers of government between Congress and the colonies proved far less troubling than might have been expected." Instead of the working-out of a vision of multilayered authority, the Articles represented a strategy for resistance and defense.[59] Thus issues such as representation, settlement of intercolonial land disputes, and administration of the military dominated the debates during the drafting process. In a letter to Patrick Henry, Silas Deane cited the New England Confederation of 1643 as a model for the new union, observing that "[i]f a reconciliation with G Britain takes place, it will be obtained on the best terms, by the Colonies being united, and be the more like to be preserved, on just and equal Terms; if no reconciliation is to be had without a Confederation We are ruined to all intents and purposes."[60] As Deane's comments suggest, the discussions of the Articles centered largely on the problems of operating as a union for purposes of external affairs relating to international relations and war—precisely the domain of Locke's federative power. The distribution of power was therefore clear: each state would continue to oversee its own internal affairs, while the confederation government would attend to exigent circumstances such as war and to the relatively narrow category of matters pertaining to what Locke termed "the management of the security and interest of the public without."[61]

The Articles thus embodied the governmental multiplicity for which American whigs had argued since the Stamp Act debates of the 1765. Moreover, as had been the case in the controversies of the 1760s and 1770s, the multiplicity in question centered on legislative power. Unlike the seventeenth-century New England Confederation, but similar to the 1754 Albany Plan, the Articles established a separate level of superlegislature that operated as an entirely new level of government—to be sure, a level of government with extremely circumscribed substantive powers, but a distinct layer nonetheless. Yet Americans in the late 1770s and early 1780s remained guarded in their enthusiasm for multiplicity, keeping a close rein on the "United States in Congress assembled" and devoting little attention to the lingering question of supremacy. As Gordon Wood puts it, "The principle of sovereignty was not probed and analyzed by

Americans in 1776–77 the way it had been in the sixties, because whatever the limitations the Confederation may have placed in fact on the individual sovereignty of the states, few believed that their union in any theoretical sense contravened that sovereignty."[62] This was multiplicity in practice, encumbered by little in the way of explicit constitutional theory.

This account is not to suggest that the outcome of the debates over the confederation was in any way inevitable, or that the rest of the delegates simply sat by and let a few knowledgeable sages dictate the future course of events. Neither is the case. Instead, the prevailing mood that emerges from the records of this period is one of uncertainty. Consider, for example, Josiah Bartlett, delegate from New Hampshire. Sometime in June or July 1776, he drafted a set of notes that included several lines detailing the representation scheme in the United Provinces of the Netherlands, followed immediately by an outline of the Albany Plan. Observations about the relative contributions of Gelderland, Holland, Zealand, Utrecht, and the other provinces virtually bumped against lines of notations concerning the situation of New Hampshire (listed first; apparently, union did not require complete self-abnegation) and the other former colonies in 1754. Bartlett was a member of the committee "to prepare and digest the form of a confederation"; clearly he assembled these notes to help order his thoughts about what form would best suit the American colonies.[63] In the uncertain years of the mid-1770s, simply knowing that one was participating in a Europe-wide conversation regarding the best forms of government, the best location of sovereignty, and the best arrangement for union must have provided some comfort.[64]

And comfort was in short supply. Recall, after all, what some of the precedents walking and talking in the congressional chamber stood for. The Albany Plan? Not adopted, and anyway, it would have subordinated the colonies to legislative approval by the Crown. The *Summary View?* Again, radical for its time, but by 1776, union within the empire held little appeal. The Anglo-Scottish union? Perhaps the worst precedent of all, in light of events after 1707: a union that arguably started federal but quickly became incorporating, while the union itself became subsumed in the dominant partner's imperial projects.

A shift had taken place from 1774 and 1775, when the proposals of Cartwright, Galloway, and Jefferson first made explicit arguments for various forms of composite unions, to 1776, when the superstructure that had framed those composites—the British Empire—no longer dictated the Americans' analysis. Cartwright's view of confederation as a means to union independent of the empire; Jefferson's idea of an imperial union attached only to the monarch; even Galloway's vision of confederation as a means to a better empire—all these had given way to a sense that a new species of confederation or union that would be altogether distinct from the empire was needed. De facto decentralization of authority under the British Empire had proven insufficient to guarantee that power would remain distributed throughout the various levels that constituted American government. Moreover, as the Scottish example showed, compound states with aspirations toward empire could be expected to chafe at apportionments of authority, resulting in a tendency toward domination by a single member of the polity—in essence, an incorporating union. Given the eighteenth century's experience with union, anxiety regarding the need to stave off empire—whether the specific peril of the British Empire or the more general fear of power asymmetries within the creole confederation—propelled the American whigs toward the best alternative they believed their precedents offered them: federal union.[65]

Federal union, to individuals in 1776, did not mean what it means to individuals in the twenty-first century, or what it meant to individuals in 1865 or even 1789. To the delegates at Philadelphia and their contemporaries, a federal union meant much the same thing that it had to James Hodges in 1703: an association "whereby Distinct, Free, and Independent Kingdoms, Dominions or States, do unite their separate Interests into one common Interest, for the mutual benefit of both, so far as relates to certain Conditions and Articles agreed upon betwixt them, retaining in the mean time their several Independencies, National Distinctions, and the different Laws, Customs, and Government of each."[66]

The "federalness" of a federal union referred to the fact that the union was built on an agreement or treaty (the Latin *foedus*), pursuant to which each component entity maintained some measure of sovereignty. This was Pufendorf's vision as well: the "system of states" in which "several States are, by some special Band, so closely united, as that they seem to compose one Body, and yet retain each of them the sovereign Command in their respective Dominions."[67]

As the debates and commentaries of the early 1770s demonstrate, British-style empire and federal union increasingly appeared to contemporaries to be potentially incompatible species of political organization. To American observers, the Scottish example indicated that empires tended toward incorporation, whatever the initial agreements. Union, in contrast, at least had the potential to be federal and so was more to the liking of Americans, who were, after all, only gradually coming to regard themselves as members of a larger political community. Concluding his argument for proportional rather than state-by-state representation, delegate Benjamin Rush summed up this hopeful vision: "I would not have it understood, that I am pleading the Cause of Pensilvania. When I entered that door, I considered myself a Citizen of America."[68] The fear of incorporating union and its imperial analogue prompted the colonists to turn toward what they viewed as the best available alternative to meld a group of polities into a single body. That option was federated union.

CHAPTER 5

The Authority of a Central Government

A S THE PREVIOUS CHAPTERS have demonstrated, the history of American federalism began decades before the Constitutional Convention of 1787. Some of federalism's central concepts, most notably the idea of constructing a government around multilayered legislative authority, had begun to emerge in the 1760s and 1770s, cobbled together by members of the colonial opposition in the midst of protracted disputes between British North Americans and their metropolitan counterparts.

Nevertheless, the debates at the Constitutional Convention in Philadelphia represented a vital moment in which British imperial precedents, colonial practices, postwar exigency, and political theory came together in the hands of particular individuals to form both a new idea of government and an actual new government. The convention debates and the Constitution that resulted created and codified federalism in important ways. Arguments about the nature and scope of Parliament's power to regulate the colonies, which began as the colonists' response to what they viewed as unconstitutional legislation from Westminster, became by the 1780s a full-blown theory of government authority. With the rebellion against Britain behind them, the members of the founding generation were able—indeed, required—to consolidate the previous two decades' many shreds and pieces of structural and political argument into a more or less coherent conception of government. In this sense, then, the discussions at Philadelphia represented neither an original moment of genius nor simply another instance of negotiation among existing groups and institutions. Rather, the period from 1787 to 1789 should be understood as a reexamination and reshuffling of fundamental ideas of government with which Americans had begun experimenting decades before. The drafting and ratification of the Constitution served to crystallize a novel, distinctively British North American theory of government that had been developing since at least the mid-1760s.

The story of federalism's development in the 1780s is thus primarily one of ideology formation. American federalism's central ideas—multilayered authority, a substantive (as opposed to territorial or personal) approach to jurisdiction, a central government with a brief and identity distinct from the combined wills of the component states—had begun to coalesce in the 1760s and 1770s, when colonial commentators used them to fend off metropolitan claims of parliamentary supremacy. Under the British Empire, the belief that a single government might legitimately contain multiple layers of authority underlay colonists' claims that their own assemblies ought to operate parallel, rather than subject, to Parliament. In a 1764 pamphlet, for example, Virginian Richard Bland acknowledged Westminster's authority over the colonies in matters of external governance but then insisted that "the legislature of the colony have a right to enact ANY law they shall think necessary for their INTERNAL government."[1] This premise of legislative multiplicity became the basis of a new ideology, in David Armitage's sense of the word: "a systematic model of how society functions" and also "a world-view which is perceived as contestable by those who do not share it."[2] This protofederal ideology of multilayered government required a great deal of explanation throughout the Revolutionary period, as colonial commentators sought to explain why their scheme of what Robert Cover has termed "jurisdictional redundancy" did not violate contemporary political theory's proscription of *imperium in imperio,* or a government within a government.[3]

Multilayered authority thus became a plausible way to arrange government in the course of the Revolutionary-era debates. The specter of *imperium in imperio,* however, continued to haunt political discourse.

One need only consider the Articles of Confederation to appreciate the uncertainty with which members of the founding generation faced the problem of giving structure to their vision of multiplicity. True, the Articles contemplated two levels of government: the several states and the United States of America. But the actual operations of the United States of America were to be carried out by an entity denominated "the United States in Congress assembled" and limited to a handful of "expressly delegated" powers in specific subject areas, including war, treaties, currency, post offices, and Indian affairs.[4] As John Adams's reference to the Massachusetts congressional delegation as "our embassy" suggests, the general government was less a distinct level of government than a shell organization that occasionally served as the venue for meetings of the constituent entities.[5] The United States existed only at the moments when its members were in Congress assembled; it claimed no executive or judiciary. The general government, in other words, was essentially an emanation from the states.

In the summer of 1787, then, when the delegates to the Constitutional Convention gathered, federalism's central idea—the possibility that a functional government could include more than one sovereign—remained largely untested. Despite the vast changes that Americans' conception of political authority had undergone since the 1760s, the Articles of Confederation represented an attempt to institutionalize the idea of multiplicity in the same forms that had hamstrung British Americans in their debates with metropolitan commentators. From the Stamp Act controversy to the many angry colloquies between royal governors and colonial assemblies to the Articles themselves, colonists had devoted their arguments to proving that multilayered authority, in the form of multiple legislatures, offered a viable method of governing a far-flung empire.

But simply stacking legislatures did not answer several crucial questions, including profound questions about institutional multiplicity's theoretical and practical significance. If the central intellectual issue of the Revolutionary-era debates was hammering out a conception of multilayered government, the central achievement of the Philadelphia convention was assembling an institutional structure to support that conception. In the course of these efforts, participants in the drafting and ratification debates offered not only a plausible form of multilayered authority but also a novel normative vision of composite government distinct from past Anglo-American practice and theory. The legislature-centered approaches to multiplicity that had characterized the 1760s and 1770s gave way in the early Republic to a reexamination of foundational questions of the location of authority within a composite polity, and to practical issues of how such a polity might actually operate. The floor of the convention became a crucial site of this reexamination.

In particular, the debate surrounding James Madison's proposal to give Congress the power to negative, or veto, state laws required delegates to work through the meaning of multiplicity. In the end, the delegates' rejection of the negative and adoption instead of a judicialized approach to the problem of multilayered authority signaled a fundamental shift from the colonial approach to such issues, and even from the Articles of Confederation. By 1787, the previous decades' embrace of multiplicity as the response to full-throated metropolitan insistence on unitary authority seemed inadequate to the pressing problems of establishing a government. Colonial commentators' refrain of multiplicity gave few specifics about what that idea might mean in practice, or what forms it would take in a postimperial state. The Revolutionary ideology of multiplicity, in other words, seemed by 1787 to demand a new institutional structure. With a mandate to assemble that new structure, the convention delegates rejected the established legislative solution embodied in Madison's negative and turned instead to another institution, the judiciary, to mediate between state and general governments. In so doing, they gave their institutional choice of a judicial approach a normative edge. The Revolutionary belief in multiplicity thus melded with a new structural commitment to a judicial solution. The result was both ideology and institution, and it was called federalism.

Participants in the drafting and ratification of the Constitution thus worked Revolutionary ideology into a new institutional structure, a process that in turn helped create a new ideology. This story, therefore, has to do with institutions, but it is not a purely institutional story; rather, it focuses on the ideas and debates that went into setting up the institutions. The debate over Madison's negative was a debate about federal thinking. The central story line of that debate was the emergence of not just an idea but an ideology of multitiered authority.

Madison in the Library and the Legislature

A critical moment for the notion of authority, particularly the species of layered authority that would characterize American federalism, came in 1786 as the American Confederation struggled to solidify its victory over its former imperial master in the face of political unrest, fiscal ruin, and sectional rivalry. Between April and June of that year, during the recess of the Virginia House of Delegates, in which he served, James Madison returned to his home in Orange County, Virginia, where he immersed himself in his extensive library of historical treatises. Two trunkfuls of books had recently arrived from Madison's friend Thomas Jefferson, who had been detailed to Paris in 1784 to replace Benjamin Franklin as American minister to the Court of Versailles, and to whom Madison had given free rein to acquire and relay as many books as possible concerning the fates of confederacies, both antique and contemporary.[6] The thirty-five-year-old Madison, already famously hardworking, settled back into his parents' Piedmont home, Montpelier, and addressed himself to the task of canvassing this precious "literary cargo."[7] His research yielded forty-one pocket-sized pages of handwritten notes that surveyed political entities from the Amphictyonic Confederacy of classical Greece to the contemporary United Netherlands.[8]

Despite some initial misgivings about the prospect of tinkering with the Republic's foundational document, Madison spent his days and nights (aside from an occasional evening game of whist) searching for answers in the experiences of other confederacies. He did find guidance, but in the form of cautionary tales rather than specific models of government.[9] In his notes he judged the ancient and modern confederacies harshly, enumerating their shortcomings under the heading "Vices of the Constitution." What was the chief failing of these storied political systems? In each case, the newly constituted "foederal authority" remained beholden to the component states, secondary in both the power it wielded and the allegiance it demanded to the entities that had created it. In their efforts to preserve the sovereignty of the members, the creators of these confederacies had rendered the central government impotent. The famed Achaean League of ancient Greece, for example, had failed, Madison believed, because the "defect [lack] of subjection in the members to the general authority ruined the whole Body." Similarly, Madison noted about the contemporary Holy Roman Empire, "Jealousy of the Imperial authority seems to have been a great cement of the confederacy."[10] The repetition of the word "authority" here is striking. Underpinning both statements is Madison's conclusion that the confederacies in question were dysfunctional because their structures failed to settle the fundamental question of authority, of which entity possessed ultimate power—the component polities or the general government.

Moreover, the way in which Madison used the term "authority" also reveals a more specific conclusion. Throughout the "Notes," the term "authority" is nearly always allied with one of three other terms: "foederal," "general," or "imperial." In the course of examining existing structures of authority, Madison also addressed the unasked question that had likely motivated his task in the first place: what was the nature of authority in a republic consisting of multiple preexisting entities that had long considered themselves independent, sovereign states? If that republic was to succeed where its predecessors had failed, the answer was clear to Madison: authority must be tied to that which was federal, general, or imperial—that is, in the case of the United States, to a national government.

Recognition of this problem led Madison to conclude that the Articles of Confederation, premised on a vague hierarchy of legislatures, were insufficient for the task of bringing the states together under a strong central government. "Our situation is becoming every day more & more critical," Madison wrote to Edmund Randolph in February 1787, as he sat in an increasingly idle Confederation Congress awaiting the approaching Philadelphia convention. "No money comes into the federal Treasury. No respect is paid to the federal authority; and people of reflection unanimously agree that the existing Confederacy is tottering to its foundation."[11] The question for Madison—and for the Constitutional Convention—became how to save the United States from the fate that he believed had reduced other confederacies to little more than impotent leagues, the power of which was limited to serving the will and convenience of their component states. Madison drew on his analysis throughout the Constitutional Convention of 1787 and the Virginia ratifying convention of 1788, as well as in his contributions to *The Federalist* during the winter and spring of 1787–1788.[12]

By the time the delegates to the Constitutional Convention began trickling into Philadelphia in May 1787, Madison had arrived at a solution that he believed would establish the supremacy of the general government.[13] In a coded letter to Jefferson, he laid out his prescription: "Over & above the positive power of regulating trade and sundry other matters in which uniformity is proper, to arm the federal head with a negative *in all cases whatsoever* on the local Legislatures. Without this defensive power experience and reflection have satisfied me that however ample the federal powers may be made, or however [c]learly their boundaries may be delineated, on paper, they will be easily and continually baffled by the Legislative sovereignties of the States."[14] Madison's remedy for the vices of the American Confederation appeared simple enough: to vest the general (federal) government with the power to veto laws passed by the state legislatures.

This "federal negative" proved to be the linchpin of Madison's plan for reforming the national charter.[15] In a trio of letters to Jefferson, Randolph, and George Washington written in March and April 1787, which Douglass Adair has called the seedbeds of "the first shoot in his thoughts of a plan of Federal Government," Madison elaborated on his vision.[16] Taking a cue from his earlier observations concerning the jealousies of the states, Madison now presented the federal negative as the cure both for the problem of authority that had dogged every other confederation and for what he viewed as the related problem of the states' increasing tendency to carry rule by majority to dangerous excess.[17] The effect of incorporating the federal negative into the amended charter, he wrote, would be "not only to guard the national rights and interests against invasion, but also to restrain the States from thwarting and molesting each other, and even from oppressing the minority within themselves by paper money and other unrighteous measures which favor the interest of the majority." The federal negative, therefore, would remedy several of the "Vices of the Political System of the United States" that Madison enumerated in his essay of the same name, written in the spring of 1787 as he prepared for the Philadelphia convention: "Failure of the States to comply with the Constitutional requisitions"; "Encroachments by the

States on the federal authority"; and "Trespasses of the States on the rights of each other"; as well as four other provisions concerning the "Multiplicity," "[M]utability," "Injustice," and "Impotence" of state laws under the Confederation.[18]

The concept of granting a central legislative authority the power to veto the acts of a subordinate legislature was not Madison's innovation, as he readily acknowledged. Indeed, his own words laid bare the source of Madison's solution to the problem of authority: the British Empire. Regarding the national government, Madison wrote to Randolph on April 8, "Let it have a negative in all cases whatsoever on the Legislative Acts of the States as the K. of G. B. heretofore had." In a more formal, less shorthand-laden letter to Washington eight days later, Madison elaborated. A "negative *in all cases whatsoever* on the legislative acts of the States, as heretofore exercised by the Kingly prerogative," was "absolutely necessary" and constituted "the least possible encroachment on the State jurisdictions."[19] The centerpiece of Madison's plan to reconstitute the Republic, therefore, sprang directly from the institutions and practices of the British Empire, the thralldom of which the American colonies had escaped only four years before.

The inspiration to import the negative to American shores seems to have been brewing in Madison's mind as early as the spring of 1786, when he composed his "Notes on Ancient and Modern Confederacies." The causal cascade among the other confederacies' lack of a mechanism by which the central government could police the laws of the component entities, the perceived failings of those confederacies, and the presence of such a mechanism in the British Empire echoed throughout his writings in 1786–1787. In order to save the Union, Madison proposed grafting onto the founding charter a provision requiring the same type of ex ante review of state legislative acts that the British Crown, through the mechanism of the Privy Council, had formerly wielded over the acts of the colonial assemblies.

A Republican Privy Council?

The Privy Council was a hybrid executive and legislative body composed of the king and his councillors, many of whom were peers and therefore also members of the House of Lords.[20] Since the early twentieth century, a few legal historians have focused on the Privy Council's appellate review of colonial legislative acts and judicial decisions. Beginning with a brace of articles published by Arthur M. Schlesinger, Sr., in 1913, scholars have argued that the structure of review established by the Privy Council influenced American colonists' understanding of the hierarchical array of legal authorities in which they lived.[21] As the legal historian Joseph Henry Smith demonstrated, medieval theories of kingship—still widely espoused in the late seventeenth century in the form of the legal fiction that the colonies qualified as "king's dominions" by right of conquest—dictated that the colonies did not fall within the ambit of domestic English appellate procedure.[22] Thus instead of bringing his case before the King's Bench, as his counterpart at home in Swindon or Bristol might, a colonist who wished to appeal an adverse decision by his highest colonial court could request a hearing before the Crown in the form of the Privy Council. These practices fell under the rubric of royal prerogative and therefore tied the colonies directly to monarchical authority.[23] Mary Sarah Bilder has elaborated on Smith's findings, arguing that the Privy Council's standard of review, which interrogated colonial laws to determine whether they were repugnant to the laws of England, connected the New World to the Old by creating a "transatlantic constitution" based on specific levels of hierarchical authority.[24]

These histories have focused primarily on one species of the Privy Council's activity—its review of colonial judicial decisions—as part of a project of tracing continuities between imperial and colonial modes of appellate jurisdiction, and ultimately the origins of American judicial review.[25] The Privy Council's power to scrutinize colonial law extended beyond reviewing the decisions of colonial courts, however. In addition to exercising this protojudicial review, the Privy Council wielded a power over the colonies that modern legal scholars would now call legislative review: that is, the power to evaluate the acts of colonial legislatures, unattached to a specific case or set of parties, and to declare those acts either valid or invalid as applied prospectively to all persons and all scenarios. Fewer scholars have focused on the impact of this parallel practice of legislative or administrative review.[26]

Certainly, as many scholars have argued, the parsing of distinctions between such modern notions as judicial and legislative review and applying them retrospectively to seventeenth- and eighteenth-century legal proceedings is fraught with peril. Anglo-American jurists of the period did not recognize a firm distinction between adjudication and legislation; this was why, as Charles McIlwain and others have ably demonstrated, the medieval English Parliament could be characterized as both a high court and a legislative body. The ambiguity endured in the American colonies.[27] Consequently, to expect the legal forms of the period to conform neatly to modern taxonomies is to court anachronism.

Nevertheless, it is possible to analyze the substance of the action at hand and to categorize it as more like one or the other form of review as jurists today understand them. The hallmark of adjudication is *specificity:* particular parties bring a particular dispute before a decision-making body, which then issues a ruling that applies primarily to the particular case at hand and, secondarily, as a precedent to aid in deciding future cases that materially resemble that case. Judicial review is similarly specific: particular parties bring before a decision-making body either the ruling of another, inferior decision-making body or a statute promulgated by a lawmaking body. Legislation and legislative review, by contrast, aspire toward *generality,* if not universality. Unlike bodies responsible for adjudicating disputes, legislative bodies issue rules that apply to all persons and scenarios covered by the terms of the legislation; moreover, the rules typically apply only prospectively.[28]

The Privy Council exercised both varieties of review with respect to the American colonies in the seventeenth and eighteenth centuries, albeit to varying degrees depending on each colony's particular legal organization. By positing that lands beyond the realm were held by the monarch alone by virtue of conquest, the doctrine of the king's dominions vested the king's council with authority to oversee colonial legislation and to review the decisions of colonial courts. The extent of the Privy Council's authority over the legislative acts and judicial decisions of a given colony therefore depended on the quantum of royal control that underpinned the colony's founding. In the initial decades of North American colonization, the general taxonomy was as follows: royal colonies were clearly subject to the maximum level of royal control, including both legislative and judicial review by the Privy Council; charter colonies were subject to varying levels of royal control depending on the specific provisions and reservations of their charters; and proprietary colonies were subject to minimal amounts of royal control and thus typically lacked appeal to the Privy Council, except as otherwise provided by local assemblies.[29] Following the 1675 and 1696 establishment of the Committee of Trade and Plantations and the Board of Trade, respectively, the Crown sought to tighten its control over the colonies by expanding the Privy Council's jurisdiction to review colonial legislative acts and judicial decisions.[30]

In cases of judicial review, an aggrieved colonial party first sought permission to appeal to the metropolitan authority via either a grant of permission from the colonial court or, failing that, a grant of a petition from the Privy Council itself. Upon receiving one or the other form of permission, which involved meeting certain procedural and jurisdictional requirements, such as a minimum damage amount, the appellant presented his or her case during a hearing before the Privy Council's Committee for Appeals. The verdict, which required the monarch's approval, came in the form of an order in council. Between 1680 and 1780, the Privy Council heard 265 such appeals from the colonies that would later become the United States.[31]

In contrast to this highly judicialized role, when the Privy Council engaged in its parallel mode of legislative review, it issued a sweeping declaration that either approved or disallowed a colonial legislative act.[32] In some special cases, the Privy Council went even further by holding a colonial act void ab initio—not only invalidating the act prospectively but declaring that the act had never been valid in the first place. Julius Goebel found only four examples of legislative declarations of nullity ab initio during the colonial period; he observed that the Privy Council seems to have preferred to issue such rulings in specific cases that came before it on appeal and that thus required it to act in its judicial capacity.[33] This preference likely arose out of prudential concerns, as well as what Goebel terms "the indurated common law tradition that issues of such moment should be settled in true adversarial proceedings."[34]

The realities of contemporary transportation meant that a declaration that a law had never been valid would almost certainly give rise to further disputes about the status of contracts and obligations entered into during the period between the passage of the act in the colonies and the arrival there of news that it had been invalidated by the Privy Council. In the majority of cases in which the Privy Council invalidated a colonial act, it held that the act had been valid during the interim period before the invalidation, and that therefore rights could vest under the act.[35] Consequently, as Goebel points out, disallowance by the Privy Council cannot accurately be likened to a veto, insofar as disallowance would permit an interim period of validity, while a veto would immediately negate the act, permitting no such period.[36] According to one estimate, the Privy Council disallowed 5.5 percent of the colonial statutes that it reviewed.[37]

The most vigorous contests between Crown and colonies concerning the Privy Council's authority originated in the chartered colonies after 1696. The administrative reorganization that resulted in the establishment of the Board of Trade heralded a renewed metropolitan effort to bring the chartered colonies to heel by drawing them into the ambit of the Crown's appellate power.[38] Although some early grants explicitly reserved to the Crown the authority to hear judicial appeals (beginning with a 1664 patent to the Duke of York), after 1696 royal officials routinely argued that such authority inhered in the very nature of the colonies as portions of the king's dominions.[39]

Along with these assertions of royal appellate power following the 1675 and 1696 reorganizations, the Crown argued during the same period for an increasingly robust power of legislative review. As was the case with judicial review, this flexing of imperial muscle through legislative review aroused a storm of controversy. No monarch employed the analogous domestic power to strike down parliamentary legislation after 1707, by which time colonists had begun to feel keenly any metropolitan challenge to the authority of their local assemblies. Intent on checking those assemblies' pretensions to power, imperial administrators ordered colonial governors in royal and proprietary colonies automatically to veto certain categories of local legislation. In addition, imperial officials increasingly required that colonial legislation include suspending clauses, which made the enactment of such legislation contingent on Privy Council approval.[40]

The statutory basis for this power of legislative review was the ninth section of the "Act for Preventing Frauds, and Regulating Abuses in the Plantation Trade," which provided, in relevant part,

> That all Lawes By-lawes Usages or Customes att this tyme or which hereafter shall bee in practice or endeavoured or pretended to bee in force or practice in any of the said Plantations which are in any wise repugnant to the before mentioned Lawes ... soe far as they doe relate to the said Plantations ... or which are wayes repugnant to this present Act, or to any other Law hereafter to bee made in this Kingdome soe farr as such Law shall relate to and mention the said Plantations are illegall null and void to all Intents and Purposes whatsoever.[41]

In addition, most colonial charters contained provisions prohibiting the enactment of laws that were contrary or repugnant to the laws of England.[42] The charter of the Massachusetts Bay Colony, for example, included a clause permitting the governor and company

> to make Lawes and Ordinances for the Good and Welfare of the saide Company, and for the Government and ordering of the saide Landes and Plantacon, and the People inhabiting and to inhabite the same, as to them from tyme to tyme shalbe thought meete, *soe as such Lawes and Ordinances be not contrarie or repugnant to the Lawes and Statuts of this our Realme of England.*[43]

The roots of the Privy Council's legislative review lay beyond the boundaries of the mainland North American colonies, in earlier English imperial projects. Ex ante legislative review by the Crown had originated in 1494 with the efforts of Henry VII to subdue Ireland by mandating that all acts of the Irish Parliament be approved by the English king and his council before passing into law. This requirement, known as Poynings' Law, endured until 1782.[44] Closer to the American case in both space and time was the situation of Jamaica, which in the 1670s attracted the attention of the Lords Committee for Trade and Plantations, which targeted the Caribbean colony as the first test case for the new policy of tightening the leash on colonial legislatures.[45] With precedents such as these, the purpose of legislative review of colonial statutes appeared clear to American colonists in the seventeenth and eighteenth centuries: to subordinate local assemblies to the twofold jurisdiction of royal prerogative and imperial administration.

The Mechanics of Federalism

In 1787, the long history of Privy Council review formed an important part of the American constitutional landscape. Madison explicitly drew on this precedent as he marshaled his arguments for giving the general government of the United States the power to negative state laws. But why look to a cornerstone of British imperial organization when searching for models of government for the new republic? Put simply, Madison believed that what had been lacking in every other confederacy in history was also lacking in the American Confederation but had been present under the British Empire: a firm authority emanating from the center that established the foundational rules of union and policed the extremes of the states' behavior. "Without this defensive power, every positive power that can be given on paper will be evaded & defeated. The States will continue to invade the national jurisdiction, to violate treaties and the law of nations & to harrass [*sic*] each other with rival and spiteful measures dictated by mistaken views of interest."[46] In short, Madison believed that the lessons of the empire could be applied to the problem of authority in the American republic.

Moreover, Madison's words demonstrate that he had imperial practice in mind when he conceived the notion of the federal negative—recall his recommendation to Washington of a "negative *in all cases whatsoever* on the legislative acts of the States, as heretofore exercised by the Kingly prerogative."[47] Madison envisioned the federal negative functioning in the same manner as the Privy Council's practice of reviewing statutes ex ante, in a general posture, before they could be applied in individual cases or challenged by specific parties. He thus selected one of the two strands of British imperial practice and sought to graft it onto the revised American charter. Without adopting what legal historians have generally recognized as the Privy Council's embryonic power of judicial review,

Madison endorsed its alternative procedure of legislative review.[48] Just as the pre-Revolutionary Privy Council had periodically reviewed new colonial acts to gauge whether they were repugnant to English law, the newly minted general government of the United States would possess a procedural mechanism by which to "prevent encroachments by the states on each other and on the general government itself."[49] As Lance Banning notes, historians of the founding period cannot help being surprised at the degree to which Madison based the architecture of his constitution on a foundation built in England: "[I]t is stunning to remark how clearly he was thinking, at this point, of a republican replacement for the old imperial regime, complete with the prerogative to overturn provincial legislation that was incompatible with the requirements of the 'empire' as a whole."[50]

To be sure, Madison's theory did diverge somewhat from British imperial practice. Most significantly, the plan aimed to remedy not just the binary problem of state laws that ran afoul of the laws of the general government—analogous to the imperial problem of colonial acts that conflicted with English law—but the more complex challenge of state laws that suppressed the will of minorities within a given state or trenched on the laws of other states. The federal negative would give the general government the power to police both a state's relationship with its inhabitants and its relationship with its fellow states. Consider the litany of woes that Madison outlined in his letter to Washington, cited earlier, that would result if the general government lacked such a power: "The States will continue to invade the national jurisdiction, to violate treaties and the law of nations & to harrass each other with rival and spiteful measures dictated by mistaken views of interest."[51] Invasions of the national jurisdiction and violations of treaties and the law of nations clearly are conflicts on the national level, classic examples of matters within the purview of the general government of even the weakest confederacy.[52] But laws passed by one state that had the effect of harassing other states? This was something new, something that had not been contemplated by the privy councillors.

For Madison, this state-on-state aggression was the real danger, for in his view the states simply could not be trusted to behave themselves. A balancing agent would have to be found, and Madison found it in the mechanism of the federal negative. "The great desideratum which has not yet been found for Republican Governments," he wrote to Washington, "seems to be some disinterested & dispassionate umpire in disputes between different passions & interests in the State."[53] A son of the Enlightenment, Madison embraced the era's vision of passions and interests as equal and countervailing elements of individual and social life, with important consequences for political order. The federal negative would import the Privy Council's legislative review mechanism to American shores, establishing the central government as an umpire over the fractious states with authority to oversee both their internal actions (e.g., "oppressing the minority within themselves") and their external actions (e.g., "thwarting and molesting each other," "invad[ing] the national jurisdiction," and "violat[ing] treaties and the law of nations").[54]

Outside the confines of Madison's study, however, the negative looked to some contemporaries like little more than a rehash of imperial procedure. Upon hearing rumors of Madison's scheme in April 1787, one month before the Philadelphia convention assembled, Virginia congressman William Grayson wrote to William Short, Jefferson's secretary in Paris: "Some of the gentlemen of the convention are here and I have conversed freely with them as to the reform; they are for going in a great way: some of them are for placing Congress in loco of the King of G.B.— besides their present powers: for giving them a perpetual duty on imports and exports. Figure to yourself how the States will relish the idea of a negative on their laws."[55] Grayson's meaning was clear: with its combination of increased central power over states' actions and an imperial lineage, Madison's negative immediately raised suspicions among some of his fellow statesmen.

The Virginia delegation, however, embraced the federal negative. Between May 14 and May 25, before the first meeting of the convention, the Virginia delegates met informally and began to hammer out a blueprint for governmental reform. Presented to the convention by Virginia governor Edmund Randolph on May 29, the scheme became known as the Virginia Plan. Although the authorship of the plan cannot be determined, the provisions closely tracked Madison's proposals as outlined in his letters to Jefferson, Randolph, and Washington in March and April.[56] The assembled convention quickly accepted the Virginia Plan as the initial template for reform and basis for debate. Most notable for our purposes was Article VI:

> Resolved that each branch [of the national legislature] ought to possess the right of originating Acts; that the national Legislature ought to be impowered to enjoy the Legislative Rights vested in Congress by the Confederation & moreover to legislate in all cases to which the separate States are incompetent, or in which the harmony of the United States may be interrupted by the exercise of individual Legislation; *to negative all laws passed by the several States, contravening in the opinion of the National Legislature the articles of Union;* and to call forth the force of the Union agst. any member of the Union failing to fulfill its duty under the articles thereof.[57]

When discussion of the plan began on May 31, one clause contained in Article VI sparked debate: the grant of lawmaking power to Congress "in all cases to which the separate States are incompetent." Several delegates took issue with the vagueness of the provision and argued that it threatened to strip the states of jurisdiction. But the subsequent clause, which set forth the federal negative, elicited no debate at all. Madison's notes, considered "the standard authority for the proceedings of the Convention," state: "The other clauses giving powers necessary to preserve harmony among the States to negative all State laws contravening in the opinion of the Nat Leg the articles of Union down to the last clause . . . were agreed to [without] debate or dissent."[58] Madison's federal negative had cleared its first hurdle. Over the course of the next two weeks, however, as the delegates debated the Virginia Plan in depth, the negative faced much more rigorous challenge.

Article VI was not the only provision of the Virginia Plan that contemplated ex ante review of legislation. Article VIII proposed "that the Executive and a Convenient number of the National Judiciary, ought to compose a Council of revision with authority to examine every act of the National Legislature before it shall operate, & every act of a particular Legislature before a Negative thereon shall be final."[59] As had been the case under the empire, a quasi-executive, quasi-judicial body would assess a new act before it became operable to determine whether the law comported with a more general, overarching body of law. In contrast to the Privy Council's legislative review and Madison's federal negative, the Council of Revision would function both horizontally (national authorities evaluating national laws) and vertically (national authorities evaluating state laws), passing on the actions of states (the "particular legislatures") as a supplement to the congressional negativing power. The purposes of the Council of Revision and the negative were similar, however: to import imperial practice to the United States as a means of checking wayward majorities that, like the colonial assemblies, might be prone to an excess of democracy or self-interest.[60]

Jack Rakove finds a link between Article VI and Article VIII on the basis of their shared suspicion of legislatures qua legislatures. He argues that "Madison thought that unchecked legislatures posed the greatest threats to the constitution of any republic."[61] Although Madison certainly feared that a legislature citing a popular mandate might overrun the other branches of government, the sixth and eighth articles shared another common theme: both offered procedural, institutional solutions to the problem of mediating among multiple levels of authority. Taken together, these key elements of the Virginia Plan sought to grant Congress ongoing supervisory power over the state legislatures, as well as creating in the Council of Revision a supralegislative body with immense power not merely over specific parties or cases but over the lawmaking process itself. In so doing, Madison, the architect of the Virginia Plan, again borrowed from British imperial precedents in constructing the new government. As had been the case under British rule, a hybrid council would measure new legislative acts against a preexisting set of general principles, and the remedy for acts repugnant to those principles would be to void them ab initio.[62] Rather than relying on a body of substantive, supreme national law, then, the Virginia Plan attempted to solve the problem of central authority through structural mechanisms dictating the relationship among different legislative powers.[63]

After the relatively warm reception that it received on May 31, the federal negative remained in the background of the convention's discussions until June 8, when it dominated debate. South Carolinian Charles Pinckney opened the proceedings with a motion expanding the scope of the negative to encompass any state law that Congress judged "improper."

The Virginia Plan, in contrast, had limited the negative to state laws that in Congress's judgment contravened the articles of union—in other words, laws that were unconstitutional. Madison, whom some scholars suspect of colluding with Pinckney (his fellow lodger at Mary House's rooms at the corner of Fifth and Market streets), seconded the motion.[64]

Despite his considerable influence on the drafting of the Virginia Plan, Madison soon made it clear that he advocated a much broader negative than the one outlined in the proposal. Only two days after making his first major speech in the convention, Madison catalogued the benefits of the negative for his fellow delegates, which he now believed ought to be "lodged in the senate alone." According to his notes of the debates, in which he consistently referred to himself in the third person, Madison issued the following opening salvo: "He could not but regard an indefinite power to negative legislative acts of the States as absolutely necessary to a perfect system. Experience had evinced a constant tendency in the States to encroach on the federal authority; to violate national Treaties[;] to infringe the rights & interests of each other; to oppress the weaker party within their respective jurisdictions. A negative was the mildest expedient that could be devised for preventing these mischiefs."[65] If any doubt had existed about Madison's position on the proper solution to the problem of authority, this speech shattered it.

Madison's remarks also invoked several shibboleths of imperial practice that likely would have resonated with his audience. For example, by speaking in the language of "encroachments," Madison signaled his debt to the Privy Council's mode of reviewing proposed legislation. His subsequent comments coupled imperial argot with the astronomical vernacular popular among the members of the founding generation: "This prerogative of the General Govt. is the great pervading principle that must controul the centrifugal tendency of the States; which, without it, will continually fly out of their proper orbits and destroy the order & harmony of the political system."[66] Just as the royal prerogative, via the Privy Council, had restrained the centrifugal, heterogeneous tendencies of the colonies by compelling their laws to conform to English norms, the republican prerogative, via Congress, would keep the states from spinning into the turmoil that had characterized the Confederation.

For Madison, then, the term "prerogative" did not immediately inspire suspicion, as it did for some of his fellow Revolutionaries, for whom the term conjured images of the seventeenth-century struggles with the Stuart monarchs over the extent of kingly power.[67] On the contrary, Madison's vision of prerogative as the source of the federal negative, and therefore as the cure for confederal chaos, was benign, even salutary. Nor does Madison appear to have been troubled by the distinction between royal and legislative sources of prerogative power for the Privy Council and the negative-wielding Congress, respectively. For Madison, the relevant characteristic of both legislative review by the Privy Council and the federal negative was that each offered an opportunity for one lawmaking body to oversee the activities of another. Whether the inferior body was a colonial assembly or a state legislature mattered little. The key element in both the imperial and the Madisonian systems was that lawmaking was at least a two-step process, requiring the assent (even if through inaction) of a superior entity in order to make legislation complete.

Madison's argument for the broadest possible version of the federal negative galvanized his fellow delegates. Elbridge Gerry of Massachusetts objected, seemingly to the federal negative in any form: "The Natl. Legislature with such a power may enslave the States." James Wilson of Pennsylvania endorsed the proposal, however, even Pinckney's broader version. "A definition of the cases in which the Negative should be exercised, is impracticable," Wilson insisted. "A discretion must be left on one side or the other[. W]ill it not be most safely lodged on the side of the Natl. Govt.?"[68] Invoking the same type of internal strife and external vulnerability that Madison had diagnosed as afflicting the ancient and modern confederacies, Wilson continued: "We must remember the language with wh. we began the Revolution, it was this, Virginia is no more, Massachusetts is no more—we are one in name, let us be one in Truth & Fact—Unless this power is vested in the Genl. Govt. the States will be used by foreign powers as Engines agt the Whole—New States will be soon formed, the Inhabitants may be foreigners and possess foreign affections, unless the Genl. Govt. can check their State laws they may involve the Nation in Tumult and Confusion."[69] Wilson, a Scot who had emigrated to America in 1765 at the age of twenty-three, placed enormous importance on union and security. The imperial heritage of the federal negative does not appear to have troubled him.

Madison's remarks at the close of the June 8 debate confirm the broad scope of his plan to reshape the relationship between the states and the general government. The key institutions in this relationship were to be the legislatures, and the node connecting the two levels of legislatures was to be the negative. As Madison explained in a letter of October 24 to Jefferson, he concurred with James Wilson's statement in the convention that "[i]t will be better to prevent the passage of an improper law, than to declare it void when passed."[70] Indeed, Madison suggested that the very existence of the negative would deter state legislatures from passing questionable acts in the first place. "The existence of such a check would prevent attempts to commit" offenses against either the nation or the other states.[71]

Other delegates were less convinced of the need for ex ante legislative review. "The proposal of it would disgust all the States," Gouverneur Morris argued. "A law that ought to be negatived will be set aside in the Judiciary departmt. and if that security should fail; may be repealed by a Nationl. law."[72] Morris, like many of his colleagues, endorsed a vision of state and national governments as interlocking at several points: first, at the moment when an injured party brought a judicial action seeking relief from a state law pursuant to the Supremacy Clause; and second, at the moment when Congress repealed the offending state law. This interlocking approach contrasted with Madison's vision of two parallel systems that crossed only at the single moment when Congress considered whether to give validity to a state act.[73]

Furthermore, Madison's comments suggest that he envisioned the legislatures operating almost as a single system—a compound legislature comprising inferior and superior bodies. Such a system required the approval of the superior body to give effect to any piece of legislation. Thus in response to criticisms that the negative would create delay and uncertainty while Congress considered a given state law, Madison linked the need for speedy action by the general government with ongoing oversight of state lawmaking processes. "The case of laws of urgent necessity must be provided for by some emanation of the power from the Natl. Govt. into each State so far as to give a temporary assent at least. This was the practice in Royal Colonies before the Revolution and would not have been inconvenient; if the supreme power of negativing had been faithful to the American interest, and had possessed the necessary information."[74]

The assumption that the assent of the general government was necessary for state laws to be effective, and the consequent call for the "emanation" of national power into the states, demonstrate that the negative was merely one side of an affirmative congressional power to ratify state legislation. Indeed, Madison appears to have envisioned that congressional approval (which, paradoxically, could be manifested only negatively, by Congress's declining to use its power to veto a state act) would function as a necessary final step in the legislative process. "The States [could] of themselves pass no operative act, any more than one branch of a Legislature where there are two branches can proceed without the other," he insisted.[75] The negative, in other words, gave the national government a permanent option to intervene in the state lawmaking process. Absent some form of assent by the general government, state laws would be incomplete and invalid, just as disapproval (or, in the case of colonies with suspending clauses, mere silence) from the Privy Council had annulled provincial legislation.

Madison's comments on June 8 made clear the political and historical precedents that informed his proposal. But for a misalignment of interests between metropolitan authorities and colonial assemblies, he seemed to say, Privy Council review would not have been at all onerous. By the end of the colonial period, imperial review might have become corrupt or misguided in reality, but the principle of supremacy on which that review was based, and the mechanism of review itself, survived intact. Therefore, Madison contended, it was an appropriate means of establishing an analogous supremacy in the United States. When the vote came at the end of that day's session, however, Madison's arguments had not prevailed. Pinckney's motion to expand the scope of the proposed negative failed by a vote of seven to three, with one state's delegation divided.[76]

After the June 8 debate, the tide seems to have turned decidedly against Madison. Eight days later, when the delegates took up the original, limited negative set forth in the Virginia Plan and endorsed in the June 13 report of the committee of the whole, John Lansing of New York and Luther Martin of Maryland spoke against the proposal.[77] Although Wilson parried their criticisms, the tenor of the debate had shifted. To be sure, the report of the committee of the whole had largely adopted the Virginia Plan, ostensibly a triumph for Madison.[78] But the defeat of the broader version of the negative, combined with the introduction of William Paterson's decentralizing New Jersey Plan on June 15, halted the momentum that had been propelling the Virginia Plan—and with it the federal negative—forward. Madison believed that the limited negative was insufficient to stave off the evils that had dogged the ancient and modern confederations, including the American Confederation. Nevertheless, he kept fighting. Even a limited negative was preferable to the New Jersey Plan's proposed return to a loose confederation of minimally connected states.

The defeat of the broader negative on June 8, however, portended the provision's ultimate fate. Despite Randolph's last-ditch effort to give states a right of appeal to the federal judiciary following an adverse exercise of the negative—a naked attempt to bridge the rift between large states and small states that the New Jersey Plan had highlighted—the negative was doomed.[79] On July 17, the delegates voted seven to three to reject the negative. Aside from a short-lived attempt by Pinckney to revive the measure on August 23, this spelled the end of Madison's proposal.[80]

How had Madison lost what he viewed as a crucial battle? What accounts for the shift in opinion that transformed the success of May 31 into the rout of July 17? Although it is impossible to identify with certainty the cause of the negative's downfall, one potential explanation stems from the rhetoric that Madison employed when he discussed the proposal in the convention. With his speech of June 8, which tied the negative closely to imperial practice, Madison may have planted the seed of opposition in his colleagues' minds. By explicitly noting that a mechanism very similar to the negative "was the practice in Royal Colonies before the Revolution," Madison invited his fellow delegates to put themselves back in the place of colonists seeking the approval of their imperial masters. Although some observers might have agreed with Virginia congressman Edward Carrington's conviction that "the negative which the King of England had upon our Laws was never found to be materially inconvenient," others such as John Lansing viewed the plan to imitate the Privy Council more critically: "Such a Negative would be more injurious than that of Great Britain heretofore was."[81] Delegates who already feared what they viewed as the centralizing tendency of the convention could not have been comforted by the prospect of the national government's having a veto over state laws. Madison's overt references to the negative's origins in British imperial practice might have seemed a harbinger of, as Martin put it, "the *destruction of the State governments, and the introduction of monarchy.*"[82]

To be sure, other factors contributed to the defeat of the federal negative. For example, in the June 8 vote on the Pinckney proposal to broaden the scope of the negative, the three states whose delegations favored expansion were also the three largest states: Virginia, Pennsylvania, and Massachusetts. At that point in the convention, the mode of representation in Congress was still very much an open question. Proportional representation based on population appeared likely to win the day; the New Jersey Plan, with its small-state-friendly proposal for equal representation, had not yet been introduced. Did the delegates from the three largest states believe that their large populations would allow them to dominate Congress and control the exercise of the federal negative, thereby insulating their own states' acts from review and veto? Perhaps; after all, as Martin pointed out, as of mid-June, the convention appeared to have reached consensus on a plan that would have given this trio a lock on the Senate: "[U]pon this plan, the three large States, Virginia, Pennsylvania, and Massachusetts, would have *thirteen senators* out of *twenty-eight,* almost *one half of the whole number.*" Spinning out his dire scenario, Martin predicted that the powerful troika "*would make what laws they pleased, however injurious or disagreeable to the other States; and that they would always prevent the other States from making any laws, however necessary and proper, if not agreeable to the views of those three States.*"[83]

But this hypothesis cannot explain the July 17 vote, which found the North Carolina delegation joining Virginia and Massachusetts in approving the limited negative, while Pennsylvania moved to the opposition camp. By that point, the New Jersey Plan had played out its brief role as a rallying point for the smaller states, and Roger Sherman's "Connecticut Compromise," establishing a bicameral Congress with a lower house based on proportional representation and an upper house based on equal representation, had won the majority's support. The vote approving the compromise plan took place on July 16, the day before the federal negative was defeated.[84] Had the acrimonious debate over representation cost so much energy and conflict that the delegates from Massachusetts and Virginia could no longer hope to muster support for the negative? If this was the case, why had they now gained the backing of North Carolina? Support for the negative had clearly been eroding since at least June 8. Prior to that date, the assembled delegates had thought well enough of the provision to incorporate it into the June 13 report of the committee of the whole, which had become the blueprint for the first weeks of debate. By mid-July, the delegates would have had the opportunity to mull over Madison's comments linking the negative to imperial practices of review. Had the references to the negative's British parentage ultimately poisoned the delegates against the negative? At a minimum, to judge from the comments of Lansing and Martin, emphasizing the family relationship had not helped Madison's cause.

For many delegates, the prospect of a sweeping congressional power to veto state laws—a power enunciated in language resembling that of the reviled Declaratory Act, no less[85]—threatened the integrity of the states themselves. The breadth of the negative was particularly offensive to these delegates. "The Natl. Legislature with such a power may enslave the States," argued Elbridge Gerry.[86] Specifically, Gerry and others contended, granting Congress the negative would permit the general government to regulate areas of activity traditionally left to the states, effectively usurping powers the states had claimed ever since they were colonies chafing against parliamentary oversight. Hugh Williamson of North Carolina, for example, based his opposition to the negative on his belief that "the State Legislatures ought to possess independent powers in cases purely local, and applying to their internal policy."[87] Even as they drafted a new constitution, some delegates resisted the notion that the general government ought to enjoy an ongoing, structurally guaranteed power to intervene in states' lawmaking processes.

Opponents of the negative thus used language of enslavement and encroachment similar to that their forbears in the 1760s and 1770s had employed against broad metropolitan oversight. Moreover, critics of the negative articulated similar fears of a central power bent on sowing discord among the component polities and stifling their efforts at self-protection. The negative, Gerry argued, "may enable the Genl. Govt. to depress a part for the benefit of another part—it may prevent the encouragements which particular States may be disposed to give to particular manufactures, it may prevent the States from train[ing] their militia, and thereby establish a military Force & finally a Despotism."[88] In Gerry's view, the chief danger of the negative lay in its potentially chilling effect on the states' autonomy, creativity, and prosperity. Gunning Bedford of Delaware, meanwhile, offered a more practical critique. "How can it be thought that the proposed negative can be exercised?" he inquired of his fellow delegates. "[A]re the laws of the States to be suspended in the most urgent cases until they can be sent seven or eight hundred miles, and undergo the deliberations of a body who may be incapable of Judging of them?"[89] On the contrary, Madison responded. State laws would receive timely consideration by "some emanation of the power from the Natl. Govt. into each State so far as to give a temporary assent at least," for which he cited "the practice in Royal Colonies before the Revolution."[90]

Gerry's vision of the states as possessing a discrete, spatially defined sphere of exclusive authority echoed colonial assemblies' claims of independent regulatory power in the face of metropolitan assertions of Parliament's supremacy. Arguments such as Bedford's, meanwhile, resembled Revolutionary-era complaints that the king and the Privy Council neglected colonial legislation, leaving acts to languish without approving them or declaring them void. The Declaration of Independence had included just such a charge against George III: "He has refused his Assent to Laws, the most wholesome and necessary for the public good. He has forbidden his Governors to pass Laws of immediate and pressing importance, unless suspended in their operation till his Assent should be obtained; and when so suspended, he has utterly neglected to attend to them."[91]

Taken together, the arguments of the negative's opponents convey a deep-seated fear of a specific array of solutions to the problem of multilayered authority. That array of solutions included prerogative-based, ex ante review of legislation, of the type that the Privy Council had used to invalidate colonial statutes, as well as more formal arrangements of hierarchical legislatures, akin to parliamentary supremacists' account of the relationship between Parliament and the colonial assemblies. The common element uniting these solutions in the eyes of the negative's opponents was their shared heritage as tools of British imperial governance. Gerry, Bedford, and others did not base their objections on simple animus toward all things British. Certainly, Luther Martin lamented after the convention, "[W]e were eternally troubled with arguments and precedents from the British government." But that complaint came in the context of a discussion of the presidential veto—a vestige of British practice that did find its way into the Constitution, and that operated at a single, horizontal level of government.[92] Criticism of the negative, in contrast, sounded a variety of themes but tended to focus on the same issue that had motivated the colonists' attacks on metropolitan oversight, whether by the Privy Council or Parliament: a multitiered governmental system built around the superior level's sweeping power to intervene in the inferior level's legislative process. For the negative's opponents, as well as the colonists, then, the problem of multiple authorities—the central problem of the era's protofederal systems—could not be solved by merging two levels of government power into one compound legislature.

From Legislative to Judicial Supremacy

Despite the outcome of the July 17 vote, Madison persisted in his belief that without the federal negative, the new government risked repeating the mistakes of the Confederation.[93] His exchange of letters with Jefferson spanning the period from June to October of 1787 reveals that Madison continued to develop his theory of the negative even after it had faded from discussion in the convention. Barred by convention rules from discussing the proceedings with outsiders, Madison did not introduce the negative into his correspondence with his friend and mentor; rather, it was Jefferson who broached the subject.[94] Clearly, word of Madison's proposal had already reached Paris. In a letter dated June 20, which appears not to have reached Madison until late August or early September, Jefferson offered his views on the proposal. "The negative proposed to be given [Congress] on all acts of the several legislatures is now for the first time suggested to my mind. Primâ facie I do not like it." Jefferson's opposition to the negative stemmed from what he viewed as the unnecessarily broad power it gave to Congress to insert itself into every piece of state legislation:

> It fails in an essential character, that the hole & the patch should be commensurate. But this proposes to mend a small hole by covering the whole garment. Not more than 1. out of 100. state-acts concern the confederacy. This proposition then, in order to give them 1. degree of power which they ought to have, gives them 99. more which they ought not to have, upon a presumption that they will not exercise the 99. But upon every act there will be a preliminary question[:] Does this act concern the confederacy? And was there ever a proposition so plain as to pass Congress without a debate? Their decisions are almost always wise; they are like pure metal. But you know of how much dross this is the result.

Rather than vesting Congress with this sweeping power of legislative review, Jefferson proposed a judicial alternative: "an appeal from the state judicature to a federal court, in all cases where the act of Confederation controled the question." Would this judicial solution not, he asked, "be as effectual a remedy, & exactly commensurate to the defect"?[95] In contrast to the legislature-centered proposal put forth by Madison, the student of political science, Jefferson the lawyer proposed that the Constitution adopt the other prong of the Privy Council's practice: judicial review of the laws of an inferior jurisdiction by a superior court.

By early September, Madison seems to have realized that the new charter would not include the negative—"the one ingredient that in his view was essential for establishing the supremacy of the central government and for protecting the private rights of individuals."[96] In response to both this defeat and Jefferson's comments, on October 24 Madison composed a seventeen-page letter to Jefferson that laid out his theory of the federal negative with great vigor and conviction. Despite the failure of such arguments to win converts in the convention, Madison continued to insist that the imperial analogy, combined with the experience of life under the Confederation, confirmed the value of the negative. "If the supremacy of the British Parliament is not necessary as has been contended, for the harmony of that Empire; it is evident I think that without the royal negative or some equivalent controul, the unity of the system would be destroyed. The want of some such provision seems to have been mortal to the antient Confederacies, and to be the disease of the modern."[97] Now, Madison feared, the national government's want of a power to veto harmful state legislation might prove mortal to the Republic.

Madison's letter demonstrated the continued influence of European and American history on his political thought. Even after the defeat of the federal negative, he could not help revisiting the precedents that he believed bolstered his case. Incorporating large segments of his "Notes on Ancient and Modern Confederacies," the letter delineated the failings of the United Netherlands and the Holy Roman Empire, among other confederacies, as Madison strove to convince Jefferson that the negative was necessary to prevent both "encroachments on the General authority" and "instability and injustice in the legislation of the States." Without this power, he feared that the national government would splinter into a collection of grasping, inferior political entities. Only the negative could save the American federation from the fate of its confederal European cousins. Without the negative, the United States would be nothing more than another example of a failed attempt at stitching multiple political entities together under a single overarching authority. In short, without the negative, the novel American project was doomed to the Old World fate of becoming "a feudal system of republics" rather than "a Confederacy of independent States."[98]

Here was the great paradox of Madison's proposal: by importing the review procedure practiced under the empire, he hoped to cement the authority of the national government, thereby allowing the United States to escape what he viewed as the doom of its European confederal predecessors. In other words, he sought to use one of the preeminent tools of British imperial practice to create a unique system of American federal government. Unfortunately for Madison, however, few of his colleagues shared his benign view of such a plan.[99] In response to Madison's October 24 discourse, Jefferson's next missive made no mention of the federal negative. Jefferson was apparently unmoved by Madison's arguments; his most relevant statement on the subject of national authority over the states echoed the concerns about overweening centralized power that his earlier letter had raised: "I own I am not a friend to very energetic government. It is always oppressive."[100]

Although Jefferson questioned whether the federal negative would create a too-energetic central government, the majority of convention delegates shared Madison's desire to shore up national authority. As Charles Warren put it, "Nearly all the delegates agreed that a curb on State legislation must be provided in the new Constitution, but the difficult question was: how shall it be applied? By the Legislature, in the shape of preventive action or corrective statutes; by the Executive, in the shape of force; or by the Judiciary, in the shape of Court decisions, in cases involving State laws?"[101] Writing to Nicholas Trist (Jefferson's grandson-in-law) in 1831, Madison provided a similar characterization of the array of options that had faced the convention. "The obvious necessity of a controul on the laws of the States, so far as they might violate the Constitution and laws of the U.S. left no option but as to the mode. The modes presenting themselves were 1. A Veto on the passage of the State Laws. 2. A Congressional repeal of them. 3. A Judicial annulment of them."[102] Having eliminated the negative from consideration, the delegates turned their attention to other mechanisms that would mediate between state and national authority.

In the aftermath of the negative's defeat, the discussion at the convention turned toward an altogether different institutional approach. Following the demise of the federal negative, with its legislative solution to the problem of establishing a hierarchy of authorities, the delegates began to consider seriously the possibility of a judicial approach. In the words of Joseph Story, writing in 1833, the delegates sought to lodge in the general government "some effectual power" that could "restrain or correct" the states. Story described the power as "either a direct negative on the state laws, or an authority in the national courts to overrule such, as shall manifestly be in contravention to the constitution." Having thus framed the delegates' decision, Story concluded, "The latter course was thought by the convention to be preferable to the former; and it is, without question, by far the most acceptable to the states."[103] As Larry Kramer and other scholars have pointed out, the Supremacy Clause must therefore be seen as following from, and causally related to, the defeat of the negative.[104] When they adopted it in late August, the delegates intended the Supremacy Clause to do what Madison had intended the negative to do.

As Jefferson's June 20 letter suggests, the idea of a judicial approach to harmonizing state and national laws had been circulating at least since the delegates convened.[105] Most notably, the New Jersey Plan contained a provision specifying that all treaties and acts of Congress "shall be the supreme law of the respective States" and directing that state courts would therefore be bound by them.[106] In a somewhat different vein, an anonymous pamphlet published in May 1787 and attributed to John Dickinson advocated the establishment of an "Equalizing Court" that would provide a forum in which states could challenge congressional acts (and, in what Dickinson implied was a secondary function, Congress could challenge state acts). Dickinson's proposal envisioned the Equalizing Court as "an umpire between Congress and the States" to which "an aggreived [*sic*] or accused State may resort for complaint, defence, or protection."[107] Like the New Jersey Plan, Dickinson's scheme focused on creating the proper forum in which disputes between state and federal legislatures would be decided. Both plans also shared an emphasis on adjudicative proceedings, albeit with individuals as parties in the case of the New Jersey Plan and states as parties in Dickinson's plan. And, unlike Madison's negative, these approaches rejected the Privy Council's practice of ex ante legislative review, instead placing the burden to challenge a particular state law on the aggrieved parties.

Madison, however, argued throughout the debates that judicial review alone could not stave off all state legislation that encroached on the national authority or that interfered with other states' laws. With Wilson, he objected to the New Jersey Plan's proposal to vest state courts with the power to decide cases involving national laws.[108] As he wrote in his October 24 letter to Jefferson, "[I]t is more convenient to prevent the passage of a law, than to declare it void after it is passed." Madison thus clearly still conceived of the negative's effect as rendering state legislation void ab initio, preventing it from becoming a law in the first instance rather than nullifying it after the fact. As for placing the burden to challenge an act on aggrieved individuals, Madison was dismissive. "[A]

State which would violate the Legislative rights of the Union, would not be very ready to obey a Judicial decree in support of them." He feared that such intransigence on the part of a state would ultimately lead to a violent confrontation between state and national power—precisely the catastrophe that his proposal had aimed to prevent. Such a "recurrence to force, which in the event of disobedience would be necessary, is an evil which the new Constitution meant to exclude as far as possible."[109] The prospect of building force into the Constitution as a last resort dismayed Madison, who had considered but ultimately rejected coercion as a tactic as early as the first meeting of the convention.[110]

By sounding the death knell for the federal negative, the July 17 vote raised the possibility of a judicial rather than a legislative remedy to the problem of competing state and national authorities. According to Madison's notes, immediately following the vote on the negative, Luther Martin introduced a resolution containing language based on the New Jersey Plan. Martin's resolution provided "that the Legislative acts of the U.S. made by virtue & in pursuance of the articles of Union, and all treaties made and ratified under the authority of the U.S. shall be the supreme law of the respective States, as far as those acts or treaties shall relate to the said States, or their Citizens and inhabitants—& that the Judiciaries of the several States shall be bound thereby in their decisions, any thing in the respective laws of the individual States to the contrary notwithstanding."[111] The resolution passed unanimously. Despite the defeat of the New Jersey Plan, its approach to the issue of national authority had triumphed. With the approval on August 23 of John Rutledge's proposal to replace the phrase "the Articles of Union" with the words "[t]his Constitution" and to relocate this reference to the national charter to the beginning of the paragraph, the provision that would become the Supremacy Clause passed into the document that would become the Constitution.[112]

Significantly, many delegates seem to have been willing to consider judicial review by this point in the convention. As Lawrence Sager has highlighted, on August 27—four days after the delegates had agreed on the final language of the Supremacy Clause—they revisited and retooled the description of the Supreme Court's powers in what would become Article III of the Constitution.[113] The jurisdictional language of the judiciary article was edited to conform to the language of the Supremacy Clause. For example, the delegates added the phrase "under this Constitution" to expand the Supreme Court's jurisdiction to include cases that were based on constitutional claims. In this way, the judiciary article was "tailored to facilitate Supreme Court enforcement" of the Supremacy Clause.[114] The Supremacy Clause, therefore, defined the final language of Article III.

Moreover, the clause's significance for vertical judicial review was clear to the delegates. In the words of Pierce Butler of South Carolina, the Constitution established a "Judiciary to be Supreme in all matters relating to the General Government, and Appellate in State Controversies."[115] The clause thus created formal authority in the central government, as well as giving that authority an institutional home in the judiciary. The Supremacy Clause, then, represented a shift in the delegates' attitude toward the problem of multilayered authorities. With the negative, Madison had offered a mechanism that adapted British imperial practice to the decidedly unimperial project of embracing multiplicity. By adopting the Supremacy Clause instead of the negative, the delegates turned instead toward a vision of federal authority that relied not on legislatures but on judges and courts to mediate among disparate sources of law.

On the larger issue of the relationship between American federalism and British imperial organization, another August 27 amendment to the draft constitution is striking. Following the approval of the changes that brought the judiciary article into line with the Supremacy Clause, Madison and Gouverneur Morris proposed replacing the phrase "the jurisdiction of the Supreme Court" with the phrase "the judicial power" in the article's description of the scope of the Supreme Court's power.[116] Thus instead of reading, "The Jurisdiction of the Supreme (National) Court shall extend to all Cases arising under Laws passed by the legislature of the United States" (as had an early draft), the language of the judiciary article as approved in late August read, "The judicial power shall extend to all cases . . . arising under this constitution, the laws of the United States, and treaties made, or which shall be made, under their authority." The proposal passed immediately, without opposition.[117] As Julius Goebel noted with respect to this change, "To speak of jurisdiction in terms of national power and not of a court was a noteworthy extension of the base of judicial authority."[118] Thus extended, judicial authority in the new republic would be qualitatively different from the judicial authority that had underpinned Britain's American empire.

Although the contours of judicial review remained uncertain and controversial for much of the early republican period, its ascendance in the aftermath of the negative's defeat suggests that many delegates viewed it as an explicit tool to mediate among levels of government.[119] This was a decided change from the more ad hoc species of judicial review that the Privy Council exercised. The Privy Council's power of judicial review followed from the council's role as an agent of royal prerogative, but the American mode of review was premised on a more fundamental relationship between judicial review and the nation itself. Federal judicial review depended on a court, to be sure, but a court that stood for—while also creating—the judicial power of the nation itself. Imperial review, whether legislative or judicial, was fairly modest in that it directed parties to seek a remedy through existing institutions: send the law in question to the Privy Council, and the Privy Council will say whether it is repugnant to the laws of England. Federal review under the Supremacy Clause, in contrast, would subject the state law in question not to a mere court, but to an entirely separate and distinct level of government, which would be embodied in, but not confined to, the Supreme Court. The power of this court would originate in the power of the nation itself, from which the court would derive authority to police the states.

The Supremacy Clause was thus an explicit statement about the nature of the relationship between state and national levels of government. Rather than depending on formal legal *structure* (the Privy Council's power to nullify colonial acts, Congress's power to veto state laws), the federal union would be kept in balance by a constitutional provision that actually invoked a category of *law*—namely, the "supreme law of the land." Rather than looking to a single institution to enforce this balance, the framers envisioned an independent, national judicial power that would be the source of both substantive content and jurisdictional requirements. Whereas the British Empire had relied on the familiar institution of legislative power to monitor the boundaries between layers of power, the American republic would look to a novel conception of judicial authority itself that contained both substantive and procedural, jurisprudential and jurisdictional, components.

A Defective Federal Republic?

Forty-four years after the Philadelphia convention had adjourned, Madison continued to ponder the events that had led to the defeat of his prized negative. In an 1831 letter to Trist, the former president again felt compelled to take up his pen in defense of the proposal. The catalyst for this renewal of the debate was the publication in 1821 of Robert Yates's *Secret Proceedings and Debates of the Convention Assembled . . . for the Purpose of Forming the Constitution of the United States.* Prior to walking out of the convention in early July along with fellow New Yorker and Hamilton foe John Lansing, Jr., Yates had recorded notes of the debates. Yates died in 1801, but in 1821 the notes were published thanks to the efforts of Lansing and Edmond Genêt. Genêt, already infamous for his exploits as the French minister to the United States during the 1790s, had in 1808 seen fit to break the silence that had governed the delegates since the convention adjourned and had published portions of Yates's notes in pamphlet form. Genêt's motivation was hardly a charitable desire to inform the public about the proceedings in Philadelphia; rather, he hoped to aid the fortunes of his father-in-law, New York Democratic kingpin George Clinton, as Clinton campaigned against Madison for the presidency. Most scholars agree that as part of this project, Genêt altered Yates's notes to paint Madison as an extreme nationalist.[120]

Madison objected strongly to the *Secret Proceedings,* which he regarded as a deliberate attempt to smear his contributions to the convention and, consequently, to the formation of the Constitution. He seemed to take greatest umbrage—as demonstrated by the amount of space he devoted to the subject in this and other letters—at the charge that he was a consolidationist bent on giving the national government the same oppressive power that the British government had wielded over the colonies. One can almost hear Madison sighing from his study at Montpelier as, yet again, he rehearsed the logic that had led him to embrace the federal negative. The *Secret Proceedings,* he wrote, "import 'that I was disposed to give Congress a power to repeal State laws,' and 'that the States ought to be *placed under the controul of the Genl Gt* at least as much as they were formerly when under the British King & Parliament.'" He offered the following rebuttal: "The opinion that the States ought to be placed not less under the Govt of the U.S. than they were under that of G. B., can provoke no censure from those who approve the Constitution as it stands with powers exceeding those ever allowed by the colonies to G. B. particularly the vital power of taxation, which is so indefinitely vested in Congs and to the claim of which by G. B. a bloody war, and final separation was preferred."[121]

In other words, Madison argued that the Constitution as ratified gave far greater power to the general government than the British government had wielded over the colonies, especially with regard to the thorny issue of taxation.[122] The structure of national power with the negative might have been the same as the structure of imperial power, he contended, but the scope of that power was different. In any event, he seemed to say, the Constitution had rejected this structure in favor of an entirely new governmental architecture, and that federal architecture bore little resemblance to the imperial approach to the problem of establishing central authority.

Madison therefore conceded that he had modeled his federal negative on imperial practice, but he denied that he had done so as part of a larger project of consolidating national power. Freely admitting that "a negative on the laws of the States, was suggested by the negative in the head of the British Empire, which prevented collisions between the parts & the whole, and between the parts themselves," Madison agreed with his critics' assertion that the federal negative traced its origin to imperial practice.[123] But he rejected the charge that his proposal for the negative stemmed from a desire to reproduce the imperial-colonial hierarchy in the form of the new federal republic. Moreover, he scoffed at the notion that despite its defeat, the negative had somehow infected the Constitution with the germ of unidirectional, top-down political power. Nevertheless, as the controversy over Yates's *Secret Proceedings* demonstrates, nearly half a century after the Philadelphia convention—even as the mounting sectional crisis gave new urgency to balancing national and state power—some Americans continued to associate Madison with the British Empire on the basis of his theory of the federal negative.

The problem of authority was the central issue for both the British Empire and the early American republic. Madison's negative attempted to bridge these two systems, proposing a relationship between national and state authority that applied one of the empire's chief mechanisms to the new American government. He selected one strand of the Privy Council's centuries-old practice of reviewing colonial laws, a practice that offered no substantive rules of decision but rather process and structure alone, as a means of bringing wayward peripheries into line with the central authority. (Indeed, even the Privy Council's protojudicial review created little new substantive law, insofar as it purported merely to measure colonial acts against the existing laws of England.) In proposing the federal negative, Madison followed this procedural approach, emphasizing the negative as a mechanism rather than any rules of deciding whether a state law conflicted with the Constitution. In this respect, the negative shared important features with Dickinson's Equalizing Court and the Virginia Plan's Council of Revision, both of which sought refuge from state-national conflict by attempting—ultimately in vain—to create an ideal forum rather than a body of legal principles according to which cases would be decided.

Of the two components of Privy Council practice, Madison chose to emphasize legislative review rather than judicial review.[124] The Constitution, however, ultimately pointed toward the opposite choice, albeit with profound changes to give judicial review more substance than it had ever possessed under the empire.[125] The Supremacy Clause offered neither an architecture nor a forum for decisions but rather an affirmative statement about the fundamental rules of the game and the power from which those rules derived: "This Constitution, and the Laws of the United States which shall be made in Pursuance thereof; and all Treaties made, or which shall be made, under the Authority of the United States, shall be the supreme Law of the Land."[126] Taken together, the Supremacy Clause and Article III communicated that American federalism would emanate from a national judicial power and be based on a body of substantive "law of the land," indeed, the very body of substantive law that contained the Supremacy Clause.[127] The defeat of the negative thus marked an important transition from a system in which multiple levels of government existed in uneasy tension with a theoretical commitment to unitary sovereignty to a system expressly designed to mediate among multiple bases of authority.

In the federal republic, the principal institution responsible for this mediation was to be the judiciary. Immediately following the definition of "the supreme Law of the Land," the Supremacy Clause stated that "the Judges in every State shall be bound thereby, any Thing in the Constitution or Laws of any State to the Contrary notwithstanding."[128] The federal negative offered a legislative solution to the problem of co-ordinating conflicts between the levels of government, while the Supremacy Clause offered a judicial solution. This judicial approach subsequently became the basis of American federalism as federal judicial review was confirmed in the Judiciary Act of 1789 and was expounded by the Supreme Court in cases such as *Fletcher v. Peck* (1810) and *Martin v. Hunter's Lessee* (1816).[129] Although the nature and scope of the federal judiciary's role remained controversial into the nineteenth century, the fiery debates of that later period proceeded from the assumption that the judiciary was the crucial fulcrum on which the federal-state balance pivoted.

The defeat of the negative and the adoption of the Supremacy Clause heralded the arrival of an explicitly judiciary-based approach to the problem of multiple authorities. This shift in the 1780s was profoundly connected to ideological and institutional changes dating to the proto-Revolutionary debates of the 1760s. As colonists and royal governors confronted each other over the legitimacy of the Stamp Act, and as provincial assemblies and Parliament stood in altercation over the respective powers of colonial and metropolitan legislatures, a new conception of authority was emerging in British North America. At the core of many colonists' arguments lay the radical assumption that multiplicity was not evidence of a defective system of government, but rather a basis on which to build an entirely new vision of government. Massachusetts governor Thomas Hutchinson insisted in 1773 that "[i]t is impossible there should be two independent Legislatures in one and the same State, for . . . the two Legislative Bodies will make two Governments as distinct as the Kingdoms of England and Scotland before the Union."[130] The Scots-American jurist James Wilson, in contrast, argued that "all the different members of the British empire are distinct states, independent of each other, but connected together under the same sovereign in right of the same crown."[131] As these divergent views suggest, the Revolutionary period witnessed a profound conflict regarding the possibility that more than one sources of authority might legitimately exist within a single government. By 1777, when the Articles of Confederation constructed a union from fourteen separate legislatures, multiplicity had itself become a central value for many members of the founding generation. The ideology of early U.S. constitutionalism, in other words, was multiplicity.

The debate over Madison's negative was the moment in which the theories that had underpinned the Revolutionary-era debates came together with the affirmative need to build a government that took into account the reality of postcolonial America's numerous jurisdictions. The ideology of authority in British North America had changed dramatically in the 1760s and 1770s; the debate over the negative demonstrated that the structure of that authority—the form it took on the ground—was equally unsettled. One of the most pressing questions facing the delegates in Philadelphia was thus how to translate a broad commitment to multiplicity into a functioning government. Given a more or less shared conviction that a single government might contain more than one level of authority, what institutions would best allow these authorities to remain distinct while also providing for occasional interactions between them?

For Madison, the solution was to borrow the Privy Council's power to review colonial statutes, putting Congress in the place of the council as the final arbiter and enacter of state law. As with the Privy Council's process, Congress's review would operate prospectively; its approval would be necessary to complete the legislation in question, as had been the case when the council reviewed legislation from a colony with a suspending clause in its charter. Moreover, had Madison succeeded in securing the broadest possible form of the negative, granting Congress the ability to intervene "in all cases whatsoever," Congress could have blocked any state law with which it disagreed, exercising a preemptive reach far greater than the contours of the powers that were eventually allocated to Congress under Article I of the Constitution.[132] In addition to the finished Constitution's requirements of bicameral passage and presidential approval to make congressional legislation effective, Madison's proposal would have made congressional approval—in the form of silence—a prerequisite to make state legislation effective. This broadest possible negative would have inextricably bound the two levels of lawmaking power together, eliminating any meaningful distinction between the scope of congressional power, on one hand, and state legislative power, on the other.

Despite Madison's efforts, his fellow delegates ultimately decided not to adopt the compound legislative structure that the negative offered. Instead, blending the Virginia Plan's concern with national power and the New Jersey Plan's preference for courts as mediating institutions, they cobbled together a structure that in turn refined the ideology of multiplicity. This structure centered on the Supremacy Clause, which bound state-court judges to follow congressional statutes, treaties, and the Constitution itself. In contrast to the negative, courts and judges would be the mediating agents between the national and state governments, ensuring the supremacy of the general government in its particular areas of competence while minimizing the size of the shadow that national oversight cast onto the states.

Moreover, in conjunction with the enumerated powers of Article I, section 8, the solution of the Supremacy Clause joined with judicial review maintained an important degree of separation between national and state lawmaking processes. The negative implied concurrence: every matter that the states could reach and regulate could also be reached and regulated by Congress by virtue of its power to negate state laws. Reading the Supremacy Clause in conjunction with the rest of the Constitution, meanwhile, told a different, more complicated story. The Supremacy Clause identified and created a body of supreme law of the land that was, according to Article I, circumscribed along subject-specific lines such that there was no concurrence with the substantive areas of state law.

To be sure, the clause looked to judges in the states to enforce this supreme law of the land. It thus set up a procedural overlap between the two levels of government. For this reason, Bernard Bailyn describes the Supremacy Clause as "linking the states' officers, no less than the nation's officers, to the enforcement of federal law," resulting in "a functional merger of—not conflict between—the two levels of authority."[133] But Bailyn's point overlooks the change that the Supremacy Clause represented from the nearly total merger that Madison's negative entailed, with its compound state lawmaking process. Furthermore, the conflict-merger dichotomy misses the distinction that the Supremacy Clause offered between the two levels of authority as a matter of substantive law, despite the procedural overlap that followed from the involvement of the state judges. The judges might be nodes of connection between the functional levels of government, but their more significant role was as nodes of separation between the supreme (national, enumerated) law of the land and the ordinary (state) law that operated in all other contexts.[134]

The rejection of the negative and the turn toward a judiciary-centered solution to the problem of authority thus signaled a transformation in American constitutional thought. The radical concept of multiplicity that undergirded Revolutionary challenges to unitary authority had demanded robust new structures to replace the tentative efforts of the Articles of Confederation. In this way, the new ideology of multiplicity had both created and required new institutions, setting the scene for the convention's confrontation between the negative and the Supremacy Clause. With the culmination of those debates in the adoption of the Supremacy Clause and a notion (albeit sketchy) of judicial review, the idea of multiplicity found an institutional mooring in the judiciary. This coupling of multiplicity as an idea with courts as a mode of mediating among multiple levels of government in turn created a new ideology: federalism.

The central constitutional question of the late-eighteenth-century Anglo-American world was whether more than one source of governmental authority could legitimately exist within a single state—the *imperium in imperio* question. Bailyn identifies the issue as crucial to the debates surrounding the ratification of the Constitution. "The key doctrine of federalism could survive criticism only to the extent that it could somehow be distinguished from the ancient belief that *imperium in imperio* was an illogical and unresolvable solecism. So [the federalists] reexamined that old formula, took it apart, and showed not its falsity, but its irrelevance in the American situation."[135]

Although Bailyn's is a plausible functional account of the federalists' arguments, it does not answer the question of how the ideas that underlay those arguments were changing, thereby allowing the arguments to be made. On Bailyn's view, a doctrine called "federalism" emerged from the convention debates and immediately entered the fray of political discourse, and it was only the need to defend the doctrine that led its proponents to fill in its theoretical basis after the fact. Thus, according to Bailyn, federalism came into existence first, followed by its ideological underpinnings, which were largely the product of the instrumental concerns of the Constitution's advocates, such as the authors of *The Federalist.*

But this sequence misses the long development of federal ideas prior to the ratification campaign, from the colonists' assertions of the possibility of legislative multiplicity, to the convention delegates' struggles to assemble an institutional framework that could support multilayered government, to the Constitution's normative vision of multitiered authority mediated through a newly potent judiciary. Jack Greene, Mary Sarah Bilder, and other scholars argue that the British Empire was an essentially federal entity, with federalness a kind of de facto condition, contested at the time by metropolitan authorities but defined in retrospect by factors such as institutions and practices. Even if one accepts such experiential factors as the relevant criteria, however, the shift in institutional focus that took place in the late 1780s offers a counterpoint to these scholars' overarching story of imperial-to-federal continuity.

Instead of stacked legislatures generating several varieties of positive law, the combined efforts of the delegates at Philadelphia produced a judicial mode of organizing federalism that was altogether different from previous approaches to the problem of multiple authorities. The rejection of the negative and adoption of the Supremacy Clause gave state judges the power to interpret the law of the federal polity while, in the same stroke, bringing those judges under the occasional control of that polity. This judicially driven federalism was a new species of government, embracing multiplicity and giving it an institutional home in the judicial branches of both levels of government.[136] The negative's demise heralded the emergence not just of an idea but also of an ideology of multilayered authority. After more than two decades of controversy and experimentation, multiplicity was no longer an embarrassment, a pathological or dysfunctional "solecism" that had infected American government. Nor was it an uncomfortable reality at variance from political theory. On the contrary, the replacement of the mechanical negative with the spare, elliptical phrases of the Supremacy Clause signaled that multiplicity had become the defining concept of the new republic, a new normative vision distinct from past Anglo-American practice and ideology.

CHAPTER 6

Jurisdiction as the Battlefield

T HE DEFEAT OF MADISON'S NEGATIVE and the adoption by the convention of the Supremacy Clause spelled a significant transition in federal thought. Instead of focusing exclusively on legislative power, federal thinkers began discussing courts; instead of working to limn the perfect subject-matter boundary around each level of governmental authority, commentators devoted increasing attention to the concept of concurrent jurisdiction. As part of these efforts, two congressional statutes—the Judiciary Act of 1789 and the Judiciary Act of 1801—stand out as important early attempts to define the scope of federal judicial power.

Legal historians and constitutional scholars have tended to approach the judiciary acts of 1789 and 1801 as though the two statutes were separated not only by a dozen years but also by a fundamental, unbridgeable conceptual gulf. While the Judiciary Act of 1789 is celebrated as "probably the most important and the most satisfactory Act ever passed by Congress," as Justice Henry B. Brown hailed it in 1911, the Judiciary Act of 1801 is frequently regarded as a forgettable relic of early national political squabbling.[1] The storied heritage of the 1789 act began with its passage into law more than four months before the Supreme Court convened for its first session, and therefore well in advance of the date when the entire federal government can truly be said to have begun function-ing;[2] the 1801 act, in contrast, is remembered principally for a pair of controversial distinctions: first, creating the circuit courts to which President John Adams appointed the so-called midnight judges on the eve of his departure from office; and second, suffering repeal at the hands of the newly Republican Congress one year later, in the aftermath of the acrimonious election of 1800. As Kathryn Turner Preyer observed, "[A]wareness of the Act seems to have been kept alive chiefly because it must be summoned to serve as the cause of its own repeal in March 1802."[3] If the 1789 act stands for the fulfillment of the "Madisonian com-promise" reached at Philadelphia, in which the delegates agreed to post-pone the divisive issue of inferior federal courts to the First Congress, the 1801 act represents the failure of compromise, when the first party system collided with unsettled questions about the structure of the fed-eral judiciary.[4]

Clearly, the two acts have received quite disparate treatment over the course of the past two centuries. But this difference fails to take into ac-count their meaning and context in light of their shared historical mo-ment. Too often, each judiciary act has been treated as an isolated piece of legislation complete in itself rather than as an intellectual vestige of a particular moment in American legal and political discourse. But the acts have more to tell us than this. Considering the two acts as disjunc-tive and dichotomous overlooks the vital role that both statutes played in the development of American federalism. Instead of lionizing the 1789 act and attempting to excuse or dismiss the 1801 act, reading the two to-gether offers new insights into the crucial years between 1787 and 1802, when theorists and politicians turned their focus to giving meaning to the Constitution's phrase "the judicial power of the United States."

If one regards the years from 1787 to 1802 as a single period and then situates that period at the end of a larger sweep of Anglo-American con-stitutional ferment, the two judiciary acts take on new significance be-yond simply completing the founding settlement. On this view, the im-portance of the acts lies beyond their immediate consequences for the balance between state and federal judicial power, or even for the broader question of the meaning of union at the dawn of the nineteenth century. Rather, the debate over the judiciary acts implicates federal ideas in the broadest sense—that is, the specifically late-eighteenth-century/early-nineteenth-century effort to bring together multiple levels of authority within a single government while maintaining lines of demarcation between the levels. In other words, the judiciary acts must be understood as important sites for the development of federal theory, not simply as component parts in the heroic story of the construction of the modern American republic.

The passage of the judiciary acts, then, should be examined in the context of the continuing development of American federal ideas *as ideas* in the early republican period. The acts of 1789 and 1801 are vital to the story of federalism because their passage signaled a shift from legislative-focused theorizing, which had characterized the years roughly between 1765 and 1787, to a new emphasis on the role of judicial power in establishing and delineating boundaries between the levels of authority within a multilayered polity. Some scholars have pointed out the significance of the acts, especially the 1789 act, for establishing the federal judiciary in the separation-of-powers framework. Other commentators have explored the institutional role of the courts vis-à-vis other actors, such as Congress or the states, in maintaining (or, in some cases, confounding) the federal structure.[5] Rather than focusing on judicial supremacy at either the horizontal level of separation-of-powers theory or the vertical level of state-federal relations, however, my analysis seeks to situate the judiciary acts in the context of the Revolutionary and early republican struggles to construct a federal union that was more centralized than the old Confederation but less unitary in its distribution of sovereignty than the British Empire.[6] On this view, the judiciary acts should be understood not only as markers in the retrospective, modern narrative of how the United States came to have the courts that it now has, but also as experiments in fleshing out the sometimes-ill-defined scheme of federal government that had slowly been emerging in America since the 1760s.

The two acts must be seen on their own terms, as attempts by particular individuals to confront functional questions of governmental authority that more than two decades' worth of thought and debate had left unaddressed. The turn to the judiciary in 1789 represented a subtle but important departure from the prominent role that the legislature

had played in the previous several decades' theories of divided authority. Anglo-American theorists of the pre- and post-Revolutionary eras
had for the most part shared their metropolitan cousins' emphasis on
the legislative power as the most significant player in the contemporary
constitutional arrangement. Many Americans, however, declined to follow this theory to the conclusion that was increasingly gaining adherents
in Britain, among them Sir William Blackstone: that the legislature—
specifically, Parliament—possessed complete and indivisible sovereign
authority.[7] Consequently, in the transatlantic debates of the 1760s and
1770s, Anglo-Americans had begun to articulate a vision of political
authority that explored new methods of segmenting power among many
levels of legislatures rather than vesting power entirely in one supreme
legislature. In so doing, they rejected the growing orthodoxy of domestic British constitutional theory, as well as the broader applications of
that theory to the British Empire. Not until 1787, however, did the demands of the constitution-drafting process impel American thinkers to
put aside the legislative focus of their political heritage and begin experimenting with the judicial power as a key component of the federal
arrangement.

To be sure, by 1789, the notion that the judiciary might potentially
play a specific structural role in the architecture of the federal republic
remained a highly contested idea. It continued to be controversial for
many years, as the rancor surrounding the 1801 act and its repeal demonstrated. But the period beginning around 1789 differed from the colonial, Revolutionary, and ratification periods in at least one crucial respect. The final decade of the eighteenth century and the early decades
of the nineteenth century witnessed a transformation from sovereignty
to jurisdiction as the central organizing principle—and battlefield—of
American federalism.

As this chapter will demonstrate, pre- and postwar debates about the
essential nature of sovereignty—an inquiry that had occupied political
theorists since the early modern era—slowly gave way in the early republican period to a search for the proper jurisdictional arrangement to mediate between the multiple levels of government contemplated in the Constitution. This quest to find the appropriate structural mechanisms to
avoid the "solecism" of *imperium in imperio,* or a government within a

government, continued to haunt early republicans, just as it had plagued their predecessors during the Stamp Act crisis of the 1760s and the confrontations between colonial assemblies and royal governors of the 1770s.[8] But although they employed this inherited vocabulary, theorists and politicians in the 1790s and 1800s conceived of their problem not in terms of locating the initial source of governmental authority but instead as a question of delineating the boundaries among the judicial bodies that would guide the exercise of that authority. This second-generation process sought to fill in gaps and decipher hints left by the Constitutional Convention. In so doing, early republican theorists seized on Article III and the Supremacy Clause to guide their efforts to establish institutions that would carry out the federal project. The goal of this project was to build a structure to support the federal aspirations of the Constitution. The material of this structure was a theory of federal jurisdiction.

This chapter examines the rise of jurisdiction as the defining element of American federalism. Beginning around 1789, the organization of the federal judiciary became the locus of debates over both the practical and the ideological meaning of federalism. Commentators as diverse as Alexander Hamilton, Thomas Jefferson, John Marshall, Theodore Sedgwick, Joseph Story, and St. George Tucker focused on jurisdiction as they hammered out their own working understandings of federalism and confronted those of their contemporaries. This account thus challenges the assumption underlying some modern federalism scholarship that nationalization through the federal judiciary is a relatively new, post-1937 phenomenon. My argument demonstrates the anachronistic nature of such assumptions by highlighting the centrality of the judiciary in the nation's earliest debates over the scope and extent of national power. To be sure, general federal question jurisdiction, according to which federal courts had the power to hear a broad category of cases arising under the Constitution, federal statutes, or treaties, did not become a stable fixture of American law until 1875. That date does not mean, however, that for the previous eighty-six years a consensus had held that the scope of federal courts' jurisdiction was limited, and properly so. On the contrary, viewing the expansion of federal jurisdiction as purely a post-Reconstruction or a twentieth-century phenomenon ignores important early republican antecedents to those later developments.

Defining the Judicial Power, 1787–1789:
Convention and Constitution

The period between 1787 and 1802 witnessed a transformation in American constitutional discourse from the language of legislative power and sovereignty to that of judicial power and jurisdiction. In order to see this subtle but fundamental transformation in early national modes of thought, we must in a sense undomesticate the judiciary acts by examining them outside the familiar tropes of, on the one hand, the state-versus-federal dichotomy that often preoccupies American constitutional history and, on the other hand, twentieth- and twenty-first-century debates over the scope of modern federal courts' jurisdiction. Without question, those debates are important, and they occupy a deservedly central place in constitutional law and federal courts scholarship.[9] But in order to comprehend the significance of the judiciary acts for the historical narrative of federalism's origins, a wider perspective is necessary. This perspective begins with an inquiry into the particular legal and political context in which the acts were created.

When the First Congress convened in April 1789, fifty-four of the congressmen and senators had recently served as members of the Constitutional Convention or of the state ratification conventions.[10] As part of those earlier deliberations, the members had been involved in discussions concerning two measures that had emerged in the course of the debates at Philadelphia and that shaped the role of the judiciary in the new republic. Although the provisions had different aims, taken together, they suggested that judicial institutions would feature prominently in the new government that was being cobbled together.

The first such measure, the so-called Madisonian compromise, consisted of a provision that "the National Legislature be empowered to institute inferior tribunals"; the measure was adopted by the convention on June 5, 1787, after substantial debate.[11] It was a compromise in that it staved off a motion by John Rutledge of South Carolina to delete all references to inferior federal courts from the draft constitution, but it did not go as far as mandating the establishment of inferior federal courts, as had been proposed in Edmund Randolph's Virginia Plan or South Carolinian Charles Pinckney's draft constitution.[12] Instead, the compromise was incorporated into Article III, which vested the "judicial Power of the United States" in "one supreme Court, and in such inferior Courts as the Congress may from time to time establish."[13]

In addition to the Madisonian compromise, which established the potential for, but not the certainty of, inferior federal courts, the delegates at Philadelphia and in the state ratifying conventions engaged in a related debate that concerned not the horizontal relationship between Congress and lower federal courts but instead the vertical interaction between the general government and the states. Madison and other delegates such as Pinckney and James Wilson of Pennsylvania feared that the states might continue the unruly and independent behavior that they had displayed throughout the 1780s. A government capable of accommodating multiple levels of authority had been many colonists' desideratum since the 1760s, but the disorder of the 1780s forced observers to reconsider the structure of this multitiered polity. How might the state legislatures be checked in their rush to issue paper currency, pass debtor-relief laws, deny the provisions of the peace treaty with Britain, and otherwise follow state rather than larger, national interests?[14] Madison and some of his convention colleagues believed that a mechanism had to be found by which the states might be both restrained from exploiting each other and coaxed into aligning their interests with those of the Union.

As the previous chapter discussed, the mechanism that the delegates settled on was a bold statement of federal supremacy that emerged more or less simultaneously with the demise of Madison's negative.[15] In contrast to the negative, which had embraced a legislative solution to the problem of mediating between the levels of authority within the federal republic, the Supremacy Clause presented the judiciary as a potential site of intergovernmental ordering. In this way, the clause addressed Madison's twin goals, as he subsequently described them in a letter to Jefferson: "1. to prevent encroachments on the General authority. 2. to prevent instability and injustice in the legislation of the States."[16] By identifying "the Laws of the United States" as the "supreme Law of the Land," which would in turn bind the "Judges in every State," the clause spoke the language of court-made law. One reads the Supremacy Clause and thinks of the interpretation of law through processes of adjudication, not the creation of law through the legislative process.

The evidence suggests that at least some members of the founding generation believed that the shift from the negative to the Supremacy Clause as a key federalism-enforcing mechanism meant that the Supreme Court very likely possessed the power to review actions by both state legislatures and state courts.[17] For Thomas Jefferson, allowing an injured party to appeal from a state court to a federal court was preferable to building an ex ante system of legislative review into the Constitution.[18] On the floor of the convention, delegates such as Gouverneur Morris similarly argued that the alternative to the negative was case-by-case review by courts.[19]

But this vision of the judicial power of the United States concerned only the Supreme Court. It said nothing about the lower federal courts that Congress might eventually choose to establish, and therefore it provided no clear picture of what the full judicial power of the United States might look like. Explication of those issues awaited the First Congress, where the veterans of the ratification debates and their colleagues together took up the question that, among a host of divisive issues that had vexed the Constitutional Convention, had been postponed to be dealt with by the legislature.

In the nineteen months between the end of the convention and the first meeting of Congress, the subject of inferior federal courts generated prolonged and intense discussion. During the ratification debates in the states, pamphlets and speeches had focused on the issue as one of the key sites of dispute between supporters and opponents of the new constitution.[20] The fervor with which commentators attacked the question of the federal courts suggests that they regarded jurisdictional decisions as central to defining the new republic.

Indeed, the provisions of the Constitution concerning the judicial power gave rise to some of the most vehement disagreements between Federalists and Anti-Federalists. The establishment of the Supreme Court proved relatively uncontroversial.[21] The prospect of an entirely new echelon of federal courts in addition to the Supreme Court, however, tested many observers' deepest constitutional commitments. In *The Federalist* No. 81, Alexander Hamilton argued that inferior federal courts ought to be viewed merely as ancillae of the Supreme Court and not as independent forces of consolidation. Calling the establishment of federal district courts "highly expedient and useful," Hamilton concluded, "This plan appears to me at present the most eligible of any that could be adopted."[22] A few weeks later, John Marshall offered Virginia's ratifying convention a practical argument for the new courts: "Does not every Gentleman here know, that the causes in our Courts are more numerous than they can decide, according to their present construction?" The future chief justice then exhorted his colleagues to "[l]ook at the dockets. You will find them crowded with suits, which the life of man will not see determined."[23]

But strong voices such as that of Maryland's Luther Martin lambasted the plan. Permitting Congress to appoint inferior courts "would eventually *absorb* and *swallow* up the *State judiciaries* by drawing all business from them to the courts of the general government, which the *extensive* and *undefined* powers, legislative and judicial, of which it is possessed, would *easily enable* it to do."[24] George Mason of Virginia, meanwhile, feared potential expansion of federal power under Article III. "The inferior Courts are to be as numerous as Congress may think proper," he warned. "Read the 2d section, and contemplate attentively the jurisdiction of these Courts; and consider if there be any limits to it."[25]

Controversy over the establishment of the inferior federal courts thus swelled during the ratification period, with each side in the debate invoking the first sentence of Article III ("The judicial Power of the United States, shall be vested in one supreme Court, and in such inferior Courts as the Congress may from time to time ordain and establish") as evidence of either Philadelphian prudence or consolidationist connivance.[26] Few observers could have been surprised, then, when on April 7, 1789, the First Congress took up the issue as its first item of business. Throughout the spring and summer of 1789, public attention was fixed on Federal Hall in Wall Street. Virginia congressman Alexander White commented in a letter to Madison, "At the inns on the road, I was surprised to find the knowledge which the landlords, and the country people who were at some of them, had acquired of the debates and proceedings of Congress."[27]

Believing themselves to be crafting one of the new nation's foundational institutions, members of Congress brought strong convictions and a sense of gravity to the drafting and passage of the 1789 act.[28] A Senate committee with ten members (one from each state that had ratified the Constitution and sent senators by that point) produced a first version of the bill, which the committee circulated to select attorneys and officials for comment during the summer of 1789.[29] On July 17, the Senate approved the bill by a vote of fourteen to six. The House of Representatives, which had been occupied drafting the amendments that formed the basis of the Bill of Rights, took up the judiciary bill on August 24. After extensive debate—much of it concerning the propriety of establishing inferior federal courts at all—and the addition of fifty-two amendments, the House passed the bill on September 17 by a vote of thirty-seven to sixteen. The House and the Senate then conducted speedy negotiations on some of the amendments before sending the bill to President Washington, who signed it into law on September 24.

The most important provisions of the act for our purposes centered on two structural aspects: the jurisdiction of the Supreme Court and the organization and powers of the inferior federal courts, which the act broke down into the two categories of district courts and circuit courts. As students of *Marbury v. Madison* will recall, the act sought to grant certain heads of original jurisdiction to the Court in addition to those contained in Article III. The act also established the Court's appellate jurisdiction, which extended to the lower federal courts, as well as the state courts.[30] Despite the later importance of section 25's grant to the Court of the power to review state-court decisions, as demonstrated in such cases as *Martin v. Hunter's Lessee* and *Cohens v. Virginia*, in 1789 this provision generated less debate than did the architecture of inferior federal courts that the act set up.[31]

The structure of the lower federal courts consisted of two parts: (1) thirteen district courts (one for each of the eleven states that had then ratified the Constitution, plus Maine and Kentucky, which at that time were still part of Massachusetts and Virginia, respectively), each with its own district judge; and (2) three circuit courts, each requiring a quorum of two justices of the Supreme Court and the district judge of the particular district in which the court was sitting at a given time. The district courts possessed exclusive jurisdiction over admiralty cases and cases involving minor federal crimes, as well as concurrent jurisdiction with the circuit and state courts with respect to certain tort suits by aliens and certain suits by the United States. The circuit courts' original jurisdiction, meanwhile, extended to "all suits of a civil nature at common law or in equity, where the matter in dispute exceeds . . . the sum or value of five hundred dollars, and the United States are plaintiffs, or petitioners; or an alien is a party, or the suit is between a citizen of the State where the suit is brought, and a citizen of another State." Although this jurisdiction was original, however, it was not exclusive but rather concurrent with the state courts. In addition, the circuit courts were given exclusive jurisdiction over all major federal crimes and appellate jurisdiction with respect to district-court cases.[32] Thus, in the words of Julius Goebel, "If the District Courts were viewed primarily as courts of special jurisdiction, the Circuit Courts were erected as courts of general original jurisdiction."[33]

As many modern commentators have noted, the 1789 act did not grant general federal question jurisdiction to the inferior federal courts. Indeed, Congress did not decisively embrace the modern, broadened version of federal question jurisdiction until 1875.[34] To twentieth- and twenty-first-century eyes, this is a startling fact.[35] But this sense of surprise results from the assumption that the Judiciary Act of 1789 belongs only to our own age rather than also to the late eighteenth century. After all, the language seems familiar: the act introduced district courts and circuit courts, access to federal courts for cases between citizens of different states(diversity jurisdiction), amount-in-controversy requirements, and many other staples of a modern course in federal courts. As the foregoing discussion illustrates, however, these were not "our" district courts or circuit courts. One need only consider the lack of a circuit-court bench, the relative autonomy of the district courts, and the absence of the type of firm appellate hierarchy that exists today to grasp how different the federal courts of 1789 were from those of today.

This pervasive sense of surprise is useful, however, because it demonstrates the importance of historicizing the judiciary act. The question "Why did Congress not grant general federal question jurisdiction until 1875?" gets the analysis backward. A better, less teleological approach might be to ask, "Why did Congress grant federal question jurisdiction in 1875?"—or, indeed, "Did Congress attempt to grant federal question jurisdiction before 1875?" Such questions permit a more expansive view of the impetus behind the 1789 act, as well as a richer, more contextualized picture of constitutional thought in the early Republic, because they provide a means to connect the 1789 act with the 1801 act—which did, in fact, establish general federal question jurisdiction, albeit only temporarily. The 1801 act's modern identity as an item of trivia in a federal courts course could not seem more remote from the grave attention with which the 1789 act is greeted by scholars, law students, and constitutional commentators generally. But the Judiciary Act of 1801 and, perhaps even more important, the vituperative political debate that preceded it in the 1790s are important precisely because they remind us of the essential foreignness of jurisdiction theory in the early Republic. Federal jurisdiction is an idea, and like all ideas, it had a before and an after, a time when it did not exist and a later time when it did.

Even before President Washington signed the Judiciary Act of 1789 into law, supporters and critics alike had begun to wonder aloud whether a better system might be possible. Madison termed the act "pregnant with difficulties, not only as relating to a part of the constitution which has been most criticised, but being in its own nature peculiarly complicated & embarrassing."[36] (When the bill came before the House a few weeks later, however, Madison spoke in its favor; according to published reports, the delegate from Virginia argued that "[t]he bill may not exactly suit any one member of the House, in all its parts—but it is as good as we can at present make it.")[37] The Anti-Federalist Elbridge Gerry, who represented Massachusetts in the First Congress, said of the judiciary, "[T]his department I dread as an awful tribunal." He cited the federal courts' broad jurisdiction over common-law, equity, and admiralty cases, as well as the potential for abuse of power by judges who could not be removed by Congress.[38]

In keeping with the controversy that had surrounded the drafting of the act, within a year of its passage, two reform plans were proposed. In December 1790, in response to a request from the House, Attorney General Edmund Randolph submitted a report containing recommendations for restructuring the federal judiciary. Randolph's report was followed just over two months later by a set of amendments to Article III drawn up by New York congressman Egbert Benson. Neither reform plan made much headway; on the contrary, both ended their days by languishing in committee. Randolph's plan attracted substantial press notice, however, suggesting that at least some portion of the public was interested in judicial reform.[39] Both plans will be discussed at greater length later.

Concurrence: Drawing Lines, Again

The intellectual transition from defining questions of political and legal authority in terms of sovereignty to defining them in terms of jurisdiction manifested itself most profoundly in the decade following the passage of the Judiciary Act of 1789. In early September of that year, a few weeks before the act became law, Massachusetts congressman Fisher Ames sent a letter to his friend John Lowell (soon to become federal judge for the newly created district of Massachusetts) in which Ames detailed a speech that he had recently delivered on the House floor. Ames's remarks included the following passage: "What is jurisdiction? Authority to judge, derived from a superior power___ The law of the U.S. is the law of the land, but not the law of a state___ . . . Many tell me, the state judges must decide according to law, & the offences &c are defined by law. . . . If we ascend to the first principles of the Judicia[l] power, I think we shall find them analogous to my doctrine."[40] Ames clearly regarded jurisdiction as the fundamental currency of the federal republic and an ordered system of jurisdiction as the sine qua non of that republic's success. And what was jurisdiction, in Ames's view? "Authority to judge, derived from a superior power"—in other words, court-based authority, the source of which was a still higher level of power.

Ames's comments are, it must be said, somewhat elliptical, but they demonstrate the degree to which the concept of jurisdiction occupied the thoughts of politicians and theorists by 1789.[41] The debates of the 1790s, which led to the passage of the Judiciary Act of 1801, centered on a pair of related themes. Both concerned the vertical distribution of authority between the states and the federal government—or, more broadly, between the component entities and the general government in a federal structure. The two themes were, first, the notion of concurrent jurisdiction, according to which bodies at multiple levels of government had the power to hear cases on a given topic or involving a given type of party; and second, the possibility of vesting the lowest-level authorities with the power and duty to carry out the commands of higher-level authorities. In the 1790s, then, commentators explored the possibilities of embracing concurrent jurisdiction in state and federal courts, as well as designating the state courts essentially as inferior federal courts.

In one sense, these were new issues. As subjects of the British Empire, Americans had devoted most of their political attention not to institutional arrangements within a largely agreed-upon system but rather to challenging the fundamental nature of the system itself. Thus in their efforts to rebut the hegemonic system of empire on which metropolitan authorities insisted, members of the colonial opposition had cobbled together an alternative vision of compound government that would come to be called "federalism." Early republicans, meanwhile, viewed their main task as settling on the mechanisms by which the new federal system would be maintained—a no less important or potentially acrimonious dispute, for the system was so new that its structure would in important respects determine its substance.

In another sense, however, the questions presented quandaries similar to those that had occupied the colonial opposition since the imperial struggles of the 1760s and 1770s. The crucial issue no longer concerned the nature of sovereignty in a compound political entity, but instead the new variable of jurisdiction—Ames's "authority to judge"—and its allocation among the United States' hard-won multiple sovereigns. Perhaps, then, it is not surprising that early republicans thought about these problems through some of the same intellectual lenses that had served them during the intraimperial conflict. As we will see, when Americans in the 1790s considered how best to arrange their multilayered authorities, they frequently returned to the familiar notions of *imperium in imperio* and line drawing that had informed colonial discussions.

The idea of concurrent jurisdiction was absolutely central to the early national efforts to theorize what federalism meant in practice. Yet various observers used the term in different senses that proceeded from distinct understandings of the appropriate baseline distribution of authority between the federal government and the states. At times, "concurrence" seems to have referred to very broad notions of how to manage multiple sovereigns operating within the same space; at other times, the term referred to a more finely grained vision of the institutional distribution of authority among various levels of courts and legislatures. Moreover, contemporaries disagreed over the direction of the sharing of power. Was concurrence in effect when an all-powerful general government allowed states to exercise some authority over federal issues, as Alexander Hamilton argued? Or was it the opposite situation, in which a state granted some of its plenary power to the general government, as Thomas Jefferson maintained? Although the meaning of concurrence remained contested throughout the early republican period, the term—and the basic concept of overlapping power—informed theorists on all sides of the debate.

The term "concurrence" referred in this context to a structure in which multiple levels of government within a single polity possessed overlapping authority to regulate, legislate, or adjudicate. This was the sense in which Hamilton employed the label in *The Federalist* No. 32. Addressing the Constitution's grant to Congress of the power to "lay and collect Taxes, Duties, Imposts and Excises," Hamilton reassured skeptics that the states would nonetheless retain the "independent and uncontrolable [*sic*] authority to raise their own revenues for the supply of their own wants"—a power that had been central to the colonies' claims of independence since the 1760s. Because the Constitution "aims only at a partial Union or consolidation," Hamilton reasoned, the states necessarily retained "all of the rights of sovereignty which they before had" and which were not by the Constitution "*exclusively* delegated to the United States." The consequence of this arrangement would, Hamilton concluded, mean that in certain areas—such as taxation of "all articles other than exports and imports"—citizens might be subject to "a concurrent and coequal authority in the United States and in the individual States."[42] In other words, not all powers associated with the federal government were vested exclusively in the federal government.

Since the 1760s, the taxation issue had implicated questions about overlapping, or concurrent, legislative powers. By 1789, however, the debate had shifted to include concurrent judicial power. Here, too, Hamilton, writing as Publius, had something to say. In *The Federalist* No. 82, Hamilton took up the question of the relationship between the state courts and the federal courts. (Note that at the time at which Hamilton was writing, the federal courts consisted only of the Supreme Court; however, Hamilton's reference to "the national tribunals" suggests that he, like many of his contemporaries, assumed that the First Congress would indeed establish inferior federal courts.)[43] Here again, Hamilton was sanguine about the prospects for concurrent jurisdiction. Reading Article III, section 1, as a nonexclusive description of the "organs" through which the federal judicial power was to be exercised, Hamilton argued that the states retained jurisdiction "of causes of which the state courts have previous cognizance." This concurrence did not extend, however, to "cases which may grow out of, and be *peculiar* to the constitution to be established." The guiding principle for Hamilton, then, was that the state courts might permissibly hear cases "arising under the laws of the union," as long as the Constitution or an act of Congress did not expressly commit that class of case to the federal courts.[44]

Hamilton's justifications for this concurrent judicial power are interesting because they represent a subtle but important shift from the pre-Revolutionary vision of the proper allocation of authority in a federal government. Beginning in the 1760s, colonists had objected to increased taxation and regulation by Parliament on the basis of their belief that such measures violated what they regarded as the essential structure of the imperial union. That structure, the colonists argued, did not depend on the territory-based view of authority on which metropolitan officials insisted, and which maintained that the colonies were integrated into the British dominions and therefore were subject to the full range of regulation by Parliament. Rather, Anglo-Americans argued for a subject-matter conception of political and legal power that allocated jurisdiction among multiple governmental actors (in their case, between Parliament and the colonies' own assemblies), depending on the particular thing or activity to be regulated.

By embracing concurrent powers as a natural consequence of the Constitution's structure, Hamilton implied that this strict demarcation along subject-matter lines might not be relevant to the new republic. Indeed, his formulation of the jurisdiction question did not refer at all to the separation of authority that had obtained within the British Empire. Rather, his description of those powers suggested a certain degree of ambiguity, at least with respect to concurrent state- and federal-court jurisdiction. State courts might permissibly take cognizance of cases arising under federal law, Hamilton stated, as long as the state had jurisdiction over the persons of the parties. "The judiciary power of every government looks beyond its own local or municipal laws, and in civil cases lays hold of all subjects of litigation between parties within its jurisdiction though the causes of dispute are relative to the laws of the most distant part of that globe," he wrote in *The Federalist* No. 82. "Those of Japan not less than of New-York may furnish the objects of legal discussion to our courts."[45]

According to this line of analysis, subject matter was irrelevant; the only pertinent consideration for a court was whether the parties were physically within its jurisdiction. Such a regime would necessarily lead to overlaps and would therefore run afoul of the parallelism principle articulated by prewar colonial commentators.[46] But Hamilton took a slightly different approach when he argued that the Supreme Court would necessarily possess appellate jurisdiction over state-court cases involving federal law. "The objects of appeal, not the tribunals from which it is to be made, are alone contemplated" when determining whether a case was eligible for appeal to the Supreme Court, Hamilton wrote.[47] Here, then, the relevant criterion was that the case arose under the law of the United States, not the largely happenstance fact of the geographic location in which it originated. Subject-matter questions were thus largely irrelevant to Hamilton for purposes of expanding state-court jurisdiction to include federal causes of action, but they were dispositive in determining the scope of the Supreme Court's jurisdiction.

The interest in exploring at least the possibility of concurrence as a basis for the federal republic therefore set the constitutional debates of the ratification and early republican periods apart from those of the

1760s and 1770s. Whereas many colonists had resisted concurrence and pressed for subject-matter-specific boundaries between local and metropolitan authorities, Hamilton and other commentators in 1787 treated overlapping boundaries between states and the federal government as a potential means of granting a measure of power to the states. This may seem counterintuitive; after all, the colonists viewed concurrence not as an opportunity to stake their claim to a piece of the larger government but as a transfer of power back to Westminster. How, then, could Hamilton present concurrence as an acknowledgment of the states' "primitive jurisdiction"?[48] Consider again his statement in *The Federalist* No. 32: "[T]he plan of the Convention aims only at a partial Union or consolidation," and therefore "the State Governments would clearly retain all the rights of sovereignty which they before had and which were not by that act *exclusively* delegated to the United States."[49] In a world such as that of the 1760s and 1770s, where the central controversy concerned not membership in and control of a central government but independence from that government, concurrence provided a means for the center to overreach itself and exert power over the provinces. But perhaps in the world of 1787, where complete union or consolidation appeared to be a possibility, retaining concurrent jurisdiction might reasonably be construed as a victory for the states.[50]

Still, one important difference between the colonial and the early republican discussions of concurrence was the institutional focus of each. Whereas the colonists devoted themselves to analyzing competing legislative claims to power (the provincial assemblies versus Parliament), commentators in the ratification period and afterward increasingly emphasized the judicial side of concurrence. Hamilton's analysis in *The Federalist* contemplated both species of concurrence. Increasingly after 1789, however, the drive to establish the inferior federal courts shifted the emphasis of structural discussions away from issues of legislative competition, with their colonial resonance, and toward the new problem of organizing multiple judiciaries within a single overarching polity. The advent of the lower federal courts added new urgency to this inquiry. Thus by 1803, Virginia jurist St. George Tucker could observe that the "grand boundary" that "mark[ed] the obvious limits between the federal and state jurisdictions" coexisted with "some few cases, where, by a special provision contained in the constitution either concurrent, or exclusive, jurisdiction is granted to the federal government."[51] Notably, in contrast to Hamilton's view, Tucker's vision of concurrence amounted to a special invitation to the federal courts, not the state courts, to take jurisdiction over a select group of cases. The two theorists thus differed in their baseline assumptions about which level of courts was the norm and which the exception, but they both presented some degree of judicial concurrency as necessary to the larger federal system.

But the fact that concurrence was a frequent topic of discussion in the ratification period does not mean that contemporaries had uniformly warm regard for it. Some observers opposed any form of concurrence, believing that any overlap between the state and federal judiciaries would only lead to confusion and either centralization or disintegration, depending on the observer's particular array of anxieties about federalism. Virginia judge Joseph Jones wrote to Madison in July 1789 to note his discomfort with the draft judiciary bill, which he believed muddied rather than clarified the relationships among the various courts. "[T]he different powers and jurisdictions of the Courts would have been more clearly seen had they been taken up in several bills, each describing the province and boundary of the Court to which it particularly applied." But his objections extended beyond the form of the bill. To Jones, even the act's few references to the state courts (section 9's language regarding concurrent jurisdiction with state courts for cases involving tort claims by aliens in violation of the law of nations or a treaty and section 25's provision regarding appeals to the Supreme Court) obscured the true scope of the federal courts' reach. "[W]here there is danger of clashing jurisdictions, the limits should be defined as acurately [*sic*] as may be, and this danger will exist where there are concurrent jurisdictions."[52] Congressman John Brown, who represented the Kentucky district of Virginia, sounded a similar note of caution, describing his fear that "great difficulties will arise from the concurrent Jurisdiction of the Federal with the State Court, which will unavoidably occasion great embarrassment & clashing." Despite sharing Madison's concern about "embarrassment," Brown arrived at a guarded endorsement of the act, calling it "as good I believe as we at present could make it."[53]

Edmund Randolph's 1790 plan to amend the 1789 act, meanwhile, offered reforms while also attempting to correct some of the act's ambiguities concerning concurrence. As has been noted, the attorney general's proposals failed to gain sufficient support to be adopted. Nevertheless, they demonstrate the ways in which observers were working to reconceptualize and reconfigure jurisdiction in the years following the passage of the 1789 act. Randolph's scheme offered several significant changes to the structure erected by the act. First, his plan whittled away the states' jurisdiction over nominally federal matters to such a degree that concurrent authority was rendered virtually nonexistent. As Maeva Marcus notes, Randolph's "central premise" was that "federal and state jurisdictions should be completely separate."[54] From this premise followed a much more sweeping grant of authority to the district and circuit courts, as well as language that explicitly stripped the state courts of the power to take cognizance of several of the most common federal causes of action.

The plan's broad grant to the inferior federal courts included original jurisdiction "of all cases in law and equity, arising . . . [under] the Constitution of the United States . . . [t]he laws of the United States . . . and [t]reaties made, or which shall be made under their authority."[55] In other words, Randolph sought to vest the lower federal courts with the full range of original jurisdiction under Article III—that is, general federal question jurisdiction.[56] State courts, meanwhile, were expressly prohibited from hearing a number of types of cases, including admiralty and maritime cases, cases in which the United States or a particular state was a defendant (except in case of consent by the state), cases involving land grants by different states, treason cases, federal criminal cases (in the absence of a specific congressional provision establishing state courts' jurisdiction), and cases involving congressionally created rights with federal remedies. Moreover, an apparent narrowing of the Supreme Court's power to review state-court decisions accompanied this expansion of the lower federal courts' jurisdiction, although the precise contours of the restriction were not entirely clear.[57]

Randolph's proposals appear to have confounded his contemporaries. Alfred Moore, a future justice of the Supreme Court, remarked to North Carolina senator Samuel Johnston that "there appears an utter confusion in Mr Attorney's Ideas." Moore noted in particular the apparent conflict between Randolph's claim that "the State Courts ought to be *excluded* [from federal jurisdiction] because *not under the Control* of the federal Courts" and his claim that the state courts' proceedings "are in some instances subject to the federal Judiciary, because that Judiciary must *ex natura rei* control determinations that counteract the operation of the Constitution."[58]

Despite these apparent ambiguities, Randolph's plan is important because it demonstrates the degree to which the scope and nature of federal jurisdiction remained a contested issue in the 1790s. Furthermore, the proposal clearly shows that Randolph endorsed an expanded vision of "arising under" jurisdiction at the same time that he was struggling to articulate clearer boundaries between federal and state courts than those set forth in the 1789 act.[59] In this way, Randolph's plan eschewed the relatively welcoming attitude toward concurrent jurisdiction that Hamilton had adopted in his *Federalist* essays and moved instead toward a notion of the judicial power of the United States as something extraordinary and perhaps beyond the ken of state courts.

Of course, Randolph's plan did not mandate that cases arising under the laws of the United States fell exclusively within the jurisdiction of the federal courts; the report merely stated that the lower federal courts possessed original jurisdiction over such cases. This capacious view of the federal judicial power, however, harked back to the subject-matter-driven analyses of the 1760s and 1770s insofar as it looked not to the nature of the parties or the jurisdiction in which their case arose but rather to the character of the claim at issue. Randolph's conception thus also represented a shift away from the 1789 act's focus on the parties' identity or location and toward the underlying subject of the cause of action as decisive of jurisdiction.[60] In other words, the jurisdictional lines drawn by the attorney general resembled the prewar notion of sovereignty as attaching to specific subjects of regulation.

In addition to contemplating concurrent arrangements, in which the judicial powers of the federal and state governments overlapped, some theorists in the 1790s considered whether the state courts could themselves be integrated into the emerging judicial structure. In this scenario, the state courts would in effect function as inferior federal courts.

The idea had circulated since the Philadelphia and ratifying conventions; after all, the language of the Supremacy Clause stated that "the Judges in every State" were to be bound by "the supreme Law of the Land."[61] Because the state courts were thus already obliged to follow and enforce the laws of the United States, the argument ran, inferior federal courts were not necessary to the constitutional structure; on the contrary, Congress could permissibly refrain from establishing such courts altogether.

Such an argument appealed especially to Anti-Federalists who worried that the creation of inferior federal courts amounted to the thin edge of the nationalizing wedge, intruding and encroaching on the reserved powers of the states. Indeed, outspoken critics of broad national power such as Luther Martin had initially supported the Supremacy Clause precisely because they believed that its reliance on state courts threatened less intrusion on state prerogatives than did the federal negative.[62] "[W]hat is there left to the State Courts?" George Mason inquired of his colleagues in the Virginia ratifying convention as they debated Article I's grant to Congress of the power to establish inferior federal courts. "When we consider the nature of these Courts, we must conclude, that their effect and operation will be utterly to destroy the state governments. . . . The discrimination between their judicial power and that of the States, exists, therefore, but in name."[63] For Mason and others who advocated a general government with circumscribed powers, the prospect of swelling ranks of federal courts—with concomitant growth in claims of federal jurisdiction—threatened nothing less than "the annihilation of the state judiciaries."[64]

In the 1790s, following ratification, some commentators continued to make the case for relying on state courts to conduct the first level of federal judicial business. "[T]he whole judicial system is a giddy profusion, and quite unnecessary," lamented the pseudonymous "Rusticus" in Boston's *Independent Chronicle*. "The business might have been done in the State Courts, with a balance or check, raised by giving a Court of the Union, power to examine and correct those cases where foreigners or persons of different States are concerned. And all this unweildy [*sic*] and useless machinery of Circuit, District and Supreme Courts might have been omitted."[65]

Such criticisms briefly gained momentum in March 1791 when New York congressman Egbert Benson introduced a set of amendments to Article III that echoed Rusticus's sentiments. The centerpiece of Benson's plan was a provision requiring Congress to establish in each state a "General Judicial Court," either by thus denominating the highest existing state court or by creating a new court. The general judicial court, which was to be "regulated as the Congress shall prescribe," would have original jurisdiction "in all cases to which the judicial power of the United States doth extend," as well as appellate jurisdiction over cases from other courts within the state. Moreover, although the judges of this new court would receive their salaries from the federal government and be subject to the good-behavior standard, they could be impeached by either the House of Representatives or the state legislature. Judges from state courts that were declared general judicial courts by Congress would become judges of the new courts "by force of their appointments" as state-court judges, and the powers and duties of the state court would "devolve on the judges of the general judicial court." The plan concluded with an explicit statement of the new courts' dual nature: state judicial officers would be "held to execute their respective offices for carrying into effect the laws of the United States," as well as "the duties assigned to them by the laws of the state."[66] Benson's amendments thus shunted aside fine distinctions relating to concurrence between state and federal courts and instead essentially deputized the state courts to serve Congress and the federal judicial power.

Although Benson's proposal received widespread attention in the press, it too was dispatched to committee and never heard of again.[67] Despite this ignominious fate, Benson's amendments highlight a tension in the arguments for increased reliance on state courts. The arguments of anticonsolidationists such as Martin and Mason could easily slide into plans such as Benson's; putative goals of state autonomy might quickly give way to schemes to subordinate the states into mere departments, administrative subdivisions of the general government. State courts might be able to hear diversity cases and cases involving congressional statutes, treaties, and other federal causes in the first instance, but would not such an arrangement amount to the state courts' becoming co-opted by the general government rather than maintaining their prized autonomy?

Some commentators, such as one writing under the nom de plume "Curtius," expressed suspicion along these lines in considering Benson's amendments and similar plans: "[O]n taking a candid and impartial survey of the amendments in question, it is obvious that the sole scope and intention of them is to absorbe [*sic*] and annihilate those very governments, to which the general one owes its existence; or at best, to convert them into extensive but feeble CORPORATIONS."[68]

Throughout the 1780s and 1790s, observers with a wide array of agendas and commitments argued that the state courts ought to be part of the new federal edifice. Some hoped that the state courts, as already-extant and functioning adjudicatory bodies, could be folded directly into the federal apparatus. Others wanted robust state judiciaries to act as buffers against what they viewed as the creeping expansion of federal question jurisdiction (and, with it, the homogenizing, centralizing force of union). Opponents of a broader brief for the state courts, however, offered a wide array of arguments against further incorporating them into the federal structure. While some of these critics hoped that the state courts might for their own protection be cordoned off from the federal judiciary, others argued that the state courts must be kept out because they were untrustworthy and might corrupt the federal system.

Taking the former, protective view of state courts, Pennsylvania congressman William Maclay suggested that the states were already implicated in the federal structure, whether they liked it or (as in his case) not. Just as the Constitution had "meant to swallow up all the state Constitutions by degrees," he insisted, the 1789 act aimed to "[s]wallow by degrees all the State Judiciaries." Despite his role as a member of the committee that had drafted the 1789 act, Maclay ultimately could not bring himself to vote for the act, which he called "a Vile law System, calculated for Expence, and with a design to draw by degrees all law business into the federal Courts."[69]

Federalist Fisher Ames of Massachusetts had different concerns, however. Ames contended that the state courts possessed the power to range freely over the full landscape of both federal and state matters. But how, if at all, could the state courts ever be checked? Vesting state courts with any significant jurisdiction over federal questions risked profound problems of representation insofar as it lodged decision-making power in officials whose allegiance was only to their local community, not the interests of the Union as a whole. "Will the state judges act quasi state judges or as federal[?]" Ames inquired. "If as state judges, how can you add duties not required by the states who commissioned them and how can you compel them to perform such duties, or punish for the violation or neglect[?]." Furthermore, would one even be able to determine in what capacity a state judge was acting at any given moment? "The jurisdictions being concurrent, how will you distinguish when they act as state, and when as federal judges___ sometimes a nice question this."[70]

The map created by the 1789 act expressed this prevailing uncertainty about how the state courts ought to be treated. The act's structure not only accepted the states as preexisting polities but actually overlaid the new federal districts on the existing map of the states—even borrowing the states' names. Thus the districts were described in the act as "one to consist of the State of Connecticut, and to be called Connecticut District; one to consist of the State of New York, and to be called New York District," and so forth through the other nine states and two subsets of states (Maine and Kentucky).[71] This overlap between the state and federal maps appears not to have raised significant objections during the debates on the act. Notably, an amendment to breach state boundaries by creating a multistate district covering portions of Maryland, Virginia, and Delaware failed in the House. This failure suggested that maintaining the states' territorial integrity, rather than drawing entirely new political boundaries solely for federal purposes, was important to members.[72]

Was this political and legal congruence evidence of the federal government's desire to press the states into its service, or was it an acknowledgment of the states' importance, perhaps even a sign of respect? Many contemporaries regarded the layout and number of the districts as an attempt to ensure that the judicial power of the United States could be felt throughout the nation while also establishing it as superior to the judiciary of any one state.[73] During the 1790s, however, many observers complained that the seats of federal government within any given state were too remote. One commentator suggested that the upshot of this arrangement—which created, in the words of Julius Goebel, "a species of artificial federal entity"[74]—was confusion leavened with a lack of popular identification with the federal government. "The laws of the United

States, coming into discussion only in one court in each state, are but little known, and, at a distance from that court they are considered as foreign laws," lamented "A Citizen" in the *Washington Federalist*. "The contrast between the state and the federal administration of justice appears strong, and the advantage manifest against the federal judiciary."[75] Thus despite efforts by Randolph and others to keep separate the multiple levels of judicial power, the complexities of concurrence—both of subject matter and of territorial space—were very much on commentators' minds throughout the 1790s.

Here was another respect in which the debates of the postratification period echoed the arguments of the 1760s and 1770s: commentators in the early Republic employed a vocabulary of line drawing and *imperium in imperio* similar to that of their predecessors a few decades earlier. Even as they experimented with concurrence and considered deputizing state courts to act as inferior federal courts, early republican theorists continued to think about governmental structure in terms of the boundaries between different sovereigns and different sources of authority. The drive to delineate governmental spheres had preoccupied Thomas Hutchinson and the members of Boston's colonial opposition in 1773, and it continued to needle Americans in the postratification period.

The urgency was even more profound in the later years as "the judicial" (as Ames and others termed it) increasingly became the institutional site for hashing out the competing versions of federalism that had emerged since the 1760s.[76] In this anxious context, the old tropes of sovereignty gained new force and meaning. During the 1789 debates, William Paterson conjured up the specter of *imperium in imperio:* "We are a Combination of Republics____ a number of free States confederated together, & forming a social League." Within this league, Paterson went on, the Union and each of the several states possessed "a Head____each operating upon different Objects." Given such an arrangement, could the state courts reach outside the state realm to take cognizance of federal causes of action? No, Paterson answered. Granting federal authority to judges "chosen by the respective States; in whose Election the Union has no Voice, and over whom they have little or no Control" was nothing less than "a Solecism in Politicks—a Novelty in Govt."[77] By 1791, Massachusetts Federalist Theodore Sedgwick was bemoaning the problems that "arise from an administration of justice by two distinct & independent sovereignties over the same persons, in the same place and at the same time."[78] Sedgwick made his observations just a few weeks before Justice James Wilson wrote to Washington with a proposal for a digest of federal law, observing that "the difficult and delicate Line of Authority . . . must be run."[79] Born in the provincial legislatures of a mercantile, transatlantic empire, the vocabulary of federalism found new significance among the multiple judiciaries of the early Republic.

The ongoing constitutional debates of the 1790s demonstrated the fragile nature of the definitions of political and legal authority that many Americans believed they had worked out in the course of the conflict with Britain. Now, conscious of their inheritance as the second generation since the founding, early republican observers turned worriedly back to old themes of *imperium in imperio,* multiple sovereigns, and line drawing. At the same time, however, they became fascinated with ideas of concurrence—of multiple and overlapping powers, especially judicial powers.[80] Addressing the Connecticut ratification convention in 1788, Oliver Ellsworth urged his colleagues to disregard another delegate's dire invocations of *imperium in imperio.* "Two legislative powers, says he, cannot exist together in the same place. I ask, Why can they not? It is not enough to say they cannot. I wish for some reason. . . . It is vain to say they cannot exist, when they actually have done it." Ellsworth then made a key analytic move, pointing to the judiciary as the remedy for *imperium in imperio.* "If the general legislature should at any time overleap their limits, the judicial department is a constitutional check."[81] These warring perspectives on authority gained intensity throughout the 1790s until, fueled by partisan rancor that few in the first generation had anticipated, they exploded in the tumults of 1800 and 1801.

From *federal* to *Federal* Judicial Power: The Act of 1801

As the preceding discussion has suggested, beginning in 1789, judicial power emerged as the focus of both practical and theoretical disputes about the nature of multilayered authority. The judiciary became the key site of federalism during this period, and jurisdiction was the tool by which theorists and politicians carved up the levels of power among governments and people.

That was the scene in 1789 and for much of the subsequent decade. Around 1800, however, that picture changed. From the domain of federalism as a theory in the 1780s and 1790s, judicial power became the redoubt of Federalism as a party in the 1800s. The controversial presidential election (or "revolution," as Jefferson termed it) of 1800 signaled the rise of the Jeffersonian-Republican Party and the eclipse of the Federalists.[82] As part of this tale, historians often emphasize the flight of the Federalists to the judiciary in the wake of the schism that resulted in the first party system and the "loss" of the presidency and Congress to the Jeffersonians.[83]

This story, however, often treats the Judiciary Act of 1801 as an artifact of the election of 1800, a manifestation of partisan rancor with little to tell us about constitutional thought. Hence the emphasis, as suggested in the quotation from Kathryn Turner Preyer earlier, on the Judiciary Act's passage in 1801 as a mere prelude to its repeal in 1802.[84] But there is more to the 1801 act than this narrative of Federalist overreaching and Republican chastisement suggests. Like the 1789 act, the 1801 act should be viewed not simply from the modern perspective of the forward march of the federal courts to the twenty-first century, but rather from the early republican angle of making divided government work. To be sure, party politics are central to this account; as Joanne Freeman points out, a "crisis mentality" had seized the American political scene by 1800, stemming in large part from the hardening of party lines in a time when "normalcy" was understood as "the *absence* of organized national parties, *not* a well-functioning national party system."[85] But more was at issue in the 1801 act than the partitioning of the federal empire between Federalist and Republican claimants to rule. Ideas were at stake in the debates over the 1801 act, just as they had been in 1789.

The turn-of-the-century constitutional struggle was thus not simply a cover for partisan conflict. This interpretation falls prey to the temptation to paint the 1790s as the fall from grace, the sullied and sordid aftermath of the original moment of 1787–1789. Certainly the rancor of the 1790s was real; the allegiances had hardened, and the threat that ongoing warfare in Europe would engulf the United States added a new level of global consequence to the continuing uncertainty about the Republic's future.

The point is simply that the partisan din of the 1790s should not confuse modern observers into thinking that the source of the conflict was political gain or power alone.[86] Rather, the source of the conflict was political gain and power, as well as ongoing and fundamental disagreement about just what the "federal" in "federal republic" was to mean, and what role the judiciary would play in that federal republic.

The debates that culminated in the passage and repeal of the 1801 act demonstrate the degree to which early-nineteenth-century theories of jurisdiction took on the full weight of the sovereignty discourse of the eighteenth century, transforming questions of political authority in the broadest sense into issues of judicial power and the degree to which the federal and state systems would or would not overlap. By 1801, jurisdiction had replaced sovereignty as the lodestar of American constitutional debate. The 1801 act thus continued the 1789 act's project of adjusting federal judicial structure as a means of adjusting the structure of federalism—the relationship between the states and the general government—itself.

Many of the premises underpinning the 1801 act differed markedly from those that informed the 1789 act, however. One crucial difference concerned the scope of the federal judicial power in the respective acts. As we have seen, the 1789 act took a cautious, even conciliatory, approach to the states' claims to jurisdiction. For example, the federal districts replicated the boundaries of the states rather than asserting new districts that swallowed or subdivided the states; in addition, supporters of the act pointed to its acknowledgment of concurrent state and federal jurisdiction as evidence that the lower federal courts were not intended to supplant the state courts. The drafters of the 1801 act, in contrast, spent little time reassuring the states and instead presented a significantly more robust federal judiciary—both in terms of the number of courts and in the nature of their jurisdiction—with the potential for far greater intrusion into the states. The 1801 act, in other words, combined the colonial impulse to draw lines between levels of authority with the ratification era's focus on the judiciary as the principal axis of that division.

Throughout the 1790s, Congress engaged in relatively modest reforms of the federal judiciary, despite complaints from many quarters about the 1789 act. The chief criticism centered on the requirement that

Supreme Court justices ride circuit, which meant not only fatigue for the justices but also occasional conflicts because a given justice might hear the same case twice, once at the circuit level and once in the Supreme Court.[87] Following John Adams's December 1799 address to Congress, the members of the Sixth Congress began to consider a comprehensive overhaul. In his address, the president insisted that "a revision and amendment of the judicial system" was "indispensably necessary" to "give due effect to the civil administration of Government, and to ensure a just execution of the laws."[88] Congress appeared to take Adams's recommendation seriously. In February 1800, a House committee met with Justices William Paterson and Bushrod Washington to receive their recommendations for reform. The committee consisted of five members, all Federalists: Robert Goodloe Harper of South Carolina, Chauncey Goodrich of Connecticut, James A. Bayard of Delaware, Samuel Sewall of Massachusetts, and John Marshall of Virginia.[89] Shortly thereafter, on March 11, Harper introduced the committee's draft bill to the House.

The centerpiece of the Harper bill, as it was known, was a proposal to increase the number of federal judicial districts from thirteen to thirty, and the circuit courts from three to nine. As these numbers suggest, the districts in the Harper bill did not conform to state boundaries; instead, most states were divided into multiple districts. The bill also proposed new names for the districts, given that they could no longer share nomenclature with the state with which they overlapped. The counties of Essex, Suffolk, Norfolk, Middlesex, Bristol, Plymouth, Barnstable, Duke, and Nantucket in Massachusetts were to constitute the district of Boston. The remaining Massachusetts counties (Berkshire, Hampshire, Worcester), meanwhile, would be combined into the district of Warranoch. Virginia's counties were to be divided among the Potowmac, Fluvanna, and Kenhawa districts. Rhode Island would not be divided but would constitute the district of Narragansett; similarly, Vermont would constitute the single district of Champlain, although Connecticut's district would be called Connecticut.[90] As for the nine circuits, each was described according to the districts it included:

> The first circuit shall consist of the districts of Kennebeck, Merrimac, Boston, and Narragansett; the second, of the districts of Con-

necticut, Warranock [*sic*], and Champlain; the third, of the districts of Hudson, Saratoga, and Ontario; the fourth, of the districts of Rariton, Schuylkill, Delaware, and Choptank; the fifth, of the districts of Chesapeake, Susquehanna, and Alleganey; the sixth, of the districts of Potomac [*sic*], Fluvannah [*sic*], and Kenhawa; the seventh, of the districts of Pamplico, Catawba, and Saluda; the eight, of the districts of Santee, Alatamaha, and Savannah; and the ninth, of the districts of Holston, Cumberland, Ohio, and Rockcastle.[91]

Besides this realignment of the districts and circuits, the bill proposed to expand the circuit courts' jurisdiction over several types of cases, including "all actions and suits, matters or things, cognizable by the judicial authority of the United States, under and by virtue of the constitution thereof," as long as the amount in question was at least one hundred dollars and exclusive jurisdiction was not otherwise vested in the Supreme Court by the Constitution or in the admiralty courts pursuant to the new bill.[92]

Despite the committee's efforts (including John Marshall's "lengthy defence of the new system" on the floor of the House), the Harper bill immediately stirred enormous controversy both inside and outside Congress.[93] Much of the criticism focused on the provision to increase and rearrange the district courts. Georgia senator Abraham Baldwin, writing to his brother-in-law, the diplomat and poet Joel Barlow, characterized the Harper bill as intended "to new model the judiciary" and called it "a very broad stroke to draw all the powers to the general government and to do away as far as possible [with] not only state powers, but even boundaries."[94] The *Philadelphia Aurora,* meanwhile, lambasted the reorganization of the districts, chortling, "[I]nstead of calling *Jersey* by that name the district is to be denominated *(alamode de Paris)* the *department* or *district of Rariton,* and so on throughout the United States!"[95] Given the frequency with which Federalists accused the *Aurora* and other Republican newspapers of Jacobin sympathies, this critique of the Harper bill as carrying out renaming projects akin to those of revolutionary France's Committee of Public Safety is particularly noteworthy. In a letter to his brother John Quincy Adams, U.S. minister to Prussia, Thomas Boylston Adams, the youngest son of the president, despaired of such suspicions but expressed some of his own.

"[T]here is an evident reluctance in many gentlemen towards these great national acts, because they tend to strengthen the bonds of union & give an influence to the general Government, that interferes with their malignant designs."[96]

Facing this opposition, on March 31 Harper introduced an amended bill in which the number of districts was reduced to nineteen and the number of circuits to six. In the amended bill, the names and boundaries of the district courts followed the names and boundaries of the states (with the exceptions of Massachusetts, New York, Pennsylvania, Virginia, and Tennessee, each of which was divided into two districts). This scaling back of the federal courts' presence was accompanied, however, by an extension of their jurisdiction.[97] Pursuant to the amended bill, the circuit courts' jurisdiction would encompass "all cases in law or equity, arising under the constitution and laws of the United States, and treaties made, or which shall be made, under their authority."[98] The scope of this grant stood in sharp contrast to the 1789 act's grant of original jurisdiction to the circuit courts in, first, "all suits of a civil nature at common law or in equity" in which the amount in controversy was at least five hundred dollars, and the United States was a plaintiff or petitioner, or an alien was a party; and second, diversity suits.[99] The amended bill's jurisdictional grant was not as broad as that of the original Harper bill, however, which, as we have seen, proposed expanding the scope of federal jurisdiction to "all actions and suits, matters or things, cognizable by the judicial authority of the United States, under and by virtue of the constitution thereof"—that is, to the full extent of judicial power under Article III.[100]

The amended bill made little progress in the first session of the Sixth Congress. In the second session, however, a new committee, including some Republicans, took up the judiciary question again and presented a substantially similar bill to the full House.[101] At the beginning of the session, Adams had again pressed for judicial reform in a speech to Congress that Marshall, now secretary of state, had helped prepare.[102] After some discussion of the propriety of permitting state courts to exercise jurisdiction over federal cases, the bill passed the House on January 20, 1801, and the Senate on February 7. Titled "An Act to provide for the more convenient organization of the Courts of the United States," the bill became law upon receiving Adams's signature on February 13. The final form of the provision regarding the circuit courts' original jurisdiction closely paralleled the language of the amended Harper bill. Section 11 of the act provided "[t]hat the said circuit courts respectively shall have cognizance . . . of all cases in law or equity, arising under the constitution and laws of the United States, and treaties made, or which shall be made, under their authority." In addition, the act provided for easier removal of cases from state to federal court.[103] Four days after the law's enactment, on February 17, the House finally settled the disputed presidential election by electing Jefferson on the thirty-sixth ballot.

As this chronology demonstrates, and as several scholars have noted, the movement that led to the Judiciary Act of 1801 predated the election of 1800 by several months. Thus, as Turner notes, "the Act was clearly not occasioned by the Republican victory in 1800."[104] Indeed, commentators on both sides of the partisan divide had anticipated an attempted expansion of the federal judicial power for some time before the 1801 act came to pass. In August 1799, Jefferson had confided his fears about the expansion of the federal government—in particular, the federal judiciary—in a letter to Edmund Randolph. Specifically, Jefferson worried that the growth of federal courts' jurisdiction would lead to a body of federal common law separate from state law that would become a tool of federal oppression. Jefferson's use of pronouns to refer to the government—and thus to the Federalists—is particularly illuminating:

> Of all the doctrines which have ever been broached by the federal government, the novel one, of the common law being in force & cognisable as an existing law in *their* courts, is to me the most formidable. [A]ll their other assumptions of un-given powers have been in the details. [T]he banklaw, the treaty doctrine, the sedition act, alien act . . . &c. &c. have been solitary unconsequential timid things in comparison of the audacious, barefaced and sweeping pretension to a system of law for the US. without the adoption of *their* legislature and so infinitely beyond *their* power to adopt.[105]

For Jefferson, jurisdiction was a mere cover for the spread of substantive federal law, objectionable not only because it could potentially serve as an agent of nationalization but also, and perhaps more important, because such a body of law could not be checked by the people in the states.

Jefferson's democratic critique of the trend toward broader federal jurisdiction finds an echo in the writings of some leading Federalists, who harbored similar but differently directed concerns about the relationship between the people and the federal government. In contrast to Jefferson's claim that the general government was covertly absorbing the powers of the states, and therefore of the people, Federalists such as Hamilton and Sedgwick envisioned the spread of federal power as conducive both to the public good and, not incidentally, to the power of the current government. "An accurate view of the internal situation of the UStates presents many discouraging reflections to the enlightened friends of our Government and country," Hamilton lamented in October 1799. Despite the "instructive comments afforded by the disastrous & disgusting scenes of the french Revolution," he observed that "sentiments dangerous to social happiness have not been diminished." Given this situation, "vigorous measures of counteraction" were required of the friends of the government, including the "Extension of the Judiciary system" by dividing each state into smaller districts and appointing federal justices of the peace in local areas.[106] Sedgwick recommended a similar program of extending federal power further into the states. "If the real federal majority can act together much may and ought to be done to give efficiency to the government, and to repress the efforts of the Jacobins against it," he wrote to Rufus King. "We ought to spread out the judicial so as to render the justice of the nation acceptable to the people, to aid national economy, to overawe the licentious, and to punish the guilty." Like Hamilton, Sedgwick noted that these lofty goals also offered more immediate benefits: "[W]e ought, at the same time, that we promote the real happiness & welfare of the people, to court thereby their favor."[107]

These comments from Hamilton and Sedgwick emphasize the nature of the Federalists' program of expanded federal judicial power. In contrast to Hamilton's earlier acceptance of concurrent powers when writing as Publius in *The Federalist* 32, by 1799 he was no longer attempting to thread the needle of concurrent power while still maintaining a forceful general government. Instead, Hamilton—and Sedgwick as well—embraced a vision of federal power that resembled the one that Randolph had struggled to articulate in his report of 1790. That vision in turn owed a debt to the opposition theories that colonists had launched against parliamentary power in the 1760s and 1770s, according to which each level of the composite imperial government would possess the authority to regulate a defined set of subjects. Common to these early approaches and the views of Hamilton, Sedgwick, and others in the 1790s and 1800s was a belief that the federal and state governments would operate best as parallel powers, each with its own area of competence, with little concurrence or crossover. A decade earlier, however, as we have seen, many commentators had emphasized the opposite, insisting that concurrent powers of legislation, as well as adjudication, were inevitable and perhaps even desirable in the new federal republic.

The language of the two judiciary acts illustrates this difference in emphasis. While the 1789 act makes many references to concurrent state- and federal-court jurisdiction, the only mention of concurrence in the 1801 act concerns the concurrent jurisdiction of district and circuit courts with respect to bankruptcy proceedings.[108] Similarly, contrast the apparatus of inferior federal courts established by the 1789 act with that of the 1801 act. While the drafters of the 1789 act took pains to make the new districts conform to state boundaries as much as possible, thereby avoiding the suggestion that the general government was working to subsume the states within its own artificial boundaries and structures, the drafters of the 1801 act broke the states down into smaller, more administrable districts, showing little concern for the integrity of the states as they did so. Indeed, the Harper bill provides an even more striking example of this apparent lack of respect for state boundaries by selecting regional, geographic, or Native American names for the districts rather than using the names of the states. Thus the goal of separating the levels of government—with the dual effects of undoing past blurring and asserting national power—increasingly informed the Federalists' federalizing policy after 1789. Moreover, they viewed the expansion of the federal courts' general federal question jurisdiction, which had begun with the Randolph and Harper proposals and culminated in the "arising under" jurisdiction of the 1801 act, as the key to this separation.

Of course, the Federalists did not long enjoy the fruits of their plan. Upon the election of Jefferson by the House of Representatives in February 1801, many observers predicted the course of subsequent events. The 1801 act was repealed on March 8, 1802, by a repealing act that "annulled the 1801 act's broad grant of federal question jurisdiction and discarded the newly created circuit courts, forcing the Supreme Court justices again to ride circuit and act as circuit judges."[109] In 1803, six days after handing down the decision in *Marbury v. Madison,* the Supreme Court upheld the validity of the repealing act.[110]

In the waning days of the Adams administration, as the president filled the sixteen new circuit judgeships that the 1801 act had created, murmurings of repeal had already begun to surface.[111] In his first annual message to Congress, Jefferson stated (without actually stating) the obvious: "The Judiciary system of the United States, and especially that portion of it recently erected, will, of course, present itself to the contemplation of Congress." The president noted that he had already requested an account of all cases that had been decided since 1789 and of the number of cases that had been pending when the 1801 act took effect.[112] The act of 1801 had established six new circuit courts and seven new district courts.[113] Jefferson and his associates insisted that the Federalists had erected this apparatus as a means of entrenching their power in the face of popular opposition.[114] In their view, concurrence was not a bone to be thrown—or not—to the cowering states at the pleasure of a mighty federal government, but quite the opposite: a gesture of goodwill on the part of the states as they shared a measure of their plenary power, their sovereignty, with the general government.

Hamilton, writing as "Lucius Crassus" in the *New-York Evening Post,* sneered at Jefferson's attempt to prove that the new courts were unnecessary. "No bad thermometer of the capacity of our Chief Magistrate for government is furnished by the rule which he offers for judging of the utility of the Federal Courts," Hamilton said of Jefferson's plan to tally the number of federal-court cases decided as a means of assessing the need for additional courts. "There is hardly any stronger symptom of a pigmy mind, than a propensity to allow greater weight to *secondary* than to *primary* considerations."[115] Hamilton and his allies contended that expanding the federal judicial power was the best solution to the problem of multiple authorities, or *imperium in imperio,* that had dogged the Republic since before its founding. In an address to the New York City bar shortly before the repeal of the 1801 act, Hamilton warned of the consequences that he feared would follow. According to a newspaper report, "He declared in the most emphatic manner, that if the bill for the repeal passed, and the independence of the Judiciary was destroyed, the constitution was but a shadow, and we should, e'er long, be divided into separate confederacies, turning our arms against each."[116]

"Separate confederacies, turning our arms against each"—the famously eloquent Hamilton appears to have selected his words carefully to elicit a response from his audience. But Hamilton's choice of the language of confederation at this moment reveals more than simply rhetorical talents. For many observers in the early years of the nineteenth century, the murky abstraction of Article III's "judicial power of the United States" had taken shape only through the institutions of the courts themselves, and only through the device of federal jurisdiction. The years between 1789 and 1802 saw a constant drive to reshape and reconfigure the courts and their jurisdiction in a period of institutional transformation that was unique to the judiciary. Interestingly, the early Republic witnessed few debates of similar scale regarding the meaning and form of the legislative or executive powers. The language of Article III, combined with the Madisonian compromise, had deliberately left a lacuna in the constitutional structure. By choosing not to fill that gap at Philadelphia, the drafters of the Constitution had ensured that any institution that eventually did fill it would always be seen as provisional, as an attempt but not necessarily a complete solution. The gap was visible from the beginning and would remain so, despite contemporaries' efforts to fill it—with the 1789 act, with the Harper bills, with the 1801 act, and with the 1802 repealing act. In some sense, then, the judiciary of any particular era might always appear to its contemporaries as nothing more than "a new wheel . . . introduced into the federal machine to which the union was before a stranger, and which is not necessary to its genuine motives."[117]

By 1789, the concept of jurisdiction had become one of the principal contested terrains of constitutional discourse. Instead of the emphasis on the legislature that had fascinated colonial and Revolutionary-era commentators, Americans of the ratification period and the early Republic devoted substantial thought to the structure of the judiciary. The lines of judicial authority thus replaced sovereignty as the great mystery to be unraveled by lawyers, politicians, and thinkers. But contemporaries' normative conception of jurisdiction was not stable throughout the period of the early Republic; rather, conflicting visions of jurisdiction—specifically, federal-court jurisdiction—collided and shifted throughout the period between the passage of the Judiciary Act of 1789 and the repeal of the Judiciary Act of 1801 in 1802.

The 1801 act must be understood not as an outlier but on its own terms, as—among other things—an attempt by Federalists to install a particular version of small-*f* federalism in the Constitution.[118] That small-*f* federalism built on theories that colonial commentators had developed beginning in the 1760s, during the struggle with the British Empire. Colonial spokespeople had argued for a system of divided authority in which power was allocated along subject-matter lines, allowing for multiple levels of government to exist in the same system while each exercised a sovereignty defined by the subject of the regulation in question. In the 1801 act, unlike the 1789 act, Federalists sought to return to this idea of subject-matter jurisdiction by establishing broad federal jurisdiction over cases arising under the Constitution, the laws of the United States, and treaties made under their authority. This subject-matter focus was necessarily limited by the Supremacy Clause, which explicitly contemplated some interaction between state judges and federal law and therefore appeared to preclude all federal questions from being vested exclusively in federal courts. But the Federalists succeeded briefly, most notably by broadening "arising under" jurisdiction and easing the requirements for removal of cases from state to federal courts. The election of 1800 and the ensuing repeal of the 1801 act, however, spelled the temporary demise of this idea of jurisdiction and the return of the type of concurrence and overlap that had characterized the system set up by the 1789 act. After 1801, Jeffersonian Americans pulled back from the federal idea that British North Americans had developed in the imperial crisis of several decades earlier. One of the main impulses that had driven early American federalism thus shifted location after 1802, relocating to the Supreme Court, where claims of broad and distinctively federal jurisdiction accompanied the expansion of federal judicial power.[119] The fate of Federalism, therefore, fundamentally altered the landscape of federalism.

Epilogue:
Federalism Demystified

W E HAVE CALLED by different names, brethren of the same principle. [W]e are all republicans, we are all federalists." These words are familiar to virtually every student of early United States history. They were delivered by Thomas Jefferson on March 4, 1801, in his first inaugural address, which followed the ugly scenes of the deadlocked presidential election of 1800.[1]

Neither Jefferson's handwritten draft nor his reading copy of the speech capitalized the initial "r" and "f" in the words "republicans" and "federalists." Many printed, scholarly versions of Jefferson's address do capitalize the letters, however.[2] Such changes are often part of the process of editing manuscript sources for publication; indeed, as the brackets in the quotation suggest, Jefferson's holographic versions of the address employed few capital letters, even for the first words of sentences.

Jefferson's address is often cited to illustrate his desire to lead the nation past the turmoil and hostility of one of the most hard-fought presidential elections in American history.[3] Certainly the peacemaking impulse is evident in even these few lines. But the references to "republicans" and "federalists" suggest something more, something relevant to this book's story of the development of federal ideas. By 1801, the *foedus* family of words had expanded from a clan of adjectives to encompass a noun describing an individual who advocated federal ideas—a "federalist."[4]

To be sure, the term had existed before 1801; one need only think of the collection of essays by Alexander Hamilton, James Madison, and John Jay titled *The Federalist* (or, as the original typesetting in the *New York Independent Journal* had it, *The Foederalist*) to find an earlier usage, and a more obviously politically charged one. In 1801, as in 1787, the term carried manifold connotations, from the abstract idea of a believer in more centralized government to the less genteel sense of a backer of a political junto bent on Anglicization, commercial development, and entrenched social hierarchy (possibly with titles of nobility, but at least with a firmly established elite class).[5]

As Jefferson used it, the term "federalist" appeared to bear little relationship to the debates of the 1760s, 1770s, and 1780s or to the question of the British imperial legacy. But this was not the case; on the contrary, much of the power of Jefferson's language stemmed from the richly layered meanings that the term "federal" and its cognates had accumulated as part of early modern Anglo-American constitutional debates. From an adjective describing a general category of political union, the term "federal" metamorphosed over the course of the eighteenth century into a necessary attribute of one particular union. All agreed by 1801 that the United States was a federal union; as the debates over the judiciary acts demonstrated, however, arguments flared when one attempted to define precisely what "federal union" meant. Jefferson's use of the word "federalist" captures the partisan, early republican, large-*F* connotation of the term ("Federalist"). In the same breath, the new president also conjured up the more philosophical, Revolutionary, small-*f* sense of the term ("federalist"), and with it the sense that federalness did not simply refer to one group's bundle of political commitments, but rather to a basic characteristic of the nation itself.

～

As Jefferson's inaugural address illustrates, both the small-*f* and large-*F* versions of federalism endured into the nineteenth century. For this reason, the emergence of large-*F* federalism during the ratification debates was a significant moment in the history of federalism as an ideology. Let us examine another commentary—this one by Alexander Hamilton, writing as Publius in *The Federalist* No. 9, slightly less than fourteen years before Jefferson took the oath of office:

> The definition of a *Confederate Republic* seems simply to be, an "assemblage of societies" or an association of two or more States into one State. . . . So long as the separate organisation of the members be not abolished, so long as it exists by a constitutional necessity for local purposes, though it should be in perfect subordination to the general authority of the Union, it would still be, in fact and in theory, an association of States, or a confederacy. The proposed Constitution, so far from implying an abolition of the State Governments, makes them constituent parts of the national sovereignty by allowing them a direct representation in the Senate, and leaves in their possession certain exclusive and very important portions of sovereign power. This fully corresponds, in every rational import of the terms, with the idea of a Foederal Government.[6]

This paragraph is one of the most striking in the series of eighty-five *Federalist* essays because it accomplishes an enormous amount in a relatively small space and without seeming to cost much effort. Consider the first line: a "confederate republic," Hamilton states, is nothing more than a joining of two states into another, different state. This composite state, or union, becomes the confederate republic; the only requirement for maintaining this status appears to be permitting the component states to retain both their separateness and their jurisdiction over "local purposes." Hamilton next walks the reader through the application of this general rule to the specific case of the American states under the proposed constitution. Not only does that constitution permit the states to retain their distinct identities and "certain exclusive and very important portions of sovereign power," but it also makes the states *as states* indispensable to the sovereignty of the general government by granting them representation in the Senate. So far, all seems straightforward. Then comes Hamilton's conclusion: this relationship between the states and the general government "fully corresponds" with "the idea of a Foederal Government." A foederal government? Did this paragraph not begin by talking about a confederate republic? Where did the "foederal" idea come from?

At this point, the tremendous work being carried out by this paragraph starts to become evident. As we have seen, the term "federal" was not unknown before the 1780s; on the contrary, participants in the Anglo-Scottish union debates who hoped for some degree of continued Scottish autonomy argued that the union ought to be established on a federal rather than an incorporating basis. By "federal," these commentators referred to what James Hodges had termed "Distinct, Free, and Independent Kingdoms, Dominions, or States . . . unit[ing] their separate Interests into one common Interest . . . retaining in the mean time their several Independencies, National Distinctions, and the different Laws, Customs, and Government of each."[7] This meaning of "federal," therefore, closely resembled Pufendorf's model of a system of states, as well as the ancient and modern confederations that Madison studied. In other words, the old meaning of "federal" was quite close to that of "confederal" or "confederation."

But unlike these more or less equivalent early-eighteenth-century usages, Hamilton's description of the structure of the confederate republic differs from his description of a federal government. Toward the end of the paragraph, Hamilton's mention of the Senate and the "national sovereignty" makes clear what his references to the confederate republic (following, as the next paragraph makes clear, Montesquieu) had obscured. The system of government that the proposed constitution creates is not a mere bundle of agreements forming a lean league or an "assemblage of societies"; on the contrary, it is an entirely new level of government, with its own level of sovereign authority and its own theory of legitimacy.

Peter Onuf and Nicholas Onuf have characterized this tour de force as "manipulation to the point of obfuscation" by Hamilton, and an attempt to use "federal" in the old sense while also giving it a wholly new meaning.[8] Whatever Hamilton's intent, this paragraph demonstrates the slipperiness of the terms used by commentators in the founding and ratification periods, and the rapidity with which meanings could change. In this paragraph, we can see one of the many moments in which the meaning of "federal" shifted from denoting the federal union of the Anglo-Scottish debates to something more like a hybrid between a federal and an incorporating union. This hybrid was not a federal union in the old

sense, because it created a new general government with some amount
of sovereignty; neither was it an incorporating union in the old sense,
because, again, it created a new level of government rather than merging
one entity into another, preexisting one.

⌒

Now let us consider a later moment: the Supreme Court's opinion in
Cohens v. Virginia (1821), in which Chief Justice John Marshall, writing
for a unanimous Court, held that the Supreme Court possessed jurisdiction to review state-court criminal cases: "The constitution and laws of
a State, so far as they are repugnant to the constitution and laws of the
United States, are absolutely void. These States are constituent parts of
the United States. They are members of one great empire—for some purposes sovereign, for some purposes subordinate."[9] Here, in the fourth
decade of the federal republic's existence, we begin to see the full, practical force of Hamilton's subtle shift. Borrowing the repugnancy language of the Privy Council's review of colonial court decisions, as Mary
Sarah Bilder has demonstrated, Marshall suggested that the Supreme
Court's appellate jurisdiction stemmed from the substantive body of
"laws of the United States" first articulated in the debates at Philadelphia concerning the Supremacy Clause.[10]

Marshall's language did not entirely replicate imperial structures of
review and supremacy, however. Since the 1760s, colonial observers had
argued that the colonies possessed powers that were not derived from
the empire or from metropolitan authorities. Instead, they contended, a
given colony—for example, Virginia—possessed a corpus of sovereign
lawmaking authority over certain specific things and activities that were
inherently internal, domestic, or related to taxation or raising revenue.
Metropolitan officials, meanwhile, argued that any legislative powers
that Virginia had were mere delegations from the empire itself, and that
therefore Virginia could claim no independent lawmaking authority.
The latter position was the official imperial position; the colonial arguments were just that—arguments. The holding in *Cohens*, in contrast,
adopted a version of the colonial arguments insofar as it acknowledged
some essential corpus of sovereignty within each state. Despite the invo-
cation of "empire," then, the Court did not insist that the federal govern-

ment possessed the full spectrum of plenary power that British imperial officials had claimed for their empire.[11]

Marshall's language did insist on one crucial power, however. By claiming for the Court the authority to determine whether a state was sovereign or subordinate in a given situation, the chief justice articulated a bold vision of federal judicial supremacy. The debates of the previous decades had concerned the legitimacy of divided authority and had ultimately arrived at a vision of divided authority as not a defect but rather a virtue. Marshall's contribution to this ideology of multiplicity was an institutional one. The basis of the American union was divided authority, with the Court taking upon itself the role of the dividing authority.

∾

One final voice, from the nineteenth century:

> The human understanding more easily invents new things than new words, and we are thence constrained to employ a multitude of improper and inadequate expressions. When several nations form a permanent league and establish a supreme authority, which . . . acts upon each of the confederate States in a body, this government, which is so essentially different from all others, is denominated a Federal one. Another form of society is afterwards discovered, in which several peoples are fused into one and the same nation with regard to certain common interests, although they remain distinct, or at least only confederate, with regard to all their other concerns. . . . Here the term Federal government is clearly no longer applicable to a state of things which must be styled an incomplete national government: a form of government has been found out which is neither exactly national nor federal; but no further progress has been made, and *the new word which will one day designate this novel invention does not yet exist.*[12]

This observation comes from Alexis de Tocqueville's *Democracy in America* of 1835. Tocqueville was writing as the first federal moment of American history was drawing to a close, marked by the death of John Marshall in July of that year. Meanwhile, new incarnations of old conflicts and

uncertainties loomed, from the lasting rancor of the 1832–1833 nullification crisis, in which South Carolina defied both President Andrew Jackson and Congress by claiming the power to negate a federal tariff, to the
brewing sectional conflict concerning slavery in the territories. Tocqueville captured the growing ambiguity of federalism as the idea
changed, and was changed by, the messy processes of politics and law in
the early Republic.[13] A new conception of layered governmental authority had been invented during the colonists' struggles with metropolitan
powers and refined during the early republicans' debates over the institutional mechanisms by which that authority would operate. That conception ended up bearing the name "federalism," a theoretically and
historically significant label that immediately began to accumulate new
meanings and new significances as it rolled onward in time.

This book has argued for an ideological approach to understanding
the origins of American federalism. The federal idea has origins because
it was created; it is an intellectual artifact, not a transcendent or timeless
idea that has always hovered around waiting to be applied to a particular
political project. To paraphrase Reinhart Koselleck, American federalism possesses a "beforehand not yet"—a before and an after, like all intellectual artifacts.[14] Whether we can discern the dividing point between
these moments of before and after is a different question altogether.

As this book has shown, the process of creative transformation took
decades to unfold and engaged the imaginations of many individuals.
Understanding this transformation requires stripping away some of the
supposed miraculousness of the founding while still recognizing the extraordinary confluence of theory, circumstance, and innovation at a particular legal and political moment in late-eighteenth-century North
America. This book has thus sought both to demystify and to appreciate
the history of the American federal idea. To demystify federalism, we
must estrange ourselves from its familiar modern-day incarnations—
both the ones that use "federal" interchangeably with "national" ("the
federal government," "federal authorities") and those that associate
"federalism" with oppositional claims about the reserved sphere of state
sovereignty. Indeed, federalism's modern dichotomy between national
and state power offers little insight into the question how federalism itself became the frame through which such questions must be viewed.

Instead, estrangement requires that we tie federalism's emergence and development to particular moments and particular debates, finding the appropriate balance of theory, experience, contingency, and expediency. To appreciate the significance and novelty of American federalism, we must connect it to larger eighteenth-century debates about the nature, location, and ultimate hierarchy of political and legal authorities.

Between the middle decades of the eighteenth century and the early years of the nineteenth century, federal thought was transformed from a heterodox willingness to tolerate messy, multilayered government into an affirmative belief that such multiplicity—untidy though it might be—could form the basis for a new species of union. Throughout Anglo-America and then the United States, commentators and statecrafters as varied as Britannus Americanicus, George Grenville, James Otis, Thomas Hutchinson, James Madison, John Witherspoon, Luther Martin, Robert Goodloe Harper, and John Marshall struggled to define the meaning and limits of governmental authority in a world in which multiplicity suddenly seemed possible, even if it appeared illegitimate to some. The Philadelphia delegates' decision to use courts rather than legislatures as the principal mechanism to balance multiplicity with union gave concrete, institutional meaning to the emerging federal vision. Moreover, the rejection of Madison's negative and the adoption of judicial review under the Supremacy Clause ushered in the early republican fascination with using federal-court jurisdiction as a device to modulate the system's commitment to multiplicity.

Between the 1760s and the early nineteenth century, then, a loose array of Anglo-American federal ideas fused into an American ideology of federalism. This ideology was larger and more profound than a constitutional doctrine or a structural principle of government. Rather, it was the frame through which Americans came to view their political and legal world, as well as the foundation of the nation itself.

Notes

INTRODUCTION

1. Jack P. Greene, *Peripheries and Center: Constitutional Development in the Extended Polities of the British Empire and the United States, 1607–1788* (Athens: University of Georgia Press, 1986), 3. See also, e.g., Andrew C. McLaughlin, "The Background of American Federalism," *American Political Science Review* 12 (1918): 215–240; McLaughlin, *A Constitutional History of the United States* (New York: D. Appleton-Century Co., 1935).

2. For "composite empire" language, see McLaughlin, "Background of American Federalism," 216.

3. Jack P. Greene, *Negotiated Authorities: Essays in Colonial Political and Constitutional History* (Charlottesville: University Press of Virginia, 1994); McLaughlin, "Background of American Federalism," 216.

4. I am grateful to David Armitage for suggesting the distinction between experience and arguments.

5. Daniel J. Hulsebosch, *Constituting Empire: New York and the Transformation of Constitutionalism in the Atlantic World, 1664–1830* (Chapel Hill: University of North Carolina Press, 2005), 7; Mary Sarah Bilder, *The Transatlantic Constitution: Colonial Legal Culture and the Empire* (Cambridge, Mass.: Harvard University Press 2004), 4, 7. Eric Slauter has offered a cultural account of the Constitution's emergence. See Eric Slauter, *The State as a Work of Art: The Cultural Origins of the Constitution* (Chicago: University of Chicago Press, 2009).

6. The quotes are from, respectively, Bernard Bailyn, *The Ideological Origins of the American Revolution,* enl. ed. (1967; Cambridge, Mass.: Belknap Press of Harvard University Press, 1992), xiv; and Gordon S. Wood, *The Creation of the American Republic, 1776–1787* (Chapel Hill: University of North Carolina Press, 1969), viii. Bailyn was responding to the work of Charles Beard, which had emphasized the role of economic, social, and other material factors in bringing about first the Revolution and then the Constitutional Convention. See Charles A. Beard, *An Economic Interpretation of the Constitution of the United States* (New York: Macmillan, 1913).

7. *U.S. Term Limits, Inc. v. Thornton,* 514 U.S. 779, 838 (1997) (Kennedy, J., concurring). The literature on federalism as a normative question in American constitutional theory is enormous. See, e.g., Raoul Berger, *Federalism: The Founders' Design* (Norman:

University of Oklahoma Press, 1987); Edward A. Purcell, Jr., *Originalism, Federalism, and the American Constitutional Enterprise: A Historical Inquiry* (New Haven, Conn.: Yale University Press, 2007); Harry N. Scheiber, *Federalism: Studies in History, Law, and Policy* (Berkeley: Institute of Governmental Studies, University of California, 1988); Harry N. Scheiber and Malcolm M. Feeley, eds., *Power Divided: Essays on the Theory and Practice of Federalism* (Berkeley: Institute of Governmental Studies, University of California, 1989); David L. Shapiro, *Federalism: A Dialogue* (Evanston: Northwestern University Press, 1995); Daniel J. Elazar, "Federalism as Grand Design," *Publius* 9 (1978): 1–8; Philip P. Frickey and Steven S. Smith, "Judicial Review, the Congressional Process, and the Federalism Cases: An Interdisciplinary Critique," *Yale Law Journal* 111 (2002): 1707–1756; Larry D. Kramer, "Understanding Federalism," *Vanderbilt Law Review* 47 (1994): 1485–1561; Henry P. Monaghan, "Our Perfect Constitution," *New York University Law Review* 56 (1981): 353–396; Judith Resnik, "Afterword: Federalism's Options," *Yale Law and Policy Review* 14 (1996): 465–503; Edward L. Rubin and Malcolm Feeley, "Federalism: Some Notes on a National Neurosis," *UCLA Law Review* 41 (1994): 903–952; and Peter J. Smith, "Sources of Federalism: An Empirical Analysis of the Court's Quest for Original Meaning," *UCLA Law Review* 52 (2004): 217–287.

8. For example, Wood describes federalism as "an emerging doctrine" derived from the pro-Constitution federalists' reworking of the idea of popular sovereignty. See Wood, *Creation of the American Republic,* 545.

9. See, e.g., Greene, *Peripheries and Center,* 205 ("In many respects . . . in its organization, the United States after 1788 looked very much like the early modern British Empire. Certainly, in contriving the Constitution, the framers had clearly drawn, if in many cases half-consciously, upon the experience and precedents of the empire").

10. On the relationship between language and institutions in intellectual and political history, see Quentin Skinner, "Meaning and Understanding in the History of Ideas," in James Tully, ed., *Meaning and Context: Quentin Skinner and His Critics* (Princeton, N.J.: Princeton University Press, 1988), 29–67.

11. David Armitage, *The Ideological Origins of the British Empire* (Cambridge: Cambridge University Press, 2000), 5.

12. The phrase "well constructed Union" is from [James Madison], "The Federalist No. 10," in Jacob E. Cooke, ed., *The Federalist* (Middletown, Conn.: Wesleyan University Press, 1961), 56. Madison's observations are from [Madison], "The Federalist No. 51," in Cooke, *Federalist,* 353. See also Lance E. Banning, *The Sacred Fire of Liberty: James Madison and the Founding of the Federal Republic* (Ithaca, N.Y.: Cornell University Press, 1995), 210–211.

13. Max M. Edling, *A Revolution in Favor of Government: Origins of the U.S. Constitution and the Making of the American State* (New York: Oxford University Press, 2003), 219; David C. Hendrickson, *Peace Pact: The Lost World of the American Founding* (Lawrence: University Press of Kansas, 2003), ix.

14. William Blackstone, *Commentaries on the Laws of England* (1765–1769; reprint, with an introduction by Stanley N. Katz, Chicago: University of Chicago Press, 1979), 1:49.

15. To borrow David Hendrickson's useful formulation from a different context, the issue centered not on the proposition that the general government was to decide every-

thing, but that it—through the mechanism of the Supremacy Clause and Congress's enumerated powers under Article I, section 8—"was to decide where everything was to be decided." Hendrickson, *Peace Pact,* 88 (discussing the situation in 1774, upon passage of the Coercive Acts).

1. THE FEDERAL IDEA

1. The vast literature on the rise of the colonial assemblies provides crucial insights into these important bodies. On the assemblies and the decades-long history of institutional conflict within the colonial governments, see Evarts B. Greene, *The Provincial Governor in the English Colonies of North America* (New York: Longmans, Green, and Co., 1898); Jack P. Greene, *The Quest for Power: The Lower Houses of Assembly in the Southern Royal Colonies, 1689–1776* (New York: Norton, 1963); Michael G. Kammen, *Deputyes and Liber-. tyes* (New York: Knopf, 1968); Leonard Woods Labaree, *Royal Government in America: A Study of the British Colonial System before 1783* (New Haven, Conn.: Yale University Press, 1930); and Herbert Osgood, *The American Colonies in the Eighteenth Century* (New York: Columbia University Press, 1924). For a more recent institutional analysis, see Christine A. Desan, "The Constitutional Commitment to Legislative Adjudication in the Early American Tradition," *Harvard Law Review* 111 (1998): 1381–1503.

2. 24 Hen. 8, c. 12; J. G. A. Pocock, "A Discourse of Sovereignty: Observations on the Work in Progress," in Nicholas Phillipson and Quentin Skinner, eds., *Political Discourse in Early Modern Britain* (Cambridge: Cambridge University Press, 1993), 381. On the contested concept of sovereignty, see Ken MacMillan, *Sovereignty and Possession in the English New World: The Legal Foundations of Empire, 1576–1640* (Cambridge: Cambridge University Press, 2006).

3. See Michael Mendle, "Parliamentary Sovereignty: A Very English Absolutism," in Phillipson and Skinner, *Political Discourse in Early Modern Britain,* 97.

4. Jack N. Rakove, "Making a Hash of Sovereignty, Part I," *Green Bag,* 2d ser., 2 (1998): 36.

5. Jean Bodin, *On Sovereignty: Four Chapters from "The Six Books of the Commonwealth,"* ed. and trans. Julian H. Franklin (Cambridge: Cambridge University Press, 1992), 1, 49–50. Franklin describes Bodin's theory of sovereignty as "the assertion that there must exist, in every ordered commonwealth, a single center of supreme authority, and that this authority must necessarily be absolute." See also Julian H. Franklin, *Jean Bodin and the Rise of Absolutist Theory* (Cambridge: Cambridge University Press, 1973), 23.

6. Thomas Hobbes, *Leviathan,* ed. C. B. Macpherson (Harmondsworth: Penguin, 1968) (chap. 18).

7. Mendle, "Parliamentary Sovereignty," in Phillipson and Skinner, eds., *Political Discourse in Early Modern Britain,* 100, 97 (noting that Bodin was cited in the debates on the Petition of Right in 1628).

8. See Thomas C. Grey, "Origins of the Unwritten Constitution: Fundamental Law in American Revolutionary Thought," *Stanford Law Review* 30 (1978): 866–67 (discussing the rise of parliamentary sovereignty in eighteenth-century English legal thought). The

indivisibility of sovereignty had also made its way into French political thought, notably that of Jean-Jacques Rousseau. Rousseau's *Social Contract* (1762) described sovereignty as "the exercise of the general will"; therefore, as a "collective entity," it was "indivisible for the same reason that it is untransferable: a will is either general, or it is not; it is the will of the body of the people, or of a part only." Jean-Jacques Rousseau, *The Social Contract*, trans. Christopher Betts (Oxford: Oxford University Press, 1994), 63–64.

9. William Blackstone, *Commentaries on the Laws of England* (1765–1769; reprint, with an introduction by Stanley N. Katz, Chicago: University of Chicago Press, 1979), 1:156–157.

10. See Morton J. Horwitz, "Why Is Anglo-American Jurisprudence Unhistorical?" *Oxford Journal of Legal Studies* 17 (1997): 555 ("Blackstone .. needed to reconcile the waning seventeenth century Whig tradition of fundamental law with the gradually unfolding recognition during the second half of the eighteenth century of the reality of parliamentary supremacy"). On the relationship between Blackstone, the common law, and emerging ideas of popular sovereignty, see Horwitz, *The Transformation of American Law, 1780–1860* (Cambridge, Mass.: Harvard University Press, 1977), 19–20.

11. Blackstone, *Commentaries on the Laws of England*, 4:114. Some of Blackstone's contemporaries were less willing to grant him authority than subsequent generations of jurists would be. After terming as "sophistry" Blackstone's treatment of representation and referring to him as a "*court* lawyer," The American diplomat and London-trained lawyer Arthur Lee noted that "*Mr. Blackstone is solicitor to the queen*" (Blackstone had become solicitor general to the queen in 1763). Bernard Bailyn, *The Ideological Origins of the American Revolution*, enl. ed. (1967; Cambridge, Mass.: Belknap Press of Harvard University Press, 1992), 171 (quoting Lee).

12. Bernard Bailyn refers to the "ancient belief that *imperium in imperio* was an illogical and unresolvable solecism." Bailyn, *Ideological Origins,* 358. Why the term "solecism" should so often have been employed to dismiss the concept of *imperium in imperio* remains a question. Daniel Hulsebosch has demonstrated that the pejorative dated back at least to 1720, when Henry St. John, Viscount Bolingbroke, referred to *imperium in imperio* as a "Solecism in Politicks." Daniel J. Hulsebosch, *"Imperia in Imperio:* The Multiple Constitutions of Empire in New York, 1750–1777," *Law and History Review* 16 (1998): 340 n.58 (citing [Bolingbroke], *The Country Journal, or the Craftsman,* no. 172, October 18, 1729)).

13. For an especially impassioned critique of feudal law, see John Adams, "A Dissertation on the Canon and Feudal Law," in Charles Francis Adams, ed., *The Works of John Adams, Second President of the United States* (Boston: Charles C. Little and James Brown, 1851), 3:447–464.

14. Blackstone, *Commentaries on the Laws of England,* 1:156–157.

15. See Bailyn, *Ideological Origins,* 198–202. The combination of parliamentary sovereignty with empire yielded a situation following the Seven Years' War that Bailyn describes as "anomalous": "extreme decentralization of authority within an empire presumably ruled by a single, absolute, undivided sovereign." Ibid., 204.

16. See, for example, English jurist and historian James Bryce's reference to "the omnipotence of the British Parliament," which he remarked "seems to have fostered the notion

that all Parliaments ought to be free to do wrong as well as to do right." James Bryce, *Studies in History and Jurisprudence* (Oxford: Clarendon Press, 1901), 1:495.

17. See Charles Howard McIlwain, *The American Revolution: A Constitutional Interpretation* (1923; Ithaca, N.Y.: Cornell University Press, 1958); Robert Livingston Schuyler, *Parliament and the British Empire: Some Constitutional Controversies Concerning Imperial Legislative Jurisdiction* (New York: Columbia University Press, 1929); Andrew C. McLaughlin, *A Constitutional History of the United States* (New York: D. Appleton-Century Co., 1935); Barbara A. Black, "The Constitution of Empire: The Case for the Colonists," *University of Pennsylvania Law Review* 124 (1976): 1157–1211; Jack P. Greene, *Peripheries and Center: Constitutional Development in the Extended Polities of the United States, 1607–1788* (Athens: University of Georgia Press, 1986); Jack P. Greene, "From the Perspective of Law: Context and Legitimacy in the Origins of the American Revolution," *South Atlantic Quarterly* 85 (1986): 56–77; John Phillip Reid, *Constitutional History of the American Revolution*, 4 vols. (Madison: University of Wisconsin Press, 1986–1993). The quotation is from Schuyler, *Parliament and the British Empire*, v.

18. McIlwain, *American Revolution*, 17.

19. Schuyler, *Parliament and the British Empire*, 33.

20. McLaughlin, *Constitutional History*, 82.

21. Black, "Constitution of Empire," 1210–1211.

22. See Bailyn, *Ideological Origins;* Bernard Bailyn, *The Origins of American Politics* (New York: Knopf, 1968; New York: Vintage, 1970); and Gordon S. Wood, *The Creation of the American Republic, 1776–1789* (Chapel Hill: University of North Carolina Press, 1969). Citations to Bailyn, *Origins of American Politics*, are to the Vintage edition.

23. Martin S. Flaherty, "History 'Lite' in Modern American Constitutionalism," *Columbia Law Review* 95 (1995): 543.

24. Daniel J. Hulsebosch, *Constituting Empire: New York and the Transformation of Constitutionalism in the Atlantic World, 1664–1830* (Chapel Hill: University of North Carolina Press, 2005), 7.

25. Throughout his four-volume *Constitutional History of the American Revolution*, Reid emphasizes this conflict between what he views as the seventeenth-century constitution embraced by the American whigs and the eighteenth-century constitution developing in Britain. Reid thus insists that the American position drew on ancient and still-valid constitutional principles, in contrast to the arguments of historians such as Schuyler and McIlwain, who suggested that colonial opposition ideas were constructed opportunistically, in the face of superior British arguments. John Phillip Reid, *The Authority to Legislate*, vol. 3 of *Constitutional History of the American Revolution* (Madison: University of Wisconsin Press, 1991), 6.

26. See, e.g., Jack P. Greene, *Negotiated Authorities: Essays in Colonial Political and Constitutional History* (Charlottesville: University Press of Virginia, 1994), xviii (noting "the importance of negotiation in imperial governance and the significant role of peripheral entities in constructing authority in the extended polities represented by the new transatlantic empires"). For a full elaboration of the tensions over competing theories of authority, see Greene, *Peripheries and Center*, 181–211.

27. Wood, *Creation of the American Republic*, 51.

28. See Patrick Thomas Riley, "Historical Development of the Theory of Federalism, 16th–19th Centuries" (Ph.D. diss., Harvard University, 1968), 119–190; Peter S. Onuf and Nicholas Onuf, *Federal Union, Modern World: The Law of Nations in an Age of Revolutions, 1776–1814* (Madison, Wis.: Madison House, 1993), 65–66; Richard Tuck, introduction to *The Rights of War and Peace,* by Hugo Grotius (Indianapolis: Liberty Fund, 2005), 1:xxxiii; and Edward Keene, *Beyond the Anarchical Society: Grotius, Colonialism, and Order in World Politics* (Cambridge: Cambridge University Press, 2002), 3 (discussing Grotius's views of "divisible sovereignty" and arguing that these ideas both informed and grew out of European colonialism and imperialism).

29. Samuel Johnson, *Taxation No Tyranny: An Answer to the Resolutions and Address of the American Congress,* 4th ed. (London: T. Cadell, 1775), 24.

30. Keene, *Beyond the Anarchical Society,* xi.

31. Hagen Schulze, foreword to *German Federalism: Past, Present, Future,* ed. Maiken Umbach (Basingstoke, Hants: Palgrave, 2002), viii.

32. See Peter Schröder, "The Constitution of the Holy Roman Empire after 1648: Samuel Pufendorf's Assessment in His *Monzambano,*" *Historical Journal* 42 (1999): 961–983.

33. Samuel von Pufendorf, *The Law of Nature and Nations: or, a General System of the most Important Principles of Morality, Jurisprudence, and Politics,* trans. Basil Kennet, 5th ed. (London, 1749) (1672), 681–683.

34. The Fundamental Orders of Connecticut (1639), by which the towns of Windsor, Hartford, and Wethersfield resolved to "enter into Combination and Confederation together," provided an even earlier example of confederal government within the empire. The Fundamental Orders provided that each town would send deputies to a General Court, in which would be vested "the supreme power of the Commonwealth." The chief purpose of the confederation was "to maintain and preserve the liberty and purity of the Gospel of our Lord Jesus" and "the discipline of the Churches," as well as to govern "civil affairs." Fundamental Orders of Connecticut (1639), in Donald Lutz, ed., *Colonial Origins of the American Constitution: A Documentary History* (Indianapolis: Liberty Fund, 1998), 211–215.

35. Articles of Confederation of the United Colonies of New England (1643), in Lutz, *Colonial Origins of the American Constitution,* 365–369. On the New England Confederation, see Herbert L. Osgood, *The American Colonies in the Seventeenth Century,* 3 vols. (New York: Macmillan, 1904).

36. Articles of Confederation of the United Colonies of New England, 366.

37. The Dominion of New England lasted only until 1691, when Massachusetts became a royal colony. On this transition and its administrative aftermath generally, see Viola Florence Barnes, *The Dominion of New England: A Study in British Colonial Policy* (New Haven, Conn.: Yale University Press, 1923); see also Labaree, *Royal Government in America.*

38. One commentator has termed the New England Confederation "the first major attempt at federalism in America." Donald S. Lutz, ed., *Documents of Political Foundation Written by Colonial Americans: From Covenant to Constitution* (Philadelphia: Institute for the Study of Human Issues, 1986), 207. Although this statement flattens the many important differences between the confederal efforts of the seventeenth century and the related but distinct species of thought that developed in the eighteenth century, it does convey the

importance of the New England Confederation for understanding the long tradition of proposals for colonial unions and leagues in British North America.

39. On the "Jumonville affair" and the Seven Years' War, see Fred Anderson, *Crucible of War: The Seven Years' War and the Fate of Empire in British North America, 1754–1766* (New York: Vintage Books, 2001).

40. Some scholars have argued that the Iroquois Confederacy—also known as the Iroquois League or the Six Nations—provided the inspiration for British North American efforts at union. Edmund Morgan, for example, observes that the example of the Iroquois Confederacy spurred British officials to think of a league as the appropriate form to counter the French threat. According to Morgan, Franklin believed that "[i]f the Iroquois could form a powerful union that had lasted from time immemorial, some kind of union ought not to be beyond the capacity of a dozen English colonies 'to whom it is more necessary, and must be more advantageous.'" Edmund S. Morgan, *Benjamin Franklin* (New Haven, Conn.: Yale University Press, 2002), 81 (quoting Franklin in 1751). Scholars engaged in a lively debate in the 1980s and 1990s on the degree to which the Iroquois Confederacy influenced the Albany Plan in particular and colonial ideas of confederation in general; on balance, the consensus appears to be that although British North Americans were certainly aware of the confederal nature of Iroquois government, the case for causation has not been made. On the causation side, see Bruce E. Johansen, *Forgotten Founders: Benjamin Franklin, the Iroquois, and the Rationale for the American Revolution* (Ipswich, Mass.: Gambit, 1982) (arguing that Franklin and others drew on the Iroquois Confederacy for their theories of government). On the skeptical side, a nuanced account is Timothy J. Shannon, *Indians and Colonists at the Crossroads of Empire: The Albany Congress of 1754* (Ithaca and Cooperstown, N.Y.: Cornell University Press and New York State Historical Association, 2000); see also Donald Lutz, "The Iroquois Confederation: An Analysis," *Publius* 28, no. 2 (1998), 99–127; and Elisabeth Tooker, "The United States Constitution and the Iroquois League," *Ethnohistory* 37 (1988): 305–336. The "Iroquois influence" thesis was the subject of an influential forum in the *William and Mary Quarterly* in 1996. See "Forum: The 'Iroquois Influence' Thesis—Con and Pro," *William and Mary Quarterly*, 3d ser., 53 (1998), 587–636.

41. For a discussion of Hutchinson's role in the Albany Congress, see Lawrence Henry Gipson, "Thomas Hutchinson and the Framing of the Albany Plan of Union, 1754," *Pennsylvania Magazine of History and Biography* 74, no. 1 (1950): 5–35.

42. Albany Plan of Union, in Lutz, *Colonial Origins of the American Constitution*, 370–375.

43. Morgan, *Benjamin Franklin*, 83–84, 86. David Hendrickson also provides a useful analysis of the Albany Plan's provisions. See David C. Hendrickson, *Peace Pact: The Lost World of the American Founding* (Lawrence: University Press of Kansas, 2003), 118–121.

44. Albany Plan of Union, 374.

45. Franklin to Peter Collinson, May 28, 1754, quoted in Morgan, *Benjamin Franklin*, 86.

46. Morgan, *Benjamin Franklin*, 89. On the failure of the Albany Plan, see Alison Gilbert Olson, "The British Government and Colonial Union, 1754," *William and Mary Quarterly*, 3d ser., 17 (1960): 22–34.

47. Morgan, *Benjamin Franklin*, 85, 90.

48. On the corporate nature of the New England colonies before the English Civil War, see Anthony McFarlane, *The British in the Americas, 1480–1815* (London: Longman, 1994), 40–42. A more recent exploration of the consequence of early modern English corporation law for the development of judicial review is Mary Sarah Bilder, "The Corporate Origins of Judicial Review," *Yale Law Journal* 116 (2006): 502–566. Official metropolitan attitudes toward colonial trade changed in the 1650s and 1660s, first under the Commonwealth and then under the restored Stuart monarchy. This shift, which began with the Navigation Act of 1651, tended toward greater reliance on—and therefore regulation of—colonial commerce as an integral piece of English national policy. Michael Kammen notes, "After 1660 trade and commerce became, as never before, matters of immediate governmental concern. In consequence mercantilist thinking gained even greater prominence." Michael Kammen, *Empire and Interest: The American Colonies and the Politics of Mercantilism* (Philadelphia: J. B. Lippincott Co., 1970), 20. On the wider context of the colonial economy, see Claire Priest, "Law and Commerce, 1580–1815," in Christopher Tomlins and Michael Grossberg, eds., *The Cambridge History of Law in America*, vol. 1, *Early America (1580–1815)* (Cambridge: Cambridge University Press, 2008), 400–446.

49. David Armitage, *The Ideological Origins of the British Empire* (Cambridge: Cambridge University Press, 2000), 22, 60.

50. Brian P. Levack, *The Formation of the British State: England, Scotland, and the Union, 1603–1707* (Oxford: Clarendon Press, 1987), 1.

51. See, e.g., "Novanglus No. VII" and "Novanglus No. VIII," in Charles Francis Adams, *Works of John Adams*, 4:99–150. In response to the arguments of his opponent, "Massachusettensis," that allowing the colonies to have distinct legislatures would make them distinct states, as had been the case for England and Scotland before 1707, Adams insisted, "There is no absurdity at all in it. Distinct states may be united under one king. And these states may be further cemented and united together by a treaty of commerce." "Novanglus No. VII," 4:113.

52. John Robertson, "An Elusive Sovereignty: The Course of the Union Debate in Scotland, 1698–1707," in John Robertson, ed., *A Union for Empire: Political Thought and the Union of 1707* (Cambridge: Cambridge University Press, 1995), 206 and passim.

53. [James Hodges], *The Rights and Interests of the Two British Monarchies, Inquir'd Into, and Clear'd; with a Special Respect to an United or Separate State, Treatise I* (London, 1703), 2, 3. Hodges's reference to two British monarchies demonstrates his commitment to the equality of Scotland with England. The epigraph on the cover of the pamphlet, which Hodges attributed to the book of Ecclesiastes, repeats this theme: *"Two are better than One."*

54. In all three cases, the name of the new incorporated kingdom differed from that of each of the subkingdoms, suggesting that by joining together, the components had created a new political entity. Thus, according to Hodges, the seven kingdoms of the Kentish Saxons, the South Saxons, the East Angles, the East Saxons, the Marcians, the Northumbers, and the West Saxons joined to form a new kingdom called England. Hodges's theory thus did not contemplate annexation or another unequal relationship between preexisting kingdoms in which one simply absorbed the other. Ibid., 3.

55. Ibid., 4.

56. See Robertson, "Elusive Sovereignty," 209–210. Throughout the course of the union debates, these and other thinkers' positions shifted in multiple and subtle ways. At various points, for instance, both Hodges and Ridpath argued that the union of crowns had in fact created an incorporating union in which each country's sovereignty endured. Although Robertson notes that such a shift "ran against the grain of the powerful conceptual association built up over the previous two centuries between 'incorporation' and territorial 'empire,'" he describes these commentators as demonstrating "a willingness to think again" about how authority was to be divided between Scottish and English institutions once joined. Ibid., 215. On Fletcher's vision of a union of equals, see ibid., 209. Robertson quotes Fletcher as stating before the Scottish Parliament in 1703 that the rest of the world regarded Scotland as a "conquered province." See ibid., 204; see also "Speeches by a Member of the Parliament," in Andrew Fletcher, *Political Works,* ed. John Robertson (Cambridge: Cambridge University Press, 1997), 133. Robertson notes that Fletcher's library contained copies of Pufendorf's works. See Fletcher, *Political Works,* 208n.

57. Robertson, "Elusive Sovereignty," 202–204. On the pre-1707 history of Scotland's relationship with England and emerging notions of Britishness and empire, see David Armitage, "Making the Empire British: Scotland in the Atlantic World, 1542–1707," *Past and Present,* no. 155 (May 1997): 34–63. On the economic situation of the two nations before the union of parliaments, see T. C. Smout, "The Anglo-Scottish Union of 1707: The Economic Background," *Economic History Review,* n.s., 16 (1964): 455–467.

58. Despite Scotland's loss of its independent parliament, Robertson points out that some Scottish unionists insisted that Scotland had not given up its sovereignty, but rather had gained the possibility of greater rights as a member of the union. At least one spokesman invoked the writings of Hugo Grotius to elucidate their theories, especially his statement in *De jure belli ac pacis (The Rights of War and Peace)* of 1625 that "[w]henever two nations become united, their rights, as distinct states, will not be lost, but will be communicated to each other. . . . The same reasoning holds good respecting states, which are joined, not by a FEDERAL union, but by having one sovereign for their head." Hugo Grotius, *The Rights of War and Peace: Including the Law of Nature and Nations,* trans. A. M. Campbell (London: B. Boothroyd, 1814), bk. 9, chap. 9, § 8. William Seton of Pitmedden cited this section of *The Rights of War and Peace* in a speech before the Scottish Parliament on the articles of union. Quoted in Robertson, "Elusive Sovereignty," 221 and n.78.

59. John Robertson, "Empire and Union: Two Concepts of the Early Modern European Political Order," in John Robertson, ed., *A Union for Empire: Political Thought and the British Union of 1707* (Cambridge: Cambridge University Press, 1995), 9–10. The 1533 date comes from the Act in Restraint of Appeals of that year, the preamble to which stated that "this Realme of Englond is an Impire." An Acte that the Appeles in suche cases as have ben used to be pursued to the See of Rome shall not be from hensforth had ne used but wythin this Realme, 24 Hen. 8, c. 12 (quoted in Robertson, "Empire and Union," 8). See also Armitage, *Ideological Origins of the British Empire,* 60 (describing "British state-building and British empire-building" as "continuous with one another in their origins as in their outcomes").

60. Armitage, *Ideological Origins of the British Empire,* 148, 25. On Ireland's position within the British Empire, see Nicholas Canny, *Kingdom and Colony: Ireland in the Atlantic World, 1560–1800* (Baltimore: Johns Hopkins University Press, 1988); Canny, "The Ideology of English Colonization: From Ireland to America," *William and Mary Quarterly,* 3d ser., 30 (1973): 575–598. On parallels between American and Irish claims, see John Phillip Reid, *In a Defiant Stance: The Conditions of Law in Massachusetts Bay, the Irish Comparison, and the Coming of the American Revolution* (University Park: Pennsylvania State University Press, 1977).

61. 10 Hen. VII, c. 4 (1495); repealed 21 & 22 Geo. III, c. 47 (1781).

62. William Molyneux, *The Case of Ireland's Being Bound by Acts of Parliament in England, Stated* (Dublin: Joseph Ray, 1698), 149.

63. John Adams, "Novanglus No. XI," in Charles Francis Adams, *Works of John Adams,* 4:168.

2. DIVIDING LAWMAKING POWER

1. Britannus Americanicus [pseud.], *A serious Address to the Inhabitants of New-York* (New York, 1765). A handwritten note at the bottom of the version available through the Early American Imprints series states, "This paper was distributed all over New York & stuck up at the Coffee-h[ouse] at Noon Day." Early American Imprints, 1st ser.: Evans, 1639–1800, no. 10041.

2. Ibid.

3. Ibid. On responses in America to the Glorious Revolution of 1688–1689, see Jack P. Greene, "The Glorious Revolution and the British Empire, 1688–1783," in Lois G. Schwoerer, ed., *The Revolution of 1688–1689: Changing Perspectives* (Cambridge: Cambridge University Press, 1992); and David S. Lovejoy, *The Glorious Revolution in America* (Middletown, Conn.: Wesleyan University Press, 1987).

4. See Greene, "Glorious Revolution and the British Empire."

5. See Bernard Bailyn, introduction to James Otis, "The Rights of the British Colonies Asserted and Proved," in Bernard Bailyn, ed., *Pamphlets of the American Revolution, 1750–1765* (Cambridge, Mass.: Belknap Press of Harvard University Press, 1965), 412–413; see also J. G. A. Pocock, *The Ancient Constitution and the Feudal Law: A Study of English Historical Thought in the Seventeenth Century; A Reissue with a Retrospect* (New York: Norton, 1987), 229–251. William Blackstone was the leading contemporary exponent of this view. See William Blackstone, *Commentaries on the Laws of England* (1765–1769; reprint, with an introduction by Stanley N. Katz, Chicago: University of Chicago Press, 1979), 1:156–157.

6. On the notion of the king-in-Parliament, see H. T. Dickinson, "Britain's Imperial Sovereignty," in H. T. Dickinson, ed., *Britain and the American Revolution* (London: Longman, 1998): 64–96; J. G. A. Pocock, "Political Thought in the English-Speaking Atlantic, 1760–1790, Part I: The Imperial Crisis," in J. G. A. Pocock, ed., *The Varieties of British Political Thought, 1500–1800* (Cambridge: Cambridge University Press, 1993), 246–282; Pocock, "Political Thought in the English-Speaking Atlantic, 1760–1790, Part II:

Empire, Revolution and the End of Early Modernity," in Pocock, *Varieties of British Political Thought,* 283–317; and Pocock, "A Discourse of Sovereignty: Observations on the Work in Progress," in Nicholas Phillipson and Quentin Skinner, eds., *Political Discourse in Early Modern Britain* (Cambridge: Cambridge University Press, 1993), 377–428.

7. On colonial lawyers' challenges to Parliament's power, see Barbara A. Black, "The Constitution of Empire: The Case for the Colonists," *University of Pennsylvania Law Review* 124 (1976): 1157–1211; and John Phillip Reid, *The Authority to Legislate,* vol. 3 of *Constitutional History of the American Revolution* (Madison: University of Wisconsin Press, 1991), 4–5.

8. An Act for Granting and Applying Certain Stamp Duties, and Other Duties, in the British Colonies and Plantations in America, 5 Geo. 3, c. 12.

9. Rhode Island Patent (1643), in John Russell Bartlett, ed., *Records of the Colony of Rhode Island and Providence Plantations in New England* (Providence: A. C. Greene, 1856–1865), 1:143–146.

10. Jack P. Greene, "The Colonial Origins of American Constitutionalism," in Jack P. Greene, ed., *Negotiated Authorities: Essays in Colonial Political and Constitutional History* (Charlottesville: University Press of Virginia, 1994), 39.

11. On the parliament/Parliament distinction, see Black, "Constitution of Empire," 1181.

12. For the related phrase "negotiated authorities," see Jack P. Greene, "Negotiated Authorities: The Problem of Governance in the Extended Polities of the Early Modern Atlantic World," in Greene, *Negotiated Authorities,* 1–24.

13. The degree of lawmaking authority granted to the provincial assemblies varied throughout the seventeenth and eighteenth centuries. The Glorious Revolution, in particular, brought renewed efforts to increase metropolitan regulation of the colonies. See Richard R. Beeman, *The Varieties of Political Experience in Eighteenth-Century America* (Philadelphia: University of Pennsylvania Press, 2004), 8–30; and Brendan McConville, *The King's Three Faces: The Rise and Fall of Royal America, 1688–1776* (Chapel Hill: University of North Carolina Press, 2006), 39–48.

14. Reid, *Authority to Legislate,* 228–230.

15. Ibid.

16. John Phillip Reid, *Constitutional History of the American Revolution,* abr. ed. (Madison: University of Wisconsin Press, 1995), 13–14.

17. See J. M. Bumsted, "'Things in the Womb of Time': Ideas of American Independence, 1633 to 1763," *William and Mary Quarterly,* 3d ser., 31 (1974): 534 (discussing the "undercurrent of concern about, and anticipation of, eventual American separation from the Empire in the years before 1763").

18. John Adams, *Diary and Autobiography of John Adams,* ed. L. H. Butterfield, vol. 1 (Cambridge, Mass.: Belknap Press of Harvard University Press, 1961) (entry of December 18, 1765), 263.

19. Speech of George Grenville, Commons Debates, March 9, 1764, in P. D. G. Thomas, ed., "Parliamentary Diaries of Nathaniel Ryder, 1764–7," in *Camden Miscellany,* 4th ser., 23 (London: Camden Society, 1969), 7:234–235. The text of Grenville's March 9 speech has not survived, but portions of the remarks have been preserved in contemporary accounts. See Edmund S. Morgan, "The Postponement of the Stamp Act," *William and Mary Quarterly,*

3d ser., 7 (1950): 355. Morgan's article canvasses several of the contemporary summaries of Grenville's speech.

20. Quoted in John Phillip Reid, *The Authority to Tax,* vol. 2 of *Constitutional History of the American Revolution* (Madison: University of Wisconsin Press, 1987), 12.

21. Edmund S. Morgan and Helen Morgan, *The Stamp Act Crisis: Prologue to Revolution,* rev. ed. (New York: Collier Books, 1962), 75, 42 (quotation). This provision was not included in the final version of the act.

22. Morgan, "Postponement of the Stamp Act," 358.

23. Morgan and Morgan, *Stamp Act Crisis,* 78. The Morgans are skeptical of the genuineness of Grenville's offer to allow the colonies to tax themselves, pointing to the abortive efforts by members of the Massachusetts House of Representatives to convene a special legislative session to consider alternative methods of taxation. When the colonists broached the issue to Governor Francis Bernard, he responded that "it was impossible at present to proceed to an actual taxation, untill [*sic*] the demands of the ministry should be further explained." From this exchange, the Morgans conclude that Grenville consciously omitted to back up his offer with actual instructions to the governor or other specific guidelines. Quoted ibid., 84–85.

24. Available evidence suggests that three individuals drafted proposed versions of stamp legislation: Henry McCulloh, Thomas Cruwys, and Thomas Whately. Ibid., 78 n.8. Whately was at the time Grenville's secretary to the Treasury. McCulloh had in 1755 published a pamphlet discussing the nature of British authority over the colonies, discussed later in this chapter. Whately later gained infamy in America for his role as a correspondent with Thomas Hutchinson, the royal governor of Massachusetts; the release of their letters in 1773 fueled Massachusetts colonists' opposition to the governor and his perceived sabotage of their constitutional arguments. In addition to airing the possibility of a stamp duty, Grenville recommended certain changes to the colonial customs levies, in particular a reduction in the duty on molasses imported into the colonies from non-British producers in an effort to stimulate consumption and thereby increase the revenue flow from the molasses trade into the imperial fisc. See Robert Middlekauff, *The Glorious Cause: The American Revolution, 1763–1789,* rev. and expanded ed. (New York: Oxford University Press, 2005), 63. In April 1764, the reduction in the molasses duty (in addition to new duties on other foreign goods, such as indigo, "coffee and pimento," certain wines, linen, calico, and "all wrought silks, bengals, and stuffs, mixed with silk or the herbs of the manufacture of Persia, China, or East India") passed into law in what was titled the Revenue Act of 1764 but quickly became known as the Sugar (or Molasses) Act. On the context of the Sugar Act, see Morgan and Morgan, *Stamp Act Crisis,* 36–58.

25. On imperial interest in strengthening ties between Britain and the North American colonies, see, e.g., Jack P. Greene, "Metropolis and Colonies: Changing Patterns of Constitutional Conflict in the Early Modern British Empire, 1607–1763," in Greene, *Negotiated Authorities,* 75; Charles F. Mullett, "English Imperial Thinking, 1764–1783," *Political Science Quarterly* 45 (1930): 548–579; and Randolph G. Adams, *Political Ideas of the American Revolution: Britannic-American Contributions to the Problem of Imperial Organization, 1765 to 1775,* 3d ed. (Durham, N.C.: Trinity College Press, 1922; New York: Barnes and Noble, 1958). Citations are to the Barnes and Noble edition. On Grenville's place in

this narrative, see, e.g., P. D. G. Thomas, *British Politics and the Stamp Act Crisis: The First Phase of the American Revolution* (Oxford: Clarendon Press, 1975), the first chapter of which is titled "George Grenville Comes to Power." On Grenville's determination to reform revenue collection, see John L. Bullion, *A Great and Necessary Measure: George Grenville and the Genesis of the Stamp Act, 1763–1765* (Columbia: University of Missouri Press, 1982), 62–113 (describing Grenville's ascendance and his focus on reducing clandestine trade and identifying new sources of revenue). On Britain's growing national debt and estimates of troop costs, see Morgan and Morgan, *Stamp Act Crisis*, 36, 37.

26. On the Board of Trade in this period, see Ian K. Steele, "Metropolitan Administration of the Colonies, 1696–1775," in Jack P. Greene and J. R. Pole, eds., *The Blackwell Encyclopedia of the American Revolution* (Cambridge, Mass.: Basil Blackwell, 1991), 9–16; see also Thomas, *British Politics and the Stamp Act Crisis,* especially chapter 2, "The Hub of Empire: Whitehall and Westminster" (noting on page 27 that although "[n]o central machinery for the government of the first British Empire existed," the Board of Trade "did supply some unofficial cohesion"). For an earlier period, see Ian K. Steele, *Politics of Colonial Policy: The Board of Trade in Colonial Administration, 1696–1720* (Oxford: Clarendon Press, 1968). On its successor, the Colonial or American Department, see Margaret Marion Spector, *The American Department of the British Government, 1768–1782* (New York: Columbia University Press, 1940).

27. Morgan and Morgan, *Stamp Act Crisis,* 38 (revenues), 39 (absentee collectors). The many impediments to officials' collection of customs duties are discussed in Middlekauff, *Glorious Cause,* 63–64. One scholar has argued that many metropolitan officials viewed rampant smuggling and illegal imports as signs that the colonies needed to be reminded of their due subordination; the new tax legislation provided a means to achieve this end. Thomas C. Barrow, "Background to the Grenville Program, 1757–1763," *William and Mary Quarterly,* 3d ser., 22 (1965): 93–104.

28. Other commentators, however, contend that Parliament had a long history of issuing colonial regulations that were quite similar to the acts of the 1760s. These scholars typically cite the Molasses Act of 1733 as a significant precedent in this regard. See, e.g., Reid, *Authority to Tax,* 28–29 (describing the 1733 act and its origin in a metropolitan drive to steer colonists toward British West Indian sugar and away from cheaper sugar produced in the French islands) and 158–180 (chapter 15). The Hat Act of 1732, which was intended to discourage the colonial manufacture of hats and therefore encourage imports of British hats, is also mentioned frequently in this regard. 5 Geo. 2, c. 22; see, e.g., Reid, *Authority to Tax,* 368–369 n.8.

29. Morgan and Morgan, *Stamp Act Crisis,* 39.

30. Ibid., 40. Admiralty courts had operated in the colonies since 1697, but jurisdictional struggles and control of judges by local merchants had limited their ability to enforce the navigation acts. Ibid. Beginning in the 1760s, metropolitan efforts to police colonial trade increasingly relied on the Royal Navy as an arm of the customs service. Under the Grenville ministry, for example, British naval officers stationed in America received Treasury warrants investing them with the power of deputy customs officers. See Michael Kammen, *Empire and Interest: The American Colonies and the Politics of Mercantilism* (Philadelphia: J. B. Lippincott Co., 1970), 120.

31. An Act for Granting Certain Duties in the British Colonies and Plantations in America . . . and More Effectually Preventing the Clandestine Conveyance of Goods to and from the Said Colonies and Plantations, and Improving and Securing the Trade between the Same and Great Britain, 4 Geo. 3, c. 15. John Dickinson also noted the similarities between the Sugar and Stamp acts in his 1768 *Letters from a Farmer;* he concluded that both statutes' stated aims of raising a revenue was "a most dangerous innovation." [John Dickinson], *Letters from a Farmer in Pennsylvania, to the Inhabitants of the British Colonies* (Boston: Mein and Fleeming, 1768), 17–19. The Morgans also note that in 1742, Sir William Keith had proposed a stamp tax on the ground that it would instill American colonists with "a more just and favourable opinion of their dependency on a British Parliament, than what they generally have at present." Quoted in Morgan and Morgan, *Stamp Act Crisis,* 87.

32. Morgan, "Postponement of the Stamp Act," 358; Grenville to the House of Commons, April 26, 1770; quoted in Bullion, *Great and Necessary Measure,* 210.

33. The range of duties was extremely broad: two pence for "any almanack or calendar . . . printed on one side only of any one sheet"; three pence per sheet of paper (or "every skin or piece of vellum or parchment") used for "any declaration, plea, replication, rejoinder, demurrer, or other pleading, or any copy thereof, in any court of law"; one shilling per sheet, skin, or piece for "any bond for securing the payment of any sum of money above twenty pounds, and not exceeding forty pounds of sterling money"; twenty shillings per sheet, skin, or piece for "any licence for retailing of spirituous liquors"; and ten pounds per sheet, skin, or piece for "any license, appointment, or admission of any counsellor, solicitor, attorney, advocate, or proctor, to practice in any court, or of any notary within the said colonies and plantations." The act clearly placed a substantial burden on attorneys and other legal actors. The duty for a license to practice in court (ten pounds) amounted to twenty times the rate per page of the duty for an appeal, writ of error, or writ of dower (ten shillings) and eight hundred times that of a declaration, plea, replication, or other pleading in a court of law (three pence).

34. Middlekauff, *Glorious Cause,* 81, 98.

35. The declaration of rights, petitions, and memorial are reprinted in Edmund S. Morgan, ed., *Prologue to Revolution: Sources and Documents on the Stamp Act Crisis, 1764–1766* (Chapel Hill: University of North Carolina Press, 1959), 62–69.

36. For the great weight that colonists placed on avoiding establishing any precedent for enforcement of the duty, see Reid, *Constitutional History of the American Revolution,* abr. ed., 31.

37. See, e.g., New York Merchants Non-Importation Agreement, October 31, 1765, *New York Mercury* (November 7, 1765) (according to which two hundred "principal merchants" agreed "not to buy any goods, wares, or merchandises of any person or persons whatsoever that shall be shipped from Great Britain after the first day of January next unless the Stamp Act shall be repealed"). For a discussion of popular uprisings and protests during this period, see Gary B. Nash, *The Unknown American Revolution: The Unruly Birth of Democracy and the Struggle to Create America* (New York: Viking, 2005), 44–149.

38. Middlekauff, *Glorious Cause,* 113.

39. Ibid.

40. William Cobbett, ed., *Parliamentary History of England: From the Earliest Period to the Year 1803* (London: R. Bagshaw, 1806–1820), 16:107–108.

41. The Parliamentary Diary of James Harris, quoted in R. C. Simmons and P. D. G. Thomas, eds., *Proceedings and Debates of the British Parliament Respecting North America, 1754–1783,* vol. 2 (Millwood, N.Y.: Kraus International Publications, 1983), 81.

42. Horace Walpole, *Memoirs of the Reign of King George the Third,* ed. G. F. Russell Barker (London, 1894), 184–191, quoted in Simmons and Thomas, *Proceedings and Debates of the British Parliament,* 2:81. Cobbett notes that the member for Bristol, Edmund Burke, made his maiden speech in Parliament during this debate, on which Pitt complimented him ("in terms," according to Pitt's autobiography, "peculiarly flattering to a young man"). Quoted in Cobbett, *Parliamentary History of England,* 16:108 fn.

43. Cobbett, *Parliamentary History of England,* 16:105.

44. See Quentin Skinner, "Meaning and Understanding in the History of Ideas," in James Tully, ed., *Meaning and Context: Quentin Skinner and His Critics* (Princeton, N.J.: Princeton University Press, 1988), 64.

45. Reid, *Authority to Legislate,* 8. Reid also notes that by referring to the Stamp Act as an "internal" tax, the colonists deliberately emphasized its novelty—which, in a legal universe that prized precedent as dearly as did the eighteenth-century Anglo-American common-law world, was tantamount to denouncing the act as unconstitutional. Reid, *Authority to Tax,* 39.

46. Reid, *Authority to Tax,* 8–12.

47. R. G. Adams, *Political Ideas of the American Revolution,* 91; Middlekauff, *Glorious Cause,* 129. The previous edition of Middlekauff's *Glorious Cause* made a stronger argument in this vein, as Reid notes. See Robert Middlekauff, *The Glorious Cause* (New York: Oxford University Press, 1982); Reid, *Authority to Legislate,* 7–8.

48. Specifically, Bailyn describes the Townshend duties of 1767 as "cynically devised to satisfy the colonists' incautious concession of 'external' taxes" by levying extensive customs duties on tea, glass, paper, and paint. Such duties were external in that they had to be paid at the point of importation, but the preamble to the act clearly stated that the act's objective was to raise a revenue in the colonies. See Bernard Bailyn, introduction to "A Dialogue between an American and a European Englishman by Thomas Hutchinson," in Donald Fleming and Bernard Bailyn, eds., *Perspectives in American History* 9 (Cambridge, Mass.: Charles Warren Center for Studies in American History, Harvard University, 1975): 347; see also Reid, *Authority to Tax,* 33 (describing the "mistaken belief" of Charles Townshend, chancellor of the Exchequer, that Americans would permit external but not internal taxes, despite Townshend's stated belief that the distinction was "ridiculous in every body's opinion except the Americans").

49. See Edmund S. Morgan, "Colonial Ideas of Parliamentary Power, 1764–1766," *William and Mary Quarterly,* 3d ser., 5 (1948): 340, 341; and Morgan and Morgan, *Stamp Act Crisis,* 152–154.

50. Much like modern commentators, contemporary observers disagreed over whether the internal-external rhetoric had originated in Britain or in America. In 1774, one member of Parliament asserted in debate that "the Americans . . . have taken that strange distinction between internal and external," suggesting that the trope was unfamiliar to him, at

least. Quoted in the Parliamentary Diary of Henry Cavendish, quoted in R. C. Simmons and P. D. G. Thomas, eds., *Proceedings and Debates of the British Parliament Respecting North America, 1754–1783,* vol. 4 (Millwood, N.Y.: Kraus International Publications, 1985), 182. The outstanding works in this regard are Reid's, particularly *The Authority to Tax* and *The Authority to Legislate,* both from his four-volume *Constitutional History of the American Revolution.*

51. [Henry McCulloh], *A Miscellaneous Essay Concerning the Courses pursued by Great Britain in the Affairs of her Colonies; with some Observations on the Great Importance of our Settlements in America, and the Trade thereof* (London: R. Baldwin, 1755), 14, 69, 16–17. Ned Landsman identifies McCulloh with the group of Scottish and Scottish-American officials who wrote on the relationship between colonies and empire in the mid-eighteenth century. See Ned Landsman, "The Legacy of British Union for the North American Colonies: Provincial Elites and the Problem of Imperial Union," in John Robertson, ed., *A Union for Empire: Political Thought and the British Union of 1707* (Cambridge: Cambridge University Press, 1995), 304–305.

52. [McCulloh], *Miscellaneous Essay,* 16.

53. See [Archibald Kennedy], *Observations on the Importance of the Northern Colonies under Proper Regulations* (New York: James Parker, 1750), 9, 20; [Kennedy], *An Essay on the Government of the Colonies. Fitted to the Latitude Forty-one, but may, without sensible Error, serve all the Northern Colonies* (New York: J. Parker, 1752), 20–21, 35.

54. Landsman, "Legacy of British Union," 305.

55. [McCulloh], *Miscellaneous Essay,* 92; Landsman, "Legacy of British Union," 305.

56. Bernard Bailyn, introduction to "The Colonel Dismounted," in Bailyn, *Pamphlets of the American Revolution,* 707 n.11. Bland claimed that he had written the pamphlet eight months earlier, which would put its composition in December 1763. Ibid., 297.

57. Common Sense [Richard Bland], *The Colonel Dismounted: or the Rector Vindicated. In a Letter Addressed to His Reverence: Containing a Dissertation upon the Constitution of the Colony* (Williamsburg: Joseph Royle, 1764), 22–23.

58. In addition to Bland, many other writers produced tracts examining the relationship between metropolitan and colonial power in terms of the internal-external distinction. In December 1764, a pamphlet written by Rhode Island governor Stephen Hopkins and approved by the Rhode Island Assembly put forth a similar vision of imperial legislative power as allotted to Parliament for certain matters and to the colonial assemblies for others. The pamphlet, titled *The Rights of Colonies Examined,* observed that although "each of the colonies hath a legislature within itself to take care of its interests and provide for its peace and internal government," other matters of a "more general nature, quite out of the reach of these particular legislatures," also needed to be "regulated, ordered, and governed." The obvious regulator of such matters, Hopkins stated, was Parliament. Among the "general concerns," Hopkins listed "the commerce of the whole British empire, taken collectively, and that of each kingdom and colony in it as it makes a part of that whole." Other general matters included "keeping the peace," money and paper credit ("those grand instruments of all commerce"), and "everything that concerns the proper interest and fit government of the whole commonwealth." [Stephen Hopkins], *The Rights of Colonies Examined* (Providence: William Goddard, 1765), 10–11.

59. James Otis, *The Rights of the British Colonies Asserted and Proved* (Boston: Edes and Gill, 1764), 32–33, 59. Bailyn notes of *Rights of the British Colonies*, "Of all the pronouncements issued by the colonists in the agitated year between the passage of the Sugar Act and that of the Stamp Act . . . none was more widely known or commented upon." A London edition of the pamphlet was issued by the end of 1764, and at least three more editions appeared by 1766. Bernard Bailyn, introduction to Otis, "The Rights of the British Colonies," in Bailyn, *Pamphlets of the American Revolution*, 409.

60. Otis, *Rights of the British Colonies*, 42.

61. Ibid., 32–33, 38.

62. Ibid., 70–71. On Otis's role in the writs of assistance case, see Bernard Bailyn, *The Ideological Origins of the American Revolution*, enl. ed. (1967; Cambridge, Mass.: Belknap Press of Harvard University Press, 1992), 176–181.

63. On the American whigs' uses of Enlightenment theory generally, see Bailyn, *Ideological Origins*, 26–28. Although Bailyn notes that "[t]he citations are plentiful" but "the knowledge they reflect . . . is at times superficial," other scholars have emphasized that at least some of the American whigs delved deeply into the study of political theory. Ibid., 28. See, e,g., Anthony M. Lewis, "Jefferson's *Summary View* as a Chart of Political Union," *William and Mary Quarterly*, 3d ser., 5 (1948): 34–51 (discussing Jefferson's immersion in the writings of Locke, Jean Jacques Burlamaqui, Montesquieu, and others beginning in 1769, on the basis of notes in his commonplace book). Bailyn notes that Otis was a "thorough scholar of ancient texts." Bailyn, *Ideological Origins*, 25. For purposes of the discussion in this chapter, his related point that the Americans read selectively in both ancient and modern philosophy is less important than the evidence of what, given their selective tastes, they chose to read.

64. Otis, *Rights of the British Colonies*, 25–27. Bailyn notes that the passage from Grotius, based on a 1738 translation published in London, is "correct in both wording and citation." Bailyn terms the Pufendorf quotation "essentially correct" and identifies it as taken from an English translation by Basil Kennet and William Percivale that first appeared in 1703. He also notes that Hopkins's tract quotes the same passages. Bailyn, introduction to Otis, "The Rights of the British Colonies" in Bailyn, *Pamphlets of the American Revolution*, 720 n.10.

65. On this divergence between metropolitan and provincial sources of political theory, see Pocock, "Political Thought in the English-Speaking Atlantic, 1760–1790, Part I," 263–264.

66. Otis, *Rights of the British Colonies*, 38. As has already been noted, Blackstone's *Commentaries* was published in England beginning in 1765. Bailyn notes that Otis saw a copy of the first volume in that year. Bailyn, introduction to James Otis, "A Vindication of the British Colonies," in Bailyn, *Pamphlets of the American Revolution*, 546 and 738 n.6; see also Otis's own references to "Mr. Blackstone's accurate and elegant analysis of the laws of England" on the subject of the liberties of Englishmen. Otis, *A Vindication of the* British Colonies, a*gainst the Aspersions of the* Halifax *Gentleman, in His Letter to a Rhode Island Friend* (Boston: Edes and Gill, 1765), 9. It is worth noting that Otis's contemporary Stephen Hopkins displayed a similar interest in looking to Europe for political ideas and models of government in his effort to rebut metropolitan claims of supreme parliamentary authority. For

example, in *The Rights of Colonies Examined,* Hopkins cited "the empire of Germany" as evidence for his claim that laws concerning the empire as a whole ought to be within the jurisdiction of the whole and not of one part alone. Hopkins derived from this example the general principle that in an "imperial state . . . all laws and all taxations which bind the whole must be made by the whole." [Hopkins], *Rights of Colonies Examined,* 19–20.

67. Otis, *Vindication,* 14, 10, 5. Otis discussed these themes in a different pamphlet published in 1765: *Brief Remarks on the Defense of the Halifax Libel on the British-American Colonies.* Many scholars, in addition to many of Otis's contemporaries, regard these 1765 works as abandoning the earlier arguments in *Rights of the British Colonies* in favor of a vision of unfettered parliamentary supremacy. See, e.g., Middlekauff, *Glorious Cause,* rev. and expanded ed., 91–92. Bailyn finds more continuity between *Rights* and the two later tracts but notes that *Vindication* "permanently compromis[ed] its author's reputation as a spokesman for the colonies." Bailyn, introduction to Otis, "A Vindication of the British Colonies," in *Pamphlets of the American Revolution,* 546. Some observers, then and now, attributed this seemingly wild shift to Otis's growing mental instability. In late 1765, John Adams described Otis as "fiery and feverous." Quoted ibid., 546. Nevertheless, the pamphlets—particularly the first two—shared the view that the internal-external distinction was invalid.

68. Merrill Jensen, ed., *Tracts of the American Revolution, 1763–1776* (Indianapolis: Bobbs-Merrill Co., 1967), 94.

69. [Daniel Dulany], *Considerations on the Propriety of Imposing Taxes in the British Colonies for the Purpose of Raising a Revenue by Act of Parliament,* 2d ed. (Annapolis: Jonas Green, 1765), 15. Despite his early prominence as a critic of British policy, Dulany remained a loyalist during the Revolution, and his property was confiscated by the state.

70. The "who decides?" question is suggested in David Hendrickson, *Peace Pact: The Lost World of the American Founding* (Lawrence: University Press of Kansas, 2003), 88–89 ("The burden of the British case [for the Coercive Acts of 1774] rested not on the proposition that Parliament was to decide everything, but that it was to decide where everything was to be decided.").

71. See Daniel J. Hulsebosch, *Constituting Empire: New York and the Transformation of Constitutionalism in the Atlantic World, 1664–1830* (Chapel Hill: University of North Carolina Press, 2005), 3 (describing the imperial agents as "a corps of officials trying to reform imperial administration," in contrast to "a provincial elite jealous of its local power"). On the colonial agents, perhaps the most in-between of these groups, see Michael G. Kammen, *A Rope of Sand: The Colonial Agents, British Politics, and the American Revolution* (Ithaca, N.Y.: Cornell University Press, 1968).

72. This point is not intended to suggest that law as defined in London was in some sense monolithic throughout the empire, or that the formal legal pronouncements that issued from authorities in either the metropolitan center or the provincial capitals necessarily described conditions beyond these centers of power. As Jack Greene has noted, in British North America, "authority structures [were] created not strictly by imposition from the top down or from the center out but through an elaborate process of negotiation among the parties involved." It is not the aim of this chapter to challenge this thesis; on the contrary, the recognition that the practice of imperial governance entailed more or less constant

conflict and compromise regarding the location of authority makes necessary a reexamination of imperial theory as another site of negotiation (and, indeed, a site of another negotiation), in this case among political and constitutional ideas. On this general point, see Greene, "Negotiated Authorities: The Problem of Governance in the Extended Polities of the Early Modern Atlantic World," in Greene, *Negotiated Authorities,* 4; see also Hulsebosch, *Constituting Empire* (especially chapter 3, "The Multiple Constitutions of Empire in New York, 1750–1777"); Christine A. Desan, "The Constitutional Commitment to Legislative Adjudication in the Early American Tradition," *Harvard Law Review* 111 (1998): 1281–1502; and Desan, "Remaking Constitutional Tradition at the Margin of Empire: The Creation of Legislative Adjudication in Colonial New York," *Law and History Review* 16 (1998): 257–317.

73. The group that I term "metropolitan" thus included both "imperial agents" and the "creole provincial elite"—two categories of individuals that Daniel Hulsebosch identifies as holding distinct views of the imperial constitution. Hulsebosch, *Constituting Empire,* 76.

74. Bailyn notes that Otis was citing the first edition of Pownall's book. See Bailyn, introduction to Otis, "The Rights of the British Colonies," in *Pamphlets of the American Revolution,* 721 n.20.

75. Thomas Pownall, *The Administration of the Colonies,* 2d ed. (London: J. Dodsley and J. Walter, 1765), 9–10, A5, table of contents, 12–18. As one scholar of the imperial administration has noted, Pownall's reforms proposed substantial changes to colonial governance, which had to that point been carried out by an assortment of institutions and offices, with "no one individual or department primarily responsible for the coordination of the efforts of these various branches of administration. In 1766 the Earl of Chesterfield gloomily reflected that 'if we have no Secretary of State with full and undisputed powers for America, in a few years we may as well have no America.'" Spector, *American Department,* 11–12. On Pownall in particular and competing visions of imperial continuity in general, see Peter N. Miller, *Defining the Common Good: Empire, Religion and Philosophy in Eighteenth-Century Britain* (Cambridge: Cambridge University Press, 1994). Pownall's brother John Pownall, who had served as permanent secretary to the Board of Trade since 1741, became one of two undersecretaries in the American Department after its establishment in 1768.

76. Pownall, *Administration of the Colonies,* 36.

77. Ibid., 41.

78. Ibid., 90–91 (emphasis added).

79. Ibid., 91.

80. Francis Bernard, *Select Letters on the Trade and Government of America; and the Principles of Law and Polity, Applied to the American Colonies* (London: T. Payne, 1774), 1–2.

81. Ibid., 30.

82. See Morgan and Morgan, *Stamp Act Crisis,* 339–340.

83. Bernard, *Select Letters,* 72.

84. Ibid., 78.

85. Answer of the House of Representatives to Governor Bernard, October 23, 1765, in Alden Bradford, ed., *Speeches of the Governors of Massachusetts, from 1765 to 1775: and the*

Answers of the House of Representatives to the Same; with Their Resolutions and Addresses
for That Period and Other Public Papers Relating to the Dispute between This Country and
Great Britain Which Led to the Independence of the United States (Boston: Russell and
Gardner, 1818), 45.

86. Virginia Resolves, quoted in Samuel Eliot Morison, ed., *Sources and Documents Il-*
lustrating the American Revolution, 1764–1788, and the Formation of the Federal Constitu-
tion, 2d ed. (New York: Oxford University Press, 1965), 17 (second emphasis added).

87. On the traditional rights of Englishmen, see Pocock, *Ancient Constitution and the*
Feudal Law, 30–55.

88. An Act Repealing the Stamp Act, 6 Geo. 3, c. 11; An Act for the Better Securing the
Dependency of His Majesty's Dominions in America upon the Crown and Parliament of
Great Britain, 6 Geo. 3, c. 12 (the Declaratory Act). The Declaratory Act stated, in relevant
part, "That the said colonies and plantations in America have been, are, and of right ought
to be, subordinate unto, and dependent upon the imperial crown and parliament of Great
Britain; and that the King's majesty, by and with the advice and consent of the lords spiritual and temporal, and commons of Great Britain, in parliament assembled, had, hath, and
of right ought to have, full power and authority to make laws and statutes of sufficient force
and validity to bind the colonies and people of America, subjects of the crown of Great
Britain, in all cases whatsoever."

89. Richard Bland, *An Inquiry into the Rights of the British Colonies* (Williamsburg:
Alexander Purdie, 1766), 20–21.

90. Middlekauff, *Glorious Cause,* rev. and expanded ed., 161.

91. [Dickinson], *Letters from a Farmer in Pennsylvania,* 17.

92. Ibid., 24, 17.

93. Ibid., 26.

94. See also colonial agent William Bollan's assertion that the "care of common rights"
should be left to Parliament. In the midst of what was essentially an apologia for parliamentary supremacy, Bollan thus implied, first, that some noncommon rights existed, and second, that protecting such rights might be within the purview of an authority other than
Parliament. [William Bollan], *A Succinct View of the Origin of our Colonies, with heir Civil*
State, Founded by Queen Elizabeth, Corroborated by Succeeding Princes, and Confirmed by
Acts of Parliament . . . (London, 1766), 40.

95. [William Hicks], *The Nature and Extent of Parliamentary Power Considered, in*
Some Remarks upon Mr. Pitt's Speech in the House of Commons, previous to the Repeal of the
Stamp-Act: With an Introduction, Applicable to the present Situation of the Colonies (Phila-
delphia: William and Thomas Bradford, 1768), 12.

96. Ibid., 175–177.

97. On the background and context of the dialogue, see Bailyn, introduction to "A Dialogue between an American and a European Englishman," in Fleming and Bailyn, *Perspec-*
tives in American History 9:343–410.

98. Thomas Hutchinson, "A Dialogue between an American and a European Englishman," in Fleming and Bailyn, *Perspectives in American History* 9:407.

99. Bailyn, introduction to "A Dialogue between an American and a European Englishman," 363.

100. Knox continued: "It is this *new invention* of *collecting taxes* that makes them burdensome to the Colonies; and an infringement of their rights and privileges." William Knox, *The Controversy between Great Britain and her Colonies Reviewed; The Several Pleas of the Colonies, in Support of Their Right to all the Liberties and Privileges of British Subjects, and to Exemption from the Legislative Authority of Parliament, Stated and Considered: and the Nature of Their Connection with, and Dependence on, Great Britain, Shewn, upon the Evidence of Historical Facts and Authentic Records* (Boston: Mein and Fleeming, 1769), 37, 19.

101. Jack P. Greene, "The Debate over Parliamentary Imperial Jurisdiction," *Parliamentary History* 14 (1995): 51.

102. Pauline Maier, *From Resistance to Revolution: Colonial Radicals and the Development of American Opposition to Britain, 1765–1776* (New York: Norton, 1972), 113–114.

103. In his *History of the Colony and Province of Massachusetts-Bay,* which he began writing while serving as lieutenant governor, Hutchinson himself adopted the distinction between metropolitan regulation of commerce and of internal colonial affairs. Of the situation prior to the Stamp Act, Hutchinson wrote, "In a very few instances had the interior government of any of the colonies been regulated, or controlled, by acts of parliament. By far the greatest part in force were for the regulation of commerce, which the colonies had at all times acknowledged to be reasonable." Thomas Hutchinson, *The History of the Colony and Province of Massachusetts-Bay,* ed. Lawrence Shaw Mayo (Cambridge, Mass.: Harvard University Press, 1936), 3:254.

104. See Skinner, "Meaning and Understanding in the History of Ideas," 64 (describing "context" as "an ultimate framework for helping to decide what conventionally recognizable meanings, in a society of *that* kind, it might in principle have been possible for someone to have intended to communicate").

105. As Eliga Gould notes, the majority of colonists—even those who opposed the Stamp Act—"were quick to assert that their opposition did not mean they disputed the general principle of Parliament's imperial sovereignty; nor, they insisted, did they object to contributing to the costs of government in Britain." Indeed, throughout the 1760s, many colonial commentators stressed the degree to which the colonies voluntarily and willingly underwrote the empire by obeying the Navigation Acts' trade restrictions. Eliga H. Gould, *The Persistence of Empire: British Political Culture in the Age of the American Revolution* (Chapel Hill: University of North Carolina Press, 2000), 123–126.

3. THE DEBATES OVER SOVEREIGNTY

1. On the relationship between the governor and the assembly in Massachusetts in this period, see Richard R. Beeman, *The Varieties of Political Experience in Eighteenth-Century America* (Philadelphia: University of Pennsylvania Press, 2004), 69–94; Richard L. Bushman, *King and People in Provincial Massachusetts* (Chapel Hill: University of North Carolina Press, 1985). Bushman notes that the salary controversy was particularly acute because of the contemporary "conception of politicians as bound together in networks of interest, with each official serving those powers that advanced his interests. . . . Unless the governor

was tied to the province by the salary, he would serve his own interests, and perhaps the crown's, but not the colony's." Ibid., 129.

2. Massachusetts colonists presented additional grievances to the king in early 1773 through their agent, Benjamin Franklin. These complaints, which dated back to 1772, included the following: the expansion of the powers of royal revenue officers and admiralty courts in the colonies; a recent act of Parliament regulating dockyards that required colonists to face trial in Britain on the basis of events occurring in America; the occupation of Castle William in Boston Harbor by a garrison of British regulars who were not under even the governor's authority; a prohibition on meetings of the Council (the upper house of the colonial legislature) without the governor's approval; a bar on colonial taxation of Crown-appointed officials' salaries if those salaries were paid from outside the colony; and a prohibition on the payment of salary to any colonial agents not authorized by the governor, as well as the Council and House of Representatives. See K. G. Davies, introduction to *Documents of the American Revolution, 1770–1783 (Colonial Office Series)* (Dublin: Irish University Press, 1974), 6:4–5; "House of Representatives of Massachusetts to Earl of Dartmouth" and "House of Representatives of Massachusetts to the King," ibid., 6:96–102.

3. *Boston Evening Post,* January 11, 1773.

4. The leading contemporary exponent of this view was William Blackstone, who argued, "[T]here is and must be in all [governments] a supreme, irresistible, absolute, uncontrolled authority, in which the *jura summi imperii,* or the rights of sovereignty, reside." See William Blackstone, *Commentaries on the Laws of England* (1765–1769; reprint, with an introduction by Stanley N. Katz, Chicago: University of Chicago Press, 1979), 1:49. For a modern view, see Stephen D. Krasner, *Sovereignty: Organized Hypocrisy* (Princeton, N.J.: Princeton University Press, 1999), 11 (quoting F. H. Hinsley, *Sovereignty,* 2d ed. (Cambridge: Cambridge University Press, 1986)). Krasner terms this "domestic sovereignty," in contrast to three other species of sovereignty (Westphalian, international legal, and interdependence).

5. On the provincial assemblies and the decades-long history of institutional conflict within the colonial governments, see Evarts B. Greene, *The Provincial Governor in the English Colonies of North America* (New York: Longmans, Green, and Co., 1898); Jack P. Greene, *The Quest for Power: The Lower Houses of Assembly in the Southern Royal Colonies, 1689–1776* (New York: Norton, 1963); Michael G. Kammen, *Deputyes and Libertyes* (New York: Knopf, 1968); Leonard Woods Labaree, *Royal Government in America: A Study of the British Colonial System before 1783* (New Haven, Conn.: Yale University Press, 1930); and Herbert Osgood, *The American Colonies in the Eighteenth Century* (New York: Columbia University Press, 1924).

6. Antagonism between colonial assemblies and governors was common throughout the eighteenth century, arising out of institutional competition for power at a provincial level, as well as friction between the governor's (and sometimes the council's) role as an imperial agent and the assembly members' role as representatives of imperial subjects. See, e.g., Christine A. Desan, "The Constitutional Commitment to Legislative Adjudication in the Early American Tradition," *Harvard Law Review* 111 (1998): 1381–1503. On the nature and consequences of the "plural legal order" that characterized colonial political structure, see

Lauren Benton, "Colonial Law and Cultural Difference: Jurisdictional Politics and the Formation of the Colonial State," *Comparative Studies in Society and History* 41 (1999): 563–588. On the broader context of changing ideas of authority and state power in the eighteenth-century British Atlantic world, see Peter N. Miller, *Defining the Common Good: Empire, Religion and Philosophy in Eighteenth-Century Britain* (Cambridge: Cambridge University Press, 1994).

7. John Phillip Reid, "The Ordeal by Law of Thomas Hutchinson," in Hendrik Hartog, ed., *Law in the American Revolution and the Revolution in the Law* (New York: New York University Press, 1981), 33–34. The debates are reprinted in John Phillip Reid, ed., *The Briefs of the American Revolution: Constitutional Arguments between Thomas Hutchinson, Governor of Massachusetts Bay, and James Bowdoin for the Council and John Adams for the House of Representatives* (New York: New York University Press, 1981).

8. The delay between Bernard's departure and Hutchinson's officially becoming governor was due in part to ongoing political turmoil in Boston. The personal attacks on Hutchinson that had begun during the Stamp Act crisis intensified during this period. Most significant was the aftermath of the Boston Massacre, which pitted Hutchinson against the Boston selectmen when the latter demanded that Hutchinson order the British troops to withdraw from the town. Hutchinson had previously attempted to remove himself from consideration for the governorship; a few weeks after the Massacre, he actually sent a letter of resignation to London, but it did not arrive there until his commission had been sent. After much awkwardness on both sides, Hutchinson accepted the commission in June 1770. See Bernard Bailyn, *The Ordeal of Thomas Hutchinson* (Cambridge: Belknap Press of Harvard University Press, 1974), 156–168. Other biographies of Hutchinson include William Pencak, *America's Burke: The Mind of Thomas Hutchinson* (Washington, D.C.: University Press of America, 1982); and James Kendall Hosmer, *The Life of Thomas Hutchinson, Royal Governor of the Province of Massachusetts Bay* (Boston: Houghton, Mifflin, 1896). The quotation is from Bailyn, *Ordeal of Thomas Hutchinson*, 196.

9. Bailyn, *Ordeal of Thomas Hutchinson*, 204 (quoting Hutchinson's letter of July 21, 1772); Message from Hutchinson to House, July 14, 1772, in Alden Bradford, ed., *Speeches of the Governors of Massachusetts, from 1765 to 1775: and the Answers of the House of Representatives to the Same; with Their Resolutions and Addresses for That Period and Other Public Papers Relating to the Dispute between This Country and Great Britain Which Led to the Independence of the United States* (Boston: Russell and Gardner, 1818), 332 (hereafter cited as *Speeches of the Governors*).

10. Thomas Hutchinson to Lord Dartmouth, November 3, 1772, Hutchinson Correspondence, 1741–1774, Massachusetts Archives, Harvard University Library (microfilm) (hereafter cited as Hutchinson Correspondence). On the organization of the Colonial Department in Whitehall, see Margaret Marion Spector, *The American Department of the British Government, 1768–1782* (New York: Columbia University Press, 1940).

11. *The Votes and Proceedings of the Freeholders and Other Inhabitants of the Town of Boston, in Town Meeting Assembled, According to Law* (Boston, 1772), iii.

12. Hutchinson to Dartmouth, December 22, 1772, Hutchinson Correspondence. The earlier letter was dated October 30, 1772, and characterized the town meeting—or "the

Inhabitants of the Town of Boston," as Hutchinson referred to the assemblage—as addressing the governor in the language "of the News papers which have so much inflamed the
minds of the people." Examination of Hutchinson's correspondence with Dartmouth during this period suggests that the officials' letters typically took approximately two months to
travel between Boston and London or vice versa. In a letter to Dartmouth dated January 7,
1773, Hutchinson noted that he had the day before received Dartmouth's letter of November
4. Similarly, Dartmouth began a March 3, 1773, letter to Hutchinson by reporting that he
had received Hutchinson's letters of December 30, 1772, and January 7, 1773. Throughout
their correspondence, Hutchinson and Dartmouth numbered each letter, enabling them to
monitor which letters had arrived and in what sequence. Hutchinson to Dartmouth, January
7, 1773, Hutchinson Correspondence; Dartmouth to Hutchinson, March 3, 1773, in Davies,
Documents of the American Revolution, 6:94. This travel time comports with scholars' estimates of the typical speed of eighteenth-century transoceanic correspondence. See Ian K.
Steele, *The English Atlantic, 1675–1740: An Exploration of Communication and Continuity*
(New York: Oxford University Press, 1986), 10, 91, 335 n.19.

13. John Phillip Reid, *The Authority of Law*, vol. 4 of *Constitutional History of the
American Revolution* (Madison: University of Wisconsin Press, 1993), 92.

14. Davies, introduction to *Documents of the American Revolution*, 6:4.

15. Andrew C. McLaughlin, *A Constitutional History of the United States* (New York:
D. Appleton-Century Co., 1935), 69–70.

16. Bailyn, *Ordeal of Thomas Hutchinson*, 297. The chapter in Bailyn's book that deals
with this period of Hutchinson's life is titled "The Failure of Reason."

17. Randolph G. Adams, *Political Ideas of the American Revolution: Britannic-
American Contributions to the Problem of Imperial Organization, 1765 to 1775*, 3d ed. (Durham, N.C.: Trinity College Press, 1922; New York: Barnes and Noble, 1958), 115. Citations
are to the Barnes and Noble edition.

18. In a 1775 draft of what he termed a "vindication" of his conduct, Hutchinson wrote,
"Britain and its Colonies are alike dependent upon the supreme authority of the whole
Empire." Using the third person to refer to himself, he continued, "The King, Lords, and
Commons—this supreme authority appeared to him to be the sole bond which kept the
several parts of the Empire together." Thomas Hutchinson, *The Diary and Letters of His
Excellency Thomas Hutchinson, Esq.*, ed. Peter Orlando Hutchinson (Boston: Houghton,
Mifflin, 1884–1886), 1:577. Writing between 1749 and 1751, Dr. William Douglas of Boston
had made a similar comparison. The colonial governments, he wrote, paralleled the structure of the British government in that "by the governor, representing the King, the colonies
are monarchical; by the Council, they are aristocratical; by a house of representatives or
delegates from the people, they are democratical: these three are distinct and independent
of each other. . . . I should call it a *trinity in unity*." Quoted in Bernard Bailyn, *The Origins of American Politics* (New York: Vintage Books, 1967), 59. On the consequences of the
Glorious Revolution for metropolitan and colonial political theory, see Jack P. Greene,
"The Glorious Revolution and the British Empire, 1688–1783," in Lois G. Schwoerer, ed.,
The Revolution of 1688–1689: Changing Perspectives (Cambridge: Cambridge University
Press, 1992); David S. Lovejoy, *The Glorious Revolution in America* (Middletown, Conn.:
Wesleyan University Press, 1987); and Jack M. Sosin, *English America and the Revolution*

of 1688: Royal Administration and the Structure of Provincial Government (Lincoln: University of Nebraska Press, 1982).

19. In particular, "the British had developed since the Glorious Revolution the constitutional doctrine of the sovereign legislature of king-in-parliament as the ultimate, absolute and irresistible authority in the state." H. T. Dickinson, "Britain's Imperial Sovereignty," in H. T. Dickinson, ed., *Britain and the American Revolution* (London: Longman, 1998), 81.

20. Samuel Johnson, *Taxation No Tyranny: An Answer to the Resolutions and Address of the American Congress*, 4th ed. (London: T. Cadell, 1775), 24.

21. *The Speeches of His Excellency Governor Hutchinson, to the General Assembly of the Massachusetts-Bay . . . with the Answers of His Majesty's Council and the House of Representatives . . .* (Boston: Edes and Gill, 1773), 3–4.

22. Speech of the Governor to the Two Houses, January 6, 1773, in Bradford, *Speeches of the Governors,* 337. The question of the precise legal status of the colonies and the distinctions between membership in kingdom, realm, and dominion (the last distinguishable between the dominions of England and those of the king himself) is treated in Joseph Henry Smith, *Appeals to the Privy Council from the American Plantations* (New York: Columbia University Press, 1950), especially chapter 8, "The Privy Council and the Extension of English Law." For a discussion of pre-Revolutionary Americans' own understandings of the status and origin of the colonies, see Michael Kammen, "The Meaning of Colonization in American Revolutionary Thought," *Journal of the History of Ideas* 31 (1970): 337–358. Kammen notes that by 1763, "it was manifest to imperial bureaucrats in London that colonization was somehow a subversive process viewed altogether differently by men living on opposite sides of the Atlantic." Ibid., 351.

23. The fact that Hutchinson, scion of one of Boston's elite merchant families and a layman in the field of law, had been appointed chief justice of the superior court stoked the ire of many of his contemporaries at the Boston bar, especially John Adams. Adams rarely missed a chance to demonstrate his scorn for Hutchinson throughout the crisis of the early 1770s, even in passing. In the midst of discussing the issue of the Crown salaries in his 1774 *Novanglus* letters, Adams took a swipe at Hutchinson's plural officeholding as lieutenant governor, chief justice, probate court judge, and a member of the Council. Indeed, Adams began the *Novanglus* series by referring to Hutchinson by name as a "destroying angel" whose "hypocrisy and perfidy" had long become apparent to the people of Massachusetts. John Adams, "Novanglus No. I" and "Novanglus No. V," in Charles Francis Adams, ed., *The Works of John Adams, Second President of the United States* (Boston: Charles C. Little and James Brown, 1851), 4:12, 72. The web of marriage connections among the Hutchinsons and the Olivers, two of the leading families of merchants and public officials, lent some credence to Adams's concerns. Combined with Hutchinson's numerous public positions, his family connections help explain the animosity that some of his fellow colonists displayed toward him. Bernard Bailyn sums up after laying out this interwoven pair of family trees, "No one but a Hutchinson or an Oliver had been lieutenant governor of Massachusetts after 1758 or chief justice after 1760." Bailyn, *Ordeal of Thomas Hutchinson,* 31. Interested readers may consult Peter Oliver's own account of the events of this period in a manuscript dated 1781. See Peter Oliver, *Origin and Progress of the American Rebellion: A Tory View,* ed. Douglass Adair and John A. Schutz (Stanford, Calif.: Stanford University

Press, 1961). In Bailyn's view, however, Adams's dislike of Hutchinson was "obsessive" and rooted in Adams's own "excruciatingly sensitive self-esteem." Bailyn, *Ordeal of Thomas Hutchinson*, 50–51.

24. *Speeches of His Excellency Governor Hutchinson*, 8. On the concept of repugnancy in the British Empire, see Mary Sarah Bilder, *The Transatlantic Constitution: Colonial Legal Culture and the Empire* (Cambridge, Mass.: Harvard University Press, 2004).

25. *Speeches of His Excellency Governor Hutchinson*, 5, 11.

26. On the rise of the theory of parliamentary sovereignty, see J. G. A. Pocock, *The Ancient Constitution and the Feudal Law: A Study of English Historical Thought in the Seventeenth Century; A Reissue with a Retrospect* (New York: Norton, 1987), especially the conclusion to part 1, titled "1688 in the History of Historiography."

27. David Armitage, *The Declaration of Independence: A Global History* (Cambridge, Mass.: Harvard University Press, 2007), 41. Armitage notes that Franklin informed the volume's editor in December 1775 that the book "has been continually in the hands of our congress, now sitting." Ibid.

28. Richard Bland, *An Inquiry into the Rights of the British Colonies* (Williamsburg, 1766; reprint, Richmond, Va.: Appeals Press, 1922), 9 (misidentifying the title of Vattel's work as *Law of Nature*); Richard Tuck, introduction to *The Rights of War and Peace*, by Hugo Grotius (Indianapolis: Liberty Fund, 2005), xi.

29. Peter Onuf and Nicholas Onuf, *Federal Union, Modern World: The Law of Nations in an Age of Revolutions, 1776–1814* (Madison, Wis.: Madison House, 1993), 5–7.

30. David Hendrickson terms the federal republic "an American system of states inside a larger system of states." David C. Hendrickson, *Peace Pact: The Lost World of the American Founding* (Lawrence: University Press of Kansas, 2003), 22.

31. *Speeches of His Excellency Governor Hutchinson*, 96–97 (debates of March 6, 1773) (emphasis on "united by a Sort of unequal Confederacy" added).

32. Ibid., 121–122.

33. Evidence that John Adams was the author of the House's statements comes from the obvious familiarity with the works of Grotius and Pufendorf that Adams displayed in his *Novanglus* letters. No. VI, for example, provided not just a passing reference but an actual footnote to *The Law of Nature and Nations*, volume 1, book 7, chapter 8, §§ 5–6, on the question of the subject's power to resist a tyrannical prince. John Adams, "Novanglus No. VI," in Charles Francis Adams, *Works of John Adams*, 4:79. Adams's footnote also cited a note by Jean Barbeyrac, the French translator of Pufendorf, whose notes were included in the English translation by Basil Kennet that Adams and his peers read. On Barbeyrac and the complex history of his translations, see David Saunders, "The Natural Jurisprudence of Jean Barbeyrac: Translation as an Art of Political Adjustment," *Eighteenth-Century Studies* 36 (2003): 473–490.

34. See Hendrickson, *Peace Pact*, 29 ("The long line of ancient and modern thinkers who had probed the foundations of balanced government . . . had virtually nothing to say on the question of how a multitude of commonwealths might concert their common action").

35. As evidence of Hutchinson's dedication to a positivistic vision of Parliament's authority, Reid reports the following story, which was repeated in Massachusetts in 1770: "At a dinner, Hutchinson was asked by a fellow Bostonian: 'Pray Sir do you think if the Parlia-

ment of Great Britain should pass a Law to deprive me of my Estate without my having been guilty of any crime to forfeit it that I should be bound in duty & loyalty to comply. [Mr. Hutchinson] answer'd very solemnly & seriously Without doubt Sir.'" Reid, "Ordeal by Law of Thomas Hutchinson," 27.

36. "An Elector," *Boston-Gazette and Country Journal,* January 11, 1773.

37. Ibid.

38. Mercy Otis Warren, *The Adulateur: A Tragedy, as It Is Now Acted in Upper Servia* (Boston: New Printing-Office, 1773). The first installments of the drama were published in the *Massachusetts Spy* in March 1772. See Bailyn, *Ordeal of Thomas Hutchinson,* 201–202.

39. *Boston-Gazette and Country Journal,* February 1, 1773. The members of the House, in particular, went to great lengths to ensure that their response would deal adequately with the challenge that Hutchinson's dense, polemical address posed. House leaders did not scruple to search beyond the chamber's membership to find the strongest advocate for their cause. After their overtures to Daniel Dulany and John Dickinson were rejected, House managers selected members Samuel Adams and Joseph Hawley to lead the opposition. Bailyn, *Ordeal of Thomas Hutchinson,* 208. They also drafted the rising Boston lawyer John Adams to aid in drafting responses to Hutchinson. The Council's committee, which consisted of William Brattle, Harrison Gray, James Pitts, James Humphrey, and Benjamin Greenleaf, produced a response approximately one-third the length of the House's. According to Alden Bradford, the authors of the Council's response included James Bowdoin, Harrison Gray, James Otis, and at least one other person. Bradford, *Speeches of the Governors,* 351.

40. *Speeches of His Excellency Governor Hutchinson,* 18–19. By invoking the ancient constitution to rebut claims of parliamentary sovereignty, the Council was both embarking on a novel interpretation of traditional English constitutional arguments and returning to old understandings of those arguments. The trope of the ancient constitution had emerged in the early seventeenth century as a challenge to Stuart absolutism, a means of outflanking the claims of James I that his power and prerogative were based not on his will but on ancient custom. Promoted by the seventeenth-century jurist Edward Coke, the myth of the ancient constitution became ascendant after Parliament succeeded in forcing out James II and installing William and Mary as constitutional monarchs in 1689. The Council's use of the ancient constitution to oppose parliamentary sovereignty therefore turned the principle to the very opposite of its original objective. See Pocock, *Ancient Constitution and the Feudal Law,* 233–236. John Phillip Reid terms this a "constitutional step backwards from the Glorious Revolution," but it is possible to see this revolution of the ancient constitution as an adaptation to changed circumstances rather than as a retreat along a linear spectrum of constitutional progress. John Phillip Reid, *Constitutional History of the American Revolution,* abr. ed. (Madison: University of Wisconsin Press, 1995), 98.

41. John Phillip Reid, *The Authority to Legislate,* vol. 3 of *Constitutional History of the American Revolution* (Madison: University of Wisconsin Press, 1991), 8, 82 ("[T]he concept of 'supremacy' was more a topic of dispute than an element of definition. It was used as much to argue about constitutionalism as to explain it"), 85, 83 (discussing the relative nature of the term "supreme").

42. On the relationship between nation and empire in this period, see Eliga H. Gould, *The Persistence of Empire: British Political Culture in the Age of the American Revolution* (Chapel Hill: University of North Carolina Press, 2000). Randolph G. Adams points out that John Adams's *Novanglus* letters distinguished between the dual nature of Parliament as both an imperial and a national legislature. In John Adams's view, "Parliament had a double capacity, and when it acted as a Parliament of Great Britain, it had no relation to the colonies. When acting in its imperial capacity it had only such relation to the colonies as they by their consent accorded to it." Britain, meanwhile, "conceived the empire as a unicellular state wherein sovereignty was possessed, according to the Lockeian dogma, by the legislative, that is, by the High Court of Parliament at Westminster. Britons talked about 'our sovereignty' over the colonies." R. G. Adams, *Political Ideas of the American Revolution*, 120, 175.

43. On emerging notions of Britishness in this period, see Linda Colley, *Britons: Forging the Nation, 1707–1837* (New Haven, Conn.: Yale University Press, 1992).

44. John Adams, "Novanglus No. III," in Charles Francis Adams, *Works of John Adams*, 4:37–38. John Adams has been called a "Britannic statesman" for, among other achievements, his rare ability to think systematically about sovereignty. This was no small feat: "Few thinkers of this or any other age can really think clearly in terms of sovereignty," points out Randolph G. Adams. "As the political thought of the Revolution unfolds, we observe that thinker after thinker drops by the wayside as the problem approaches this question of sovereignty." R. G. Adams, *Political Ideas of the American Revolution*, 107, 168.

45. Reid, *Authority to Legislate*, 84.

46. *Speeches of His Excellency Governor Hutchinson*, 38.

47. Ibid., 40. Parliament's own Navigation Act of 1660 endorsed the theory of the king's dominions, characterizing the colonies as "Lands, Islands Plantations or Territories to his Maiesty belonging or in his possession." Quoted in Smith, *Appeals to the Privy Council*, 470. As Smith's discussion makes clear, the House's use of this history was somewhat opportunistic, for the status of English law in the colonies was the subject of much confusion as late as 1700. Ibid., 473–475. Yet again the imprecision of eighteenth-century syntax is worth noting. The terms "realm" and "kingdom" were often used in perplexingly similar contexts during this period. John Adams seems to have been aware of this lack of precision. Of the Massachusetts Bay Company, he commented, "[A]s soon as they arrived here, they got out of the English realm, dominions, state, empire, call it by what name you will, and out of the legal jurisdiction of parliament. The king might, by his writ or proclamation, have commanded them to return; but he did not." John Adams, "Novanglus No. VII" and "Novanglus No. XII," in Charles Francis Adams, *Works of John Adams*, 4:102, 177. Ultimately, it seems fair to say that Adams believed that the colonies were under the control of the Crown but were not part of the realm. The histories of Wales and Ireland, he believed, demonstrated the relevant point for the colonies: "[T]here is a distinction between the crown and realm, and that a country may be annexed and subject to the former, and not to the latter." "Novanglus No. XI," ibid., 4:159. On the "realm question" and the confusion that resulted from the "haphazard, unsystematic fashion" in which British colonization had taken place, see Peter N. Miller, *Defining the Common Good: Empire, Religion, and Philosophy in Eighteenth-Century Britain* (Cambridge: Cambridge University Press, 1994), 215–239. Miller concludes that "[b]ecause of the extent of

their self-rule the Americans effectively constituted a kingdom within this composite monarchy" (216).

48. See Bernard Bailyn, *The Ideological Origins of the American Revolution,* enl. ed. (1967; Cambridge, Mass.: Belknap Press of Harvard University Press, 1992), 201. Daniel Hulsebosch notes that the colonists cited royal prerogative "just as such rhetoric was becoming anachronistic in England." Nevertheless, that principle, not the notion of parliamentary sovereignty, "was their mainstay throughout the colonial period." Daniel J. Hulsebosch, *"Imperia in Imperio:* The Multiple Constitutions of Empire in New York, 1750–1777," *Law and History Review* 16 (1998): 328–329. Even after the Restoration, but before the Glorious Revolution, some charters continued to be made directly with the king rather than with Parliament. See Martha C. Nussbaum, *Liberty of Conscience: In Defense of America's Tradition of Religious Equality* (New York: Basic Books, 2008), 48–50 (discussing Charles II's grant of a charter to Roger Williams for Rhode Island and Providence Plantations in 1663).

49. Reid, *Constitutional History of the American Revolution,* abr. ed., 5.

50. The phrase "dominion status" comes from Charles Page Smith, who notes in his biography of James Wilson that Wilson may "be credited with formulating the idea of dominion status six years ahead of [John Adams] and some seventy years ahead of the British Foreign Office." Charles Page Smith, *James Wilson: Founding Father, 1742–1798* (Chapel Hill: University of North Carolina Press, 1956), 58. The phrase "doctrine of allegiance" is that of Randolph G. Adams. R. G. Adams, *Political Ideas of the American Revolution,* 116–117.

51. James Wilson, "Considerations on the Nature and Extent of the Legislative Authority of the British Parliament," in Robert Green McCloskey, ed., *The Works of James Wilson* (Cambridge, Mass.: Belknap Press of Harvard University Press, 1967), 2:745. The advertisement that announced the publication of this work noted that Wilson had originally written this pamphlet in 1768, during the nonimportation controversy that followed the passage of the Townshend Acts, but it was not published until 1774.

52. John Adams, "Novanglus No. VII," in Charles Francis Adams, *Works of John Adams,* 4:107. Adams took great care to distinguish between the British Empire, the existence of which he questioned, and the situation of the American colonies with respect to the king, which he regarded as unique. "I say we are not a part of the British empire; because the British government is not an empire. . . . It is a limited monarchy. . . . [T]he British constitution is nothing more nor less than a republic, in which the king is first magistrate." Ibid., 4:106.

53. R. G. Adams, *Political Ideas of the American Revolution,* 44. Adams notes that at the time of his writing, in 1922, the commonwealth idea was widely discussed with respect to the dominions of the British Empire and the establishment of the League of Nations. Ibid., 36, 44 n.6. The move to establish something more like a commonwealth system, according to which the colonies would be subject to the Crown alone, gained momentum in 1774. See Thomas Jefferson, "Draft of Instructions to the Virginia Delegates in the Continental Congress (MS Text of *A Summary View,* &c.)" (1774), in Julian P. Boyd, ed., *The Papers of Thomas Jefferson* (Princeton, N.J.: Princeton University Press, 1950), 1:135; see also John Cartwright, *American Independence the Glory and Interest of Great Britain* (London: H. S.

Woodfall, 1774); Joseph Galloway, "A Plan of a Proposed Union, &c." (1774), in Ernest H. Baldwin, ed., *Joseph Galloway: Selected Tracts* (New York: Da Capo Press, 1974), 1:27–29.

54. Brian P. Levack, *The Formation of the British State: England, Scotland, and the Union, 1603–1707* (Oxford: Clarendon Press, 1987), 1.

55. On the connections between the Scottish union debates and eighteenth-century Anglo-American constitutional thought, see Ned C. Landsman, "The Provinces and the Empire: Scotland, the American Colonies and the Development of British Provincial Identity," in Lawrence Stone, ed., *An Imperial State at War* (London: Routledge, 1994); Landsman, "The Legacy of British Union for the North American Colonies: Provincial Elites and the Problem of Imperial Union," in John Robertson, ed., *A Union for Empire: Political Thought and the British Union of 1707* (Cambridge: Cambridge University Press, 1995), 297–317; and John Robertson, "Empire and Union: Two Concepts of the Early Modern European Political Order," ibid., 3–36.

56. On the influence of Wilson's Scottish background on his political thought, see Mark David Hall, *The Political and Legal Philosophy of James Wilson, 1742–1798* (Columbia: University of Missouri Press, 1997), 68–72; McCloskey, introduction to *The Works of James Wilson*, 1:14–16.

57. John Adams, "Novanglus No. VII" and "Novanglus No. VIII," in Charles Francis Adams, *Works of John Adams*, 4:113, 123, 124. Levack explains how the arrangement between Scotland and England functioned during the reign of James VI and I: "The crown of England remained distinct from the crown of Scotland, even though James possessed and embodied both of them. James held the two crowns in the way that an ecclesiastical pluralist held two benefices. . . . The Union of the Crowns should, in fact, be considered primarily as a dynastic achievement." Levack, *Formation of the British State*, 1–2, 3.

58. In his *Dissertation on the Canon and the Feudal Law* of 1765, Adams had explicitly linked what he viewed as increasing British arbitrary rule and tyranny over the colonies with the despised legal systems of his title. Unrestrained, the "desire of dominion" threatened the rights of the people, rights "that cannot be repealed or restrained by human laws" because they "derived from the great Legislator of the universe." John Adams, "A Dissertation on the Canon and the Feudal Law," in Charles Francis Adams, ed., *The Works of John Adams, Second President of the United States*, vol. 3 (Boston: Charles C. Little and James Brown, 1851), 449.

59. *Speeches of His Excellency Governor Hutchinson*, 9.

60. See, e.g., Simeon L. Guterman, *The Principle of the Personality of Law in the Germanic Kingdoms of Western Europe from the Fifth to the Eleventh Century* (New York: P. Lang, 1990); Guterman, *From Personality to Territorial Law: Aspects of the History and Structure of the Western Legal-Constitutional Tradition* (Metuchen, N.J.: Scarecrow Press, 1972); and Walter Ullmann, *Law and Jurisdiction in the Middle Ages* (London: Variorum Reprints, 1988).

61. *Speeches of His Excellency Governor Hutchinson*, 45.

62. Ibid., 45–46. No colonist wanted to be seen as an apologist for unfettered royal prerogative. For this reason, the House's insistence that the king had stipulated to their rights was significant insofar as it suggested that the king had recognized preexisting rights rather than granting new ones. The latter, many colonists argued, would have been beyond the

scope of royal power. As one commentator denominated "An Old Friend" wrote in the *Boston-Gazette,* "Let it ever be remembered, That the Rights of the Prince are the *Gift of the People.*—He can have no legal Prerogative but what *they* give him—Therefore Charters, or no Charters, the People have a Right to all their natural Rights which they have not given away." The author argued, therefore, that colonies that had not been founded pursuant to a royal charter nevertheless possessed the same freedoms as colonies that had charters, and that both types of colony could therefore challenge parliamentary authority. "An Old Friend," *Boston-Gazette and Country Journal,* February 8, 1773.

63. *Speeches of His Excellency Governor Hutchinson,* 35.

64. Ibid., 39, 56.

65. Ibid., 57.

66. "A True Friend," *Boston Evening-Post,* February 1, 1773.

67. "A Friend to the Community," *Boston-Gazette,* February 8, 1773.

68. *Boston Evening-Post,* February 8, 1773; *Boston-Gazette and Country Journal,* February 1, 1773.

69. Dartmouth to Hutchinson, March 3, 1773, in Davies, *Documents of the American Revolution,* 6:94–95.

70. Hutchinson to Dartmouth, February 1, 1773, Hutchinson Correspondence. The manuscript of this letter shows that Hutchinson originally wrote "give both the House &" but then crossed out "House &" so that the final version read "give both the Council & House a full reply." Did the force and scope of the House's arguments perhaps make the governor initially lose sight of the proper hierarchy of the two houses of the General Court, such that he considered the House's answer as the primary one that needed to be answered? As in other colonies, the Council in Massachusetts was the upper house of the legislature; in contrast to other colonies' practice, however, the members of the Council in Massachusetts were elected by the lower house rather than appointed by the king or the governor. See Bailyn, *Ordeal of Thomas Hutchinson,* 112 (discussing the May 1766 "purge" of the Council, when the House removed all executive officeholders [including Hutchinson and the Olivers] from the Council); and Anthony McFarlane, *The British in the Americas, 1480–1815* (London: Longman, 1992), 205–206 (describing the various colonial governments).

71. *Speeches of His Excellency Governor Hutchinson,* 61, 73.

72. Ibid., 5, 86–87.

73. See, e.g., Bland, *Inquiry into the Rights of the British Colonies,* 20 (describing the colonies' long-standing identity as "independent, as to their *internal* Government," but united with Britain, "as to their *external* Polity, in the closest and most intimate League and Amity, under the same Allegiance, and enjoying the Benefits of a reciprocal Intercourse"). See also Adams's argument in "Novanglus No. VII": "It is . . . our interest and duty to continue subject to the authority of parliament, in the regulation of trade, as long as she shall leave us to govern our internal policy . . . and no longer." John Adams, "Novanglus No. VII," in Charles Francis Adams, *Works of John Adams,* 4:120–121. See also Bailyn, *Ideological Origins,* 215.

74. Blackstone, *Commentaries on the Laws of England,* 1:49.

75. Edmund S. Morgan, *Inventing the People: The Rise of Popular Sovereignty in England and America* (New York: Norton, 1988), 267.

76. Bailyn, *Ideological Origins,* 228.

77. Kramer, *The People Themselves: Popular Constitutionalism and Judicial Review* (New York: Oxford University Press, 2004), 35–36. Cf. Morton J. Horwitz, "A Historiography of *The People Themselves* and Popular Constitutionalism," *Chicago-Kent Law Review* 81 (2006): 817 ("If for Bailyn and Wood, the basic change in political theory brought about by the American Revolution was the shift from British parliamentary to American popular sovereignty, for Kramer popular sovereignty was already a powerful force even before the conflicts leading up to the Revolution").

78. *Speeches of His Excellency Governor Hutchinson,* 115, 124 (emphasis on "returned" added). Although he subscribed to the orthodox but ahistorical whig view that the Glorious Revolution settlement had declared for all time the transcendent authority of Parliament, Hutchinson's interest in history here compelled him to distinguish between the feudal system as practiced on the Continent and the "corrected" feudalism that emerged after 1066, when, he argued, English custom tempered European feudalism to produce, among other things, mixed government and a distinct legislative power. Ibid., 118.

79. Ibid., 114. Hutchinson initially prorogued the legislative session until April 21. On April 8, however, he issued a proclamation that dissolved the General Court in light of the approaching beginning of the next session, which the charter decreed must convene on the last Wednesday of May. *Boston Evening-Post,* April 12, 1773.

80. Hutchinson to Gage, March 27, 1773, Hutchinson Correspondence.

81. Bailyn, *Ordeal of Thomas Hutchinson,* 212.

82. Hutchinson to——, March 10, 1773, Hutchinson Correspondence; Hutchinson to Dartmouth, April 25, 1773, Hutchinson Correspondence.

83. Bailyn, *Ordeal of Thomas Hutchinson,* 215 (quoting Dartmouth's letter).

84. Ibid., 217 (quoting Cushing's letter).

85. Ibid., 218–219 (quoting Dartmouth).

86. Hutchinson to Dartmouth, June 1773 (unsent), Hutchinson Correspondence.

87. Hutchinson to Dartmouth, June 12 and 26, 1773, Hutchinson Correspondence.

88. Bailyn, *Ordeal of Thomas Hutchinson,* 227. Bailyn's chapter titled "The Scape-Goat" provides an in-depth discussion of the release of the Whately letters by Benjamin Franklin and the uproar that followed.

89. Hutchinson, *Diary and Letters of His Excellency Thomas Hutchinson, Esq.,* 151. Hutchinson's departure was almost certainly a melancholy occasion for the governor, who was, after all, a creole and a great-great-grandson of the religious dissident Anne Hutchinson.

90. Bailyn, *Ordeal of Thomas Hutchinson,* 273; 14 Geo. 3, cc. 19, 39, 45, 54, 83.

91. Reid, *Authority to Legislate,* 309. Similarly, Jack Rakove notes "the clarifying impact" of the Coercive Acts insofar as they demonstrated that "in the British view there were no practical or theoretical limits to the exercise of parliamentary sovereignty over the colonies." Thus "previously tangled constitutional issues had now been reduced to a stark simplicity." Jack N. Rakove, *The Beginnings of National Politics: An Interpretive History of the Continental Congress* (New York: Alfred A. Knopf, 1979; Baltimore: Johns Hopkins University Press, 1982), 35. Citations are to the Johns Hopkins edition.

92. An Act for the Better Securing the Dependency of His Majesty's Dominions in America upon the Crown and Parliament of Great Britain, 6 Geo. 3, c. 12 (the Declaratory Act).

93. Occasionally a modern scholar has argued that divided sovereignty violates the *imperium in imperio* principle, and that therefore American federalism must be based on some other premise. See, e.g., Andrew C. McLaughlin, *The Foundations of American Constitutionalism* (New York: New York University Press, 1932), 135–136. McLaughlin's view, however, has become increasingly anomalous in the decades since he wrote.

94. John Dickinson, "An Essay on the Constitutional Power of Great Britain over the Colonies in America," in John B. Linn and William H. Egle, eds., *Pennsylvania Archives*, 2d ser. (Harrisburg: B. F. Meyers, 1875), 3:565, 569.

95. James Iredell, "To the Inhabitants of Great Britain," in Griffith J. McRee, ed., *Life and Correspondence of James Iredell, One of the Associate Justices of the Supreme Court of the United States* (New York: D. Appleton and Co., 1857), 1:219.

96. This distinction between subject-matter and territorial bases of sovereignty is conceptually similar to Daniel Hulsebosch's distinction between "jurisdictional" and "jurisprudential" visions of law. According to the former, as articulated by Sir Edward Coke, "the common law was inseparable from the institutions that applied, practiced, and taught the common law." A jurisprudential notion of law, in contrast, "refers to a rationally organized body of rules and principles defined primarily in reference to each other, not to the remedies and personnel enforcing them." Daniel J. Hulsebosch, "The Ancient Constitution and the Expanding Empire: Sir Edward Coke's British Jurisprudence," *Law and History Review* 21 (2003): 445–446.

97. [Alexander Hamilton], "The Federalist No. 27," in Jacob E. Cooke, ed., *The Federalist* (Middletown, Conn.: Wesleyan University Press, 1961), 174. This effort to divide lawmaking authority along substantive lines subsequently influenced the drafting of the Supremacy Clause of the U.S. Constitution. The clause distinguishes between "this Constitution, and the Laws of the United States," which the clause denominates "the supreme law of the land," and all other laws (e.g., state laws), which are relegated to subordinate status insofar as they conflict with the supreme law. U.S. Constitution, art. VI, cl. 2.

4. FORGING A FEDERATED UNION

1. The Revolutionary writer Mercy Otis Warren later noted, "It was frequently observed, that the only melioration of the present evils was, that the recal [*sic*] of Mr. Hutchison accompanied the bills, and his leaving the province at the same period the port-bill was to be put in operation, seemed to impress a dawn of hope from time, if not from his immediate successor." Mercy Otis Warren, *History of the Rise, Progress and Termination of the American Revolution, Interspersed with Biographical, Political and Moral Observations* (Boston: Manning and Loring, 1805), 1:123.

2. I thank David Armitage for suggesting the implicit-explicit formulation.

3. On ideas of confederation during this period, see J. G. A. Pocock, "States, Republics, and Empires: The American Founding in Early Modern Perspective," in Terence Ball and J. G. A. Pocock, eds., *Conceptual Change and the Constitution* (Lawrence: University Press of Kansas, 1988), 55–77; see also Samuel H. Beer, *To Make a Nation: The Rediscovery of*

American Federalism (Cambridge, Mass.: Belknap Press of Harvard University Press, 1993).

4. Murray Forsyth, *Unions of States: The Theory and Practice of Confederation* (New York: Holmes and Meier, 1981), 60.

5. [John Cartwright], *American Independence the Interest and Glory of Great Britain; or, Arguments to prove, that not only in Taxation, but in Trade, Manufactures, and Government, the Colonies are entitled to an entire Independency on the British Legislature; and that it can only be by a formal Declaration of these Rights, and forming thereupon a friendly League with them, that the true and lasting Welfare of both Countries can be promoted. In a Series of Letters to the Legislature. To which are added copious Notes; containing Reflections on the Boston and Quebec Acts; and a full Justification of the People of Boston, for destroying the British-taxed Tea; submitted to the Judgment, not of those who have none but borrowed Party-opinions, but of the Candid and Honest* (London: H.S. Woodfall, 1774), 2 (describing these as the "two grand questions now to be decided").

6. Ibid., 6 (internal quotation marks omitted), 8.

7. [Cartwright], *American Independence the Interest and Glory of Great Britain,* 10. On virtual representation, see Edmund S. Morgan, *Inventing the People: The Rise of Popular Sovereignty in England and America* (New York: Norton, 1988), 240–245; and Gordon S. Wood, *The Creation of the American Republic, 1776–1787* (Chapel Hill: University of North Carolina Press, 1969), 173–181.

8. [Cartwright], *American Independence the Interest and Glory of Great Britain,* 22, 41, 23.

9. Ibid., 53 (quoting Josiah Tucker, *Four Tracts on Political and Commercial Subjects,* 2d ed. [Gloucester, England: R. Raikes, 1774]), 165, 172). On Tucker in general, and his relationship with Cartwright in particular, see J. G. A. Pocock, "Political Thought in the English-Speaking Atlantic, 1760–1790, Part I: The Imperial Crisis," in J. G. A. Pocock, ed., *The Varieties of British Political Thought, 1500–1800* (Cambridge: Cambridge University Press, 1993), 275–276; and Pocock, "Josiah Tucker on Burke, Locke, and Price: A Study in the Varieties of Eighteenth-Century Conservatism," in J. G. A. Pocock, ed., *Virtue, Commerce and History* (Cambridge: Cambridge University Press, 2002), 157–192.

10. [Cartwright], *American Independence the Interest and Glory of Great Britain,* 62, 66.

11. Ibid., 65, 66.

12. Ibid., 63–64. This distinction between empire and union draws on that put forth in John Robertson, "Empire and Union: Two Concepts of the Early Modern European Political Order," in John Robertson, ed., *A Union for Empire: Political Thought and the British Union of 1707* (Cambridge: Cambridge University Press, 1995): 3–36.

13. This sketch draws on the biography presented in Ernest H. Baldwin, "Joseph Galloway: The Loyalist Politician," in Ernest H. Baldwin, ed., *Joseph Galloway: Selected Tracts* (New York: Da Capo Press, 1974), 1:ix–xcviii.

14. Baldwin attributes some of the hostility to Galloway's plan to the arrival of John Dickinson in Congress. Since the conflict of the 1760s between supporters of royal government and those who supported the proprietary government, Galloway and Dickinson had stood on opposite sides of Pennsylvania politics. Ibid., lxix.

15. Joseph Galloway, "A Plan of a Proposed Union, &c.," in Baldwin, *Joseph Galloway,* 1:27–29.

16. Edmund S. Morgan, *Benjamin Franklin* (New Haven, Conn.: Yale University Press, 2002), 211 (quoting Franklin).

17. Baldwin, "Joseph Galloway," lxxxx (describing discussions of both plans in the pages of the *Pennsylvania Journal* and *Pennsylvania Gazette*).

18. Galloway, "Plan of a Proposed Union," 29, 27, 28. More than a year after Galloway proposed his plan in Congress, Edmund Burke suggested a different but related approach to integrating the colonies into the legislative authority of Parliament. Whereas Galloway had seen a coordinate provincial legislature as the answer, Burke's "Speech on Conciliation with the Colonies" of March 22, 1775, contemplated permitting the colonists some representation in Parliament itself but stopped short of offering a formal proposal. "Speech on Conciliation with the Colonies," in Isaac Kramnick, ed., *The Portable Edmund Burke* (New York: Penguin Books, 1999), 265, 269.

19. The first edition of the *Summary View* was printed by Clementina Rind of Williamsburg, Virginia's first female newspaper editor and printer, whom the House of Burgesses appointed public printer to the colony in May 1774. Jefferson later noted that "the title, the motto and the preface" of the pamphlet "were of the editors." See "Appendix I: Historical and Bibliographical Notes on *A Summary View of the Rights of British America*," in *The Papers of Thomas Jefferson,* ed. Julian P. Boyd (Princeton, N.J.: Princeton University Press, 1950) (hereafter *PTJ*), 1:672.

20. Thomas Jefferson, "Autobiography" (1821), in Thomas Jefferson, *Writings,* ed. Merrill D. Peterson (New York: Library of America, 1984), 8–10. Jefferson credited Randolph with publicizing his essay, which Randolph—the chairman of the Virginia convention—did by "inform[ing] the convention he had received such a paper from a member prevented by sickness from offering it in his place, and he laid it on the table for perusal." Whatever Jefferson's view of Henry in 1774, by 1821 he regarded the famous orator as "the laziest man in reading I know" and opined that this was the reason Henry had not circulated the *Summary View* among the delegates. Ibid., 9. For a description of the essay's publication history in America and Britain, see "Appendix I: Historical and Bibliographical Notes," in *PTJ*, 1:669–676.

21. Thomas Jefferson, "Draft of Instructions to the Virginia Delegates in the Continental Congress (MS Text of *A Summary View,* &c.)" (1774), in *PTJ*, 1:135 (hereafter "Summary View"). The Williamsburg version of the pamphlet contained the phrase "union *and a* generous plan," but, as the editor of the *Papers of Thomas Jefferson* notes, Jefferson's own draft and his later, corrected copy of the pamphlet use "union *on a* generous plan" (emphases added). See notes, ibid., 1:135–137, especially note 40.

22. The idea of the Crown-in-Parliament originated in Charles I's *Answer to the Nineteen Propositions of Parliament* (1642). By the mid-1780s, Pocock notes, "[t]here was no need for 'absolute monarchy' as the alternative to a 'republic' if the Crown's authority in Parliament could be confirmed. . . . What was taking shape . . . was the true shape of English absolutism: the undisputed sovereignty of the king-in-parliament." See J. G. A. Pocock, "Political Thought in the English-Speaking Atlantic, 1760–1790, Part II: Empire, Revolution and the End of Early Modernity," in Pocock, *Varieties of British Political Thought,* 299. On the king-in-Parliament, see also Pocock, "A Discourse of Sovereignty: Observations on the Work in Progress," in Nicholas Phillipson and Quentin Skinner, eds., *Political Discourse in Early Modern Britain* (Cambridge: Cambridge University Press,

1993), 377–426; and Pocock, "Political Thought in the English-Speaking Atlantic, 1760–1790, Part I: The Imperial Crisis."

23. Thomas Jefferson, "Summary View," in *PTJ*, 1:122. As David Armitage has pointed out, Jefferson's use of the term "state" here is significant because it was unusual at the time, and because it anticipated the similar diction he later used in the Declaration of Independence (e.g., "[t]hat these United Colonies are, and of Right ought to be, FREE AND INDEPENDENT STATES"). See David Armitage, *The Declaration of Independence: A Global History* (Cambridge, Mass.: Harvard University Press, 2007), 17–20, 170. On the novelty of the word "state" as the basic term for political entities, see Pocock, "States, Republics, and Empires," 57–58.

24. Jefferson, "Summary View," in *PTJ*, 1:122.

25. Ibid., 1:126.

26. Ibid., 1:125, 128.

27. Ibid., 1:129. Jefferson did not cite the most recent—and, as it turned out, the final—Crown veto of an act of Parliament: Anne's veto of the Scottish Militia Bill in 1707. The leading explication of whig political philosophy and its resonance in the colonies is Bernard Bailyn, *The Ideological Origins of the American Revolution,* enl. ed. (1967; Cambridge, Mass.: Belknap Press of Harvard University Press, 1992).

28. Jefferson, "Summary View," in *PTJ*, 1:129. The classic work on the Board of Trade and the role of the Privy Council in reviewing acts of the colonial assemblies is Joseph Henry Smith, *Appeals to the Privy Council from the American Plantations* (New York: Columbia University Press, 1950), 523–654; more recent treatments include Ian K. Steele, *Politics of Colonial Policy: The Board of Trade in Colonial Administration, 1696–1720* (Oxford: Clarendon Press, 1968); and Mary Sarah Bilder, *The Transatlantic Constitution: Colonial Legal Culture and the Empire* (Cambridge, Mass.: Harvard University Press, 2004).

29. Jefferson, "Summary View," in *PTJ*, 1:130.

30. Ibid., 1:131.

31. Ibid., 1:132, 134.

32. Jefferson's statement that "[i]t is neither our wish nor our interest to separate" from Britain is notable in this respect. Ibid., 1:135.

33. The phrase "commonwealth of nations" comes from Randolph G. Adams, *Political Ideas of the American Revolution: Britannic-American Contributions to the Problem of Imperial Organization, 1765 to 1775,* 3d ed. (Durham, N.C.: Trinity College Press, 1922; New York: Barnes and Noble, 1958), 45. Citations are to the Barnes and Noble edition. For the theory of "imperial federalism," see Jack N. Rakove, *The Beginnings of National Politics: An Interpretive History of the Continental Congress* (New York: Alfred A. Knopf, 1979; Baltimore: Johns Hopkins University Press, 1982), 36. Citations are to the Johns Hopkins edition. Adams presents the commonwealth of nations as the third strand in a three-part taxonomy of the various theories of empire circulating between 1765 and 1775. The other two are the "colonial dependency" theory—essentially the official metropolitan position that the colonies were entirely subordinate and that Parliament was supreme both domestically and imperially—and the "imperial federation" theory, which held that an empirewide legislature representing both the colonies and Britain was necessary. See R. G. Adams, *Political Ideas of the American Revolution,* 43–46. For a discussion of federation ideas in

Britain beginning in the seventeenth century and extending to current debates, see John Kendle, *Federal Britain* (London: Routledge, 1997).

34. See, e.g., Jefferson, "Summary View," in *PTJ*, 1:126 ("Not only the principles of common sense, but the common feelings of human nature must be surrendered up, before his majesty's subjects here can be persuaded to beleive [*sic*] that they hold their political existence at the will of a *British* parliament") (emphasis added). That the colonial assemblies, not Parliament, were the rightful repositories of the legislative sovereignty secured by the Glorious Revolution was a commonly held belief in British North America. See Barbara A. Black, "The Constitution of Empire: The Case for the Colonists," *University of Pennsylvania Law Review* 124 (1976): 1157–1211; and Jack P. Greene, "The Glorious Revolution and the British Empire, 1688–1783," in Lois G. Schwoerer, ed., *The Revolution of 1688–1689: Changing Perspectives* (Cambridge: Cambridge University Press, 1992): 260–271.

35. James Wilson, "Considerations on the Nature and Extent of the Legislative Authority of the British Parliament," in Robert Green McCloskey, ed., *The Works of James Wilson* (Cambridge, Mass.: Belknap Press of Harvard University Press, 1967), 2:745n. Wilson's biographer Page Smith used the phrase "dominion status," which Robert McCloskey describes as the "working compromise" that would later preserve the nineteenth-century British empire—"namely, that Parliament has *no* authority over the colonies, which are bound to the Empire only by their obedience and loyalty to the British King." McCloskey, introduction to *The Works of James Wilson*, 1:3 (citing Page Smith, *James Wilson, Founding Father, 1742–1798* [Chapel Hill: University of North Carolina Press, 1956], 58).

36. John Dickinson, "Essay on the Constitutional Power of Great Britain over the Colonies in America," in John B. Linn and William H. Egle, eds., *Pennsylvania Archives*, 2d ser. (Harrisburg, Pa.: B. F. Meyers, 1875), 3:601–602.

37. James Iredell, "To the Inhabitants of Great Britain," in Griffith J. McRee, ed., *Life and Correspondence of James Iredell, One of the Associate Justices of the Supreme Court of the United States* (New York: D. Appleton and Company, 1857), 1:219.

38. Jefferson, "Autobiography," 9. Merrill Peterson notes that one of Jefferson's instructors at the College of William and Mary was William Small, a Scot and "the only layman on a faculty of Anglican clerics." Jefferson later noted that his studies and acquaintance with Small "probably fixed the destinies of my life." Chronology, in Jefferson, *Writings*, 1519.

39. Thomas Jefferson's Notes of Proceedings in Congress, in Paul H. Smith, ed., *Letters of Delegates to Congress, 1774–1789* (Washington, D.C.: Library of Congress, 1979), 4:161 (emphasis added in the second quotation).

40. Ibid., 4:161–162. With respect to this and the previous quotation, it is worth bearing in mind the surmise of the editor of the *Letters of Delegates to Congress* that Jefferson's notes may have contained after-the-fact accounts of debates, as well as notes taken down as the discussions were happening. Whether Jefferson reconstructed the debates later or recorded them as they occurred, however, his use of the language of federal and incorporating unions, and the fact that such language appears in the notes of other observers such as John Adams, suggests that these terms were used in the course of the discussions in 1776. P. H. Smith, *Letters of Delegates to Congress*, 4:164 n.2.

41. [James Hodges], *The Rights and Interests of the Two British Monarchies, Inquir'd into, and Clear'd: With a Special Respect to an United or Separate State, Treatise I* (London, 1703), 3.

42. Ned Landsman, "The Legacy of British Union for the North American Colonies: Provincial Elites and the Problem of Imperial Union," in Robertson, *Union for Empire,* 298. On Scots' and Americans' shared provincial identity, see John Clive and Bernard Bailyn, "England's Cultural Provinces: Scotland and America," *William and Mary Quarterly,* 3d ser., 11 (1954): 200–213.

43. As Landsman puts it, these Scottish imperial representatives' "persistence in addressing the problem of imperial union constituted an important link between the Union debates of 1707 and the later American consideration of empire, confederation, and union that emerged in the latter part of the century." Landsman, "Legacy of British Union," 299.

44. Ibid., 311.

45. John Witherspoon's Speech in Congress, in P. H. Smith, *Letters of Delegates to Congress,* 4:587. The date of this speech—which survives only in fragments and is sometimes referred to as Witherspoon's "Speech in Congress upon the Confederation"—is uncertain, although Smith puts it on July 30, 1776. Ibid., 4:587 n.1.

46. John Adams' Notes of Debates, ibid., 4:593.

47. Jefferson, "Autobiography," 29.

48. Ibid.

49. The passages from the debates in the Continental Congress discussed in the foregoing paragraphs have been subject to some misinterpretation in the scholarly literature. Some scholars have misread Witherspoon's comments about the nature of the English-Scottish union to refer to the nature of the British Empire in North America and have conflated these comments with those articulated by Adams, Wythe, and others regarding the nature of the colonies' connection to the Crown and Parliament. See, e.g., Jack P. Greene, *Peripheries and Center: Constitutional Development in the Extended Polities of the British Empire and the United States, 1607-1788* (Athens: University of Georgia Press, 1986), 172; Martin S. Flaherty, "More Apparent than Real: The Revolutionary Commitment to Constitutional Federalism," *University of Kansas Law Review* 45 (1997): 1000. According to these interpretations, the passages from the debates in the Continental Congress appear to suggest that the British Empire was essentially federal throughout its history, and that therefore the constitutional debates of the period from 1765 to 1789 represented little original thought but rather an application of existing ideas of governmental structure from the colonies to the states. This argument, however, ignores the specific historical and political meaning that the terms "federal" and "incorporating" carried for observers such as Witherspoon and his fellow delegates in 1776 and the particular examples they associated with each species of union.

50. On the Scottish Enlightenment's distinctive background in the law of nature and nations, see John Fabian Witt, *Patriots and Cosmopolitans: Hidden Histories of American Law* (Cambridge, Mass.: Harvard University Press, 2007), in particular, chapter 1, "The Pyramid and the Machine: Founding Visions in the Life of James Wilson."

51. Anthony M. Lewis, "Jefferson's *Summary View* as a Chart of Political Union," *William and Mary Quarterly,* 3d ser., 5 (1948): 35.

52. Gilbert Chinard, ed., *The Commonplace Book of Thomas Jefferson: A Repertory of His Ideas on Government* (Baltimore: Johns Hopkins Press, 1926), 205, 369, 327. Chinard estimates that these notations date from the period between 1774 and 1776. Ibid., 9.

53. Ibid., 269, 316.

54. Ibid., 317; Wilson, "Considerations on the Nature and Extent of the Legislative Authority of the British Parliament," 2:745n.

55. [Alexander Hamilton], "The Farmer Refuted," in Harold C. Syrett, ed., *The Papers of Alexander Hamilton* (New York: Columbia University Press, 1961), 1:86.

56. Articles of Confederation, art. III.

57. Ibid., art. II.

58. Forsyth, *Unions of States,* 55. Although the Articles did not contemplate a separate executive branch of government, Jerrilyn Greene Marston argues that the text vested the Confederation Congress with many of the most important executive functions for which the Crown had formerly been responsible—in particular, the powers to conduct foreign relations, to control the military, and to regulate Indian affairs. "Many of the basic imperial powers exercised by the king had been thrust upon a reluctant Congress from 1775 on," Marston notes. "Until the great problems of federalism were resolved, there would be no frame of government that would guarantee the union of the colonies." Jerrilyn Greene Marston, *King and Congress: The Transfer of Political Legitimacy, 1774–1776* (Princeton, N.J.: Princeton University Press, 1987), 205.

59. Rakove, *Beginnings of National Politics,* 136, 145 ("What seemed to be at stake in 1775 was not the creation of an enduring nation state but the continued legitimation of a resistance movement whose responsibilities were rapidly growing more extensive and complex").

60. Silas Deane to Patrick Henry, January 2, 1775, in Charles Isham, ed., *The Deane Papers, 1774–1790* (New York: New-York Historical Society, 1887), 1:38.

61. John Locke, *Second Treatise of Government* (1690; reprint, with an introduction by C. B. Macpherson, Indianapolis: Hackett Publishing Co., 1980), 77 (emphasis removed). On the role of the Articles as a first attempt at situating the United States within the world community, see David C. Hendrickson, *Peace Pact: The Lost World of the American Founding* (Lawrence: University Press of Kansas, 2003), 156–157.

62. Wood, *Creation of the American Republic, 1776–1787,* 354–355.

63. Josiah Bartlett's Notes on the Plan of Confederation, in P. H. Smith, *Letters of Delegates to Congress,* 4:199–200, 200n.1.

64. On the European, as opposed to British, context of these debates, see Robertson, "Empire and Union," 4.

65. By the time of the debates more than a decade later over the ratification of the Constitution, and especially for Federalists, the term "empire" connoted the territorial ambitions of the United States rather than the historical example of the British Empire. See, e.g., [Alexander Hamilton], "The Federalist No. 1," in Jacob E. Cooke, ed., *The Federalist* (Middletown, Conn.: Wesleyan University Press, 1961), 3 (describing the debate over ratification as concerning "the fate of an empire, in many respects, the most interesting in the world"); see also Peter S. Onuf, *Jefferson's Empire: The Language of American Nationhood* (Charlottesville: University Press of Virginia, 2000).

66. [James Hodges], *The Rights and Interests of the Two British Monarchies, Inquir'd into, and Clear'd; With a special respect to An United or Separate State, Treatise I* (London, 1703), 3.

67. Samuel von Pufendorf, *The Law of Nature and Nations: or, A General System of the most Important Principles of Morality, Jurisprudence, and Politics,* trans. Basil Kennet, 5th ed. (London, 1749) (1672), 681.

68. John Adams' Notes of Debates, August 1, 1776, in P. H. Smith, *Letters of Delegates to Congress,* 4:593.

5. THE AUTHORITY OF A CENTRAL GOVERNMENT

1. Common Sense [Richard Bland], *The Colonel Dismounted: or the Rector Vindicated. In a Letter addressed to His Reverence: Containing a Dissertation upon the Constitution of the Colony* (Williamsburg: Joseph Royle, 1764), 22–23.

2. David Armitage, *The Ideological Origins of the British Empire* (Cambridge: Cambridge University Press, 2000), 5.

3. Robert M. Cover, "The Uses of Jurisdictional Redundancy: Interest, Ideology, and Innovation," *William and Mary Law Review* 22 (1981): 639–682. On the concept of *imperium in imperio,* see Daniel J. Hulsebosch, "*Imperia in Imperio:* The Multiple Constitutions of Empire in New York, 1750–1777," *Law and History Review* 16 (1998): 319–379.

4. Articles of Confederation, arts. II, IX.

5. Articles of Confederation, art. II; Merrill Jensen, *The Articles of Confederation: An Interpretation of the Social-Constitutional History of the American Revolution, 1774–1781* (Madison: University of Wisconsin Press, 1940), 164 (quoting Adams).

6. Editorial Note, in Robert A. Rutland et al., eds., *The Papers of James Madison,* ed. (Chicago: University of Chicago Press, 1975), 9:3–4 (hereafter *PJM*).

7. Madison to Jefferson, March 18, 1786, *PJM,* 8:501. Madison's devotion to his studies had always been remarkable: upon completion of his bachelor's degree at Princeton in two years, Madison was forced to remain in New Jersey an additional year in order to regain his strength while continuing with private studies. Despite taking this care, however, when Madison returned to Montpelier in April 1772, he suffered something like a nervous breakdown. At least one historian posits that the matriculation decision a few years later of another founder, Alexander Hamilton, may have been dictated by Princeton president John Witherspoon's desire to avoid a repeat of Madison's experience. Witherspoon denied Hamilton's request to proceed through the curriculum at his own (rapid) pace; consequently, Hamilton traveled to New York to study at King's College. See Ron Chernow, *Alexander Hamilton* (New York: Penguin Press, 2004), 48; see also Ralph Ketcham, *James Madison: A Biography* (Charlottesville: University Press of Virginia, 1990), 51–52.

8. Ketcham, *James Madison,* 184.

9. Ibid.

10. James Madison, "Notes on Ancient and Modern Confederacies," *PJM,* 9:8, 22.

11. Madison to Randolph, February 25, 1787, *PJM,* 9:299. On Madison's conclusion that any federal system based on voluntary compliance of the states was likely to fail, see

Jack N. Rakove, *James Madison and the Creation of the American Republic,* 2d ed. (New York: Longman, 2002), 52–53.

12. *The Federalist* No. 18 focuses on the ancient confederacies, especially the Amphicty-onic and Achaean leagues; *The Federalist* No. 19 discusses contemporary confederacies, including the Holy Roman Empire, Poland, and the Swiss confederacy; and *The Federalist* No. 20 considers the contemporary United Netherlands. Jacob E. Cooke, ed., *The Federalist* (Middletown, Conn.: Wesleyan University Press, 1961).

13. Madison arrived in Philadelphia on May 5, in time for the convention's first sched-uled meeting on May 14, but the lack of a quorum postponed the initial session until May 25. Madison reported these events to Jefferson on May 15, noting, "The number as yet assembled is small. . . . There is a prospect of a pretty full meeting on the whole, though there is less punctuality than was to be wished. Of this the late bad weather has been the principal cause." Madison to Jefferson, May 15, 1787, *PJM,* 9:415.

14. Madison to Jefferson, March 19, 1787, *PJM,* 9:318. Larry Kramer points out that the phrase "in all cases whatsoever" echoed the language of the hated Declaratory Act of 1766. He further notes that "Madison could not have picked language more likely to arouse anxi-eties about centralized authority." Larry D. Kramer, "Madison's Audience," *Harvard Law Review* 112 (1999): 628.

15. Scholars have employed a variety of terms to refer to Madison's proposed negative, including "the negative on state laws," "the federal veto," and "the federal negative." In his intellectual biography of Madison, Lance Banning uses the latter two phrases. See Lance E. Banning, *The Sacred Fire of Liberty: James Madison and the Founding of the Federal Republic* (Ithaca, N.Y.: Cornell University Press, 1995), 117, 188. This chapter will use the term "federal negative."

16. Douglass Adair, "James Madison's Autobiography," *William and Mary Quarterly,* 3d ser., 2 (1945): 202.

17. Many scholars who have studied Madison's federal negative have emphasized its role as a weapon against majoritarian tyranny and have therefore viewed it as inextricably linked with Madison's discussion in *The Federalist* No. 10 of the problem of faction and the consequent need for a large republic. See, e.g., Kramer, "Madison's Audience"; Jack N. Rakove, *Original Meanings: Politics and Ideas in the Making of the Constitution* (New York: Knopf, 1996), 51, 197. These and other scholars have viewed it as evidence of a creep-ing nationalist, even consolidationist, tendency in Madison's thought. See, e.g., Charles F. Hobson, "The Negative on State Laws: James Madison, the Constitution, and the Crisis of Republican Government," *William and Mary Quarterly,* 3d ser., 36 (1979): 258; Forrest McDonald, *States' Rights and the Union: Imperium in Imperio, 1776–1876* (Lawrence: University Press of Kansas, 2000), 18; Rakove, *Original Meanings,* 51. Banning disputes the latter position, saying that one of his purposes is "to utterly deny—in the face of very old and very influential emphases on the reactionary character of constitutional reform—that there was any hint of such a counterrevolutionary attitude in Madison himself." Banning also notes that Hobson later retreated somewhat from his stance. See Banning, *Sacred Fire of Liberty,* 127, 442 n.22. Although this debate is obviously significant, this chapter will fo-cus on the negative in the context of the transition from imperial to federal modes of authority.

18. Madison to Jefferson, March 19, 1787, *PJM*, 9:318; James Madison, "Vices of the Political System of the United States," Spring 1787, in *PJM*, 9:348–357.

19. Madison to Randolph, April 8, 1787, *PJM*, 9:370; Madison to Washington, April 16, 1787, *PJM*, 9:383. Several historians have discussed the influence of imperial practice on Madison's thinking about the federal negative. Most notable are Banning, *Sacred Fire of Liberty*, 118; Mary Sarah Bilder, *The Transatlantic Constitution: Colonial Legal Culture and the Empire* (Cambridge, Mass.: Harvard University Press 2004), 191–192; Andrew C. McLaughlin, *The Foundations of American Constitutionalism* (New York: New York University Press, 1932), 153; Michael P. Zuckert, "A System without Precedent: Federalism in the American Constitution," in Leonard W. Levy and Dennis J. Mahoney, eds., *The Framing and Ratification of the Constitution* (New York: Macmillan, 1987), 144–145; and Jack N. Rakove, "Making a Hash of Sovereignty, Part I," *Green Bag*, 2d ser., 2 (1998): 40–41.

20. Blackstone defined the Privy Council as "the principal council belonging to the king" and described its composition as follows: "The king's will is the sole constituent of a privy counsellor; and this also regulates their number." See William Blackstone, *Commentaries on the Laws of England* (1765–1769; reprint, with an introduction by Stanley N. Katz, Chicago: University of Chicago Press, 1979), 1:222–223. See also Henry Campbell Black, *Black's Law Dictionary*, 6th ed. (St. Paul, Minn.: West, 1990), s.v. "Privy Council": "In England, the principal council of the sovereign, composed of the cabinet ministers, and other persons chosen by the king or queen as privy councillors."

21. Arthur Meier Schlesinger, "Colonial Appeals to the Privy Council," pts. 1 and 2, *Political Science Quarterly* 28, no. 2 (1913): 279–297; no. 3 (1913): 433–450. My discussion of the hierarchical underpinnings of colonial and early American appellate review is informed by Philip Hamburger's discussion of the "hierarchical assumptions" that undergirded seventeenth- and eighteenth-century understandings of superior and inferior law. See Philip Hamburger, "Law and Judicial Duty," *George Washington Law Review* 72 (2003): 9–12.

22. Joseph Henry Smith, *Appeals to the Privy Council from the American Plantations* (New York: Columbia University Press, 1950).

23. Ibid., 464–523. The doctrine of the king's dominions was a holdover from the Middle Ages, when English kings held lands outside the realm, such as Aquitaine or Normandy. By the time English colonization of the New World began in 1607, however, these overseas holdings had dwindled to the Channel Islands, which alone possessed the standing to claim a right of appeal to the Crown. See Julius Goebel, Jr., *Antecedents and Beginnings to 1801*, vol. 1 of *The Oliver Wendell Holmes Devise History of the Supreme Court of the United States*, ed. Paul A. Freund (New York: Macmillan, 1971), 36. Technically, the forum for such appeals was a specially designated committee of the Privy Council. From 1675 to 1696, that committee was initially denominated the Committee of Trade and Foreign Plantations and subsequently the Committee for Trade and Plantations; the members of both entities were also known as the Lords Committee of Trade and Plantations. Between 1675 and 1696, the committee fluctuated in size from as few as twelve to as many as thirty-three members, occasionally including the entire membership of the Privy Council. A 1696 act of William III reorganized the committee and renamed it the Board of Trade and the Committee for Hearing Appeals from the Plantations. See Smith, *Appeals to the Privy*

Council, 71–72, 132–138; Goebel, *Antecedents and Beginnings,* 60–65. Smith notes that "all these committees were conciliar derivatives—their decisions gained force only through Orders in Council issued by the Council Board itself." See Smith, *Appeals to the Privy Council,* 72. This chapter therefore follows the terminology of Smith and others and employs the general phrase "Privy Council" to refer to the body responsible for hearing appeals from the colonies and evaluating colonial acts for conformity to the laws of England.

24. Bilder, *Transatlantic Constitution,* 1–4. See Randolph G. Adams, *Political Ideas of the American Revolution: Britannic-American Contributions to the Problem of Imperial Organization, 1765 to 1775,* 3d ed. (Durham, N.C.: Trinity College Press, 1922; New York: Barnes and Noble, 1958), 117–118 (discussing eighteenth-century conceptions of the repugnancy principle). Citations are to the Barnes and Noble edition.

25. See, e.g., Bilder, *Transatlantic Constitution,* 6; Hamburger, "Law and Judicial Duty."

26. Goebel refers to such practices as "administrative control of colony legislation," while Smith terms them "legislative review." Goebel, *Antecedents and Beginnings,* 60; see also Smith, *Appeals to the Privy Council,* 523. In modern jurisprudence, a challenge to a law's operation in all situations and with respect to all parties is termed a "facial challenge," in contrast to an as-applied challenge, which takes on the statute only as it is applied to a particular type of party or set of facts. In both cases, however, an aggrieved party must bring the challenge; courts will not take up the issue of their own volition, because such an act would violate the Constitution's case or controversy requirement. See U.S. Constitution, art. III, § 2. Because the application of facial challenges is so broad, courts have erected substantial barriers to their successful prosecution, rendering them relatively rare. Examples are the Supreme Court's holdings in *National Endowment for the Arts v. Finley,* 524 U.S. 569, 580 (1998), and *United States v. Salerno,* 481 U.S. 739, 745 (1987). On this distinction generally, see Richard H. Fallon, Jr., "As-Applied and Facial Challenges and Third-Party Standing," *Harvard Law Review* 113 (2000): 1321–1370.

27. The classic text on the dual characterization of the English Parliament is Charles H. McIlwain, *The High Court of Parliament: An Historical Essay on the Boundaries between Legislation and Adjudication* (New Haven, Conn.: Yale University Press, 1910). A more recent interpretation of this issue in the American context is Barbara A. Black, "The Constitution of Empire: The Case for the Colonists," *University of Pennsylvania Law Review* 124 (1976): 1157–1211. For a discussion of the link between the development of bicameral legislatures in the colonies and the judicial-legislative distinction, see Mark DeWolfe Howe and Louis F. Eaton, Jr., "The Supreme Judicial Power in the Colony of Massachusetts Bay," *New England Quarterly* 20 (1947): 291–316.

28. At the risk of spoiling the ending of the story, I should point out that the case or controversy requirement ultimately found its way into the Constitution in order to prevent just such practices as the Privy Council's ex ante legislative review from taking root in the federal courts. U.S. Constitution, art. III, § 2. The alternative to a case or controversy standard is to permit courts to issue advisory opinions—that is, judicial determinations of a law's validity without an aggrieved party's having first challenged the law. For more on this distinction and the rationale behind it, see Erwin Chemerinsky, *Federal Jurisdiction,* 4th ed. (New York: Aspen Publishers, 2003), 44–56.

29. On royal colonies, see Smith, *Appeals to the Privy Council,* 77–78 (discussing the early precedents of the Channel Islands), 79–82 (discussing Virginia and New Hampshire). In both royal and proprietary colonies, the local assembly was subject to an additional level of imperial oversight in the form of the governor's veto. See Bernard Bailyn, *The Origins of American Politics* (New York: Knopf, 1968; New York: Vintage, 1970), 67. Citations are to the Vintage edition. On charter colonies, see Smith, *Appeals to the Privy Council,* 45–46 (discussing "the recalcitrance of Massachusetts Bay" in repeatedly challenging the royal power to hear appeals from the colony during the first half of the seventeenth century), 51–54 (canvassing Connecticut, Rhode Island, and the Carolinas). On proprietary colonies, see ibid., 85–86 (discussing New Jersey and Maryland).

30. See Anthony McFarlane, *The British in the Americas, 1480–1815* (London: Longman, 1992), 198; see also Goebel, *Antecedents and Beginnings,* 40, 60–65.

31. Schlesinger, "Colonial Appeals to the Privy Council," pt. 2, 437–438, 446. Schlesinger notes that after 1734 or 1735, the Privy Council records drop the phrase "for Appeals" and refer to the decision-making body simply as "the Committee." Ibid., 439.

32. The breadth of the Privy Council's reach prompted Charles M. Andrews to emphasize the relationship between disallowance and the royal prerogative. Andrews described disallowance as "an executive rather than a legislative act" because it was "performed not by the king but by the Council as his executive agent." The power of disallowance was thus "an exercise of the royal prerogative, an expression of the king's supreme authority in the enacting of laws by inferior law-making bodies, whose right to make laws at all rested on the king's will." Andrews concluded, therefore, that disallowance was "not a veto but an act of regulation and control." Charles M. Andrews, "The Royal Disallowance," *Proceedings of the American Antiquarian Society* 24 (1914): 343. See also A. G. Dorland, "The Royal Disallowance in Massachusetts," *Bulletin of the Departments of History and Political and Economic Science in Queen's University, Kingston, Ontario, Canada,* no. 22 (1917).

33. Here Goebel and Smith differ in their interpretations. While Goebel suggests that the Privy Council in its judicial capacity declared void ab initio a small handful of colonial acts, Smith states that there was only one such case: *Winthrop v. Lechmere* (P.C. 1728), reprinted in *Public Records of the Colony of Connecticut* (Hartford: Lockwood and Brainard Co., 1873), 7:578, in which a 1699 Connecticut intestacy law was held void as contrary to English law and the colonial charter. The two scholars agree, however, that the mechanism of voiding a colonial statute ab initio was used when the Privy Council was acting both in its legislative and in its judicial capacities. See Goebel, *Antecedents and Beginnings,* 72–73; Smith, *Appeals to the Privy Council,* 537.

34. Goebel, *Antecedents and Beginnings,* 72.

35. Goebel distinguishes thus between declarations of nullity ab initio and disallowance: "A declaration of nullity was something close to catastrophic, for everything that might have been done under [the act] was rendered nugatory." Ibid., 69. Goebel notes that some colonial acts included a suspending clause explicitly stating that the act was not final, and therefore that no rights and duties could be created pursuant to it until it was affirmatively validated by the Privy Council. The Crown pressed for such clauses as a means of emphasizing the incompleteness of colonial legislative authority. Goebel states, however,

that many—perhaps the majority—of colonial acts went into effect with no ruling one way or the other by metropolitan authorities. Thus he concludes that "whatever the theory, the Crown was practically not an indispensable party." Ibid., 68.

36. In other words, rights could vest pursuant to an act even if that act was subsequently disallowed, but no rights could vest pursuant to an act that was vetoed and thus never took effect. Ibid., 68–72.

37. Elmer Beecher Russell, *The Review of American Colonial Legislation by the King in Council* (New York: Columbia University Press, 1915), 221. Forrest McDonald gives a similar number, reporting that the Board of Trade disallowed 469 of the 8,563 mainland colonial acts that it reviewed, or 5.48 percent. See McDonald, *States' Rights and the Union*, 2.

38. See Smith, *Appeals to the Privy Council*, 138; and Bilder, *Transatlantic Constitution*, 74.

39. The relevant language on Crown authority to hear judicial appeals appeared in the Grant of the Province of Maine from Charles II to the Duke of York and reserved to the Crown "ye receiving hearing and determining of the appeal and appeales of all or any person or persons, of in or belonging to ye territoryes or islands aforesaid in or touching any judgment or sentence to be there made or given." Grant of the Province of Maine (1664), in Francis Newton Thorpe, *The Federal and State Constitutions, Colonial Charters, and Other Organic Laws of the States, Territories, and Colonies Now or Heretofore Forming the United States of America, Compiled and Edited under the Act of Congress of June 30, 1906* (Washington, D.C.: Government Printing Office, 1909), 3:1638–1639; see also Smith, *Appeals to the Privy Council*, 53. On the arguments of royal officials, see Goebel, *Antecedents and Beginnings*, 40–41. Opponents of this expanded royal power, among the most vocal of which were Connecticut and Massachusetts, countered that the Crown possessed appellate jurisdiction only to the extent that such jurisdiction was expressly reserved by charter. Without a specific reservation of appellate power to the Crown, as was found, for example, in the charter of the proprietary colony of Pennsylvania, opponents of royal appellate power argued that the Privy Council had no business reviewing the decisions of colonial courts. Charter for the Province of Pennsylvania (1691), in Thorpe, *Federal and State Constitutions*, 5:3038. Massachusetts judges apparently felt little obligation to assist parties in bringing appeals: those who sought appeal from the decisions of the colony's highest court were often frustrated by the court's refusal to provide a written record or to order execution of its final judgment. See William E. Nelson, *Americanization of the Common Law: The Impact of Legal Change on Massachusetts Society, 1760–1830* (Athens: University of Georgia Press, 1994), 16. Crown officials strenuously resisted such interpretations, fueling a dispute that lasted well into the eighteenth century.

40. See Bailyn, *Origins of American Politics*, 67.

41. *Statutes of the Realm*, 7 & 8 Wm. III, c. 22, §8 (1696).

42. See Smith, *Appeals to the Privy Council*, 525. Rhode Island was an exception: the terms of its charter did not require acts of the colonial assembly to be reviewed by the Privy Council before taking effect. See Bilder, *Transatlantic Constitution*, 55–56.

43. Massachusetts Bay Charter (1629), in Thorpe, *Federal and State Constitutions*, 3:1853 (emphasis added). The subsequent Massachusetts charter of 1691 provided that

colonial acts would take effect if the Crown did not take contrary action within a set time period. See Goebel, *Antecedents and Beginnings,* 66.

44. 10 Hen. VII, c. 22 (1495); amended by 21 & 22 Geo. III, c. 47 (1782).

45. See Bilder, *Transatlantic Constitution,* 54–55; Goebel, *Antecedents and Beginnings,* 61–65.

46. Madison to Washington, April 16, 1787, *PJM,* 9:383–384.

47. Ibid., 9:383.

48. On the Privy Council's power of judicial review, see, e.g., Smith, *Appeals to the Privy Council;* see also Black, "Constitution of Empire"; McIlwain, *High Court of Parliament.*

49. See Zuckert, "System without Precedent," 144.

50. Banning, *Sacred Fire of Liberty,* 126–127.

51. Madison to Washington, April 16, 1787, *PJM,* 9:384.

52. For example, the Holy Roman Empire, a loose confederation in Madison's own time, exercised authority over imperial legislation, treaties, and declarations of war. See Madison, "Notes on Ancient and Modern Confederacies," *PJM,* 9:19. Several decades earlier, John Locke had listed such powers among the "federative powers" of the commonwealth, which he defined as relating to "the management of the *security and interest of the public without.*" John Locke, *Second Treatise of Government* (1690; reprint, with an introduction by C. B. Macpherson, Indianapolis: Hackett Publishing Co., 1980), 77.

53. Madison to Washington, April 16, 1787, *PJM,* 9:384.

54. See Madison to Jefferson, March 19, 1787, *PJM,* 9:318 ("oppressing" and "thwarting and molesting"); Madison to Washington, April 16, 1787, *PJM* 9:384 ("invad[ing]" and "violat[ing]"). Here I differ markedly from Banning, who argues that "Madison's reference to a 'dispassionate umpire' over contending interests applies specifically and solely to a federal referee over contentions within individual states," and that therefore "he does not envision a federal legislature capable of dispassionately supervising national conflicts of interest." Banning, *Sacred Fire of Liberty,* 445 n.52. In both the March 19 letter to Jefferson and the April 16 letter to Washington, however, Madison seems clearly to contemplate that the federal negative would apply to inter- as well as intrastate conflicts. On ideas of passions and interests in this period, see Albert O. Hirschman, *The Passions and the Interests: Political Arguments for Capitalism before Its Triumph,* rev. ed. (Princeton, N.J.: Princeton University Press, 1997), 47.

55. Grayson to Short, April 16, 1787, in Edmund C. Burnett, ed., *Letters of Members of the Continental Congress* (1936; reprint, Gloucester, Mass.: Peter Smith, 1963), 8:581.

56. See Editorial Note, *PJM,* 10:12–13.

57. "The Virginia Plan," *PJM,* 10:16 (emphasis added). Interestingly, the scope of the negative as set forth in the Virginia Plan was narrower than Madison's earlier formulations had contemplated. While the plan's language referred to laws "contravening in the opinion of the National Legislature the articles of Union," Madison's proposal in his earlier letter to Jefferson had given the central government broader power to negative *"in all cases whatsoever."* Madison to Jefferson, March 19, 1787, *PJM,* 9:318. Madison did not endorse this alteration, as will be discussed later.

58. Max Farrand, ed., *The Records of the Federal Convention of 1787* (New Haven, Conn.: Yale University Press, 1937), 1:xvi, 54 (brackets showing Madison's revisions of ca.

1821 omitted). Farrand's authoritative *Records of the Federal Convention* includes the notes taken by several delegates to the convention but consistently treats Madison's as the most accurate and comprehensive.

59. "The Virginia Plan," *PJM,* 10:16.

60. The Philadelphia convention was not the first instance in which a council of revision was considered. The New York constitution of 1777 featured such a council, and the Virginia legislature had contemplated adopting a similar measure in 1782–1783. See "The Virginia Plan," *PJM,* 10:17 n.3; see also Alfred B. Street, *The Council of Revision of the State of New York* (Albany: William Gould, 1859); Gordon S. Wood, *The Creation of the American Republic, 1776–1787* (Chapel Hill: University of North Carolina Press, 1969), 435–436, 455.

61. Rakove, *James Madison and the Creation of the American Republic,* 73. Madison's uneasy attitude toward legislative power manifested itself most strongly in his *Federalist* essays. See "The Federalist No. 48," in Cooke, *Federalist,* 334 ("where the legislative power is exercised by an assembly, which is inspired by a supposed influence over the people with an intrepid confidence for its own strength . . . it is against the enterprising ambition of this department, that the people ought to indulge all their jealousy and exhaust all their precautions").

62. Richard Henry Lee had made a similar point in a May 1787 letter to George Mason: "Do you not think, sir, that it ought to be declared, by the new system, that any state act of legislation that shall contravene, or oppose, the authorized acts of Congress, or interfere with the expressed rights of that body, shall be ipso facto void, and of no force whatsoever." Lee to Mason, May 15, 1787, in James Curtis Ballagh, ed., *The Letters of Richard Henry Lee* (New York: Da Capo Press, 1970), 2:422. Lee's belief that unconstitutional state laws were void ab initio seems to have led him to a different conclusion from Madison's, however. Both Lee and Mason ultimately opposed the Constitution on the ground that it granted too much power to the central government. From this result, it is possible to deduce that Lee thought that unconstitutional state laws were by definition void, and therefore that no decree of invalidity was necessary from Congress.

63. This distinction between structural and substantive approaches to authority is conceptually similar to Daniel Hulsebosch's distinction between "jurisdictional" and "jurisprudential" visions of law. According to the former, as articulated by Sir Edward Coke, "the common law was inseparable from the institutions that applied, practiced, and taught the common law." A jurisprudential notion of law, in contrast, "refers to a rationally organized body of rules and principles defined primarily in reference to each other, not to the remedies and personnel enforcing them." Daniel J. Hulsebosch, "The Ancient Constitution and the Expanding Empire: Sir Edward Coke's British Jurisprudence," *Law and History Review* 21 (2003): 445–446.

64. See Hobson, "Negative on State Laws," 266; Marty D. Matthews, *Forgotten Founder: The Life and Times of Charles Pinckney* (Columbia: University of South Carolina Press, 2004), 40, 45.

65. Madison Chronology, *PJM,* 10:xxv; Madison's Notes, June 8, 1787, in Farrand, *Records,* 1:168, 164. Charles Hobson speculates that the limited negative outlined in the Virginia Plan was the work of Randolph and George Mason. See Hobson, "Negative on State Laws," 266.

66. Madison's Notes, June 8, 1787, in Farrand, *Records*, 1:165. Michael Zuckert makes the connection to encroachments explicit, noting that Madison "conceived the Congress of the general government playing the role in the American system that the king played in the British empire through his veto power over the laws of the individual legislatures of the empire. That royal veto could be and in fact was used to prevent encroachments of the sort Madison feared." Zuckert, "System without Precedent," 145.

67. Acrimony over the scope of the royal prerogative dated back to the English Civil War and the Glorious Revolution. See Bernard Bailyn, *The Ideological Origins of the American Revolution,* enl. ed. (1967; Cambridge, Mass.: Belknap Press of Harvard University Press, 1992), 55–93; Edmund S. Morgan, *Inventing the People: The Rise of Popular Sovereignty in England and America* (New York: Norton, 1988); J. G. A. Pocock, *The Ancient Constitution and the Feudal Law: A Study of English Historical Thought in the Seventeenth Century; A Reissue with a Retrospect* (1967; New York: Norton, 1987), 233–236.

68. Madison's Notes, June 8, 1787, in Farrand, *Records*, 1:165–166.

69. Rufus King's Notes, June 8, 1787, in Farrand, *Records*, 1:172.

70. Madison's Notes, August 23, 1787, in Farrand, *Records*, 1:391; Madison to Jefferson, October 24, 1787, in *PJM*, 10:211.

71. Madison's Notes, June 8, 1787, in Farrand, *Records*, 1:164.

72. Madison's Notes, July 17, 1787, in Farrand, *Records*, 2:28.

73. Michael Zuckert makes a similar point, noting that according to Madison's view, "for the sake of the separateness and independent operation of the different governments, the governments must occasionally operate on each other." Zuckert, "System without Precedent," 144.

74. Madison's Notes, June 8, 1787, in Farrand, *Records*, 1:168.

75. Ibid., 1:165.

76. The seven states whose delegations voted against the motion were Connecticut, New York, New Jersey, Maryland, North Carolina, South Carolina, and Georgia. Voting in favor were Virginia, Pennsylvania, and Massachusetts. The Delaware delegation was split. See ibid., 1:168.

77. See Charles Warren, *The Making of the Constitution* (1937; reprint, New York: Barnes and Noble, 1967), 317.

78. The editors of *The Papers of James Madison* refer to June 13 as the "high point" of Madison's influence at the convention. Editorial Note, *PJM*, 10:3.

79. See Warren, *Making of the Constitution,* 317.

80. Madison's Notes, July 17, 1787, in Farrand, *Records*, 2:28. The votes broke down slightly differently from those cast on June 8. Voting in favor of the negative were Massachusetts, Virginia, and North Carolina; voting against were Connecticut, New Jersey, Pennsylvania, Delaware, Maryland, South Carolina, and Georgia. The New York delegation had collapsed shortly before when Robert Yates and John Lansing had walked out, leaving only Hamilton. Madison's Notes, August 23, 1787, Farrand, *Records*, 2:390–391.

81. Carrington to Jefferson, June 9, 1787, in Farrand, *Records*, 3:39; Madison's Notes, June 20, 1787, in Farrand, *Records*, 1:337.

82. Luther Martin, "Genuine Information" (1788), in Farrand, *Records*, 3:180.

83. Ibid., 3:177. All italics are Martin's own.

84. Journal of the Convention, July 16, 1787, in Farrand, *Records,* 2:14.

85. Kramer, "Madison's Audience," 628.

86. Madison's Notes, June 8, 1787, in Farrand, *Records,* 1:165.

87. King's Notes, June 8, 1787, in Farrand, *Records,* 1:171.

88. Ibid., 1:171–172.

89. Madison's Notes, June 8, 1787, in Farrand, *Records,* 1:167–168.

90. Madison's Notes, June 8, 1787, in Farrand, *Records,* 1:168.

91. Declaration of Independence (1776).

92. Luther Martin, "Genuine Information," in Farrand, *Records,* 3:203. Although the Constitution borrowed the executive veto from the English constitution, it must be noted that the last instance of a royal veto was Anne's negative of the Scottish Militia Bill in 1707.

93. Madison's August 28 comments in the convention made clear that he had not dropped the subject of the federal negative. During debate on a provision prohibiting the states from issuing bills of credit in order to ensure the nation's financial stability, Madison added this coda to his statement supporting the ban: "He conceived however that a negative on the State laws could alone secure the effect. Evasions might and would be devised by the ingenuity of the Legislatures." Madison's Notes, August 28, 1787, in Farrand, *Records,* 2:440. The records are silent about his fellow delegates' reactions to this reference to the defeated negative.

94. A few days before the convention adjourned on September 17, Madison did break his silence concerning the proceedings in a letter to Jefferson. After sketching the outlines of the proposed constitution, he concluded, "I hazard an opinion nevertheless that the plan should it be adopted will neither effectually answer its national object nor prevent the local mischiefs which every where excite disgusts agst the state governments." Madison to Jefferson, September 6, 1787, *PJM,* 10:163–164.

95. Jefferson to Madison, June 20, 1787, *PJM,* 10:64. One source of news of Madison's proposal was William Grayson's April 16 letter to Jefferson's secretary William Short, discussed earlier. On the date of Madison's receipt of Jefferson's letter, see Madison to Jefferson, September 6, 1787, *PJM,* 10:163.

96. Editorial Note, *PJM,* 10:205. At least one observer of the convention, however, held out hope until the final days that the delegates would see the wisdom of the negative. On August 22, James McClurg, who had recently left the Virginia delegation, wrote to Madison, "I still have some hope that I shall hear from you of the reinstatement of the Negative—as it is certainly the only means by which the several Legislatures can be restrained from disturbing the order & harmony of the whole; & the Governmt. render'd properly national, & one." McClurg to Madison, August 22, 1787, *PJM,* 10:154.

97. Madison to Jefferson, October 24, 1787, *PJM,* 10:210.

98. Ibid., 10:209–210.

99. See Kramer, "Madison's Audience," 649–653 (positing the delegates' "insensibility to the theory and agenda" of Madison's negative, especially the vital role that it played in his vision of the extended republic).

100. Jefferson to Madison, December 20, 1787, *PJM,* 10:338. Jefferson was evidently similarly unmoved by the arguments that another of his correspondents, James Monroe, offered in favor of the negative, which "will if [Congress] is well organiz'd, be the best way

of introducing uniformity in their proceedings that can be devis'd." Monroe to Jefferson, July 27, 1787, in Farrand, *Records*, 3:65.

101. Warren, *Making of the Constitution,* 166.

102. Madison to Trist, December 1831, in Gaillard Hunt, ed., *The Writings of James Madison* (New York: G. P. Putnam's Sons, 1910), 9:473.

103. Joseph Story, *Commentaries on the Constitution of the United States,* abr. ed. (Boston: Hilliard, Gray, and Co., 1833), 607.

104. See Larry D. Kramer, *The People Themselves: Popular Constitutionalism and Judicial Review* (New York: Oxford University Press, 2004), 74–75; Rakove, *Original Meanings,* 173; Jack N. Rakove, "The Origins of Judicial Review: A Plea for New Contexts," *Stanford Law Review* 49 (1997): 1046–1047; and Lawrence Gene Sager, "The Supreme Court, 1980 Term—Foreword: Constitutional Limitations on Congress' Authority to Regulate the Jurisdiction of the Federal Courts," *Harvard Law Review* 95 (1981): 46–47.

105. Daniel Hulsebosch has pointed to a set of early examples of horizontal judicial review in the 1780s, in which state courts "invoked the fundamental law of their own state constitutions or the Treaty of 1783 with Britain to minimize, revise, and even nullify state legislation targeting loyalists and interfering with transatlantic commerce." Daniel J. Hulsebosch, "A Discrete and Cosmopolitan Minority: The Loyalists, the Atlantic World, and the Origins of Judicial Review," *Chicago-Kent Law Review* 81 (2006): 826–827.

106. Journal of the Convention, August 10, 1787, in Farrand, *Records*, 2:245.

107. [John Dickinson], *Fragments on the Confederation of the American States* (Philadelphia: Thomas Dobson, 1787), 18, 20, 17. The essay was reprinted in the *Pennsylvania Gazette* on June 6, 1787. For the attribution to Dickinson, see the headnotes to Early American Imprints, 1st ser.: Evans, 1639–1800, no. 20367.

108. See Rakove, *Original Meanings,* 173. Madison and Wilson also argued that by its own terms, the New Jersey Plan did not adequately provide a means by which the new charter would be established as the supreme law of the land because the plan required not ratification in convention but ratification by the Confederation Congress alone. Ibid. As the modern doctrine of federal preemption demonstrates, Madison was right to fear that a complicated common-law (and, indeed, statutory) thicket would result from a judicial approach to policing the line between federal and state power. See, e.g., Christopher R. Drahozal, *The Supremacy Clause: A Reference Guide to the United States Constitution* (Westport, Conn.: Praeger, 2004), 89–127; Kenneth Starr et al., *The Law of Preemption: A Report of the Appellate Judges Conference, American Bar Association* (Chicago: American Bar Association, 1991); and Joseph F. Zimmerman, *Federal Preemption: The Silent Revolution* (Ames: Iowa State University Press, 1991).

109. Madison to Jefferson, October 24, 1787, *PJM,* 10:211–212.

110. Article VI of the Virginia Plan had included a grant of power to Congress "to call forth the force of the Union agst. any member of the Union failing to fulfill its duty under the articles thereof." By May 31, however, Madison had reconsidered the coercion provision and concluded that it was not the best way to proceed. "A Union of the States containing such an ingredient seemed to provide for its own destruction," he told the convention. "The use of force agst. a State, would look more like a declaration of war, than an infliction of punishment, and would probably be considered by the party attacked as a dissolution of

all previous compacts by which it might be bound." Apparently agreeing with Madison, the convention then voted to postpone the coercion measure. Madison's Notes, May 31, 1787, in Farrand, *Records,* 1:54. Martin Diamond notes that by incorporating a coercion provision, the New Jersey Plan arguably went further toward consolidation than the Virginia Plan, a point that the Virginia Plan's advocates did not fail to trumpet when they critiqued the New Jersey Plan for its reliance "upon civil war as the means to secure the blessings of union." Martin Diamond, "What the Framers Meant by Federalism," in Robert A. Goldwin, ed., *A Nation of States: Essays on the American Federal System* (Chicago: Rand McNally, 1963), 38.

111. Madison's Notes, July 17, 1787, in Farrand, *Records,* 2:28–29. Larry Kramer suggests that this proposal by Martin, an avowed foe of centralized power, was a gambit to move the debate away from what Martin likely viewed as the worst-case scenario of a congressional veto power and to adopt instead a weaker method of national oversight over state law. "From this point on, then," Kramer argues, "the delegates assumed the existence of judicial review over state laws in their deliberation." See Kramer, *People Themselves,* 75.

112. Madison's Notes, August 23, 1787, in Farrand, *Records,* 2:389. Madison's final reference to the negative during the convention is almost touching. As the delegates discussed giving the national government the power to police state export duties, Madison's notes record that he said, "The jurisdiction of the supreme Court must be the source of redress. . . . His own opinion was, that this was insufficient,—. A negative on the State laws alone could meet all the shapes which these [duties] could assume. But this had been overruled." Madison's Notes, September 12, 1787, in Farrand, *Records,* 2:589.

113. Sager, "Supreme Court," 49 (noting that on August 27—the Monday following the Thursday on which the delegates unanimously adopted amendments to the Supremacy Clause that made the Constitution, as well as acts of Congress and treaties, the "supreme law of the several States"—"the Convention spent an intense day addressing the judiciary article").

114. Ibid.; see also Madison's Notes, August 27, 1787, in Farrand, *Records,* 2:430–431.

115. Pierce Butler to Weedon Butler, October 8, 1787, in Farrand, *Records,* 3:103; see also Kramer, *People Themselves,* 280 n.1 (listing statements by delegates acknowledging judicial review as the most viable alternative to the federal negative).

116. See Madison's Notes, August 27, 1787, in Farrand, *Records,* 2:430–431.

117. Ibid., 2:431. Compare Farrand, *Records,* 2:172 (version of July 24–26), with 2:600 (final version of September 12).

118. Goebel, *Antecedents and Beginnings,* 241.

119. On the history of judicial review as a concept in American constitutional law, see Mary Sarah Bilder, "Idea or Practice: A Brief Historiography of Judicial Review," *Journal of Policy History* 20 (2008): 6–26.

120. See John P. Kaminski, review of *Notes of Debates in the Federal Convention of 1787,* by James Madison, ed. Adrienne Koch, *Common-place* 2 (July 2002), http://www.common-place.org/vol-02/no-04/reviews/kaminski.shtml. For a comprehensive discussion of what became known as "the Genêt affair," see Stanley Elkins and Eric McKitrick, *The Age of Federalism: The Early American Republic, 1788–1800* (New York: Oxford University Press, 1993), 341–354.

121. Madison to Trist, December 1831, in Hunt, *Writings of James Madison,* 9:473–474.

122. Anti-Federalists and, later, Republicans made a similar point during and after the ratification debates, arguing that the federal negative would have been preferable to the more robust centralization embodied in the Supremacy Clause and promoted by the Supreme Court under the leadership of Chief Justice John Marshall. Writing in 1828, John Taylor of Caroline lauded the rejection of the Virginia Plan but noted that "the negative power over state laws with which it was invested, was much less objectionable than that now constructively contended for on behalf of the federal government." John Taylor, *New Views of the Constitution of the United States* (Washington, D.C.: Way and Gideon, 1823), 18. In an 1833 letter in which he defended the negative, Madison cited Taylor's comments as "not unworthy of notice" and reiterated his own oft-repeated argument for "the necessity of some adequate mode of preventing the States, in their individual characters, from defeating the constitutional authority of the States in their united character, and from collisions among themselves." Madison to William Rives, October 21, 1833, in James Madison, *Letters and Other Writings of James Madison, Fourth President of the United States* (Philadelphia: J. B. Lippincott and Co., 1865), 4:313.

123. James Madison, "Preface to Debates in the Convention: A Sketch Never Finished nor Applied," in Adrienne Koch, ed., *Notes of Debates in the Federal Convention of 1787* (Athens: Ohio University Press, 1984), 16. Madison drafted the preface between 1830 and 1836 as part of preparing his notes for publication after his death. Ibid., 1.

124. Madison did contemplate a degree of judicial review according to which courts would be bound by the laws of the United States, but he seems quite clearly to have envisioned this as subordinate to the federal negative. "Let this national supremacy be extended also to the Judiciary department," he wrote to Randolph. "If the judges in the last resort depend on the States & are bound by their oaths to them and not to the Union, the intention of the law and the interests of the nation may be defeated by the obsequiousness of the Tribunals to the policy or prejudices of the States." Madison to Randolph, April 8, 1787, *PJM,* 9:370. As his comments regarding the limitations of ex post review show, however, he clearly considered judicial review to be at best a supplement to the federal negative.

125. Following the ratification of the Constitution, the phrase "legislative review" referred on at least one occasion to the process by which a legislature reviewed the decision of a court in a particular case, in contrast to the earlier sense of a legislature reviewing a piece of legislation before it came into effect. This post-1787 legislative review bore little resemblance to the Privy Council's practices or to the federal negative because it concerned a prior judicial decision rather than a potential act of legislation. The seminal case involving this variant of legislative review was *Calder v. Bull* (1798), in which the Supreme Court permitted the Connecticut legislature to set aside the verdict of a Connecticut probate court. As the Supreme Court noted in a 1995 decision, *Calder* involved "ad hoc legislative review of individual trial court judgments"—a far cry from the programmatic review of pending legislation that Madison's federal negative had contemplated. *Plaut v. Spendthrift Farm, Inc.,* 514 U.S. 211, 260 (1995) (citing *Calder v. Bull,* 3 U.S. 386 [1798]).

126. U.S. Constitution, art. VI, para. 2.

127. Also, as Richard B. Bernstein notes, "by bringing the Constitution into the sphere of judicially enforceable law, the Supremacy Clause ensure[d] that controversies over the

meaning of the Constitution [would] resolve themselves, sooner or later, into judicial questions coming before the federal judiciary and eventually the Supreme Court." Richard B. Bernstein, *Are We to Be a Nation? The Making of the Constitution* (Cambridge, Mass.: Harvard University Press, 1987), 174.

128. U.S. Constitution, art. VI, para. 2.

129. Judiciary Act of 1789, ch. 20, 1 Stat. 73; *Fletcher v. Peck*, 10 U.S. 87 (1810); *Martin v. Hunter's Lessee*, 14 U.S. 304 (1816). The Judiciary Act of 1789 established the statutory basis for implementing the Supremacy Clause by setting out three categories of state-court cases that might be appealed to the Supreme Court through a writ of error: (1) a decision invalidating a treaty, a federal statute, or an exercise of federal authority; (2) a decision invalidating a claim brought under the federal Constitution, a treaty, or a federal statute; or (3) a decision upholding a state statute or the exercise of state authority against a claim that the state action violated the Constitution, a treaty, or a federal statute. Judiciary Act of 1789, § 25, ch. 20, 1 Stat. 73. *Fletcher v. Peck* was the first case in which the Supreme Court held a state law unconstitutional. *Martin v. Hunter's Lessee* established the Supreme Court's appellate review over state-court decisions in civil cases. Before the Supreme Court's holdings in *Fletcher* and *Martin,* the principle of judicial review of state legislation by lower federal courts was established in *Champion & Dickason v. Casey,* a 1792 case in which the federal circuit court for Rhode Island (comprising U.S. district judge Henry Marchant, Chief Justice John Jay, and Associate Justice William Cushing) invalidated on Contracts Clause grounds a Rhode Island law that extended the period for merchant Silas Casey to settle his debts with London merchants Alexander Champion and Thomas Dickason. See Bilder, *Transatlantic Constitution,* 193.

130. *The Speeches of His Excellency Governor Hutchinson, to the General Assembly of the Massachusetts-Bay . . . With the Answers of His Majesty's Council and the House of Representatives. . . .* (Boston: Edes and Gill, 1773), 11.

131. James Wilson, "Considerations on the Nature and Extent of the Legislative Authority of the British Parliament," in Robert Green McCloskey, ed., *The Works of James Wilson* (Cambridge, Mass.: Belknap Press of Harvard University Press, 1967), 2:745.

132. The connection between the negative and Congress's affirmative lawmaking power is evident throughout the records of the convention. For example, the July 17 vote that defeated the negative followed immediately on a vote approving a motion to give Congress the power "to legislate in all cases for the general interests of the Union, and also in those to which the States are separately incompetent or in which the harmony of the U. States may be interrupted by the exercise of individual Legislation." Madison's Notes, July 17, 1787, in Farrand, *Records,* 2:26.

133. Bailyn, *Ideological Origins,* 358.

134. Bailyn associates this desire to merge levels of authority with the federalist proponents of the Constitution. See ibid. But it is worth noting that in the debates of the 1790s and 1800s concerning the scope of federal jurisdiction, Federalists (the label by then standing for the political party) tended to advocate federal courts with broad, and in some cases exclusive, powers of jurisdiction—i.e., more, not less, separation between the procedural levels of government.

135. Ibid.

136. By "judicially driven federalism," I mean something different from the "judicially enforced federalism" that Larry Kramer has discussed. Kramer uses the phrase in the context of what has been called the "new federalism" of the Rehnquist Court, referring to the problem of restraining Congress and maintaining limits on federal power. Larry D. Kramer, "But When Exactly Was Judicially-Enforced Federalism 'Born' in the First Place?" *Harvard Journal of Law and Public Policy* 22 (1998): 127.

6. JURISDICTION AS THE BATTLEFIELD

1. An Act to establish the Judicial Courts of the United States, ch. 20, 1 Stat. 73 (1789) (Judiciary Act of 1789); An Act to provide for the more convenient organization of the Courts of the United States, 2 Stat. 89 (1801) (Judiciary Act of 1801) (repealed by Judiciary Act of 1802, 2 Stat. 132 (1802)); Henry B. Brown, "The New Federal Judicial Code," *American Bar Association Reports* 36 (1911): 345 (1911), quoted in Charles Warren, "New Light on the History of the Federal Judiciary Act of 1789," *Harvard Law Review* 37 (1923): 52.

2. The first session of the Supreme Court—attended by only four of the six original justices—took place in New York on February 2, 1790. See Robert G. McCloskey, *The American Supreme Court,* 4th ed. (Chicago: University of Chicago Press, 2004), 1–2.

3. Kathryn Turner [Preyer], "Federalist Policy and the Judiciary Act of 1801," *William and Mary Quarterly,* 3d ser., 22 (1965): 3. See also William E. Nelson, "The Province of the Judiciary," *John Marshall Law Review* 37 (2004): 336 ("[t]he 1801 Act, as we know, was a failure").

4. On the Madisonian compromise, see Martin H. Redish and Curtis E. Woods, "Congressional Power to Control the Jurisdiction of Lower Federal Courts: A Critical Review and a New Synthesis," *University of Pennsylvania Law Review* 124 (1975): 52–56; Robert N. Clinton, "A Mandatory View of Federal Court Jurisdiction: A Guided Quest for the Original Understanding of Article III," *University of Pennsylvania Law Review* 132 (1984): 763–764.

5. On the general shift in focus from legislatures to courts—especially by the Federalists—in the ratification period, see, e.g., Nelson, "Province of the Judiciary," 340–349; and Gordon S. Wood, *The Creation of the American Republic, 1776–1787* (Chapel Hill: University of North Carolina Press, 1969), 537–538. On the significance of the acts in establishing the federal judiciary in the separation-of-powers framework, see, e.g., Akhil Reed Amar, *America's Constitution: A Biography* (New York: Random House, 2005), 227–232; and Wythe Holt, " 'To Establish Justice': Politics, the Judiciary Act of 1789, and the Invention of the Federal Courts," *Duke Law Journal* 1989 (1989): 1421. On the institutional role of the courts, see, e.g., Larry D. Kramer, *The People Themselves: Popular Constitutionalism and Judicial Review* (New York: Oxford University Press, 2004); Jesse H. Choper, *Judicial Review and the National Political Process: A Functional Reconsideration of the Role of the Supreme Court* (Chicago: University of Chicago Press, 1980), 171–259; Alexander M. Bickel, *The Least Dangerous Branch: The Supreme Court at the Bar of Politics* (Indianapolis: Bobbs-Merrill, 1962); and Herbert Wechsler, "The Political Safeguards of Federalism:

The Rôle of the States in the Composition and Selection of the National Government," *Columbia Law Review* 54 (1954): 543.

6. On the role that theories of empire played in the early Republic, see Daniel J. Hulsebosch, *Constituting Empire: New York and the Transformation of Constitutionalism in the Atlantic World, 1664–1830* (Chapel Hill: University of North Carolina Press, 2005), 203–258; and Peter S. Onuf, *Jefferson's Empire: The Language of American Nationhood* (Charlottesville: University Press of Virginia, 2000), 53–79.

7. In Blackstone's view, set forth in his *Commentaries on the Laws of England,* government required a "supreme, irresistible, absolute, uncontrolled authority . . . in which the rights of sovereignty reside." William Blackstone, *Commentaries on the Laws of England* (1765–1769; reprint, with an introduction by Stanley N. Katz, Chicago: University of Chicago Press, 1979), 1:49. For Blackstone, as noted in Chapter 1, that authority was Parliament.

8. As noted in Chapter 1, the "solecism" of *imperium in imperio* was a powerful rhetorical device invoked repeatedly throughout eighteenth-century Anglo-American debates. See, e.g., [James Madison with Alexander Hamilton], "The Federalist No. 20," in Jacob E. Cooke, ed., *The Federalist* (Middletown, Conn.: Wesleyan University Press, 1961), 128–129 (describing "a sovereignty over sovereigns, a government over governments, a legislation for communities, as contradistinguished from individuals" as "a solecism in theory" and "in practice").

9. The literature on Congress's power to regulate the scope of federal jurisdiction is enormous. The classic account is Henry M. Hart, Jr., "The Power of Congress to Limit the Jurisdiction of Federal Courts: An Exercise in Dialectic," *Harvard Law Review* 66 (1953): 1362–1402. More recent analyses include John Harrison, "The Power of Congress to Limit the Jurisdiction of Federal Courts and the Text of Article III," *University of Chicago Law Review* 64 (1997): 203–256; Akhil Reed Amar, "The Two-Tiered Structure of the Judiciary Act of 1789," *University of Pennsylvania Law Review* 138 (1990): 1499–1567; Amar, "A Neo-Federalist View of Article III: Separating the Two Tiers of Federal Jurisdiction," *Boston University Law Review* 65 (1985): 205–272; Clinton, "Mandatory View of Federal Court Jurisdiction," 741–855; and Gerald Gunther, "Congressional Power to Curtail Federal Court Jurisdiction: An Opinionated Guide to the Ongoing Debate," *Stanford Law Review* 36 (1984): 895–922.

10. Richard Morris, ed., *Encyclopedia of American History,* 6th ed. (New York: Harper and Row, 1982), 145.

11. Max Farrand, ed., *The Records of the Federal Convention of 1787* (New Haven, Conn.: Yale University Press, 1937), 1:125. For classic articulations of the Madisonian compromise, see Redish and Woods, "Congressional Power to Control the Jurisdiction of Lower Federal Courts," 52–56; and Clinton, "Mandatory View of Federal Court Jurisdiction," 763–764.

12. See Farrand, *Records,* 1:104–105, 119, 124–125; 2:45–46.

13. U.S. Constitution, art. III, § 1, cl. 1.

14. On the turmoil of the 1780s and its consequences for the drafting of the Constitution, see Wood, *Creation of the American Republic,* 393–429.

15. The final vote on the negative took place on July 17, 1787; immediately thereafter, the delegates took up the provision that would become the Supremacy Clause. See Farrand,

Records, 2:28–29. See also Kramer, *People Themselves,* 74–75; Jack N. Rakove, "The Origins of Judicial Review: A Plea for New Contexts," *Stanford Law Review* 49 (1997): 1046–1047; Rakove, *Original Meanings: Politics and Ideas in the Making of the Constitution* (New York: Knopf, 1996), 82–83; and Lawrence Gene Sager, "The Supreme Court, 1980 Term—Foreword: Constitutional Limitations on Congress' Authority to Regulate the Jurisdiction of the Federal Courts," *Harvard Law Review* 95 (1981): 46–47.

16. U.S. Constitution, art. VI, cl. 2; Robert A. Rutland et al., eds., *The Papers of James Madison* (Chicago: University of Chicago Press, 1975), 10:209–110.

17. By "federalism-enforcing mechanism," I mean federalism in the structural, mechanical sense that most concerned Madison: namely, the need to incorporate the states into the general government, and in so doing to move from a confederation—the early modern political philosophers' "system of states"—to a new species of federal republic in which the central government had some independent powers rather than acting merely as a shell for the states. The construction "system of states" is associated with the early modern theorist Samuel von Pufendorf. See Samuel von Pufendorf, *The Law of Nature and Nations: or, a General System of the most Important Principles of Morality, Jurisprudence, and Politics,* trans. Basil Kennet, 5th ed. (London, 1749) (1672), vol. 2, bk. 7, ch. 5, § 18, 682–683. The phrase "judicially enforced federalism" has been used in modern scholarship to refer to courts' acting on behalf of substantive federal values, including "limits on the power of the national government vis-à-vis the states." Larry D. Kramer, "But When Exactly Was Judicially-Enforced Federalism 'Born' in the First Place?" *Harvard Journal of Law and Public Policy* 22 (1998): 123. For the source of the related debate over the need for the federal government to protect federalism by acting on behalf of the states, see Wechsler, "Political Safeguards of Federalism," 543-560. See also Gerald Leonard, "Party as a 'Political Safeguard of Federalism': Martin Van Buren and the Constitutional Theory of Party Politics," *Rutgers Law Review* 54 (2001): 221–281; and Larry D. Kramer, "Putting the Politics Back into the Political Safeguards of Federalism," *Columbia Law Review* 100 (2000): 215–293.

18. Rutland et al., *Papers of James Madison* 10:64.

19. Morris later commented that portions of Article III had intentionally been drafted (by him) to speak in somewhat oblique terms. "[C]onflicting opinions had been maintained with so much professional astuteness, that it became necessary to select phrases, which expressing my own notions would not alarm others, nor shock their selflove, and to the best of my recollection, this was the only part which passed without cavil." Morris to Timothy Pickering, December 22, 1814, in Farrand, *Records,* 3:420. By the nineteenth century, the notion that judicial review had been adopted in place of the negative was a commonplace, at least for some theorists. See, e.g., Joseph Story, *Commentaries on the Constitution of the United States* (Boston: Hilliard, Gray, and Co., 1833), 3:504. See also William E. Nelson, "Changing Conceptions of Judicial Review: The Evolution of Constitutional Theory in the States, 1790–1860," *University of Pennsylvania Law Review* 120 (1972): 1166.

20. Compare, for example, "George Mason Fears the Power of the Federal Courts: What Will Be Left to the States?" in Bernard Bailyn, ed., *The Debate on the Constitution: Federalist and Antifederalist Speeches, Articles, and Letters during the Struggle over Ratifi-*

cation, January to August 1788 (New York: Library of America, 1993), 2:720–229, with "John Marshall on the Fairness and Jurisdiction of the Federal Courts," ibid., 2:730–741.

21. See Maeva Marcus, "Introduction: The Constitutional Origins of the Federal Judiciary," in Maeva Marcus, ed., *The Documentary History of the Supreme Court of the United States, 1789–1800* (New York: Columbia University Press, 1992), 4:10 (hereafter *DHSC*).

22. [Alexander Hamilton], "The Federalist No. 81," in Cooke, *The Federalist*, 547–548.

23. "Debates in the Convention of the Commonwealth of Virginia, on the Adoption of the Federal Constitution," in Jonathan Elliot, ed., *The Debates in the Several State Conventions on the Adoption of the Federal Constitution, as Recommended by the General Convention at Philadelphia, in 1787, Together with the Journal of the Federal Convention, Luther Martin's Letter, Yates's Minutes, Congressional Opinions, Virginia and Kentucky Resolutions of '98–'99, and Other Illustrations of the Constitution*, 2d ed. (Washington: Taylor and Maury, 1836), 3:553.

24. Luther Martin, "Genuine Information," In Farrand, *Records*, 3:206.

25. "Debates in the Convention of the Commonwealth of Virginia," in Elliot, *Debates*, 3:521.

26. U.S. Constitution, art. III, § 1, cl. 1.

27. White to Madison, August 17, 1789, in Warren, "New Light on the History of the Federal Judiciary Act of 1789," 65.

28. For a comprehensive discussion of the background to the act, see Maeva Marcus, ed., *Origins of the Federal Judiciary: Essays on the Judiciary Act of 1789* (New York: Oxford University Press, 1992); and Warren, "New Light on the History of the Judiciary Act of 1789," 49. For the debates, see *The Debates and Proceedings in the Congress of the United States; with an Appendix, Containing Important State Papers and Public Documents, and all the Laws of a Public Nature; with a Copious Index (Annals of the Congress of the United States)*, vol. 1 (Washington, D.C.: Gales and Seaton, 1834) (hereafter *Annals*).

29. The ten senators were Oliver Ellsworth (Connecticut), William Paterson (New Jersey), Caleb Strong (Massachusetts), Richard Henry Lee (Virginia), Richard Bassett (Delaware), William Maclay (Pennsylvania), William Few (Georgia), Paine Wingate (New Hampshire), Charles Carroll (Maryland), and Ralph Izard (South Carolina). Marcus notes that of the ten, "six had been members of the Continental Congress; and five had been members of their state ratifying conventions," and that "[w]ith the exception of Lee and Maclay, all were Federalists." Moreover, "[a]ll but Izard and Wingate had at least some legal training," although she describes only Ellsworth, Strong, and Paterson as having "extensive legal experience." Ellsworth handled the majority of the drafting. *DHSC* 4:22–23. William Maclay's journal suggests that tempers among the committee members occasionally flared up amid the intense efforts to produce a draft bill. On June 29, Maclay noted, "Attended at the Hall early. Sent my letters to the post-office; and now for the judiciary. I made a remark where Elsworth [*sic*] in his diction had varied from the Constitution. This vile bill is a child of his, and he defends it with the care of a parent, even with wrath and anger." William Maclay, *Journal of William Maclay, United States Senator from Pennsylvania, 1789–1791*, ed. Edgar S. Maclay (New York: D. A. Appleton and Co., 1890), 91.

30. Judiciary Act of 1789, §§ 13, 22, 25. The provision regarding original jurisdiction was invalidated in *Marbury v. Madison*, 5 U.S. 137, 176–179 (1803). At least as important are two related issues on which modern commentators frequently look to the 1789 act: (1) the extent of Congress's power over inferior federal courts vis-à-vis the jurisdictional baseline set forth in Article III; and (2) the question of which law applies in federal diversity cases, and the corollary inquiry into the existence or nonexistence of a federal common law. The former is discussed earlier in this chapter. On the latter, see Tony Freyer, *Harmony and Dissonance: The* Swift *and* Erie *Cases in American Federalism* (New York: New York University Press, 1981); Julius Goebel, Jr., *Antecedents and Beginnings to 1801*, vol. 1 of *The Oliver Wendell Holmes Devise History of the Supreme Court of the United States,* ed. Paul A. Freund (New York: Macmillan, 1971), 229–230; Felix Frankfurter and James M. Landis, *The Business of the Supreme Court: A Study of the Federal Judicial System* (New York: Macmillan, 1927); and Warren, "New Light on the History of the Judiciary Act of 1789," 49.

31. *Martin v. Hunter's Lessee,* 14 U.S. 304 (1816) (civil cases); *Cohens v. Virginia,* 19 U.S. 264 (1821) (criminal cases); *DHSC* 4:30–31. The membership of the Senate committee represented this diversity of opinion, for Lee and Wingate had both been instructed by their respective state ratifying conventions to resist granting broad powers to the lower federal courts. See *DHSC* 4:30–31; Goebel, *Antecedents and Beginnings,* 470–471.

32. Judiciary Act of 1789, §§ 9, 11.

33. Goebel, *Antecedents and Beginnings,* 475.

34. See, e.g., Maeva Marcus and Natalie Wexler, "The Judiciary Act of 1789: Political Compromise or Constitutional Interpretation?" in Marcus, *Origins of the Federal Judiciary,* 16 ("no provision was made [in the 1789 act] for 'general federal question' jurisdiction in the lower federal courts"); and Warren, "New Light on the History of the Judiciary Act of 1789," 131 ("it was eighty-six years before legislation was enacted, in 1875, vesting the Federal Circuit Courts with jurisdiction in all cases arising under the Federal Constitution and laws"). But see Wilfred J. Ritz, *Rewriting the History of the Judiciary Act of 1789: Exposing Myths, Challenging Premises, and Using New Evidence,* ed. Wythe Holt and L. H. LaRue (Norman: University of Oklahoma Press, 1990), 59–60, 222 n.9 (arguing that the act's "silence" does not amount to a denial of federal question jurisdiction, although the editors take some exception to this claim). See Act of March 3, 1875, ch. 137, § 1, 18 Stat. 470 (providing circuit-court jurisdiction "of all suits of a civil nature at common law or in equity . . . arising under the Constitution or laws of the United States, or treaties made, or which shall be made under their authority"). The modern grant of federal question, or "arising under," jurisdiction is now codified at 28 U.S.C. § 1331 ("[t]he district courts shall have original jurisdiction of all civil actions arising under the Constitution").

35. See, e.g., William R. Casto, "The First Congress's Understanding of Its Authority over the Federal Courts' Jurisdiction," *Boston College Law Review* 26 (1985): 1116 ("In retrospect, the most remarkable limitation upon the lower courts' jurisdiction was the absence of general federal question jurisdiction over civil cases").

36. Madison to Samuel Johnston, July 31, 1789, *DHSC* 4:491. "Embarrassing" here should be understood in the contemporary sense of causing hindrance or impediment. *Oxford English Dictionary,* 2d ed., s.v. "Embarrass."

37. *Gazette of the United States,* September 17, 1789, *DHSC* 4:512.

38. Gerry to John Wendell, September 14, 1789, *DHSC* 4:509.

39. *DHSC* 4:168 (on the fate of both plans), 124 (on press notice of Randolph's plan).

40. Ames to Lowell, September 3, 1789, *DHSC* 4:506. Ames had originally begun the second sentence "A power to judge" but replaced it with "Authority to judge." Ibid.

41. Ames seems to have been aware that his remarks might not be understood. Writing to Lowell ten days later, Ames commented, "I endeavoured to explain the leading idea or principle of my Speech in Fenno's paper [the Federalist *Gazette of the United States*] . . . not because I was under concern about it's [*sic*] reception with the people___ for on a legal question, I never supposed they would have either curiosity or understanding. But I was afraid that the *lawyers* wd either hurry over or misconceive my doctrine, and deny it's [*sic*] orthodoxy." Ames to Lowell, September 13, 1789, *DHSC* 4:507.

42. U.S. Constitution, art. I, § 8, cl. 1; [Alexander Hamilton], "The Federalist No. 32," in Cooke, *Federalist,* 199, 200, 201.

43. [Alexander Hamilton], "The Federalist No. 82," in Cooke, *Federalist,* 553.

44. U.S. Constitution, art. III, § 1, cl. 1; [Hamilton], "Federalist No. 82," 554, 555.

45. [Hamilton], "Federalist No. 82," 555.

46. See, for example, John Dickinson's prewar argument against concurrent authority in Parliament and the colonial assemblies over revenue matters. "The single question is whether the parliament can legally impose duties to be paid *by the people of these colonies only* FOR THE SOLE PURPOSE OF RAISING A REVENUE, *on commodities which she obliges us to take from her alone;* or, in other words, whether the parliament can legally take money out of our pockets without our consent." [John Dickinson], *Letters from a Farmer in Pennsylvania, to the Inhabitants of the British Colonies* (Boston: Mein and Fleeming, 1768), 26.

47. [Hamilton], "Federalist No. 82," 555–556.

48. Ibid., 555.

49. [Hamilton], "Federalist No. 32," 200.

50. St. George Tucker, however, took the view that concurrent powers of legislation were not a boon to state authority but rather a means of chipping away at the power of the states. Describing the "some few instances"—such as bankruptcy—in which "the grand boundary between the limits of federal and state jurisdiction . . . has not been strictly adhered to in the federal constitution," Tucker observed that such encroachments were "in derogation of the municipal jurisdiction of the several states" and therefore should be "strictly construed." St. George Tucker, *Blackstone's Commentaries: With Notes of Reference, to the Constitution and Laws, of the Federal Government of the United States; and of the Commonwealth of Virginia* (Philadelphia: William Young Birch and Abraham Small, 1803), 1:177.

51. Ibid., 1:178.

52. Jones to Madison, July 3, 1789, *DHSC* 4:441–442.

53. Brown to Harry Innes, September 28, 1789, *DHSC* 4:519–520.

54. *DHSC* 4:122–123.

55. Report of the Attorney-General to the House of Representatives, *DHSC* 4:140.

56. See *DHSC* 4:123. This general federal question jurisdiction was not exclusive to the federal courts.

57. Report of the Attorney-General to the House of Representatives, *DHSC* 4:140. Randolph's attitude toward the Supreme Court's appellate review of state-court decisions appears somewhat ambivalent. On the one hand, in the preface to the report Randolph refers to "convert[ing] the supreme court of the United States into an appellate tribunal over the supreme courts of the several states," suggesting that such a relationship would be novel; moreover, in discussing the phrase "appellate jurisdiction," Randolph contends that "this phrase must be pressed close to the matter of the third article of the Constitution, which is the *judicial power of the United States,* without blending state courts." Ibid., 4:132. Both these observations are offered as the arguments of those who object to granting the Court appellate power over state-court decisions, but Randolph at times appears to adopt these arguments as his own. The report itself did provide for the issuance of writs of certiorari from the Supreme Court to the circuit and state courts. See ibid., 4:153. Marcus reads the report as prohibiting the Court from hearing appeals from the state courts, however, and as substituting a broadened power for parties to remove cases from state to federal court. See *DHSC* 4:124 and n.14.

58. Moore to Johnston, February 23, 1791, *DHSC* 4:555–556 (translating the Latin phrase as "by the nature of the thing").

59. Writing in 1794, Columbia law professor James Kent—later chancellor of the New York Court of Chancery and author of *Commentaries on American Law* (4 vols., 1826–1830)—articulated a similarly broad vision of federal jurisdiction, although his reasoning differed somewhat from Randolph's. Kent compared the judicial power with the legislative power and concluded that the scope of federal courts' authority necessarily must at least match that of Congress "to preserve the equilibrium of the government." He concluded that the judiciary and the legislature should be regarded as "co-ordinate powers." James Kent, *An Introductory Lecture to a Course of Law Lectures: Delivered November 17, 1794* (New York: Francis Childs, 1794), 13.

60. Consider on this point Casto, "First Congress's Understanding," 1116 (noting, in the context of general federal question jurisdiction, that under the 1789 act, "the circuit courts were vested with jurisdiction keyed to the nature of the parties rather than the nature of the dispute").

61. U.S. Constitution, art. VI, cl. 2. For a discussion of the propriety of state courts acting as inferior tribunals, see James E. Pfander, "Federal Supremacy, State Court Inferiority, and the Constitutionality of Jurisdiction-Stripping Legislation," *Northwestern University Law Review* 101 (2007): 191–238.

62. See generally Charles F. Hobson, "The Negative on State Laws: James Madison, the Constitution, and the Crisis of Republican Government," *William and Mary Quarterly,* 3d ser., 36 (1979): 228. The final version of the Supremacy Clause failed to win Martin's support, however. In a related vein, "Federal Farmer" opposed the 1789 act's establishment of federal diversity jurisdiction, arguing that such jurisdiction was unnecessary because such suits could also be brought in state courts with appeal to the Supreme Court. "Letters from the Federal Farmer," in Bailyn, *Debate on the Constitution,* 1:271.

63. "Debates in the Convention of the Commonwealth of Virginia," in Elliot, *Debates,* 3:521–522.

64. "Centinel Revived, No. 26," *Independent Gazetteer* (Philadelphia), August 29, 1789.

65. "Rusticus," *Independent Chronicle* (Boston), August 26, 1790.

66. "Benson Amendments," March 3, 1791, *DHSC* 4:170, 170–171, 172.

67. Ibid., 4:168 n.4. Marcus states that the amendments were likely intended "less as a topic for debate than as a political statement" by the Hamiltonian Benson. Ibid., 4:168.

68. "Curtius," *Augusta (Ga.) Chronicle,* May 28, 1791, *DHSC* 4:559.

69. "William Maclay Diary Entry," July 17, 1789, *DHSC* 4:473.

70. Ames to John Lowell, July 28, 1789, *DHSC* 4:481.

71. Judiciary Act of 1789, § 2.

72. "An Act to establish the Judicial Courts of the United States," editorial note to § 2. *DHSC* 4:39.

73. See, for example, "A Citizen," *Washington Federalist,* January 26, 1801 ("[t]he difficulty of organizing the Judiciary of the U. States, so as, agreeably to the Constitution to vest in the General Government a judicial authority over individual States; and, at the same time to establish a commodious administration of justice, was early foreseen"). See also [Alexander Hamilton], "The Federalist No. 81," in Cooke, *Federalist,* 546–557 (arguing for the establishment of "four or five, or half a dozen districts" instead of relying on state courts to serve as inferior courts).

74. Goebel, *Antecedents and Beginnings,* 471.

75. "A Citizen," *Washington Federalist,* January 26, 1801.

76. See, e.g., Ames to Lowell, July 28, 1789, *DHSC* 4:481.

77. "William Paterson's Notes for Remarks on Judiciary Bill, [June 23, 1789]," *DHSC* 4:414, 415. Chief Justice Marshall subsequently applied similar reasoning to invalidate Maryland's tax on the Second Bank of the United States in *McCulloch v. Maryland:* "Why . . . should we suppose, that the people of any one state should be willing to trust those of another with a power to control the operations of a government to which they have confided their most important and most valuable interests? The legislature of the Union alone . . . can be trusted by the people with the power of controlling measures which concern all, in the confidence that it will not be abused." *McCulloch v. Maryland,* 17 U.S. 316, 481 (1819). On the related modern idea of the "representation-reinforcing" function of the Supreme Court's power of judicial review, see John Hart Ely, *Democracy and Distrust: A Theory of Judicial Review* (Cambridge, Mass.: Harvard University Press, 1980), 87.

78. Sedgwick to Peter Van Schaack, November 20, 1791, *DHSC* 4:566.

79. Wilson to Washington, December 31, 1791, *DHSC* 4:572.

80. On the burdens that second- and later-generation Americans perceived themselves as bearing, see generally Joyce Appleby, *Inheriting the Revolution: The First Generation of Americans* (Cambridge, Mass.: Harvard University Press, 2000) (discussing Americans born between 1776 and 1830); Perry Miller, *Errand into the Wilderness* (Cambridge, Mass.: Harvard University Press, 1956) (describing the spiritual crisis of second-generation Puritans in New England); and Henry Adams, *The Education of Henry Adams: An Autobiography* (Boston: Houghton Mifflin, 1935) (describing and illustrating later generations' sense of anxiety and fears of decline). On discussions of concurrence in the ratification debates, see Hulsebosch, *Constituting Empire,* 223, 241–242, 382–383nn.

81. Fragment of the Debates in the Convention of the State of Connecticut, January 4, 1788, in Elliot, *Debates,* 2:195–196.

82. Jefferson to John Dickinson, March 6, 1801, in Barbara Oberg, ed., *The Papers of Thomas Jefferson* (Princeton, N.J.: Princeton University Press, 2007), 33:196–197. See generally Stanley Elkins and Eric McKitrick, *The Age of Federalism: The Early American Republic, 1788–1800* (New York: Oxford University Press, 1993); and David Hackett Fischer, *The Revolution of American Conservatism: The Federalist Party in the Era of Jeffersonian Democracy* (New York: Harper and Row, 1965).

83. The outlines of this story appeared early. One day before Jefferson's inauguration, James Monroe, then Virginia's governor, wrote to the president-elect that the Federalist Party "has retired into the judiciary in a strong body where it lives on the treasury, & cannot therefore be starved out. [W]hile in possession of that ground it can check the popular current which runs against them, & seize the favorable occasion to promote reaction, w[hi]ch it does not despair of." Monroe to Jefferson, March 3, 1801, *DHSC* 4:720.

84. See Turner, "Federalist Policy and the Judiciary Act of 1801," 3.

85. Joanne B. Freeman, "The Election of 1800: A Study in the Logic of Political Change," *Yale Law Journal* 108 (1999): 1961, 1990.

86. One influential study of the political battles of the 1790s and 1800s situates partisan struggle in a broader cultural and ideological context. See Joanne B. Freeman, *Affairs of Honor: National Politics in the New Republic* (New Haven, Conn.: Yale University Press, 2001).

87. See Turner, "Federalist Policy and the Judiciary Act of 1801," 5–6.

88. Editorial Note, "Judiciary Act of 1801," *DHSC* 4:284.

89. Unfortunately, no official records of the committee's deliberations have survived.

90. Harper Judiciary Bill of 1800, §§ 7 and 10, *DHSC* 4:312–314.

91. Ibid., *DHSC* 4:314.

92. Ibid., §16, *DHSC* 4:317.

93. House of Representatives, 6th Congress, 1st Session, Thursday, March 27, 1800, *Annals* 10:646 (1800).

94. Baldwin to Joel Barlow, March 26, 1800, *DHSC* 4:640–641.

95. *Philadelphia Aurora,* March 18, 1800, *DHSC* 4:637.

96. T. B. Adams to J. Q. Adams, February 25, 1800, *DHSC* 4:627.

97. Editorial Note, "Judiciary Act of 1801," *DHSC* 4:288.

98. Judiciary Bill of 1800, § 13, *DHSC* 4:340.

99. Judiciary Act of 1789, § 11.

100. Harper Judiciary Bill of 1800, § 16, *DHSC* 4:317.

101. Editorial Note, "Judiciary Act of 1801," *DHSC* 4:289.

102. See Marshall to John Adams, November 17, 1800, in Charles F. Hobson, ed., *The Papers of John Marshall* (Chapel Hill: University of North Carolina Press, 1990), 6:11–12.

103. Judiciary Act of 1801, §§ 11, 13.

104. Turner, "Federalist Policy and the Judiciary Act of 1801," 3. See also Linda K. Kerber, *Federalists in Dissent: Imagery and Ideology in Jeffersonian America* (Ithaca, N.Y.: Cornell University Press, 1970), 136 ("Contrary to its subsequent reputation, the Judiciary Act of 1801 had been the subject of a full and responsible debate during the preceding session of Congress, and its terms represented an attempt to correct the inadequacies of the first Judiciary Act of twelve years before").

105. Jefferson to Randolph, August 18, 1799, in *Papers of Thomas Jefferson,* 31:168–169 (emphasis added).

106. Hamilton to Jonathan Dayton, October–November 1799, in Harold C. Syrett, ed., *The Papers of Alexander Hamilton* (New York: Columbia University Press, 1976), 25:599, 601.

107. Sedgwick to King, November 15, 1799, in Charles R. King, ed., *The Life and Correspondence of Rufus King* (New York: G. P. Putnam's Sons, 1896), 3:145, 147. On Hamilton and ideas of the public good, see Cecelia Kenyon, "Alexander Hamilton: Rousseau of the Right," *Political Science Quarterly* 73 (1958): 161–178.

108. Compare the Judiciary Act of 1789, §§ 9, 11, with the Judiciary Act of 1801, § 12.

109. "An Act to repeal certain acts respecting the organization of the Courts of the United States; and for other purposes," March 8, 1802, 2 Stat. 132; Editorial Note, "Judiciary Act of 1801," *DHSC* 4:294–295. On the repeal of the act, see generally George Lee Haskins and Herbert A. Johnson, *Foundations of Power: John Marshall, 1801–15* (New York: Macmillan, 1981) (especially chapters 4 and 5); and Kathryn Turner [Preyer], "The Midnight Judges," *University of Pennsylvania Law Review* 109 (1961): 494–523.

110. *Stuart v. Laird,* 5 U.S. 299 (1803). Despite the repeal, however, at least one case brought pursuant to the 1801 act's grant of federal question jurisdiction managed to survive. See Wythe Holt, "The First Federal Question Case," *Law and History Review* 3 (1985): 169–189.

111. "An Act to provide for the more convenient organization of the Courts of the United States," *DHSC* 4:295. The new judges were the so-called midnight judges. See Turner, "Midnight Judges," 495.

112. Thomas Jefferson, First Annual Message to Congress, December 8, 1801, in Syrett, *Papers of Alexander Hamilton,* 25:448 n.1.

113. [Hamilton], "The Examination No. V," *New-York Evening Post,* December 29, 1801, in Syrett, *Papers of Alexander Hamilton,* 25:477 n.4.

114. Some Federalists, such as Gouverneur Morris, agreed. But Morris took a more sympathetic view of his colleagues' strategy, observing, "They are about to experience a heavy gale of adverse wind; can they be blamed for casting many anchors to hold their ship through the storm?" Morris to Robert R. Livingston, February 20, 1801, in Jared Sparks, *The Life of Gouverneur Morris: With Selections from His Correspondence and Miscellaneous Papers: Detailing Events in the American Revolution, the French Revolution, and in the Political History of the United States* (Boston: Gray and Bowen, 1832), 3:153–154.

115. "The Examination No. V," in Syrett, *Papers of Alexander Hamilton,* 25:477.

116. Hamilton, "Remarks on the Repeal of the Judiciary Act," *New-York Gazette and General Advertiser,* February 13, 1802, in Syrett, *Papers of Alexander Hamilton,* 25:523.

117. "A Citizen," *Dunlap's American Daily Advertiser* (Philadelphia), December 20, 1791.

118. The distinction between small-*f* and large-*F* federalism borrows from Morton Horwitz's characterization of the work of Bernard Bailyn and Gordon Wood as describing a shift from small-*c* to large-*C* constitutions. See Morton J. Horwitz, "A Historiography of *The People Themselves* and Popular Constitutionalism," *Chicago-Kent Law Review* 81 (2006): 817.

119. See, e.g., *Martin v. Hunter's Lessee,* 14 U.S. 304 (1816) (holding that the Supreme Court has the power to review decisions of state courts under sec. 25 of the Judiciary Act of 1789); *Swift v. Tyson,* 41 U.S. 1 (1842) (recognizing a federal common law).

EPILOGUE

1. Thomas Jefferson, Inaugural Address, March 4, 1801, reading copy in Jefferson's hand, Papers of Thomas Jefferson, Manuscript Division, Library of Congress, http://memory .loc.gov, digital identification mssmisc pin0405.

2. See, e.g., First Inaugural Address, in Thomas Jefferson, *Writings,* ed. Merrill D. Peterson (New York: Library of America, 1984), 493.

3. See, e.g., David Waldstreicher, *In the Midst of Perpetual Fetes: The Making of American Nationalism, 1776–1820* (Chapel Hill: University of North Carolina Press, 1995), 203 ("Jefferson's inaugural assertion dissolved policy differences into ideological consensus and inspired many hopeful echoes").

4. The earliest use of the term "federalism" listed in the *Oxford English Dictionary* dates to 1793, when Edmund Burke used the term in the context of revolutionary France. *Oxford English Dictionary,* 2d ed., s.v. "federalism."

5. On the identity and unifying values of Federalists, see, e.g., David Hackett Fischer, *The Revolution of American Conservatism: The Federalist Party in the Era of Jeffersonian Democracy* (New York: Harper and Row, 1965); and Stanley Elkins and Eric McKitrick, *The Age of Federalism: The Early American Republic, 1788–1800* (New York: Oxford University Press, 1993). On their Anti-Federalist opponents and the construction of their identity, see Jackson Turner Main, *The Antifederalists: Critics of the Constitution, 1781–1788* (New York: Norton, 1974).

6. [Alexander Hamilton], "The Federalist No. 9," in Jacob E. Cooke, ed., *The Federalist* (Middletown, Conn.: Wesleyan University Press, 1961), 55.

7. [James Hodges], *The Rights and Interests of the Two British Monarchies, Inquir'd into, and Clear'd; with a Special Respect to an United or Separate State, Treatise I* (London, 1703), 3.

8. Peter Onuf and Nicholas Onuf, *Federal Union, Modern World: The Law of Nations in an Age of Revolutions, 1776–1814* (Madison, Wis.: Madison House, 1993), 56. See also J. G. A. Pocock, "States, Republics, and Empires: The American Founding in Early Modern Perspective," in Terence Ball and J. G. A. Pocock, eds., *Conceptual Change and the Constitution* (Lawrence: University Press of Kansas, 1988), 55–77.

9. *Cohens v. Virginia,* 19 U.S. 264 (1821).

10. Mary Sarah Bilder, *The Transatlantic Constitution: Colonial Legal Culture and the Empire* (Cambridge, Mass.: Harvard University Press, 2004), 192.

11. On the uses and meanings of the term "empire" in the early Republic, see Peter S. Onuf, *Jefferson's Empire: The Language of American Nationhood* (Charlottesville: University Press of Virginia, 2000); and Pocock, "States, Republics, and Empires."

12. Alexis de Tocqueville, *Democracy in America,* ed. J. P. Mayer, trans. George Lawrence (New York: HarperCollins, 2000), 157 (emphasis added).

13. For an interpretation of Tocqueville's approach to the study of ideas, see James T. Kloppenberg, "The Canvas and the Color: Tocqueville's 'Philosophical History' and Why It Matters Now," *Modern Intellectual History* 3 (2006): 495–521.

14. Reinhart Koselleck, *The Practice of Conceptual History: Timing History, Spacing Concepts,* trans. Todd Samuel Presner et al. (Stanford, Calif.: Stanford University Press, 2002), 157.

Selected Bibliography

NEWSPAPERS

Boston Evening-Post, February 1, 1773
Boston Evening-Post, February 8, 1773
Boston Evening-Post, April 12, 1773
Boston-Gazette and Country Journal, January 11, 1773
Boston-Gazette and Country Journal, February 1, 1773
Boston-Gazette and Country Journal, February 8, 1773
Dunlap's American Daily Advertiser (Philadelphia), December 20, 1791
Gazette of the United States, September 17, 1789
Independent Chronicle (Boston), August 26, 1790
Independent Gazetteer (Philadelphia), August 29, 1789
Washington Federalist, January 26, 1801

CASES

Winthrop v. Lechmere (P.C. 1728)
Champion & Dickason v. Casey (Cir. Ct. Dist. R.I., 1792)
Calder v. Bull, 3 U.S. 386 (1798)
Marbury v. Madison, 5 U.S. 137 (1803)
Stuart v. Laird, 5 U.S. 299 (1803)
Fletcher v. Peck, 10 U.S. 87 (1810)
Martin v. Hunter's Lessee, 14 U.S. 304 (1816)
McCulloch v. Maryland, 17 U.S. 316 (1819)
Cohens v. Virginia, 19 U.S. 264 (1821)
Swift v. Tyson, 41 U.S. 1 (1842)
United States v. Salerno, 481 U.S. 739 (1987)
Plaut v. Spendthrift Farm, Inc., 514 U.S. 211 (1995)
U.S. Term Limits, Inc. v. Thornton, 514 U.S. 779 (1997)

PRIMARY SOURCES

Adams, John. *Diary and Autobiography of John Adams.* Edited by L. H. Butterfield. 4 vols. Cambridge, Mass.: Belknap Press of Harvard University Press, 1961.

———. *The Works of John Adams, Second President of the United States.* Edited by Charles Francis Adams. 10 vols. Boston: Charles C. Little and James Brown, 1850–1856.

Bailyn, Bernard, ed. *The Debate on the Constitution.* 2 vols. New York: Library of America, 1993.

———, ed. *Pamphlets of the American Revolution, 1750–1765.* Cambridge, Mass.: Belknap Press of Harvard University Press, 1965.

Bernard, Francis. *Select Letters on the Trade and Government of America; and the Principles of Law and Polity, Applied to the American Colonies.* London: T. Payne, 1774.

Blackstone, William. *Commentaries on the Laws of England.* 4 vols. 1765–1769. Reprint, Chicago: University of Chicago Press, 1979.

Bland, Richard [Common Sense, pseud.]. *The Colonel Dismounted: or the Rector Vindicated. In a Letter addressed to His Reverence: Containing a Dissertation upon the Constitution of the Colony.* Williamsburg: Joseph Royle, 1764.

———. *An Inquiry into the Rights of the British Colonies.* Williamsburg: Alexander Purdie, 1766.

Bodin, Jean. *On Sovereignty: Four Chapters from "The Six Books of the Commonwealth."* Edited and translated by Julian H. Franklin. Cambridge: Cambridge University Press, 1992.

[Bollan, William]. *A Succinct View of the Origin of our Colonies, with Their Civil State, Founded by Queen Elizabeth, Corroborated by Succeeding Princes, and Confirmed by Acts of Parliament; whereby the Nature of the Empire Established in America, and the Errors of Various Hypotheses Formed Thereupon, May Be Clearly Understood. With Observations on the Commercial, Beneficial and Perpetual Union of the Colonies with This Kingdom. Being an Extract from an Essay Lately Published, Entitled the Freedom of Speech and Writing, &c..* London, 1766.

Bradford, Alden, ed. *Speeches of the Governors of Massachusetts, from 1765 to 1775: and the Answers of the House of Representatives to the Same: with Their Resolutions and Addresses for That Period: and Other Public Papers Relating to the Dispute between This Country and Great Britain Which Led to the Independence of the United States.* Boston: Russell and Gardner, 1818.

Britannus Americanicus [pseud.]. *A Serious Address to the Inhabitants of New-York.* New York, 1765.

Bryce, James. *Studies in History and Jurisprudence.* 2 vols. Oxford: Clarendon Press, 1901.

Burke, Edmund. *The Portable Edmund Burke.* Edited by Isaac Kramnick. New York: Penguin Books, 1999.

Burnett, Edmund C., ed. *Letters of Members of the Continental Congress.* 8 vols. 1936. Reprint, Gloucester, Mass.: Peter Smith, 1963.

[Cartwright, John]. *American Independence the Interest and Glory of Great Britain; or, Arguments to Prove, that Not Only in Taxation, but in Trade, Manufactures, and Government, the Colonies Are Entitled to an Entire Independency on the British Legislature; and That It Can Only Be by a Formal Declaration of These Rights, and Forming there-*

upon a Friendly League with Them, That the True and Lasting Welfare of Both Countries Can Be Promoted. In a Series of Letters to the Legislature. To Which Are Added Copious Notes; Containing Reflections on the Boston and Quebec Acts; and a Full Justification of the People of Boston, for Destroying the British-Taxed Tea; Submitted to the Judgment, Not of Those Who Have None But Borrowed Party-Opinions, But of the Candid and Honest. London: H. S. Woodfall, 1774.

Cobbett, William, ed. *Parliamentary History of England: From the Earliest Period to the Year 1803.* 36 vols. London: R. Bagshaw, 1806–1820.

Cooke, Jacob E., ed. *The Federalist.* Middletown, Conn.: Wesleyan University Press, 1961.

Davies, K. G., ed. *Documents of the American Revolution, 1770–1783 (Colonial Office Series).* Dublin: Irish University Press, 1974.

Deane, Silas. *The Deane Papers, 1774–1790.* Edited by Charles Isham. Vol. 1. New York: New-York Historical Society, 1887.

Debates and Proceedings in the Congress of the United States; with an Appendix, Containing Important State Papers and Public Documents, and All the Laws of a Public Nature; with a Copious Index (Annals of the Congress of the United States). 18 vols. Washington, D.C.: Gales and Seaton, 1834.

Dickinson, John. "An Essay on the Constitutional Power of Great Britain over the Colonies in America." In *Pennsylvania Archives,* 2d ser., edited by John B. Linn and William H. Egle. Harrisburg: B. F. Meyers, 1875.

[———]. *Fragments on the Confederation of the American States.* Philadelphia: Thomas Dobson, 1787.

[———]. *Letters from a Farmer in Pennsylvania, to the Inhabitants of the British Colonies.* Boston: Mein and Fleeming, 1768.

———. *The Political Writings of John Dickinson, 1764–1774.* Edited by Paul Leicester Ford. 1895. Reprint, New York: Da Capo Press, 1970.

[Dulany, Daniel]. *Considerations on the Propriety of Imposing Taxes in the British Colonies for the Purpose of Raising a Revenue by Act of Parliament.* 2d ed. Annapolis: Jonas Green, 1765.

Elliot, Jonathan, ed. *The Debates in the Several State Conventions on the Adoption of the Federal Constitution, as Recommended by the General Convention at Philadelphia, in 1787, Together with the Journal of the Federal Convention, Luther Martin's Letter, Yates's Minutes, Congressional Opinions, Virginia and Kentucky Resolutions of '98–'99, and Other Illustrations of the Constitution.* 2d ed. 5 vols. Washington, D.C.: Taylor and Maury, 1836–1845.

Farrand, Max, ed. *The Records of the Federal Convention of 1787.* 3 vols. New Haven, Conn.: Yale University Press, 1937.

Fletcher, Andrew. *Political Works.* Edited by John Robertson. Cambridge: Cambridge University Press, 1997.

Ford, Paul Leicester, ed. *Essays on the Constitution of the United States Published during Its Discussion by the People, 1787–1788.* Brooklyn: Historical Printing Club, 1892.

Galloway, Joseph. *Joseph Galloway: Selected Tracts.* Edited by Ernest H. Baldwin. 3 vols. New York: Da Capo Press, 1974.

Grotius, Hugo. *The Rights of War and Peace: Including the Law of Nature and Nations.* Translated by A. M. Campbell. London: B. Boothroyd, 1814.

Hamilton, Alexander. *The Papers of Alexander Hamilton.* Edited by Harold C. Syrett. 27 vols. New York: Columbia University Press, 1961–1987.

[Hicks, William]. *The Nature and Extent of Parliamentary Power Considered, in Some Remarks upon Mr. Pitt's Speech in the House of Commons, previous to the Repeal of the Stamp-Act: With an Introduction, Applicable to the present Situation of the Colonies.* Philadelphia: William and Thomas Bradford, 1768.

Hobbes, Thomas. *Leviathan.* Edited by C. B. Macpherson. Harmondsworth, UK: Penguin, 1968.

[Hodges, James]. *The Rights and Interests of the Two British Monarchies, Inquir'd into, and Clear'd; with a Special Respect to an United or Separate State, Treatise I.* London, 1703.

[Hopkins, Stephen]. *The Rights of Colonies Examined.* Providence: William Goddard, 1765.

Hutchinson, Thomas. Correspondence, 1741–1774. Massachusetts Archives. Harvard University Library.

———. "A Dialogue between an American and a European Englishman by Thomas Hutchinson." In Donald Fleming and Bernard Bailyn, eds., *Perspectives in American History,* 9:343–410. Cambridge, Mass.: Charles Warren Center for Studies in American History, Harvard University, 1975.

———. *The Diary and Letters of His Excellency Thomas Hutchinson, Esq.* Edited by Peter Orlando Hutchinson. 2 vols. Boston: Houghton, Mifflin, 1884–1886.

———. *The History of the Colony and Province of Massachusetts-Bay.* Edited by Lawrence Shaw Mayo. Cambridge, Mass.: Harvard University Press, 1936.

Hutson, James H. *Supplement to Max Farrand's "The Records of the Federal Convention of 1787."* New Haven, Conn.: Yale University Press, 1987.

Jefferson, Thomas. *The Commonplace Book of Thomas Jefferson: A Repertory of His Ideas on Government.* Ed. Gilbert Chinard. Baltimore: Johns Hopkins Press, 1926.———. Inaugural Address, March 4, 1801. Copy in Jefferson's hand. Papers of Thomas Jefferson. Manuscript Division, Library of Congress. http://memory.loc.gov, digital identification mssmisc pin0405.

———. *The Papers of Thomas Jefferson.* Edited by Julian P. Boyd and Barbara B. Oberg. 35 vols. to date. Princeton, N.J.: Princeton University Press, 1950–.

———. *Writings.* Edited by Merrill D. Peterson. New York: Library of America, 1984.

Jensen, Merrill, ed. *Tracts of the American Revolution, 1763–1776.* Indianapolis: Bobbs-Merrill Co., 1967.

Jensen, Merrill, et al., eds. *The Documentary History of the Ratification of the Constitution.* 22 vols. to date. Madison: State Historical Society of Wisconsin, 1976–.

Johnson, Samuel. *Taxation No Tyranny: An Answer to the Resolutions and Address of the American Congress.* 4th ed. London: T. Cadell, 1775.

[Kennedy, Archibald]. *An Essay on the Government of the Colonies. Fitted to the Latitude Forty-one, but May, without Sensible Error, Serve All the Northern Colonies.* New York: J. Parker, 1752.

[———]. *Observations on the Importance of the Northern Colonies Under Proper Regulations.* New York: James Parker, 1750.

Kent, James. *An Introductory Lecture to a Course of Law Lectures: Delivered November 17, 1794.* New York: Francis Childs, 1794.

King, Rufus. *The Life and Correspondence of Rufus King.* Ed. Charles R. King. 6 vols. New York: G. P. Putnam's Sons, 1896.

Knox, William. *The Controversy between Great Britain and her Colonies Reviewed; The Several Pleas of the Colonies, In Support of Their Right to all the Liberties and Privileges of British Subjects, and to Exemption from the Legislative Authority of Parliament, Stated and Considered: and the Nature of their Connection with, and Dependence on, Great Britain, Shewn, Upon the Evidence of Historical Facts and Authentic Records.* Boston: Mein and Fleeming, 1769.

Kurland, Philip B., and Ralph Lerner, eds. *The Founders' Constitution.* 5 vols. Indianapolis: Liberty Fund, 1987.

Lee, Richard Henry. *The Letters of Richard Henry Lee.* Edited by James Curtis Ballagh. 2 vols. 1911. Reprint, New York: Da Capo Press, 1970.

Letters of Mutius, Addressed to the President of the United States. Washington, D.C.: Edward Carter Stanard, 1810.

Locke, John. *Second Treatise of Government.* Edited by C. B. Macpherson. Indianapolis: Hackett Publishing Co., 1980.

Lutz, Donald, ed. *Colonial Origins of the American Constitution: A Documentary History.* Indianapolis: Liberty Fund, 1998.

———, ed. *Documents of Political Foundation Written by Colonial Americans: From Covenant to Constitution.* Philadelphia: Institute for the Study of Human Issues, 1986.

Maclay, William. *Journal of William Maclay, United States Senator from Pennsylvania, 1789–1791.* Edited by Edgar S. Maclay. New York: D. A. Appleton and Co., 1890.

Madison, James. *Letters and Other Writings of James Madison, Fourth President of the United States.* 4 vols. Philadelphia: J. B. Lippincott and Co., 1865.

———. *Notes of Debates in the Federal Convention of 1787.* Edited by Adrienne Koch. Athens: Ohio University Press, 1984.

———. *The Papers of James Madison.* Edited by William T. Hutchinson, William M. E. Rachal, and Robert A. Rutland. 17 vols. to date. Chicago: University of Chicago Press; and Charlottesville: University Press of Virginia, 1962–.

———. *The Writings of James Madison.* Edited by Gaillard Hunt. 9 vols. New York: G. P. Putnam's Sons, 1910.

Marcus, Maeva, ed. *The Documentary History of the Supreme Court of the United States, 1789–1800.* 8 vols. to date. New York: Columbia University Press, 1985–.

[McCulloh, Henry]. *A Miscellaneous Essay Concerning the Courses pursued by Great Britain in the Affairs of her Colonies; with Some Observations on the Great Importance of our Settlements in America, and the Trade thereof.* London: R. Baldwin, 1755.

Molyneux, William. *The Case of Ireland's Being Bound by Acts of Parliament in England, Stated.* Dublin: Joseph Ray, 1698.

Montesquieu. *The Spirit of the Laws.* Translated by Thomas Nugent. New York: The Colonial Press, 1900.

Morison, Samuel Eliot, ed. *Sources and Documents Illustrating the American Revolution, 1764–1788, and the Formation of the Federal Constitution.* 2d ed. New York: Oxford University Press, 1965.

Oliver, Peter. *Origin and Progress of the American Rebellion: A Tory View.* Edited by Douglass Adair and John A. Schutz. Stanford, Calif.: Stanford University Press, 1961.

Otis, James. *The Rights of the British Colonies Asserted and Proved.* Boston: Edes and Gill, 1764.

———. *A Vindication of the "British Colonies," against the Aspersions of the "Halifax" Gentleman, in His Letter to a* Rhode Island *Friend.* Boston: Edes and Gill, 1765.

Pownall, Thomas. *The Administration of the Colonies.* 2d ed. London: J. Dodsley and J. Walter, 1765.

Pufendorf, Samuel von. *The Law of Nature and Nations: or, A General System of the Most Important Principles of Morality, Jurisprudence, and Politics, in Eight Books.* Translated by Basil Kennet. 5th ed. London, 1749.

Rousseau, Jean-Jacques. *The Social Contract.* Translated by Christopher Betts. Oxford: Oxford University Press, 1994.

Simmons, R. C., and P. D. G. Thomas, eds. *Proceedings and Debates of the British Parliament Respecting North America, 1754–1783.* 6 vols. to date. Millwood, N.Y.: Kraus International Publications, 1982–.

Smith, Paul H., ed. *Letters of Delegates to Congress, 1774–1789.* 26 vols. Washington, D.C.: Library of Congress, 1976–2000.

Sparks, Jared. *The Life of Gouverneur Morris: With Selections from His Correspondence and Miscellaneous Papers: Detailing Events in the American Revolution, the French Revolution, and in the Political History of the United States.* 3 vols. Boston: Gray and Bowen, 1832.

The Speeches of His Excellency Governor Hutchinson, to the General Assembly of the Massachusetts-Bay . . . With the Answers of His Majesty's Council and the House of Representatives. . . . Boston: Edes and Gill, 1773.

Story, Joseph. *Commentaries on the Constitution of the United States.* 3 vols. Boston: Hilliard, Gray, and Co., 1833.

Taylor, John. *New Views of the Constitution of the United States.* Washington, D.C.: Way and Gideon, 1823.

Thomas, P. D. G., ed. "Parliamentary Diaries of Nathaniel Ryder, 1764–7." In *Camden Miscellany,* 4th ser., 7:234–235. London: Camden Society, 1969.

Thorpe, Francis Newton, ed. *The Federal and State Constitutions, Colonial Charters, and Other Organic Laws of the States, Territories, and Colonies Now or Heretofore Forming the United States of America, Compiled and Edited under the Act of Congress of June 30, 1906.* Washington, D.C.: Government Printing Office, 1909.

Tocqueville, Alexis de. *Democracy in America.* Translated by George Lawrence. Edited by J. P. Mayer. New York: Perennial Classics, 2000.

Tucker, Josiah. *Four Tracts on Political and Commercial Subjects.* 2d ed. Gloucester, England: R. Raikes, 1774.

Tucker, St. George. *Blackstone's Commentaries: With Notes of Reference, to the Constitution and Laws, of the Federal Government of the United States; and of the Commonwealth of Virginia.* 5 vols. Philadelphia: William Young Birch and Abraham Small, 1803.

The Votes and Proceedings of the Freeholders and Other Inhabitants of the Town of Boston, in Town Meeting Assembled, According to Law. Boston, 1772.

Warren, Mercy Otis. *History of the Rise, Progress and Termination of the American Revolution, Interspersed with Biographical, Political and Moral Observations.* 3 vols. Boston: Manning and Loring, 1805.

Wilson, James. *The Works of James Wilson.* Edited by Robert Green McCloskey. 2 vols. Cambridge, Mass.: Belknap Press of Harvard University Press, 1967.

Yates, Robert. *Secret Proceedings and Debates of the Convention Assembled at Philadelphia, in the Year 1787, for the Purpose of Forming the Constitution of the United States of America.* Albany: Websters and Skinners, 1821.

Acknowledgments

I AM DELIGHTED TO be able to acknowledge and thank the many people and institutions who have accompanied me on my quest to understand the origins of American federalism. In proper federal fashion, the book comprises many component pieces, each of which is the product of countless conversations conducted across far-flung temporal and spatial zones, and each of which reflects its own set of crucial influences, helpful suggestions, and challenging questions.

This book began in the Harvard University History Department. First of all, therefore, I thank James Kloppenberg, Morton Horwitz, David Armitage, and Christine Desan. With their help, I discovered that my two worlds of history and law could be brought together substantively and methodologically by viewing legal ideas as intellectual artifacts both dependent on and constitutive of their particular historical moment. I am deeply grateful to them for their commitment to this project and their unflagging and continuing encouragement over the past several years. In addition, I thank Joyce Chaplin and Michael Mc-Cormick, as well as my colleagues and friends Yonatan Eyal, Katherine Grandjean, Marion Gross Menzin, Margot Minardi, Daniel Wewers, and Katja Zelljadt. Finally, I am grateful to have had the privilege of beginning my graduate work with the late William Gienapp as my advisor.

For financial support during my time at Harvard, I thank the Andrew W. Mellon Fellowship in Humanistic Studies; the Charles Warren Center for Studies in American History; the Mark DeWolfe Howe Fund at Harvard Law School; the Harvard History Department; and the Harvard Graduate School of Arts and Sciences.

Great appreciation is also due to individuals who have supported this project from its early stages. I owe an enormous debt of gratitude to the Samuel I. Golieb Fellowship in Legal History at New York University Law School. At NYU, I was fortunate to have opportunities to discuss my work in particular and legal history in general with an outstanding community of scholars, including Richard B. Bernstein, Noah Feldman, Daniel Hulsebosch, Serena Mayeri, William Nelson, John Phillip Reid, Rebecca Rix, Chaim Saiman, and many others. For helpful comments as the manuscript developed, I am also grateful to Bernard Bailyn, Lauren Benton, Mary Sarah Bilder, Lisa Ford, Larry Kramer, Diane Kunz, and Jack Rakove, as well as outside readers for Harvard University Press and *Law and History Review*.

Since I arrived at my academic home, the University of Chicago Law School, many colleagues have provided intellectual guidance and support in shaping the book. I am especially grateful for the encouragement and assistance of Douglas Baird, Anu Bradford, Emily Buss, Adam Cox, Rosalind Dixon, Richard Epstein, Bernard Harcourt, Richard Helmholz, Dennis Hutchinson, Saul Levmore, Martha Nussbaum, Gerald Rosenberg, Adam Samaha, Geoffrey Stone, Lior Strahilevitz, David Strauss, Cass Sunstein, and the late David Currie. Margaret Schilt of the D'Angelo Law Library fielded countless requests for obscure sources. Evan Berkow provided excellent research assistance. In addition, conversations with the students in my fall 2006 and spring 2008 seminars on the history of federalism helped me refine my arguments. I am also thankful for the financial support of the Russell Baker Scholars Fund, the Elsie O. and Philip D. Sang Law Faculty Endowment, and the Mayer Brown Faculty Research Fund. In this great city of legal historians, I have also benefited from the comments of Felice Batlan, Daniel Hamilton, Claire Priest, Allison Tirres, and Vicky Saker Woeste. In addition,

I thank Kathleen McDermott for her encouragement and her confidence in the project from its early stages; my thanks also to Barbara Goodhouse for shepherding the book through the production process.

I have presented portions of this project at various points in its journey, and I thank the institutions and individuals who gave their time and comments. They include the Graduate Student Forum of the Colonial Society of Massachusetts, the New York University Law School Legal History Colloquium, the American Society for Legal History annual meeting, the Chicago Legal History Seminar, the American Bar Foundation Research Seminar, and the University of Chicago Law School Faculty Work-in-Progress Workshop.

Versions of Chapters 2, 4, and 5 previously appeared in "Drawing and Redrawing the Line: The Pre-Revolutionary Origins of Federal Ideas of Sovereignty," University of Chicago Law School Occasional Paper No. 47 (University of Chicago Law School, January 2008); "The Authority for Federalism: Madison's Negative and the Origins of Federal Ideology," *Law and History Review* 28 (2010); and "The New Wheel in the Federal Machine: From Sovereignty to Jurisdiction in the Early Republic," *Supreme Court Review* 2007: 345–394.

Most important, I thank my family. During the course of researching and writing this book, I traveled from Boston to New York to Chicago, with many rail and air miles in between, and with new family members arriving along the way. From childhood family trips to the Northern Neck of Virginia to recent conversations about draft chapters to even more recent grandparental assistance as I worked on the final version of the book, my parents, Terri and David LaCroix, have been essential supporters of this project and its author. My brother, David LaCroix, and sister-in-law, Helen LaCroix, have spent hours talking through research and writing issues large and small, as well as standing ready to discuss the arcana of nineteenth-century American history or to visit a historic home. Elspeth and Isolde LaCroix-Birdthistle arrived in time to help with the final revisions and to provide real-life evidence of the rewards and challenges of dividing sovereignty.

Finally, I thank my husband, William Birdthistle. More than anyone else, William has lived with this project and accompanied me into its core of vexing questions and exhilarating discoveries. At times during this process, the two of us talked about Thomas Hutchinson and James Madison so frequently and with such familiarity that they felt like friends—albeit sometimes irritatingly inscrutable friends. From feeding me to editing and proofreading text to bolstering me with period-appropriate exhortations, William has been in this project, as in all my endeavors, my partner and companion.

Index

Act for Preventing Frauds, and Regulating Abuses in the Plantation Trade, 144

Act in Restraint of Appeals, 12

Act of Union (1707), 27, 78, 87–88

Adair, Douglass, 138

Adams, Charles Francis, 230n51

Adams, John: cites Union of Crowns, 25, 28–29; on Stamp Act, 37; on Parliament, 84, 250n42; on dominion of king, 86–88; on constitutional status of colonies, 121; on government under Articles of Confederation, 134; appointment of "midnight judges" by, 176; incites change in judicial system, 204, 206; signs Judiciary Act of 1801 into law, 207; on Hutchinson, 247n23; role in Boston debates, 248n33, 249n39; as "Britannic statesman," 250n44; on Massachusetts Bay Colony, 250n47; on British Empire, 251n52, 252n58

Adams, John Quincy, 205–206

Adams, Randolph G., 43, 75, 87, 250nn42,44

Adams, Samuel, 73, 75, 249n39

Adams, Thomas Boylston, 205–206

Administration of Justice Act, 100–101

Administration of the Colonies (Pownall), 53–56

Albany Plan of Union (1754): as precedent for colonial union, 20, 126; drafting and description of, 22–24; Galloway and, 112–113; Iroquois Confederacy and, 229n40

American Department, 52, 54, 235n26, 241n75, 245n10

American Revolution, 1, 107–108, 128, 177–178

Ames, Fisher, 187, 188, 198–199, 281n41

Andrews, Charles M., 266n32

Anglo-American constitutional debates, 12–18

Anne (queen), 258n27, 271n92

Anti-Federalists, 182, 196

Appellate jurisdiction: of Supreme Court, 218–219; of Privy Council, 267n39. *See also* Supreme Court of the United States: appellate jurisdiction of

Arising under jurisdiction. *See* Jurisdiction: federal question

Armitage, David, 5, 24–25, 133

Article III of the Constitution: Supremacy Clause and, 163–164, 168–169, 179; Madisonian compromise and, 180–181; inferior federal courts and, 183, 190, 206, 211; Morris on, 278n19

Articles of Confederation: and *imperium in imperio*, 81; drafting and description of, 127–128; similarities to Albany Plan, 128; multiplicity and, 134–135; Madison's conclusions on, 137; contrasted to British Empire and federal union, 177; executive branch of government under, 261n58

Assemblies, colonial: as source of colonial law, 12, 33, 91; repugnancy standard and, 77, 85, 144, 146, 165; influence on early republican debates, 179

Authority. *See* Divided authority; Sovereignty; Unitary authority

Bailyn, Bernard: institutional approach to divided authority and, 4, 17; on parliamentary sovereignty, 32, 226n15; on taxation and trade, 63–64; on Thomas Hutchinson, 72, 75, 247n23; on popular sovereignty, 96; on Supremacy Clause, 172; on *imperium in imperio* principle, 172–173, 226n12; on Townshend Acts, 237n48; on study of political theory, 239n63
Baldwin, Abraham, 205
Banning, Lance, 146
Barbeyrac, Jean, 248n33
Barlow, Joel, 205
Bartlett, Josiah, 129
Bassett, Richard, 279n29
Bayard, James A., 204
Bedford, Gunning, 157
Benson, Egbert, 187, 197
Bernard, Francis: dual identity of, 52; titles and achievements of, 53; metropolitan perspective of, 56–58; resignation of, 72; on colonial self-taxation, 234n23; departure of, 245n8
Bernstein, Richard B., 274n127
Bilder, Mary Sarah, 4, 140, 173, 218
Bill of Rights, 184
Black, Barbara, 16, 17–18
Blackstone, William: on supreme authority, 8, 14, 76, 107, 125, 244n4; on Parliament's authority, 15, 178; Morton Horwitz on, 226n10; Arthur Lee on, 226n11; defines Privy Council, 264n20
Bland, Richard: on Parliament, 8; on taxation, 46–47; on internal-external lawmaking, 60, 71, 133
Board of Trade, 24, 38, 47, 117, 142, 143. *See also* Committee of Trade and Plantations; Privy Council
Bodin, Jean, 13, 225n5
Bollan, William, 52, 242n94
Boston debates (1773): introduction to, 68–72; controversy preceding, 72–74; Hutchinson and, 74–82, 96–100; General Court's arguments in, 82–90, 248n33, 249n40, 253n70; significance and effects of, 91–96, 100–104; events following, 105; House advocates in,

249n39; notes and reconstruction of, 259n40
Boston Evening-Post, 92
Boston-Gazette and Country Journal, 81–82, 92
Boston Massacre, 68, 245n8
Boston Port Bill, 100
Bowdoin, James, 249n39
Bradford, Alden, 249n39
Brattle, William, 249n39
Britannus Americanicus, 30–31, 36, 221
British Empire: divided authority and, 3–9; sovereignty of, 12–18; Union of Crowns and, 24–29, 120–124, 231nn56,58; tension between colonies and, 68–72; colonies as part of, 86–90, 250n47; proposals for restructuring, 105–108; Cartwright's plan for restructuring, 108–111; Galloway's plan for restructuring, 111–113; Jefferson's plan for restructuring, 113–120; Continental political theory and, 124–126; and federal union, 131; Madison's republic based on, 139, 145–146, 166–168; Jack Greene on, 224n9; combining parliamentary sovereignty and, 226n15; colonial government resembles, 246n18; John Adams's views on, 251n52, 252n58
Broadsides, 30–31, 36
Brown, Henry B., 175
Brown, John, 193
Bryce, James, 226n16
Burke, Edmund, 237n42, 257n18, 286n4
Bushman, Richard L., 243n1
Butler, Pierce, 164

Calder v. Bull, 274n125
Carrington, Edward, 154
Carroll, Charles, 279n29
Cartwright, John, 108–111
Casey, Silas, 274n129
Champion, Alexander, 274n129
Champion & Dickason v. Casey, 274n129
Charles I, 86, 257n22
Charles II, 267n39
Charter colonies, 142, 253n62

Charters, colonial, 45; construed by
Hutchinson, 77, 85, 91; as basis for
government, 85–86, 144, 251n48
Cicero, 18–19
Circuit courts, 185, 204–207. *See also*
Federal courts
Citizen, 200
Clinton, George, 166
Coercive Acts, 44, 100–101, 105, 116,
254n91. *See also* Intolerable Acts
Cohens v. Virginia (1821), 184, 218–219
Coke, Edward: on parliamentary sov-
ereignty, 13–14, 15; ancient constitution
and, 249n40; jurisdictional and juris-
prudential visions and, 255n96, 26 9n63
Colonial Department. *See* American
Department
*The Colonial Dismounted: or the Rector
Vindicated* (Bland), 47, 60
Colonial union, 20–24
Colonies: debates on authority over, 12–18,
30–37, 64–72, 91–96; Stamp Act and,
37–44; theories of legislative power in,
44–51, 60–64; metropolitan approaches
to governing, 51–59, 241n75; as part
of British Empire, 86–90, 250n47;
Intolerable Acts and, 100–101; restructuring British Empire and, 105–108;
Cartwright's views on, 108–111; Galloway's views on, 111–113; Jefferson's views
on, 113–120; Scottish precedents and,
120–124; Continental political theory
and, 124–126; Privy Council authority
over, 139–145; proprietary, 142; policing
trade in, 235n30; obedience of, 243n105;
grievances of, 244n2
Commentaries on the Laws of England
(Blackstone), 8, 14, 76, 107, 277n7
Commerce Clause (U.S. Constitution), 66
Committee of Trade and Plantations, 142,
264n23. *See also* Board of Trade; Privy
Council
Committees of correspondence, colonial,
69, 73
Concurrent jurisdiction: Judiciary Acts
and, 9–10, 209–210; Reid's views on, 36;
debates on, 187–188; in colonial and early
republican thought, 188–193; Hamilton

on, 189–192; Jefferson on, 189; opposition to, 193–200; *imperium in imperio*
principle and, 200–201; Dickinson on,
281n46; Tucker's views on, 281n50
Confederate republic, 216–218
Confederate union, 26–27
Confederations: colonial, 20–24; European
examples of, 27; Madison's research and
conclusions on, 136–139
Congress, United States: enumerated
powers of, 3, 224n15; and federal
negative, 9, 135, 147–153, 159, 161, 165,
167; as Continental Congress, 111, 112,
114, 121–123, 125, 126–128, 137; representation in, 155–156; as source of supreme
law of land, 162; as replacement for Privy
Council, 170; preemption power of, 171;
and federal courts' jurisdiction, 175,
180–186, 190, 196–197, 203–206, 210;
and election of 1800, 176, 202; institutional role of, 177; concurrent power of,
189; and state courts' jurisdiction, 194;
and nullification crisis, 220. *See also*
United States in Congress assembled
Connecticut Compromise, 155–156
Constitution, ancient, 78, 86, 249n40
Constitution, British: background of,
13–18, 25; Stamp Act debates and, 30,
31, 36; competing versions of, 86;
Hutchinson–General Court debates
and, 90, 96; divergence from American
theory and, 178
Constitution, U.S. *See* Article III of the
Constitution; Bill of Rights; Commerce
Clause; Constitutional Convention;
Supremacy Clause
Constitutional Convention: as origin
of federalism, 1–5; antecedents in
Hutchinson–General Court debate, 96,
101, 103–104; introduction to, 132–135;
Madison and, 136–139, 263n13; federal
negative proposed in, 147–153; federal
negative defeated in, 153–158; state and
federal authority in, 158–166, 168–174;
interpreted by early republicans, 179;
judicial power in, 180–187, 211
Constitutional debates, Anglo-American,
12–18

Constitutional History of the American Revolution, 35–36
Constitutional law approach to divided authority, 4–5
Continental Congress, 92, 111, 112, 114, 121–123, 125, 126–128, 137
Continental political theory, 18–20, 79–80, 124–126
Coulon de Jumonville, Joseph, 22
Council of Revision, 148–149, 269n60
Courts: federal, 182–185, 204–207; district, 184–185, 205–206; circuit, 185, 204–207; state, 191. *See also* Supreme Court of the United States
Cover, Robert, 133
Crown prerogative. *See* Prerogative
Cruwys, Thomas, 234n24
Curtius, 198
Cushing, Thomas, 98–99
Cushing, William, 274n129

Dartmouth, Lord: correspondence with, 73, 74, 245n12; supports Hutchinson, 93; rebukes Hutchinson, 98–100
Davies, K. G., 75
Deane, Silas, 127, 128
Declaratory Act, 59, 65, 71, 101, 116, 242n88
De Jumonville, Joseph Coulon. *See* Jumonville, Joseph Coulon de
De Tocqueville, Alexis. *See* Tocqueville, Alexis de
De Vattel, Emmerich. *See* Vattel, Emmerich de
Diamond, Martin, 273n110
Dickason, Thomas, 274n129
Dickinson, John: on taxation, 8, 47, 60–62; on legislative power, 71, 102; on king's dominion, 119–120; Articles of Confederation and, 127; Equalizing Court and, 162; role in Boston debates, 249n39; Galloway and, 256n14; on concurrent jurisdiction, 281n46
Disallowance, 143, 266nn32,35, 267nn36,37
District courts, 184–185, 199, 205–206. *See also* Federal courts

Divided authority: introduction to, 3–9; Bodin and Hobbes's views on, 13; colonial theories on, 18–20, 44–51; colonial resistance movement and, 30–37; Stamp Act and, 37–44; metropolitan approaches to, 51–59; Boston debates and, 68–78; theories on, 79–80; locus within composite polity and, 135–136; Supreme Court as arbiter of, 219; Pownall's views on, 241n75
Divine right of kings, 96
Doctrine of allegiance, 86
Dominion of New England, 22
Dominion status, 86, 119, 251n50, 259n35
Douglas, William, 246n18
Droit des gens (Vattel), 79
Duke of York, 267n39
Dulany, Daniel: on parliamentary authority, 8; on taxation, 47; Stamp Act and, 50–51; on legislative authority, 71; role in Boston debates, 249n39

Edling, Max, 7
Election of 1800: Congress and, 176, 202; rise of Republican party and, 202; settlement in House of Representatives, 207, 210
Elector, 81–82
Elizabeth I, 25, 38
Ellsworth, Oliver, 201, 279n29
English Civil War, 13, 15, 21, 31–32, 86
Enlightenment, 124, 147
Equalizing Court, 162–163, 168

Facial challenges, 265n26
Federal courts (lower or inferior): as subject of Madisonian compromise at Constitutional Convention, 176; early republican controversy over, 182–185, 189–193, 204–207; structure of, 184–185; state courts as substitute for, 198; judiciary acts of 1789 and 1801 and, 209–210
Federal ideology, 6–9, 34, 67, 177, 212–213, 215
The Federalist, 2, 215
The Federalist No. 1 (Hamilton), 261n65

The Federalist No. 9 (Hamilton), 216, 286n6
The Federalist No. 10 (Madison), 224n12, 263n17
The Federalist No. 18 (Madison), 263n12
The Federalist No. 19 (Madison), 263n12
The Federalist No. 20 (Madison and Hamilton), 263n12, 277n8
The Federalist No. 27 (Hamilton), 255n97
The Federalist No. 32 (Hamilton), 189–192, 281nn42–49
The Federalist No. 48 (Madison), 269n61
The Federalist No. 51 (Madison), 224n12
The Federalist No. 81 (Hamilton), 182, 279n22, 283n73
The Federalist No. 82 (Hamilton), 190–191
Federalist party, 182, 202, 208–209, 215
Federal negative: Madison's conception of, 138–139; proposal of, 145–153, 268n57; opposition to, 153–158, 171–172, 270n80; judicial review and, 158–166; defense of, 166–168, 271n93, 273n112; overview of, 168–169; Supremacy Clause and, 181–182; synonymous terms for, 263n15; scholarly views on, 263n17; support for, 271n96
Federal question jurisdiction. *See* Jurisdiction: federal question
Federal union, 26–27, 123–124, 130–131
Feudal system, 14, 254n78
Few, William, 279n29
Fletcher, Andrew, 27, 231n56
Fletcher v. Peck, 274n129
Foedera, 18
Forsyth, Murray, 108, 127
Franklin, Benjamin: Albany Plan and, 22, 23; distributes copies of Vattel's work in America, 79; reports to London on Hutchinson–General Court debates, 98; Galloway and, 112–113; on union of colonies, 123; Articles of Confederation and, 127; on Iroquois Confederacy, 229n40
Franklin, Julian H., 225n5
Freeman, Joanne, 202
French, colonial tensions with, 22
Friend to the Community, 92

Functional form of federalism, 35–36
Fundamental Orders of Connecticut, 228n34

Gage, Thomas, 97, 100, 101
Galloway, Joseph, 108, 111–113, 256n14, 257n18
Gaspée affair, 68
Genêt, Edmond, 166
George III, 41, 86–89, 115–119, 121, 157, 244n2
German Empire, 19–20
Gerry, Elbridge, 151, 156, 157, 186
Glorious Revolution, 13, 31–32, 71, 86, 97, 107, 118
Goebel, Julius, 142–143, 164–165, 185, 199, 265n26, 266n35
Goodrich, Chauncey, 204
Gould, Eliga, 243n105
Grant of the Province of Maine, 267n39
Gray, Harrison, 249n39
Grayson, William, 147, 271n94
Greene, Jack: on origins of federalism, 3–4; mentioned, 16; on transatlantic culture, 17–18; on imperial constitution, 33; on British Empire, 173, 224n9, 240n72
Greenleaf, Benjamin, 249n39
Grenville, George, 37–42, 221, 234nn23,24
Grotius, Hugo: on multiplicity, 18–19; James Otis and, 49, 239n64; availability of works in America, 79; on sovereignty, 79–80; Continental political theory and, 124; on union of states, 231n58

Hamilton, Alexander: on legislative authority, 102–103; response to Seabury, 126; on judicial power and Supreme Court, 179, 182–183; on concurrent jurisdiction, 189–192; on federal jurisdiction, 208–209; on federal judicial power, 210–211; on confederate republics, 216–218; education of, 262n7
Hampden, John, 31
Harper, Robert Goodloe, 204, 206, 221
Harper bill, 204–207, 209–210
Hat Act (1732), 116, 235n27

Hawley, Joseph, 249n39
Hendrickson, David, 7, 224n15
Henry, Patrick, 257n20
Henry VII, 144
Hicks, William, 62–63, 64
Hobbes, Thomas, 13
Hodges, James: defines incorporating and federal unions, 26–27; on colonies and Britain, 122; defines federal union, 130, 217; on English subkingdoms, 230n54
Hopkins, Stephen, 238n58, 239n66
Hulsebosch, Daniel: on nature of Anglo-American constitution, 4; on solecism, 226n12; on imperial agents, 241n73; on royal prerogative, 251n48; jurisdictional and jurisprudential visions and, 255n96, 269n63; on horizontal judicial review, 272n105
Humphrey, James, 249n39
Hutchinson, Thomas: Boston debates and, 8, 69–78, 91–100; Albany Plan and, 22; personal attacks on, 41, 245n8; mentioned, 52; arguments on legislative power, 63–64, 65; controversy caused by, 72–73; theories of sovereignty, 80, 169–170, 221, 248n33; public responses to, 81–82; General Court's responses to, 82–90; significance of, 101–104; departure of, 105, 255n1; Thomas Whately and, 234n24; on time preceding Stamp Act, 243n103; Dartmouth and, 245n12; John Adams's views on, 247n23; refers to feudal system, 254n78

Ideological approach to divided authority, 3–5. *See also* Federal ideology
Imperial agents, 52–64, 241n73
Imperial federalism, 119, 258n33
Imperial restructuring: introduction to, 105–108; Cartwright's plan for, 108–111; Galloway's plan for, 111–113; Jefferson's plan for, 113–120; Scottish precedents for union and, 120–124; Continental political theory and, 124–126
Imperium in imperio principle: in constitutional debates, 14; influence of, 81; in

Boston debates, 91, 95–96; James Iredell on, 102, 120; multiplicity and, 133–134; as central constitutional question, 172–173; in early republican debates, 178–179; concurrent jurisdiction and, 200–201; as solecism, 200, 226n12, 277n8; Hamilton and, 211
Incorporating union, 26–28, 123–124, 230n54
Inferior federal courts. *See* Federal courts
Institutional approach to divided authority, 3–5, 9–10
Interest groups, 133
Internal-external approach to imperial governance: Stamp Act and, 37–44; colonial observers' theories of, 44–51; metropolitan theories of, 51–59; debates on, 59–67, 237n50; in Hutchinson–General Court debates, 95; tracts and pamphlets on, 238n58
Intolerable Acts, 44, 100–101, 105, 116. *See also* Coercive Acts
Iredell, James, 102, 120
Ireland, 11, 28–29
Iron Act (1750), 116
Iroquois Confederacy, 22, 229n40
Izard, Ralph, 279n29

Jackson, Andrew, 220
Jamaica, 144–145
James I/James VI, 25, 87, 249n40, 252n57
James II, 22, 249n40
Jay, John, 2, 215, 274n129
Jefferson, Thomas: plan for federated union *(Summary View)*, 106, 108, 113–120; Scottish precedents and, 120–121; notes on debates in Continental Congress, 123; Continental political theory and, 125–126; Madison and, 136; on state and federal authority, 158–163; on judicial power, 182; on concurrent jurisdiction, 189, 210; on jurisdiction, 207–208; first annual message to Congress, 210; first inaugural address of, 214–215; *Summary View* and, 257n20; William Small and, 259n38; Monroe and, 271n100

Johnson, Samuel, 19, 76, 78
Johnston, Samuel, 194–195
Jones, Joseph, 193
Judicial power: defining, 176, 180–187;
concurrent jurisdiction and, 187–201;
Judiciary Act of 1801 and, 201–213
Judicial review: as distinctively American,
2; by Privy Council, 141–146; federal
negative and, 158–166; Jefferson on, 159;
Supremacy Clause and, 171–174, 221;
horizontal, 272n105; Madison and,
274n124
Judiciary Act (1789): significance of, 9–10;
Supremacy Clause and, 169; overview
of, 175–179; drafting and passage of,
180–187, 279n29; 1801 Act and, 203;
appeals and, 274n129; appellate
jurisdiction and, 280n30
Judiciary Act (1801): significance of, 9–10;
Supremacy Clause and, 169; overview
of, 175–179; federal question jurisdiction
and, 185–186; drafting and description
of, 201–213; repeal of, 202, 212
Jumonville, Joseph Coulon de, 22
Jurisdiction: substantive approach to, 133;
federal negative and, 146–147; of Supreme
Court, 164–165, 218–219; introduction
to, 179; as structural element of federalism, 180–187; diversity, 185; federal
question, 185–186, 194; Judiciary Act
of 1801 and, 185–186; 201–213; subject-
matter-based conception of, 212; royal
appellate, 267n39. *See also* Concurrent
jurisdiction
Jurisdictional and jurisprudential visions
of law, 255n96, 269n63

Kammen, Michael, 230n48
Keene, Edward, 19
Keith, William, 236n31
Kennedy, Anthony, 5
Kennedy, Archibald, 46, 122
Kennet, Basil, 248n33
Kent, James, 282n59
King: appellate jurisdiction and, 115–119,
267n39; allegiance to, 121–122
King, Rufus, 208

King-in-Parliament, 32, 113–117, 247n19,
257n22
King's dominion: colonies as, 86–88,
250n47; Cartwright's views on, 108–111;
Privy Council and, 140–145; origin of
doctrine, 264n23
Knox, William, 52, 64, 122
Koselleck, Reinhart, 220
Kramer, Larry, 96, 161–162, 273n111,
275n136

Landsman, Ned, 46, 122, 238n51, 260n43
Lansing, John, 153–154, 154–155, 156,
270n80
Lansing, John, Jr., 166
Law: politics and, 84; personal principle
of, 89; territorial principle of, 89–90;
jurisdictional and jurisprudential
visions of, 255n96, 269n63
Law of nations, 77
Law of Nations (Vattel), 79
Law of Nature and Nations (Pufendorf), 19
Lee, Arthur, 226n11
Lee, Richard Henry, 269n62, 279n29,
280n31
Legge, William. *See* Dartmouth, Lord
Legislative power: colonial theories of,
44–51; debates on, 59–67; Boston
debates and, 68–72, 74–78, 95; parliamentary acts asserting, 100–101; levels
of, 101–108; Jefferson's views on, 117–118;
Madison and, 136–139, 152, 269n61; in
Virginia Plan, 148–158; gives way to
judicial power as basis of union, 178,
180; Hopkins's views on, 238n58; of
Congress, 274n132
Legislative review: of Privy Council,
140–147; Supremacy Clause and,
168–169; facial challenges and,
265n26; shift in definition of term,
274n125
Legislatures, colonial. *See* Assemblies,
colonial
Letters from a Farmer in Pennsylvania
(Dickinson), 60–62, 102
Levack, Brian P., 252n57
Leviathan (Hobbes), 13

Locke, John, 49, 50
Lowell, John, 187, 281n41
Lower federal courts. *See* Federal courts

Maclay, William, 198, 279n29
Madison, James: on self-government, 7;
    proposes federal negative, 135, 147–153;
    comparative approach to models of
    government and, 136; Privy Council and,
    145–147, 268n54; opposition to federal
    negative and, 153–158; on state and federal
    authority, 158–163, 274n122; defends
    federal negative, 166–168, 271n93,
    273n112; on Judiciary Act of 1789, 186;
    and multiplicity, 221; education of, 262n7;
    Constitutional Convention and, 263n13;
    scholarly views on, 263n17; on legislative
    power, 269n61; on New Jersey Plan,
    272nn108,110; on judicial review, 274n124
Madisonian compromise, 180–181, 211
Magna Carta, 83, 86
Maier, Pauline, 65
Marbury v. Madison, 184, 210, 280n30
Marchant, Henry, 274n129
Marcus, Maeva, 194
Marshall, John, 179, 183, 204–206, 218–219,
    221, 283n77
Marston, Jerrilyn Greene, 261n58
Martin, Luther: Virginia Plan and, 154,
    155; on Constitutional Convention, 158;
    resolution of, 163, 273n111; opposes
    lower federal courts, 183, 196–197;
    multiplicity and, 221
Martin v. Hunter's Lessee, 184, 274n129
Mason, George, 183, 196, 197, 269n62
Massachusetts Bay Colony, 77, 85–86,
    94, 144, 250n47
Massachusetts Bay Company, 86
Massachusetts General Court: Boston
    debates and, 69–72, 74–78, 91–97;
    arguments of, 82–96, 253n70; signifi-
    cance of, 101–104; advocates for, 249n39;
    invokes ancient constitution, 249n40
Massachusetts Government Act, 100–101
Massachusetts Superior Court of Judica-
    ture, 72
McCloskey, Robert, 259n35

McClurg, James, 271n96
McColloch v. Maryland, 283n77
McCulloh, Henry, 44–45, 122, 234n24,
    238n51
McIlwain, Charles H., 16–17, 141
McLaughlin, Andrew C., 3–4, 16–17, 75
Middlekauff, Robert, 43
Molasses Act (1733), 235n27
Molyneux, William, 28
Monroe, James, 271n100, 284n83
Montesquieu, 49, 124, 125, 217
Moore, Alfred, 194–195
Morgan, Edmund: on Albany Plan, 23; on
    Grenville, 39–40, 234n23; on internal
    and external regulation, 43–44; on
    popular sovereignty, 96; on Iroquois
    Confederacy, 229n40
Morgan, Helen, 39, 43–44, 234n23
Morris, Gouverneur, 152, 164, 182, 278n19,
    285n114
Multiplicity: as foundational principle,
    6–9; continental ideas on, 18–20; change
    in attitudes toward, 33–34, 221; Boston
    debates and, 72; Articles of Confedera-
    tion and, 128–129; protofederal ideology
    and, 133–135; Supremacy Clause and,
    164, 169–170, 172, 173–174; judiciary
    and, 177; concurrent jurisdiction and,
    188–189; Supreme Court and, 219

Natural law, 49, 50
Navigation Act (1651), 230n48, 243n105,
    250n47
Negative. *See* Federal negative
New England Confederation: description
    of, 20–22; Albany Plan and, 24;
    significance of, 126, 228n38; as model
    for new union, 128
New Jersey Plan, 155, 162–163, 171,
    272nn108,110
Newspapers: on Hutchinson–General
    Court debate, 81–82, 92; on efforts to
    reform federal judiciary, 205
North, Lord, 98
Novanglus (John Adams), 84, 88
Nullification crisis, 220
Nullity ab initio, 142, 266n35

Oliver, Peter, Jr., 100
Onuf, Nicholas, 79, 217
Onuf, Peter, 79, 217
Otis, James, 46–50, 221, 239nn59,63,64, 240n67, 249n39

Parliament: authority of, 12–18, 41–44, 101–108; change in attitudes toward, 30–37; colonial theories on, 44–51; metropolitan theories on, 51–59; debates on, 59–67; Boston debates and, 68–72, 74–78, 91–96; Hutchinson's views on, 81–82, 96–97, 248n33; General Court's conclusions on, 82–90; passes Coercive Acts, 100–101; Cartwright's views on, 108–111; Galloway's views on, 111–113; Jefferson's views on, 113–120; Continental Congress delegates on jurisdiction of, 121; regulatory powers of, 132–133; as judicial and legislative body, 141; combining empire and, 226n15; Bryce on, 226n16; Bollan's views on, 242n94; John Adams's views on, 250n42
Paterson, William, 200, 204, 279n29
Personality, as basis for jurisdiction, 89
Peterson, Merrill, 259n38
Philadelphia Aurora, 205
Pinckney, Charles, 149–150, 180
Pitt, William, 41–42, 237n42
Pitts, James, 249n39
"Plan of a Proposed Union between Great Britain and the Colonies" (Galloway), 108–113, 130
Plutarch, 18–19
Pocock, J. G. A., 12
Popular sovereignty, 96
Post Office Act (1710), 116
Pownall, John, 241n75
Pownall, Thomas, 52, 53–56, 76, 106, 241n75
Poynings' Law, 28, 144
Prehistory of federalism: introduction to, 11; constitutional debates in, 12–18; multiplicity in, 18–20; colonial union in, 20–24; Scottish and Irish examples in, 24–29

Prerogative: Boston debates and, 85–89; Cartwright and, 108–111; Jefferson and, 115–119; Madison and, 150–152, 270n66; colonists cite royal, 251n48, 252n62; disallowance and, 266n32
The Principles of Law and Polity, Applied to the American Colonies (Bernard), 56–58
Privy Council: structure of review established by, 139–145; influence on Madison, 145; federal negative and, 145–147, 150–153, 166–168, 170–171, 268n54; judicial review and, 165; Blackstone's definition of, 264n20; veto power and, 266n33; invalidated colonial acts and, 266n35. *See also* Board of Trade; Committee of Trade and Plantations
Proprietary colonies, 142
Pufendorf, Samuel von: as origin of federal idea, 6; multiplicity and, 18–20; on system of states, 20, 79, 87, 103; James Otis and, 49, 239n64; on sovereignty, 79–80; Continental political theory and, 124; vision of federal union, 130

Quartering Act, 100–101
Quebec Act, 100–101

Rakove, Jack, 128, 149, 254n91
Randolph, Edmund: Madison and, 137; Virginia Plan and, 147; 1790 plan to amend Judiciary Act of 1789, 180, 186–187, 194–195; Jefferson and, 207; on Supreme Court, 282n57
Randolph, Peyton, 114, 257n20
Reconstruction, 179
Reid, John Phillip: mentioned, 16; on English constitution, 17–18; on history of federalism, 35–36; on taxation of colonies, 42–43; on Boston debates, 71, 74–78, 249n40; on Coercive Acts, 101; on conflict between constitutions, 227n25; on resistance to Stamp Act, 237n45; on Hutchinson, 248n33; on supremacy, 249n41
Representation, of states, 123–124

Republicanism, 3–5, 6–7, 10

Repugnancy standard, 77, 85, 140, 144, 146, 149, 165, 218

Revenue, raising, 60–64, 236n31

Revenue Act (1764), 234n24

Revolution, American. *See* American Revolution

Rhode Island Patent (1643), 33

Ridpath, George, 27

Rights of Englishmen, 59, 88–90

Rights of the British Colonies Asserted and Proved (Otis), 47–50

Rind, Clementina, 257n19

Robertson, John, 26, 231n56

Rousseau, Jean-Jacques, 49, 226n8

Royal colonies, 141–142, 253n62

Royal prerogative. *See* Prerogative

Rush, Benjamin, 131

Rusticus, 196

Rutledge, John, 163, 180

Sager, Lawrence, 163

Salaries, of colonial officials, 68–69, 72–73, 243n1

Schlesinger, Arthur M., Sr., 140

Schulze, Hagen, 19

Schuyler, Robert Livingston, 16–17

Scotland: as model for American political thought, 11, 24–29, 78, 87–88, 120–124, 217, 231nn56,58; ministers' and educators' presence in colonies, 122. *See also* Union of Crowns

Scottish Militia Bill, 258n27, 271n92

Seabury, Samuel, 126

Secret Proceedings and Debates of the Convention Assembled . . . for the Purpose of Forming the Constitution of the United States (Yates), 166–167

Sedgwick, Theodore, 179, 201, 208–209

Seton, William, 231n58

Seven Years' War, 22, 37–38, 41, 44, 115

Sewall, Samuel, 204

Sherman, Roger, 155

Short, William, 147, 271n94

Sidney, Algernon, 31

Six Books of the Commonwealth (Bodin), 13

Six Nations, 229n40

Small, William, 259n38

Smith, Charles Page, 251n50, 259n35

Smith, Joseph Henry, 140, 247n22

Sovereignty: subject-matter-based approach to, 7–9, 34, 103–104, 190, 218; unitary approach to, 12–18, 70, 101, 134, 169, 178; continental approach to, 18–20; Boston debates and, 68–72, 74–78, 91–96; theories on, 79–80; Hutchinson's views on, 81–82, 96–97; General Court's conclusions on, 82–90; popular, 96; of Parliament, 101–104; in failed confederacies, 136–138; federal negative and, 138–139; change in attitudes toward, 170, 178–179; relationship to jurisdiction, 203; Bodin's theory of, 225n5; Rousseau's views on, 226n8; absolute, 244n4, 257n22; John Adams and, 250n44; structural and substantive approaches to, 269n63. *See also* Divided authority

Stamp Act: resistance to, 30–34, 40–41, 236n37, 237n45; background to, 37–44; repeal of, 59–64; debates over sovereignty and, 71; Jefferson's views on, 116; continued influence of crisis surrounding, 179; drafters of, 234n24; purpose of, 236n31; duties under, 236n33

Stamp Act Congress, 40

State authority, 3–5, 158–166, 168–174

States: representation of, 123–124; national jurisdiction and, 146–147; concurrent jurisdiction and, 189–192, 194–199

St. John, Henry, 226n12

Story, Joseph, 161, 179

Strong, Caleb, 279n29

Sugar Act, 39, 40, 116, 234n24, 236n31

Summary View of the Rights of British America (Jefferson), 113–120, 257nn19,20. *See also* Jefferson, Thomas: plan for federated union

Supremacy, 83–84, 153, 246n18, 249n41

Supremacy Clause (U.S. Constitution): drafting and description of, 161–166, 168–169; judicial authority under,

171–172, 173–174, 179, 181–182, 196, 221; interpreted by Supreme Court, 218; influences on, 255n97; Bernstein on, 274n127; implementing, 274n129
Supreme Court of the United States: jurisdiction of, 164, 184; convenes for first session, 175–176; establishment of, 182–185; appellate jurisdiction of, 191, 193, 194, 218–219, 275n129, 282n57; election of 1800 and, 210
Suspending clauses, 117, 143, 153, 170, 266n35
"System of states," 19–20, 27, 79, 87, 103, 130

Tariff, federal, 220
Taxation: internal vs. external theories of, 8–9, 12, 35–36, 42–43, 48, 59, 105; Stamp Act and, 30–34, 37–44; colonial theories on, 44–51; metropolitan approaches to, 51–59; debates on, 59–67, 69; Jefferson on, 118–119; Grenville and, 234n23; smuggling and, 235n27
Taylor, John, 274n122
Tea Act, 101
Territorial principle of law, 89–90, 190
Tocqueville, Alexis de, 218–219
Townshend Acts, 59, 61, 68, 101, 116, 237n48
Trade: regulation of, 60–64; metropolitan attitudes toward, 230n48; smuggling and, 235n27; policing colonial, 235n30
Trist, Nicholas, 161, 166
Tucker, Josiah, 110
Tucker, St. George, 179, 192–193, 281n50
Turner Preyer, Kathryn, 176, 202, 207

Union: colonial, 20–24; federal, 26–27, 108, 123–124, 130–131, 177; incorporating, confederation, and federal, 26–28; Galloway's plan for, 111–113; Jefferson's plan for, 113–120; Scottish precedents for, 120–124; incorporating, 123–124, 230n54; Continental political theory and, 124–126; first American, 126–131

Union of crowns, 25–26, 28–29, 87–88, 231nn56, 58, 252n57
Unitary authority, 8, 15, 19, 65–66, 70, 78, 101. *See also* Sovereignty: unitary approach to
United States in Congress assembled, 106, 127–128, 134

Vattel, Emmerich de, 18, 79, 124
Veto power: in Albany Plan, 23; of Privy Council, 142–143, 266n33; Scottish Militia Bill and, 258n27, 271n92. *See also* Federal negative
Virginia convention (1774), 114
Virginia House of Burgesses, 58
Virginia Plan: federal negative proposed in, 147–153, 268n57; federal negative defeated in, 153–158, 171, 274n122
Virginia ratification convention (1788), 183, 196
Von Pufendorf, Samuel. *See* Pufendorf, Samuel von

Wales, 85
Walpole, Horace, 42
Warren, Charles, 161
Warren, Mercy Otis, 82, 255n1
Washington, Bushrod, 204
Washington, George, 22, 79, 146–147, 186
Watson-Wentworth, Charles, 41
Whately, Thomas, 100, 234n24
Whig party, British, 15
Whig thought, American: critique of metropolitan power, 9, 15, 36, 48, 84; theory of multiplicity and, 64–65, 90; opposition to Hutchinson, 105; on Scottish model for union, 120; influence of Continental political philosophy on, 125
Whig thought, British, 76
White, Alexander, 183
Williamson, Hugh, 156
Wilson, James: Scottish precedents and, 86–87; "dominion status" theory and, 102, 119; on states of British Empire,

Wilson, James *(continued)*
 125, 170; federal negative and, 151–152;
 fears state encroachments on federal
 supremacy, 181; proposes digest of federal
 law, 201; on New Jersey Plan, 272n108
Wingate, Paine, 279n29, 280n31
Witherspoon, John, 122–123, 221,
 260nn45,49, 262n7

Wood, Gordon S., 4, 17, 128–129, 224n8
Wythe, George, 121

Yates, Robert, 166, 270n80

Zuckert, Michael, 270nn66,73